Open
Technical
Communication

Tiffani Reardon
Tamara Powell
Jonathan Arnett
Monique Logan
Cassie Race

http://open-tc.com

Letter from the Project Manager

Welcome to *Open Technical Communication*! We're so happy that you—whether you're a student or an instructor—have decided to use our textbook.

Open TC is a freely accessible online textbook for technical communication, technical writing, workplace writing, and other related courses. Currently in its third rendition, it's had an interesting history. In 2015, Dr. Tamara Powell at Kennesaw State University gathered us, a team of like-minded colleagues, to develop an Open Educational Resource that would allow us to move away from a well-respected but very expensive textbook and towards something equally as valuable but more affordable for students. Our team applied for and received an Affordable Learning Georgia grant to fund the project, and in July 2016, we published *Sexy Technical Communication* online with a CC-BY attribution license.

What's with the title, you ask? One day, deep in the development process, our team shared a plate of dry-fried eggplant at Tasty China in Marietta, GA, and contemplated what to call the as-yet untitled project. We didn't land on a title worth keeping, but we decided to use *Sexy Technical Communication* as an in-joke working title until we thought of something better. Then, as we worked through the project, one team member (Dr. Cassie Race) wrote a fun introduction that worked well with the *Sexy TC* title, so we decided to keep it for the moment. That moment lasted four years.

The textbook's original design was as idiosyncratic as its title. Our team had a student assistant who had experience creating computer-based background art, so we handed the design reins over and asked James Monroe to design the background art for the first rendition of *Sexy TC*. The fun design worked well with the fun title.

As the years passed by, however, we ultimately decided to move in a more professional direction. Two of the original team members (Dr. Tamara Powell and I, Tiffani Reardon) applied for a smaller Affordable Learning Georgia grant to help fund a design overhaul and content edit. This second rendition of *Sexy TC* had more neutral colors as well as a consistent logo and design. We also worked hard to ensure that all chapters had consistent objectives, good accessibility and document design, and Google Analytics embedded into the back end, among other improvements. We kept the *Sexy TC* title for the time being again.

As Summer 2019 rolled in, another team member (Dr. Jonathan Arnett) pointed out that the new, professional design was great, but it doesn't mean as much without a professional title. It was only then that the team got serious about finding a more permanent title for the textbook. We considered several ideas, but we wanted something that was clear on the purpose of the textbook but also embodied the whole point of the project: affordability. Thus, *Open Technical Communication* was born.

As we roll out this third rendition of the textbook, we're excited to debut the new title as well as some new interactive activities and a few new chapters. Please feel free to reach out to me, the project manager for *Open TC*, if you ever have questions or suggestions for improvement. Whether you're an instructor designing your course around this textbook, a student using this textbook for a class, or someone who just stumbled upon our textbook by chance, the *Open Technical Communication* team hopes you find it valuable.

Yours,
Tiffani Reardon
tiffani.reardon@usg.edu

Our Team

Our amazing textbook team is made up of five faculty members at Kennesaw State University.

Ms. Tiffani Reardon

Program Manager for Affordable Learning Georgia at the University System of Georgia

PhD Student in Technical Communication and Rhetoric at Texas Tech University

Part-Time Instructor of English/Technical Communication at Texas Tech University and Kennesaw State University

tiffani.reardon@usg.edu | reardont@outlook.com

Dr. Tammy Powell

Director of the CHSS Office of Digital Education at Kennesaw State University

Professor of English at Kennesaw State University

tpowel25@kennesaw.edu

Dr. Jonathan Arnett

Program Coordinator of Technical Communication at Kennesaw State University

Assistant Professor of Technical Communication at Kennesaw State University

jarnet11@kennesaw.edu

Dr. Monique Logan

Lecturer of Technical Communication at Kennesaw State University

mlogan15@kennesaw.edu

Dr. Cassie Race

Part-Time Assistant Professor of Technical Communication at Kennesaw State University

crace@kennesaw.edu

Special thanks to the following contributors:

- Mr. David McMurrey, Author of *Online Technical Writing*
- Mr. Steve Miller, Author of Why Brilliant People Believe Nonsense
- Mrs. Cherie Miller, Author of Why Brilliant People Believe Nonsense
- Ms. Megan Gibbs, Former Instructional Designer at KSU
- Ms. Jennifer Nguyen, Former Student Assistant at KSU
- Mx. James Monroe, Former Student Assistant at KSU
- Mr. Lance Linimon, Closed Captioner, linimon@me.com

Table of Contents

Chapter 1: Introduction to Technical Writing

By: Cassandra Race

Objectives

Upon completion of this chapter, readers will be able to:

1. Define technical writing.
2. Summarize the six characteristics of technical writing.
3. Explain basic standards of good technical writing.

The Nature of Technical Writing

Did you know that you probably read or create technical communication every day without even realizing it? If you noticed signs on your way to work, checked the calories on the cereal box, emailed your professor to request a recommendation, or followed instructions to make a withdrawal from an ATM; you have been involved with technical, workplace, or professional communication.

So what? You ask. Today, writing is a more important skill for professionals than ever before. The National Commission on Writing for Americas Families, Schools, and Colleges (2004) declares that writing today is not a frill for the few, but an essential skill for the many, and goes on to state that much of what is important in American public and economic life depends on strong written and oral communication skills. A survey by the Workforce Solutions group at St. Louis Community College asserts many employers are concerned at the large number of college graduates applying for jobs who lack communication and interpersonal skills (White, 2013).

Good communication skills, particularly in writing, are essential if you are going to succeed in the workplace. The working world depends on written communication because within modern organizations, almost every action is documented in writing. Furthermore, many kinds of writing, including correspondence, presentations using visuals like PowerPoint, technical reports, and formal reports are prevalent in most workplaces. And the writing has to be good, accurate, clear, and grammatically correct. Kyle Wiens (2012) writes in an article in the Harvard Business Review: "If you think an apostrophe was one of the 12 disciples of Jesus, you will never work for me. If you scatter commas into a sentence with all the discrimination of a shotgun, you might make it to the foyer before we politely escort you from the building. I have a zero tolerance to grammar mistakes that make people look stupid."

Check out this video for more ideas about the kinds of writing that will be expected of you, especially if you are in a STEAM (Science, Technology, Engineering, Arts, and Mathematics) field.

Writing in the Workplace pt. 1

So How Do We Define this Kind of Writing?

In this text, the word "document" refers to any of the many forms of technical writing, whether it be a web page, an instruction manual, a lab report, or a travel brochure.

Technical communication is the process of making and sharing ideas and information in the workplace as well as the set of applications such as letters, emails, instructions, reports, proposals, websites, and blogs that comprise the documents you write. The Society of Technical Communications (STC) defines technical communication as a broad field that includes any form of communication that is about technical or specialized topics, that uses technology such as web pages or help files, or that provides instruction about how to do something. (n.d.)

Specifically, technical writing involves communicating complex information to a specific audience who will use it to accomplish some goal or task in a manner that is accurate, useful, and clear. Whether you write an email to your professor or supervisor, develop a presentation or report, design a sales flyer, or create a webpage, you are a technical communicator.

Where does it come from? According to the STC (n.d.), technical communications origins have actually been attributed to various eras dating back to Ancient Greece (think Rhetoric!) and to the Renaissance, but what we know today as the professional field of technical writing began during World War I from the need for technology based documentation for military and manufacturing industries. As technology grew, and organizations become more global, the need and relevance for technical communication emerged, and in 2009, the U.S. Bureau of Labor Statistics recognized Technical Writer as a profession (STC).

What does technical communication or workplace writing look like? Check out this page from the U.S. Environmental Protection Agency about climate change. Who is the target audience? What information does this document provide? What task or goal will it help to accomplish? What elements of this document do you think make it useful? Does it solve a problem? What about the style of the writing in this government document? Is it concise and accurate? This is just one example of the many kinds of technical documents you will work with in this course.

Be sure to notice the annotations in the margins of the document. Do you agree that this is an effective document? Read on for further discussion about the characteristics of technical writing.

Let's Take a Look at Characteristics of Technical Writing

Mike Markell (2015), Sidney Dobrin (2010), Elizabeth Tebeaux (2012), Sam Dragga (2012), and others all identify similar characteristics of technical writing and emphasize that it must adhere to the highest standards.

Focused on audience: Technical and workplace documents address a specific audience. The audience may be an individual or a group, and it may or may not be known to the writer. While there is always a primary audience addressed, there may be a secondary audience. Thus, an understanding of the reader or user of a technical document is important.

Rhetorical, persuasive, purposeful, and problem-oriented: Technical communication is all about helping the reader or user of a document solve a problem or compel others to act or do. For example, the syllabus of your calculus class informs the students what is expected of them; the university's web site provides information to potential students about how to apply or to current students about where to seek assistance. Identification of a specific purpose and a particular audience are the first two steps of technical writing.

Professional: Technical communication reflects the values, goals, and culture of the organization and as such, creates and maintains the public image of the organization. Look back at your university's web site to see what image it conveys, or consider the United States Government.

On October 13, 2010, President Obama signed into law the Plain Writing Act of 2010 (the Act) which is designed to promote clear government communication that the public can understand and use. The Act calls for writing that is clear, concise, and well-organized. Check out this resource on Plain Language.

Design centered: Technical communication uses elements of document design such as visuals, graphics, typography, color, and spacing to make a document interesting, attractive, usable, and comprehensible. While some documents may be totally in print, many more use images such as charts, photographs, and illustrations to enhance readability and understanding and simplify complex information.

Research and technology oriented: Because of workplace demands, technical and workplace writing is often created in collaboration with others through a network of experts and designers and depends on sound research practices to ensure that information provided is correct, accurate, and complete.

Ethical: Lastly, technical communication is ethical. All workplace writers have ethical obligations, many of which are closely linked to legal obligations that include liability laws, copyright laws, contract laws, and trademark laws. You'll learn more about these in a later chapter on ethics.

What Standards Should I Observe to Make my Writing Successful?

Good question! As a member of an organization or team, even as a student, you want to produce the absolute best writing you can. Here are the standards you must follow and some tips to help you. If you keep these in mind as you work through your learning in this text, hooray for you! You get the great writer award! You will also have a tremendous advantage in the workplace if your communication and design skills meet these standards.

- First and most important, your writing must be **honest**. Your trustworthiness in communication reflects not only on you personally but on your organization or discipline.
- Your writing has to be **clear** so that your reader can get from it the information you intended. Strive to make sure that you have expressed exactly what you mean and have not left room for incorrect interpretations.
- Next, good writing is **accurate**. Do your homework and make sure you have your facts right. There is no excuse for presenting incorrect information.
- Also make sure you have all the facts, as your writing must also be **complete**. Have you included everything that your reader needs?
- Your audience has neither time nor patience for excessive verbiage, so simplify and cut any clutter. Good writing is always concise writing.
- Your document should be **attractive** and pleasing to look at. Just as you wouldn't eat a hamburger from a dirty plate, your reader will not be moved by a document that is not carefully designed and professional.

Without exception, grammar, spelling, punctuation, and sentence structure have to be **correct**. Even a single grammatical or spelling error can cause your reader to dismiss you as not professional, as not caring enough to edit carefully. Poor writing at this level reflects poorly on your organization as well, and most companies can't mandate good writing with a law!

Accessibility in Technical Writing

Accessibility is perhaps the most important standard for excellence in technical communication. At the very least, the design of your document should be useful, easy to navigate, and with all information easy to locate. Specifically, websites and e-learning documents must meet ADA (American Disabilities Act) laws for accessibility. The link below will provide more information about ADA for you.

What is the Americans with Disabilities Act (ADA)?

What's Next? Let's Get Started!

Nobody wants to read anything you have written.

So how can you make sure they will? Say what? After years of having willing and captive audiences (i.e. your mom and your teachers) for every word you put on paper, we are telling you that nobody wants to read what you have written? Yep. They don't want to, but they have to. Technical or workplace writing is intended to solve problems, seek solutions, and provide necessary information that workers will use to, well, solve problems, seek solutions, and provide necessary information. And to do those things well, you as the writer have to do several things well.

How do you ensure that your document will be useful to your readers? Of course, you will make sure that it adheres to the standards of excellence in this chapter. But for now, let's get started with some strategies to make your writing accessible, useful, and excellent!

Here are a few simple things to practice right now. Jakob Nielsen (1997) observes that readers, or users, won't read content unless it is clear, simple, and easy to understand. The late William Zinsser (2006), author of *On Writing Well*, emphasizes the same points when he states, "Good writing has an aliveness that keeps the reader reading from one paragraph to the next, and it's not a question of gimmick to personalize the author. It's a question of using the English language in a way that will achieve the greatest clarity and strength." (p.5).

First, make sure your writing is **legible**. Legible? Sure. Is the font large enough to be read by a variety of audiences? Is it an easy to read font style that is appropriate for the content? If you are writing for the internet, these considerations are especially significant. If there are problems with legibility in your document, it will be of little use to your reader.

Then, make sure your writing is **readable**. If you have identified and analyzed your audience, you are off to a good start. Readable means that your document can be easily understood by your target audience, and refers to the formula whereby words, sentence length, and sentence complexity determine how hard or easy your sentences are to read. If your readability is too high for the audience, then they will either take more time getting what they need from your writing, or it won't be of any use to them at all. Too low? You may come across as condescending, if not a lousy writer.

Microsoft Word has a readability test built into the program under the Review heading that will give you a good starting place. However, don't rely completely on it to assess the ease or difficulty of your writing. Have a trusted colleague take a look and give you feedback. You can also use one of many free online readability formulas.

Free Readability Test!

Finally, your writing may be legible and readable, but how well can your audience comprehend, or understand it in the way you intended? Is the reader able to use the document in the manner you meant? To enhance the readers **comprehension**, use language and terminology familiar to the reader, and limit paragraphs to one main idea. Strive for brevity if your users will be reading on tablets or mobile devices. Use visuals such as charts or diagrams to present a lot of information in a graphic format. You can evaluate how easy your document is to comprehend by getting another set of eyes on it.

Ask a colleague to read your text and then tell you what the important ideas are.

Got it? Then Head for the Exercises and Activities Below.

Exercise 1: Locate some examples of what you consider technical writing. These may include correspondence, journal articles, lab reports, web pages, or advertisements. In small groups with other classmates, discuss how the documents reflect the characteristics of technical writing. After your group has analyzed the document, present it to the entire class and explain how it meets the characteristics of a technical document.

Exercise 2: Locate some of the free readability tools on the Internet and apply one to a section of writing, such as this text, to evaluate the reading level. What do you think is an ideal readability level for a bank's web site; a college history text, or even the school's website? In a memo to your instructor, discuss the importance of readability measures in creating useful technical documents.

Exercise 3: Locate an instruction manual for a product you may own. Analyze it against the standards listed in the chapter for good technical writing. Submit your analysis in a memo to your instructor.

References

Adams' S. (2014). The 10 skills employers want most in 2015 graduates. Forbes. Retrieved from http://forbes.com/sites/susanadams/2014

College Board. (2004). Writing: A ticket to work…or a ticket out. A Report of the National Commission on Writing for America's Families, Schools, and Colleges. Retrieved from http://www.collegeboard.com/prod-downloads/writingcom/writing-ticket-to-work.pdf

Defining technical communication. (n.d.). Society for Technical Communication. Retrieved from http://stc.org/about-stc/the-profession-all-about-technical-communication/defining-tc

Dobrin, S., Keller, C., Weisser, C. (2010). Technical communication in the twenty first century (2nd. ed.) Upper Saddle River, NJ: Pearson Prentice Hall.

Markell, M. (2015). Technical communication (11th ed.). Boston, MA: Bedford/St. Martins.

Nielsen, J. (1997). How users read on the web. NN/g Nielsen Norman Group. Retrieved from http://www.nngroup.com

Tebeaux, E., Dragga, S. (2012). The essentials of technical communication (2nd ed.). New York, NY: Oxford University Press.

United States Department of Labor: Bureau of Labor Statistics. (2016). Technical writers. Occupational outlook handbook. Retrieved from www.bls.gov/ooh/media-and-communications/technical-writers.htm

What is technical writing? (2016). Techwhirl. Retrieved from http://Techwhirl.com/what-is-technical-writing/

White, M. (2013). The real reason new college grads can't get hired. TIME.com. Retrieved from http://business.time.com/2013/11/10/the-real-reason-college-grads-can't-get-hired.

Wiens, K. (2012). I won't hire people who use poor grammar: Here's why. Harvard Business Review. Retrieved from https://hbr.org/2012/07/i-won't-hire-people-who-use-poor-grammar

Zinsser, W. (2006). On writing well. New York, NY: HarperCollins Publishers.

Chapter 2: Applications of Technical Writing

2.1: Business Correspondence and Resumes

By: David McMurrey

Objectives

Upon completion of this chapter, readers will be able to do the following:

1. Summarize the basics of format and style in business correspondence.
2. Explain and distinguish between three common types of business letters.
3. Explain and apply basic guidelines for resume-writing.

Introductory Advice from Dawn Davenport

Common Components of Business Letters

Heading: The heading contains the writer's address and the date of the letter. The writer's name is not included; only a date is needed in headings on letterhead stationery.

Inside address: The inside address shows the name and address of the recipient of the letter. This information can help prevent confusion at the recipient's offices. Also, if the recipient has moved, the inside address helps to determine what to do with the letter. In the inside address, include the appropriate title of respect of the recipient and copy the name of the company exactly as that company writes it. When you do have the names of individuals, remember to address them appropriately: Mrs., Ms., Mr., Dr., and so on. If you are not sure what is correct for an individual, try to find out how that individual signs letters or consult the forms-of-address section in a dictionary.

Salutation: The salutation directly addresses the recipient of the letter and is followed by a colon (except when a friendly, familiar, sociable tone is intended, in which case a comma is used). Notice that in the simplified letter format, the salutation line is eliminated altogether. If you don't know whether the recipient is a man or a woman, the traditional practice has been to write "Dear Sir" or "Dear Sirs"--but that's sexist! To avoid this problem, salutations such as "Dear Sir or Madame," "Dear Ladies and Gentlemen," "Dear Friends," or "Dear People" have been tried-- but without much general acceptance. Deleting the salutation line altogether or inserting "To Whom It May Concern" in its place, is not ordinarily a good solution either--it's impersonal.

The best solution is to make a quick, anonymous phone call to the organization and ask for a name; or address the salutation to a department name, committee name, or a position name: "Dear Personnel Department," "Dear Recruitment Committee," "Dear Chairperson," or "Dear Director of Financial Aid," for example.

Example of Block Letter Format

Subject or reference line: As shown in the order letter, the subject line replaces the salutation or is included with it. The subject line announces the main business of the letter.

Body of the letter: The actual message, of course, is contained in the body of the letter--the paragraphs between the salutation and the complimentary close. Strategies for writing the body of the letter are discussed in the section on business-correspondence style.

Complimentary close: The "Sincerely yours" element of the business letter is called the complimentary close. Other common ones are "Sincerely yours," "Cordially," "Respectfully," or "Respectfully yours." You can design your own but be careful not to create florid or wordy ones. Notice that only the first letter is capitalized, and it is always followed by a comma.

Signature block: Usually, you type your name four lines below the complimentary close and sign your name in between. If you are a woman and want to make your marital status clear, use Miss, Ms., or Mrs. in parentheses before the typed version of your first name. Whenever possible, include your title or the name of the position you hold just below your name. For example, "Technical writing student," "Sophomore data processing major," or "Tarrant County Community College Student" are perfectly acceptable.

End notations: Just below the signature block are often several abbreviations or phrases that have important functions.

- *Initials*: The initials in all capital letters in the preceding figures are those of the writer or the letter, and the ones in lower case letters just after the colon are those of the typist.
- *Enclosures*: To make sure that the recipient knows that items accompany the letter in the same envelope, use such indications as "Enclosure," "Encl.," "Enclosures (2)." For example, if you send a resume and writing sample with your application letter, you'd do this: "Encl.: Resume and Writing Sample." If the enclosure is lost, the recipient will know.
- *Copies*: If you send copies of a letter to others, indicate this fact among the end notations also. If, for example, you were upset by a local merchant's handling of your repair problems and were sending a copy of your letter to the Better Business Bureau, you'd write something like this: "cc: Mr. Raymond Mason, Attorney."

Following pages: If your letter is longer than one page, the heading at the top of subsequent pages can be handled in one of the following ways:

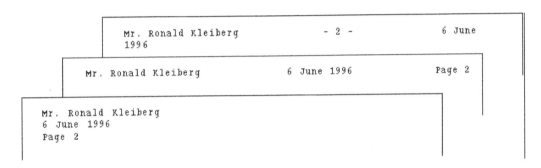

Figure 1: Examples of Second-Page Letter Headers

If you use letterhead stationery, remember not to use it for subsequent pages. However, you must use blank paper of the same quality, weight, and texture as the letterhead paper (usually, letterhead stationery comes with matching blank paper).

Business Letter Formats

If you are writing a business letter, select one of the common formats as shown in the example letters listed below. These include the block letter, the semi-block letter, the alternative block letter, and the simplified letter.

Which of these formats to use depends on the ones commonly used in your organization or the situation in which you are writing. Use the simplified letter if you lack the name of an individual or department to write to.

Style in Business Correspondence

Writing business letters and memos differs in certain important ways from writing reports. Keep thefollowing advice in mind when you write and especially when you revise your business letters or memos.

State the main business, purpose, or subject matter right away. Let the reader know from the very first sentence what your letter is about. Remember that when businesspeople open a letter, their first concern is to know what the letter is about, what its purpose is, and why they must spend their time reading it. Therefore, avoid roundabout beginnings. If you are writing to apply for a job, begin with something like this: "I am writing to apply for the position you currently have open...." If you have bad news for someone, you need not spill all of it in the first sentence. Here is an example of how to avoid negative phrasing: "I am writing in response to your letter of July 24, 1997 in which you discuss problems you have had with an electronic spreadsheet purchased from our company." The following shows an additional example.

Example of a Bad Business Letter

Example of a Better Business Letter

State the main purpose or business of the letter right away. The problem version just starts flailing away from the very outset. The revised version at least establishes the purpose of the letter (and then starts flailing).

If you are responding to a letter, identify that letter by its subject and date in the first paragraph or sentence. Busy recipients who write many letters themselves may not remember their letters to you. To avoid problems, identify the date and subject of the letter to which you respond:

Dear Mr. Stout: I am writing in response to your September 1, 19XX letter in which you describe problems that you've had with one of our chainsaws. I regret that you've suffered this inconvenience and expense and...

Keep the paragraphs of most business letters short. The paragraphs of business letters tend to be short, some only a sentence long. Business letters are not read the same way as articles, reports, or books. Usually, they are read rapidly. Big, thick, dense paragraphs over ten lines, which require much concentration, may not be read carefully—or read at all.

To enable the recipient to read your letters more rapidly and to comprehend and remember the important facts or ideas, create relatively short paragraphs of between three and eight lines long. In business letters, paragraphs that are made up of only a single sentence are common and perfectly acceptable. Throughout this chapter, you'll see examples of the shorter paragraphs commonly used by business letters.

"Compartmentalize" the contents of your letter. When you "compartmentalize" the contents of a business letter, you place each different segment of the discussion—each different topic of the letter—in its own paragraph. If you were writing a complaint letter concerning problems with the system unit of your personal computer, you might have the following paragraphs:

- A description of the problems you've had with it
- The ineffective repair jobs you've had
- The compensation you think you deserve and why

Study each paragraph of your letters for its purpose, content, or function. When you locate a paragraph that does more than one thing, consider splitting it into two paragraphs. If you discover two short separate paragraphs that do the same thing, consider joining them into one.

Provide topic indicators at the beginning of paragraphs. Analyze some of the letters you see in this chapter in terms of the contents or purpose of their individual paragraphs. In the first sentence of anybody paragraph of a business letter, try to locate a word or phrase that indicates the topic of that paragraph. If a paragraph discusses your problems with a personal computer, work the word "problems" or the phrase "problems with my personal computer" into the first sentence. Doing this gives recipients a clear sense of the content and purpose of each paragraph. Here is an excerpt before and after topic indicators have been incorporated:

Problem: I have worked as an electrician in the Decatur, Illinois, area for about six years. Since 1980 I have been licensed by the city of Decatur as an electrical contractor qualified to undertake commercial and industrial work as well as residential work.

Revision: As for my work experience, I have worked as an electrician in the Decatur, Illinois, area for about six years. Since 1980 I have been licensed by the city of Decatur as an electrical contractor qualified to undertake commercial and industrial work as well as residential work.

List or itemize whenever possible in a business letter. Listing spreads out the text of the letter, making it easier to pick up the important points rapidly. Lists can be handled in several ways, as explained in the chapter on lists. For examples of lists in business correspondence, see the block-letter format in the preceding, the inquiry letter, and order letter.

Place important information strategically in business letters. Information in the first and last lines of paragraphs tends to be read and remembered more readily. These are high-visibility points. Information buried in the middle of long paragraphs is easily overlooked or forgotten. For example, in application letters which must convince potential employers that you are right for a job, place information on your appealing qualities at the beginning or end of paragraphs for greater emphasis. Place less positive or detrimental information in less highly visible points. If you have some difficult things to say, a good (and honest) strategy is to de-emphasize by placing them in areas of less emphasis. If a job requires three years of experience and you only have one, bury this fact in the middle or the lower half of a body paragraph of the application letter. The resulting letter will be honest and complete; it just won't emphasize weak points unnecessarily. Here are some examples of these ideas:

Problem: In July I will graduate from the University of Kansas with a Bachelor of Science in Nutrition and Dietetics. Over the past four years in which I have pursued this degree, I have worked as a lab assistant for Dr. Alison Laszlo and have been active in two related organizations, the Student Dietetic Association and the American Home Economics Association. In my nutritional biochemistry and food science labs, I have written many technical reports and scientific papers. I have also been serving as a diet aide at St. David's Hospital in Lawrence the past year and a half.

The job calls for a technical writer; let's emphasize that first, then mention the rest!

Revision: In my education at the University of Kansas, I have had substantial experience writing technical reports and scientific papers. Most of these reports and papers have been in the field of nutrition and dietetics in which I will be receiving my Bachelor of Science degree this July. During my four years at the University, I have also handled plenty of paperwork as a lab assistant for Dr. Alison Laszlo, as a member of two related organizations, the Student Dietetic Association and the American Home Economics Association, and as a diet aide as St. David's Hospital in Lawrence in the past year and a half.

Problem: To date, I have done no independent building inspection on my own. I have been working the past two years under the supervision of Mr. Robert Packwood who has often given me primary responsibility for walk-throughs and property inspections. It was Mr. Packwood who encouraged me to apply for this position. I have also done some refurbishing of older houses on a contract basis and have some experience in industrial construction as a welder and as a clerk in a nuclear construction site.

Let's not lie about our lack of experience, but let's not put it on a billboard either!

Revision: As for my work experience, I have done numerous building walk-throughs and property inspections under the supervision of Mr. Robert Packwood over the past two years. Mr. Packwood, who encouraged me to apply for this position, has often given me primary responsibility for many inspection jobs. I have also done some refurbishing of older houses on a contract basis and have some experience in industrial construction as a welder and as a clerk in a nuclear construction site.

Find positive ways to express bad news in your business letters. Often, business letters must convey bad news: a broken computer keyboard cannot be replaced, or an individual cannot be hired. Such bad news can be conveyed in a tactful way. Doing so reduces the chances of an end of business relations with the recipient of the bad news. To convey bad news positively, avoid such words as "cannot," "forbid," "fail," "impossible," "refuse," "prohibit," "restrict," and "deny" as much as possible. The first versions of the example sentences below are phrased in a rather cold and unfriendly negative manner; the second versions are much more positive, cordial and tactful:

Problem: Because of the amount of information you request in your letter, I simply cannot help you without seriously disrupting my work schedule.

Revision: In your letter you ask for a good amount of information which I would like to help you locate. Because of my work commitments, however, I am going to be able to answer only a few of the questions....

Problem: If you do not complete and return this advertisement contract by July 1, 19XX, you will not receive your advertising space in this year's <u>Capitol Lines</u>. If we have not heard from you by this deadline, we will sell your advertisement space to some other client.

Revision: Please complete the enclosed contract and return it to us by July 1, 19XX. After this deadline, we will begin selling any unrenewed advertisement space in this year's <u>Capitol Lines</u>, so I hope we hear from you before then.

Problem: While I am willing to discuss changes in specific aspects of this article or ideas on additional areas to cover, I am not prepared to change the basic theme of the article: the usability of the Victor microcomputer system.

Revision: I am certainly open to suggestions and comments about specific aspects of this article, or any of your thoughts on additional areas that you think I should cover. I do want, however, to retain the basic theme of the article: the usability of the Victor microcomputer system.

Focus on the recipient's needs, purposes, or interests instead of your own. Avoid a self-centered focus on your own concerns rather than those of the recipient. Even if you must talk about yourself in a business letter a great deal, do so in a way that relates your concerns to those of the recipient. This recipient-oriented style is often called the "you-attitude," which does not mean using more you's but making the recipient the main focus of the letter.

Problem: I am writing you about a change in our pricing policy that will save our company time and money. In an operation like ours, it costs us a great amount of labor time (and thus expense) to scrape and rinse our used tableware when it comes back from large parties. Also, we have incurred great expense on replacement of linens that have been ruined by stains that could have been soaked promptly after the party and saved.

Revision: I am writing to inform you of a new policy that we are beginning, effective September 1, 19XX, that will enable us to serve your large party needs more often and without delay. In an operation like ours in which we supply for parties of up to 500, turn-around time is critical; unscraped and unrinsed tableware causes delays in clean-up time and, more importantly, less frequent and less prompt service to you the customer. Also, extra fees for stained linens can be avoided by immediate soaking after the party.

Problem: For these reasons, our new policy, effective September 1, 19XX, will be to charge an additional 15% on unrinsed tableware and 75% of the wholesale value of stained linens that have not been soaked.

Revision: Therefore, to enable us to supply your large party needs promptly, we will begin charging 15% on all unrinsed tableware and 75% of the wholesale value of stained linens that have not been soaked. This policy we hope will encourage our customers' kitchen help to do the quick and simple rinsing and/or soaking at the end of large parties. Doing so will ensure faster and more frequent service.

Avoid pompous, inflated, legal-sounding phrasing. Watch out for puffed-up, important-sounding language. This kind of language may seem business-like at first; it's actually ridiculous. Of course, such phrasing is apparently necessary in legal documents; but why use it in other writing situations? When you write a business letter, picture yourself as a plain-talking, common-sense, down-to-earth person (but avoid slang). Check out the following examples for a serious dose of bureaucratese.

Problem: The Capitol Improvements Project (hereinafter to designated as CIP) for the fiscal year 1982-1983 stipulated budget allocations in the amount not exceeding $20,000 to be designated for utilization by a program under the nomination of the 23rd Street Renaissance Market. The purpose and aim of the aforesaid program is to provide and permit basic pedestrian amenities and conveniences for a marketplace devoted to the commerce of arts and crafts to the maximum extent possible. In consideration of these dictates, the CIP has mandated that there be a geographical extension of the sidewalk no greater than 15 feet in a northerly direction. The said extension would continue to permit an opening of approximately 15 feet for the orderly flow and passage of vehicular traffic. The City Council in 1982 issued directives that mandated the temporary closure of the above-named street for a period not to exceed one calendar year. In April of the ensuing year it was directed by the City Council that this closure remains in full effect for a period not exceeding an additional six months.

This is pompous, officious-sounding prose style. People in authority positions don't have to sound like this (they might get questioned).

Revision: The Capital Improvements Program (CIP) in 1982-1983 included the amount of $20,000 for the 23rd Street Renaissance Market to provide sidewalks for an arts and crafts marketplace. The detailed plans of the CIP called for an extension of the sidewalk 15 feet north, with a 15-foot opening for automobiles.

In 1982, the City Council temporarily closed 23rd Street for a one-year period. In April of 1983, the council extended that closure for an additional six-month period which will end October 1983.

This version states the case in plain and simple language.

Avoid pompous, officious-sounding writing. Not only is the tone of the problem version offensive, it is nearly twice as long as the revised version!

Give your business letter an "action ending" whenever appropriate. An "action-ending" makes clear what the writer of the letter expects the recipient to do and when. Ineffective conclusions to business letters often end with rather limp, noncommittal statements such as "Hope to hear from you soon" or "Let me know if I can be of any further assistance." Instead, or in addition, specify the action the recipient should take and the schedule for that action. If, for example, you are writing a query letter, ask the editor politely to let you know of his decision if at all possible, in a month. If you are writing an application letter, subtlety try to set up a date and time for an interview.

As soon as you approve this plan, I'll begin contacting sales representatives at once to arrange for purchase and delivery of the notebook computers. May I expect to hear from you within the week?

Inquiry Letters

This section focuses on the inquiry letter or inquiry e-mail; let's call it the inquiry communication. The *inquiry communication* is useful when you need information, advice, names, or directions. Be careful, however, not to ask for too much information or for information that you could easily obtain in some other way—for example, by a quick trip to the library or by an Internet search.

1. Early in the letter or e-mail, identify the purpose—to obtain help or information (if it's a solicited communication, information about an advertised product, service, or program).
2. In an unsolicited letter or e-mail, identify who you are, what you are working on, why you need the requested information, and how you found out about the individual. In an unsolicited letter or e-mail, also identify the source that prompted your inquiry, for example, a journal article.
3. In the communication, list questions or information needed in a clear, specific, and easy-to-read format. If you have a number of questions, consider making a questionnaire and including a stamped, self-addressed envelope. If it's e-mail, just put the questions in the body of the e-mail or attach a separate questionnaire document.
4. In an unsolicited letter or e-mail, try to find some way to compensate the recipient for the trouble, for example, by offering to pay copying and mailing costs, to accept a collect call, to acknowledge the recipient in your report, or to send him or her a copy of your report. In a solicited letter or e-mail, suggest that the recipient send brochures or catalogs.
5. In closing an unsolicited letter or e-mail, express gratitude for any help that the recipient can provide you, acknowledge the inconvenience of your request, but do not thank the recipient "in advance." In an unsolicited letter or e-mail, tactfully suggest to the recipient will benefit by helping you (for example, through future purchases from the recipient's company).

Complaint and Adjustment Letters

This section covers two closely related types of business letters: *complaint letters*, which request compensation for problems with purchases or services, and *adjustment letters*, which are the responses to complaint letters.

Complaint Letters

A complaint letter requests some sort of compensation for defective or damaged merchandise or for inadequate or delayed services. While many complaints can be made in person, some circumstances require formal business letters. The complaint may be so complex that a phone call cannot effectively resolve the problem; or the writer may prefer the permanence, formality, and seriousness of a business letter. The essential rule in writing a complaint letter is to maintain your poise and diplomacy, no matter how justified your gripe is. Avoid making the recipient an adversary.

Note: Complaints by e-mail may not be as effective as those by regular mail, so that option is not included here.

1. Early in the letter, identify the reason you are writing—to register a complaint and to ask for some kind of compensation. Avoid leaping into the details of the problem in the first sentence.
2. Provide a fully detailed narrative or description of the problem. This is the "evidence."
3. State exactly what compensation you desire, either before or after the discussion of the problem or the reasons for granting the compensation. (It may be more tactful and less antagonizing to delay this statement in some cases.)
4. Explain why your request should be granted. Presenting the evidence is not enough; state the reasons why this evidence indicates your requested should be granted.
5. Suggest why it is in the recipient's best interest to grant your request; appeal to the recipient's sense of fairness or desire for continued business, but don't threaten. Find some way to view the problem as an honest mistake. Don't imply that the recipient deliberately committed the error or that the company has no concern for the customer. Toward the end of the letter, express confidence that the recipient will grant your request.

Adjustment Letters

Note: Adjustment communications by e-mail may not be as effective as those by regular mail so that option is not included here.

Replies to complaint letters, often called letters of "adjustment," must be handled carefully when the requested compensation cannot be granted. Refusal of compensation tests your diplomacy and tact as a writer. Here are some suggestions that may help you write either type of adjustment letter:

1. Begin with a reference to the date of the original letter of complaint and to the purpose of your letter. If you deny the request, don't state the refusal right away unless you can do so tactfully.
2. Express your concern over the writer's troubles and your appreciation that she or he has written you.
3. If you deny the request, explain the reasons why the request cannot be granted in as cordial and noncombative manner as possible. If you grant the request, don't sound as if you are doing so in a begrudging way.
4. If you deny the request, try to offer some partial or substitute compensation or offer some friendly advice (to take the sting out of the denial).
5. Conclude the letter cordially, perhaps expressing confidence that you and the writer will continue doing business.

Job Application Letters

This section focuses on the application letter (sometimes called a "cover letter"), which together with the resume is often called the "job package." You may already have written one or both of these employment-seeking documents. That's okay. Read and study this section, and then apply the guidelines here to the resumes and application letters you have created in the past.

In many job applications, you attach an application letter to your resume. Actually, the letter comes before the resume.

The role of the application letter is to draw a clear connection between the job you are seeking and your qualifications listed in the resume. To put it another way, the letter matches the requirements of the job with your qualifications, emphasizing how you are right for that job. The application letter is not a lengthy summary of the resume—not at all. It selectively mentions information in the resume, as appropriate.

Common Types of Application Letters

To begin planning your letter, decide which type of application letter you need. This decision is, in part, based on employers' requirements and, in part, based on what your background and employment needs are. In many ways, types of application letters are like the types of resumes. The types of application letters can be defined according to amount and kind of information:

- *Objective letters*: One type of letter says very little: it identifies the position being sought, indicates an interest in having an interview, and calls attention to the fact that the resume is attached. It also mentions any other special matters that are not included on the resume, such as dates and times when you are available to come in for an interview. This letter does no salesmanship and is very brief. (It represents the true meaning of "cover" letter.)
- *Highlight letters*: Another type of application letter, the type you do for most technical writing courses, tries to summarize the key information from the resume, the key information that will emphasize that you are a good candidate for the job. In other words, it selects the best information from the resume and summarizes it in the letter—this type of letter is especially designed to make the connection with the specific job.

How do you know which to write? For most technical-writing courses, write the highlight letter. However, in "real-life" situations, try calling the prospective employer; study the job advertisement for clues.

Common Sections in Application Letters

As for the actual content and organization of the paragraphs within the application letter (specifically for the *highlight* type of application letter), consider the following common approaches.

Introductory paragraph: That first paragraph of the application letter is the most important; it sets everything up—the tone, focus, as well as your most important qualification. A typical problem in the introductory paragraph involves diving directly into work and educational experience. Bad idea! A better idea is to do some combination of the following:

- State the purpose of the letter—to inquire about an employment opportunity.
- Indicate the source of your information about the job—newspaper advertisement, a personal contact, or other.
- State one eye-catching, attention-getting thing about yourself in relation to the job or to the employer that will cause the reader to want to continue.

And you try to do all things like these in the space of very short paragraph—no more than 3 to 4 lines of the standard business letter.

Main body paragraphs: In the main parts of the application letter, you present your work experience, education, and training—whatever makes that connection between you and the job you are seeking. Remember that this is the most important job you have to do in this letter—to enable the reader to see the match between your qualifications and the requirements for the job.

There are two common ways to present this information:

- Functional approach: This one presents education in one section, and work experience in the other. If there were military experience, that might go in another section. Whichever of these sections contains your "best stuff" should come first, after the introduction.
- Thematic approach: This one divides experience and education into groups such as "management," "technical," "financial," and so on and then discusses your work and education related to them in separate paragraphs.

If you read the section on functional and thematic organization of resumes, just about everything said there applies here. Of course, the letter is *not* exhaustive or complete about your background—it highlights just those aspects of your background that make the connection with the job you are seeking.

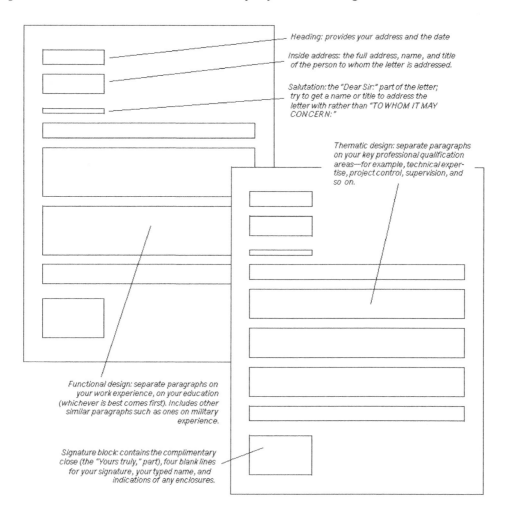

Figure 2: Common Sections of Application Letters

Another section worth considering for the main body of the application letter is one in which you discuss your goals, objectives (the focus of your career) what you are doing or want to do professionally. A paragraph like this is particularly good for people just starting their careers, when there is not much to put in the letter. Of course, be careful about loading a paragraph like this with "sweet nothings." For example, "I am seeking a challenging, rewarding career with a dynamic upscale company where I will have ample room for professional and personal growth"—come on! give us a break! Might as well say, "I want to be happy, well-paid, and well-fed."

Closing paragraph: In the last paragraph of the application letter, you can indicate how the prospective employer can get in touch with you and when are the best times for an interview. This is the place to urge that prospective employer to contact you to arrange an interview.

Background Details in the Application Letter

One of the best ways to make an application letter great is to work in details, examples, specifics about related aspects of your educational and employment background. Yes, if the resume is attached, readers can see all that details there. However, a letter that is overly general and vague might generate so little interest that the reader might not even care to turn to the resume.

In the application letter, you work in selective detail that makes your letter stand out, makes it memorable, and substantiates the claims you make about your skills and experience. Take a look at this example, which is rather lacking in specifics:

As for my experience working with persons with developmental disabilities, I have worked and volunteered at various rehabilitation hospitals and agencies in Austin and Houston *[say which ones to inject more detail into this letter]*. I have received training *[where? certificates?]* in supervising patients and assisting with physical and social therapy *[which specific therapies?]*. Currently, I am volunteering at St. David's Hospital *[doing what?]* to continue my education in aiding persons with developmental disabilities *[which specific disabilities?]*

Now take a look at the revision:

As for my experience working with persons with developmental disabilities, I have worked and volunteered at Cypress Creek Hospital in Houston and Capital Area Easter Seals/ Rehabilitation Center and Health South Rehabilitation Hospital in Austin. I have received CPR, First Aid, and Crisis Intervention certificates from Cypress Creek Hospital. Currently, I am volunteering at St. David's Hospital assisting with physical therapy to persons with developmental disabilities in the aquatics department.

Early-Career Application Letters

In the preceding, you've seen some rather impressive application letters. But what if you don't have all that experience—how do you construct a respectable application letter?

- Cite relevant projects (both in academia and community) you've worked on, even if they are not exactly related to the career that you pursue.
- Spend extra time describing college courses and programs you have been involved in. What about team projects, research projects, or reports?
- Include volunteer work that has had any trace of technical in it. (If you've not done any volunteer work, get to volunteering!)
- List any organizations you have been a member of and describe any of their activities that have any trace of technical in them. (If you've not belonged to any technically oriented organizations, get to belonging!)
- As with the resume, you can use formatting to spread what information you have to fill out the resume page.

In the example student application letter below, notice that the writer describes his coursework and the applications that he used. His reference to a professional exposition shows an active interest in a particular technical area. Moreover, his visit with an employee of the company with which he seeks employment is a crafty form of name dropping. In general, the letter expresses enthusiasm about working in the VLSI area.

Example Early-Career Application Letter

Checklist of Common Problems in Application Letters

- *Readability and white space*: Are there any dense paragraphs over 8 lines? Are there comfortable 1-inch to 1.5-inch margins all the way around the letter? Is there adequate spacing between paragraphs and between the components of the letter?
- *Page fill*: Is the letter placed on the page nicely: not crammed at the top one-half of the page; not spilling over to a second page by only three or four lines?
- *General neatness, professional-looking quality*: Is the letter on good quality paper, and is the copy clean and free of smudges and erasures?
- *Proper use of the business-letter format*: Have you set up the letter in one of the standard business-letter formats? (See the references earlier in this chapter.)
- *Overt, direct indication of the connection between your background and the requirements of the job*: Do you emphasize this connection?
- *A good upbeat, positive tone*: Is the tone of your letter bright and positive? Does it avoid sounding overly aggressive, brash, over-confident (unless that is really the tone you want)? Does your letter avoid the opposite problem of sounding stiff, overly reserved, stand-offish, blasé, indifferent?

- *A good introduction*: Does your introduction establish the purpose of the letter? Does it avoid diving directly into the details of your work and educational experience? Do you present one little compelling detail about yourself that will cause the reader to want to keep reading?
- *A good balance between brevity and details*: Does your letter avoid becoming too detailed (making readers less inclined to read thoroughly)? Does your letter avoid the opposite extreme of being so general that it could refer to practically anybody?
- *Lots of specifics (dates, numbers, names, etc.)*: Does your letter present plenty of specific detail but without making the letter too densely detailed? Do you present hard factual detail (numbers, dates, proper names) that make you stand out as an individual?
- *A minimum of information that is simply your opinion of yourself*: Do you avoid over-reliance on information that is simply your opinions about yourself? For example, instead of saying that you "work well with others," do you cite work experience that proves that fact but without actually stating it?
- *Grammar, spelling, usage*: And of course, does your letter use correct grammar, usage, and spelling?

Resumes

A *resume* is a selective record of your background—your educational, military, and work experience, your certifications, abilities, and so on. You send it, sometimes accompanied by an application letter, to potential employers when you are seeking job interviews.

A resume should be easily readable, effectively designed, and adapted to audience expectations. If you are taking a technical writing course, your instructor may be okay with your making up a few details in your resume to represent what you'll be when you graduate. However, if you're just starting your college education and have little work experience, why not try using the techniques and suggestions here to create a resume that represents your current skills, abilities, and background? Developing a decent-looking resume based on what you are now is a challenge that you have to deal with at some point—so why not now?

Resume Design: An Overview

Before personal computers, people used one resume for varied kinds of employment searches. However, with less expensive desktop publishing and high-quality printing, people sometimes rewrite their resumes for every new job they go after. For example, a person who seeks employment both with a community college and with a software-development company would use two different resumes. The contents of the two might be roughly the same, but the organization, format, and emphases would be quite different.

You are probably aware of resume-writing software: you feed your data into them and they churn out a prefab resume. You probably also know about resume-writing services that will create your resume for you for a hundred dollars or so. If you are in a time bind or if you are extremely insecure about your writing or resume-designing skills, these services might help. But often they take your information and put it into a computer database that then force it into a prefab structure. They often use the same resume-writing software just mentioned; they charge you about what the software costs. The problem is that these agencies simply cannot be that sensitive or perceptive about your background or your employment search. Nor are you likely to want to pay for their services every month or so when you are in the thick of a job search. Why not learn the skills and techniques of writing your own resume here, save the money, and write better resumes anyway?

There is no one right way to write a resume. Every person's background, employment needs, and career objectives are different, thus necessitating unique resume designs. Every detail, every aspect of your resume must start with who you are, what your background is, what the potential employer is looking for, and what your employment goals are—not with from some prefab design. Therefore, use this chapter to design your own resume, browse through the various formats, and play around with them until you find one that works for you.

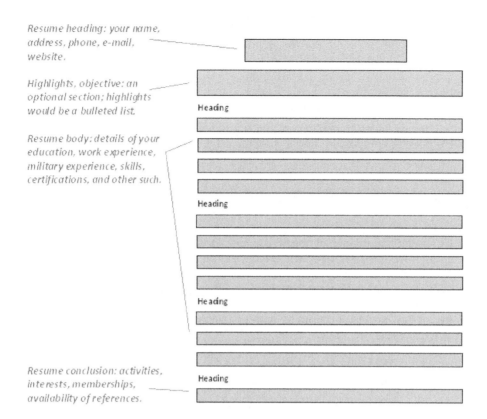

Resume heading: your name, address, phone, e-mail, website.

Highlights, objective: an optional section; highlights would be a bulleted list.

Resume body: details of your education, work experience, military experience, skills, certifications, and other such.

Resume conclusion: activities, interests, memberships, availability of references.

Figure 3: Basic Sections of a Resume

Sections in Resumes

Resumes can be divided into three sections: the heading, the body, and the conclusion. Each of these sections has fairly common contents.

Heading. The top third of the resume is the *heading*. It contains your name, phone numbers, address, and other details such as your occupation, titles, and so on. Some resume writers include the name of their profession, occupation, or field. In some examples, you'll see writers putting things like "CERTIFIED PHYSICAL THERAPIST" very prominently in the heading. Headings can also contain a goals and objectives subsection and a highlights subsection. These two special subsections are described later.

Body. In a one-page resume, the body is the middle portion, taking up a half or more of the total space of the resume. In this section, you present the details of your work, education, and military experience. This information is arranged in reverse chronological order. In the body section, you also include your accomplishments, for example, publications, certifications, equipment you are familiar with, and so on. There are *many* ways to present this information:

- You can divide it *functionally*—into separate sections for work experience and education.
- You can divide it *thematically*—into separate sections for the different areas of your experience and education.

Conclusion. In the final third or quarter of the resume, you can present other related information on your background. For example, you can list activities, professional associations, memberships, hobbies, and interests. At the bottom of the resume, people often put "REFERENCES AVAILABLE ON REQUEST" and the date of preparation of the resume. At first, you might think that listing nonwork and personal information would be totally irrelevant and inappropriate. Actually, it can come in handy—it personalizes you to potential employers and gives you something to chat while you're waiting for the coffee machine or the elevator. For example, if you mention in your resume that you raise goats, that gives the interviewer something to chat with you about during those moments of otherwise uncomfortable silence.

Resumes: Types and Design

To begin planning your resume, decide which type of resume you need. This decision is in part based on requirements that prospective employers may have, and in part based on what your background and employment needs are.

Type of organization. Resumes can be defined according to how information on work and educational experience is handled. There are several basic, commonly used plans or designs you can consider using.

- **Functional design**: Illustrated schematically below, the functional design starts with a heading; then presents either education or work experience, whichever is stronger or more relevant; then presents the other of these two sections; then ends with a section on skills and certifications and one on personal information. Students who have not yet begun their careers often find this design the best for their purposes. People with military experience either work the detail in to the education and work-experience sections as appropriate, or they create separate section specifically for military experience at the same level as education and work experience.

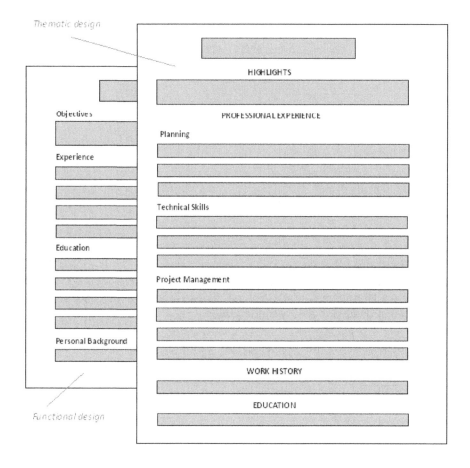

Figure 4: Two Basic Organizational Approaches to Resume Design

- **Thematic design**: Another approach to resumes is the thematic design, illustrated schematically in the preceding. It divides your experience and education into categories such as project management, budgetary planning, financial tracking, personnel management, customer sales, technical support, publications—whichever areas describe your experience. Often, these categories are based directly on typical or specific employment advertisements. If the job advertisement says that Company ABC wants a person with experience in training, customer service, and sales, then it might be a smart move to design thematic headings around those three requirements. If you want to use the thematic approach in your resume, take a look at your employment and educational experience—what are the common threads? Project management, program development, troubleshooting, supervision, maintenance, inventory control? Take a look at the job announcement you're responding to—what are the three, four, or five key requirements it mentions? Use these themes to design the body section of your resume. These themes become the headings in the body of the resume. Under these headings you list the employment or educational experience that applies. For example, under a heading like "FINANCIAL RECORDS," you might list the accounting and bookkeeping courses you took in college, the company-sponsored seminars on Excel you took, and the jobs where you actually used these skills.

Type of information. Types of resumes can be defined according to the amount and kind of information they present:

- **Objective resumes**: This type just gives dates, names, titles, no qualitative salesmanship information. These are very lean, terse resumes. In technical-writing courses, you are typically asked not to write this type. The objective-resume style is useful in resumes that use the thematic approach or that emphasize the summary/highlights section. By its very nature, you can see that the thematic approach is unclear about the actual history of employment. It's harder to tell where the person was, what she was doing, year by year.
- **Detailed resumes**: This type provides not only dates, titles, and names, but also details about your responsibilities and statements about the quality and effectiveness of your work. This is the type most people write, and the type that is the focus of most technical-writing courses. The rest of the details in this section of this chapter focus on writing the detailed resume.

Layout and Detail Format in Resumes

At some point in your resume planning, you'll want to think schematically about the layout and design of the thing. General layout has to do with the design and location of the heading, the headings for the individual sections, and the orientation of the detailed text in relation to those headings. Detail formats are the way you choose to arrange and present the details of your education and work experience.

Layout. Look at resumes in this book and in other sources strictly in terms of the style and placement of the headings, the shape of the text (the paragraphs) in the resumes, and the orientation of these two elements with each other. Some resumes have the headings centered; others are on the left margin. Notice that the actual text—the paragraphs—of resumes typically does not extend to the far-left and far-right margins. Full-length lines are not considered as readable or scannable as the shorter ones you see illustrated in the examples in this book.

Notice that many resumes use a "hanging-head" format. In this case, the heading starts on the far-left margin while the text is indented another inch or so. This format makes the heading stand out more and the text more scannable. Notice also that in some of the text paragraphs of resumes, special typography is used to highlight the name of the organization or the job title.

Detail formats. You have to make a fundamental decision about how you present the details of your work and education experience. Several examples of typical presentational techniques are shown below. The elements you work with include:

- Occupation, position, job title
- Company or organization name
- Time period you were there
- Key details about your accomplishments and responsibilities while there.

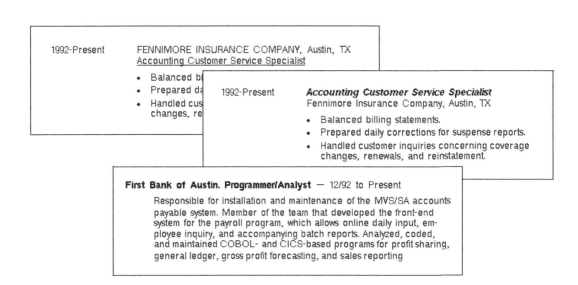

Figure 5: Examples of Detail Formats

There are many different ways to format this information. It all depends on what you want to emphasize and how much or how little information you have (whether you are struggling to fit it all on one page or struggling to make it fill one page). Several different detail formats are shown above.

Special Sections in Resumes

Here are some ideas for special resume sections, sections that emphasize your goals or qualifications.

Highlights, summary section. In the illustration below, you'll notice the "Highlights" section that occurs just below the heading (the section for name, address, phone number, etc.) and just above the main experience and education sections. This is a popular section in resumes. Resume specialists believe that the eye makes first contact with a page somewhere one-fourth to one-third of the way down the page—not at the very top. If you believe that, then it makes sense to put your very "best stuff" at that point. Therefore, some people list their most important qualifications, their key skills, their key work experience in that space on the page. Actually, this section is useful more for people who have been in their careers for a while. It's a good way to create one common spot on the resume to list those key qualifications about yourself that may be spread throughout the resume. Otherwise, these key details about yourself are scattered across your various employment and educational experience—in fact, buried in them.

Objectives, goals. Also found on some resumes is a section just under the heading in which you describe what your key goals or objectives are or what your key qualifications are. Some resume writers shy away from including a section like this because they fear it may cause certain employers to stop reading, in other words, that it limits their possibilities. A key-qualifications section is similar to a highlights section, but shorter and in paragraph rather than list form.

<u>Amplifications</u>. If you have lots of detail about what you know, this approach on page 2 of the resume may work. On the first page of this resume, the writer divides the presentation into experience and education sections and takes a chronological approach to each. On the first page, he only provides company names, job titles, dates, and discussion of duties.

Early-Career Resumes

If you are at the beginning of your career, all the advice and examples to this point may seem fine and good, but what if you have very little experience? Careers must start somewhere—and so must resumes. You can use several strategies to fill out your resume so that you appear to be the promising entry-level candidate that we all know you are.

- Cite relevant projects (both in academia and community) you've worked on, even if they are not exactly related to the career that you pursue.
- Spend extra time describing college courses and programs you have been involved in. What about team projects, research projects, or reports?
- Include volunteer work that has had any trace of technical in it. (If you've not done any volunteer work, get to volunteering!)
- List any organizations you have been a member of and describe any of their activities that have any trace of technical in them. (If you've not belonged to any technically oriented organizations, get to belonging!)
- Use formatting to spread what information you have to fill out the resume page.

In the student resume shown below, notice how much space that details about education take up. This resume writer could have included even more: Descriptions of key courses and projects could have been provided under a heading such as "Essential Coursework."

<u>Example of an Early-Career Resume</u>.

Notice too that the resume above includes plenty of co-op and part-time work. The bulleted-list format extends the length of the resume so that it fills up the page. At the bottom of the resume, the writer lists awards and organizations. These too could be amplified if necessary. Details as to what the award is about, why this writer received it, and what those organizations are—these are examples of good information that could be added, if necessary.

Subtle changes in format can also help make your resume fill a page. Top, bottom, left, and right margins can all be pushed down, up, and in from the standard 1.0 inch to 1.25 inches. You can add extra space between sections. To do so, don't just press Enter. Instead, use the paragraph-formatting feature of your software to put 6 or 9 points, for example, below the final element of each section. Line spacing is another subtle way to extend a resume. If your software by default uses 13.6 points of line spacing for Times New Roman 12-point text, experiment with changing the line spacing to exactly 15.0 points.

Resume Checklist

As you plan, write, or review your resume, keep these points in mind:

- **Readability**: are there any dense paragraphs over 6 lines? Imagine your prospective employer sitting down to a two-inch stack of resumes. Do you think she's going to slow down to read through big thick paragraphs? Probably not. Try to keep paragraphs under 6 lines long. The "hanging-head" design helps here.
- **White space**: Picture a resume crammed with detail, using only half-inch margins all the way around, a small type size, and only a small amount of space between parts of the resume. Our prospective employer might be less inclined to work through that also. "Air it out!" Find ways to incorporate more white space in the margins and between sections of the resume. Again, the "hanging-head" design is also useful.
- **Special format**: Make sure that you use special format consistently throughout the resume. For example, if you use a hanging-head style for the work-experience section, use it in the education section as well.
- **Consistent margins**: Most resumes have several margins: the outermost, left margin and at least one internal left margin. Typically, paragraphs in a resume use an internal margin, not the far-left margin. Make

sure to align all appropriate text to these margins as well. Avoid unnecessary multiple margins: they give your resume a ragged messy look.

- **Terse writing style**: It's okay to use a rather clipped, terse writing style in resumes—up to a point. The challenge in most resumes is to get it all on one page (or two if you have a lot of information to present). Instead of writing "I supervised a team of five technicians..." you write "Supervised a team of five technicians..." However, you don't leave out normal words such as articles.

- **Bold, italics, different type size, caps, other typographical special effects**: Use special typography, but keep it under control. Resumes are great places to use all of your fancy word-processing features such as bold, italics, different fonts, and different type sizes. Don't go crazy with it! Too much fancy typography can be distracting (plus make people think you are hyperactive). Also, whatever special typography you use, be consistent with it throughout the resume. If some job titles are italics, make them all italics. Avoid all-caps text—it's less readable.

- **Page fill**: Do everything you can to make your resume fill out one full page and to keep it from spilling over by 4 or 5 lines to a second page. At the beginning of your career, it's tough filling up a full page of a resume. As you move into your career, it gets hard keeping it to one page. If you need a two-page resume, see that the second page is full or nearly full.

- **Clarity of boundary lines between major sections**: Design and format your resume so that whatever the main sections are, they are very noticeable. Use well-defined headings and white space to achieve this. Similarly, design your resume so that the individual segments of work experience or education are distinct and separate from each other.

- **Reverse chronological order**: Remember to list your education and work-experience items starting with the current or most recent and working backwards in time.

- **Consistency of phrasing**: Use the same style of phrasing for similar information in a resume—for example, past tense verbs for all descriptions of past work experience.

- **Consistency of punctuation style**: For similar sections of information use the same kind of punctuation—for example, periods, commas, colons, or nothing.

- **Translations for "inside" information**: Don't assume readers will know what certain abbreviations, acronyms, or symbols mean—yes, even to the extent of "GPA" or the construction "3.2/4.00." Take time to describe special organizations you may be a member of.

- **Grammar, spelling, usage**: Watch out for these problems on a resume—they stand out like a sore thumb! Watch out particularly for the incorrect use of its and it's.

2.2: Types of Technical Documents

By: David McMurrey

Objectives

Upon completion of this chapter, readers will be able to do the following:

1. Identify common types of technical documents.
2. Summarize the purposes and formats of common types of technical documents.

Types of Technical Documents

For the final report in some technical-writing courses, you can write one of (or even a combination of) several different types of reports. If there is some other type of report that you know about and want to write, get with your instructor to discuss it.

This chapter briefly defines these different report types; some are covered in full detail elsewhere in this book; the rest are described here. But to get everything in one place, all the reports are briefly defined here, with cross-references to where their presentations occur:

Standard operating policies and procedures: These are the operating documents for organizations; they contain rules and regulations on how the organization and its members are expected to perform. Policies and procedures are like instructions, but they go much further. Standard operating procedures (SOPs) are more for procedures in which a process is performed--for example, taking a dental impression.

Recommendation, feasibility, evaluation reports: This group of similar reports does things like compare several options against a set of requirements and recommend one; considers an idea (plan, project) in terms of its "feasibility," for example, some combination of its technical, economic, social practicality or possibility; passes judgement on the worth or value of a thing by comparing it to a set of requirements, or criteria.

Technical background reports: This type is the hardest one to define but the one that most people write. It focuses on a technical topic, provides background on that topic for a specific set of readers who have specific needs for it. This report does not supply instructions, nor does it supply recommendations in any systematic way, nor does it report new and original data.

Technical guides and handbooks: Closely related to technical report but differing somewhat in purpose and audience are technical guides and handbooks.

Primary research reports: This type presents findings and interpretation from laboratory or field research.

Business plans: This type is a proposal to start a new business.

Technical specifications: This type presents descriptive and operational details on a new or updated product.

Technical Background Reports

The technical background report is hard to define—it's not a lot of things, but it's hard to say what it is. It doesn't provide step-by-step directions on how to do something in the way that instructions do. It does not formally provide recommendations in the way that feasibility reports do. It does not report data from original research and draw conclusions in the way that primary research reports do.

So, what does the technical background report do? It provides information on a technical topic but in such a way that is adapted for a particular audience that has specific needs for that information. Imagine a topic like this: renal disease and therapy. A technical background report on this topic would not dump out a ten-ton textbook containing everything you could possibly say about it. It would select information about the topic suited to a specific group of readers who had specific needs and uses for the information. Imagine the audience was a group of engineers bidding on a contract to do part of the work for a dialysis clinic. Yes, they need to know about renal disease and its therapy, but only to the extent that it has to do with their areas of expertise. Such a background report might also include some basic discussion of renal disease and its treatment, but no more than what the engineers need to do their work and to interact with representatives of the clinic.

One of the reports is an exploration of global warming, or the greenhouse effect, as it is called in the report. Notice that it discusses causes, then explores the effects, then discusses what can be done about it.

Typical contents and organization of technical background reports. Unlike most of the other reports discussed in this course guide, the technical background report does not have a common set of contents. Because it focuses on a specific technical topic for specific audiences who have specific needs or uses for the information, it grabs at whatever type of contents it needs to get the job done. You use a lot of intuition to plan this type of report. For example, with the report on renal disease and treatment, you'd probably want to discuss what renal disease is, what causes it, how it is treated, and what kinds of technologies are involved in the treatment. If you don't fully trust your intuition, use a checklist like the following:

- **Definitions**—Define the potentially unfamiliar terms associated with the topic. Write extended definitions if there are key terms or if they are particularly difficult to explain.
- **Causes**—Explain what causes are related to the topic. For example, with the renal disease topic, what causes the disease?
- **Effects**—Explain what the consequences, results, or effects associated with the topic. With the renal disease topic, what happens to people with the disease; what effects do the various treatments have?
- **Types**—Discuss the different types or categories associated with the topic. For example, are there different types of renal disease; are there different categories of treatment?
- **Historical background**—Discuss relevant history related to the topic. Discuss people, events, and past theories related to the topic.
- **Processes**—Discuss mechanical, natural, human-controlled processes related to the topic. Explain step by step how the process occurs. For example, what are the phases of the renal disease cycle; what typically happens to a person with a specific form of the disease?
- **Descriptions**—Provide information on the physical details of things related to the topic. Provide information about size, shape, color, weight, and so on. For the engineering-oriented report, this would mean size, power requirements, and other such details about the treatment technologies.
- **Comparisons**—Compare the topic, or some aspect of it, to something similar or something familiar. With the renal disease example, you could compare renal disease to some other disease; the treatment to some other treatment; the functions of the kidney to something familiar (an analogy); or even the treatment to something familiar, for example, the filter system for a swimming pool.
- **Applications**—Explore how some aspect of your topic can be used or applied. If it's some new technology, what are its applications?
- **Advantages and disadvantages**—Discuss the advantages or disadvantages of one or more aspects of your topic. In the renal disease topic, for example, what are the advantages of one treatment over another?
- **Economic considerations**—Discuss the costs of one or more aspects associated with your topic. How much does treatment for renal disease cost? How much does the equipment and personnel cost?
- **Social, political, legal, ethical implications**—Explore the implications or impact of your topic or some aspect of it in relation to social, political, legal, or ethical concerns. The renal disease example doesn't lend itself much to this area but imagine the possibilities with a topic like cryogenics—suspended animation of human beings. Often, new technologies have profound impact in these areas.
- **Problems, questions**—What problems or questions are there associated with your report topic or some aspect of it?
- **Solutions, answers**—What solutions or answers can you offer on those problems or questions raised by your topic or some aspect of it?

We could add many other categories to a checklist like this, but maybe this is enough to get you started planning the contents of your technical background report. And remember that each of these checklist items may represent a full section in the report—not a sentence or two.

As for the organization of these parts of the report, again, your intuitions are in order. Some subtopics logically come before others.

Typical format of technical background reports. Remember that in most technical-writing courses, you are expected to use a format like this exactly and precisely—unless you work out some other arrangements with your instructor.

Technical Guides and Handbooks

There's a distinction to be made between reports, on the one hand, and guides and handbooks, on the other. However, it's difficult to distinguish between the two latter types. A report, as the preceding section explains, is simply a collection of information on a topic—its background. For example, your boss might call you in and bark out this order: "Jones, our architectural firm needs to catch up with this green roof thing. See if you can pull some basic information together for me. How about in two weeks?"

A guide or handbook, on the other hand, has a somewhat different purpose. A guide would "guide" its readers in determining the feasibility of a green roof, planning, and constructing one. A handbook might contain little or no guidance but have lots of reference information about green roofs: associations supporting them, case studies, specifications, vendors, government ordinances, and so on.

But, frankly, the distinction between these two is difficult. And, in terms of format, style, and structure, there is very little difference. The abstract and executive summary have no logical place in a guide or handbook. If you are taking a technical writing course, check with your instructor about whether you still should include an abstract or executive summary.

Primary Research Reports

Primary research report is our name for that kind of report that presents original research data—no matter whether that data was generated in a laboratory or out in the "field." A secondary research report then would be a report (such as the technical background report) that presents information gained largely from printed or online information sources or from other sources such as interviews or direct observation.

You're probably already familiar with this type of report as the "lab report." The contents and organization of this type of report have a basic logic: you present your data and conclusions, but also present information on how you went about the experiment or survey. In other words, you enable the reader to replicate (the fancy scientific word for repeat) your experiment, or at least, visualize quite specifically how you went about it.

One of the examples is an experiment to see whether production of rainbow trout can be increased by varying water temperature. While there is not a one-to-one correspondence between the typical sections in primary research reports and the sections you see in the actual rainbow trout report, you'll find that most of the functions are carried out. Instead of a full paragraph, sometimes all that is needed is a single sentence. And sometimes certain functions are combined into a single sentence.

Contents of primary research reports. To enable readers to replicate your experiment or survey, you provide information like the following (each normally in its own section):

- **Introduction**—The introduction to the primary research report needs to do what any good introduction to a report needs to do—get readers ready to read the report. It may provide some background, but not more than a paragraph. Common elements, such as background, can be handled in the introduction. If they require a lot of discussion, however, they may need their own sections.
- **Problem, background**—One of the first things to do, either in the introduction, or in a separate section of its own, is to discuss the situation that has led to the research work. For example, you may have noticed something that contradicts a commonly accepted theory; you may have noticed some phenomenon that has not been studied, and so on. Explain this somewhere toward the beginning of a primary research report.
- **Purpose, objectives, scope**—Also toward the beginning of this type of report discuss what you intended to do in the research project—what were your objectives? Also, explain the scope of your work—what were you not trying to do?

- **Review of literature**—After you've established the basis for the project, summarize the literature relevant to it—for example, books, journal articles, and encyclopedias. If you are doing a study on speech recognition software, what articles have already been written on that subject? What do they have to say about the merits of this kind of software? All you do is summarize this literature briefly and enable readers to go have a look at it by providing the full bibliographic citation at the end of your report. In the context of this type of report, the review of literature shows where the gaps or contradictions are in the existing literature.
- **Materials, equipment, facilities**—Remember that one of your goals in writing this type of report is to enable the reader to replicate the experiment or survey you performed. Key to this is the discussion of the equipment and facilities you used in your research. Describe things in detail, providing brand names, model numbers, sizes, and other such specifications.
- **Theory, methods, procedures**—To enable readers to replicate your project, you must also explain the procedures or methods you used. This discussion can be step by step: "first, I did this, then I did that...." Theory and method refer more to the intellectual or conceptual framework of your project. These explain why you used the procedures that you used.
- **Results, findings, data**—Critical to any primary research report is the data that you collect. You present it in tables, charts, and graphs. These can go in the body of your report, or in appendixes if they are so big that they interrupt the flow of your discussion. Of course, some results or findings may not be presentable as tables, charts, or graphs. In these cases, you just discuss it in paragraphs. In any case, you do not add interpretation to this presentation of data. You merely present the data, without trying to explain it.
- **Discussion, conclusions, recommendations**—In primary research reports, you interpret or discuss your findings in a section separate from the one where you present the data. Now's the time to explain your data, to interpret it. This section, or area of the report, is also the place to make recommendations or state ideas for further research.
- **Bibliography**—The ideal of the primary research report is built upon or add to the knowledge in a particular area. It's the vehicle by which our knowledge advances for a specific topic. Your primary research report rests on top of all the work done by other researchers on the same topic. For that reason, you must list the sources of information you used or consulted in your project. This list occurs at the end of the report.

As for the organization of a primary research report, the typical contents just listed are arranged in an actual primary research report in just about the same order they were just discussed. Loosely, it is a chronological order. First, you discuss set-up issues such as the problem and objectives, then you discuss the procedures, then the data resulting from those procedures, then your conclusions based upon that data.

Typical format of primary research reports. In most technical-writing courses, you should use a format like the one shown in the chapter on report format. (The format you see in the example starting on page is for journal articles). In a primary research report for a technical-writing course, however, you should probably use the format in which you have a transmittal letter, title page, table of contents, list of figures, and abstracts.

Technical Specifications

Specifications are descriptions of products or product requirements. They can provide details for the design, manufacture, testing, installation, and use of a product. You typically see specifications in the documentation that comes in the package with certain kinds of products, for example, CD players or computers. These describe the key technical characteristics of the item. But specifications are also written as a way of "specifying" the construction and operational characteristics of a thing. They are then used by people who actually construct the thing or go out and attempt to purchase it. When you write specifications, accuracy, precision of detail, and clarity are critical. Poorly written specifications can cause a range of problems and lead to lawsuits.

Outline Specifications Example

Two-Column Specifications Example

Outline and two-column style used to present information in specifications. Graphics, tables, and lists are heavily used, but some details can only be provided through sentences and paragraphs. For these reasons then, specifications have a particular style, format, and organization:

- Make every effort to find out what the specific requirements are for format, style, contents, and organization. If they are not documented, collect a big pile of specifications written by or for your company, and study them for characteristics like those described in the following.
- Use two-column lists or tables to lists specific details. If the purpose is to indicate details such as dimensions, materials, weight, tolerances, and frequencies, regular paragraph-style writing may be unnecessary.
- For sentence-style presentation, use an outline style similar to the one shown in the illustration above. Make sure that each specification receives its own number–letter designation. In sentence-style specifications, make sure each specific requirement has its own separate sentence.
- Use the decimal numbering system for each individual specification. This facilitates cross-referencing.

Graphics and tables used to present information in specifications.

- Use either the open (performance) style or the closed restrictive style, depending on the requirements of the job. In the open or performance style, you can specify what the product or component should do, that is, its performance capabilities. In the closed style, you specify exactly what it should be or consist of.
- Cross-reference existing specifications whenever possible. Various government agencies as well as trade and professional associations publish specifications standards. You can refer to these standards rather than include the actual specifications details.
- Use specific, concrete language that identifies as precisely as possible what the product or component should be or do. Avoid words that are ambiguous—words that can be interpreted in more than one way. Use technical jargon the way it is used in the trade or profession.
- Test your specifications by putting yourself in the role of a bumbling contractor—or even an unscrupulous one. What are the ways a careless or incompetent individual could misread your specifications? Could someone willfully misread your specifications in order to cut cost, time, and thus quality? Obviously, no set of specifications can ultimately be "foolproof" or "shark-proof," but you must try to make them as clear and unambiguous as possible.
- For specifications to be used in design, manufacturing, construction, or procurement, use "shall" to indicate requirements. In specifications writing, "shall" is understood as indicating a requirement. (See the outline-style specifications in the first illustration on specifications for examples of this style of writing.)
- Provide numerical specifications in both words and symbols: for example, "the distance between the two components shall be three centimeters (3 cm)."
- Writing style in specifications can be very terse: incomplete sentences are acceptable as well as the omission of functions words such as articles and conjunctions that are understood.
- Exercise great caution with pronouns and relational or qualifying phrases. Make sure there is no doubt about what words such as "it," "they," "which," and "that" refer to. Watch out for sentences containing a list of two or more items followed by some descriptive phrase—does the descriptive phrase refer to all the list items or just one? In cases like these, you may have to take a wordier approach for the sake of clarity.
- Use words and phrasing that have become standard in similar specifications over the years. Past usage has proven them reliable. Avoid words and phrases that are known not to hold up in lawsuits.
- Make sure your specifications are complete—put yourself in the place of those who need your specifications; make sure you cover everything they will need.

Contents and Organization of Specifications. Organization is critical in specifications—readers need to be able to find one or a collection of specific details. To facilitate the process of locating individual specifications, use headings, lists, tables, and identifying numbers as discussed previously. But a certain organization of the actual contents is also standard:

- **General description** — Describe the product, component, or program first in general terms—administrative details about its cost, start and completion dates, overall description of the project, scope of the specifications (what you are not covering), anything that is of a general nature and does not fit in the part-by-part descriptions in the following.
- **Part-by-part description** — In the main body, present specifications part by part, element by element, trade by trade—whatever is the logical, natural, or conventional way of doing it.
- **General-to-specific order** — Wherever applicable, arrange specifications from general to specific.

Graphics in specifications. In specifications, use graphics wherever they enable you to convey information more effectively. For example, in the specifications for a cleanroom for production of integrated circuits, drawings, diagrams, and schematics convey some of the information much more succinctly and effectively than sentences and paragraphs.

Literature Reviews

A literature review summarizes what is known about a specific research topic, narrates the milestones of the research history, indicates where current knowledge conflicts, and discusses areas where there are still unknowns.

A literature review can be a standalone document or a component of a primary research report (as discussed previously). Research journals often contain articles whose sole purpose is to provide a literature review. As a component of a research report, a literature review can be as long as a whole chapter in book, only a paragraph in a research article, or as short as a few sentences in an introduction. In all cases, the function of the literature review is the same: to summarize the history and current state of research on a topic.

As you know from the preceding section, a primary research report (such as those in engineering research journals) focuses on a question: for example, the effect of weightlessness on growing vegetables. The literature-review section of that report would summarize what is known about this topic, indicate where current knowledge conflicts, and discuss areas where there are still unknowns.

A well-constructed literature review tells a story. It narrates the key events in the research on a particular question or in a particular area:

1. Who were the first modern researchers on this topic? What were their findings, conclusions, and theories? What questions or contradictions could they not resolve?
2. What did researchers following them discover? Did their work confirm, contradict, or overturn the work of their predecessors? Were they able to resolve questions their predecessors could not?

You narrate this series of research events in a literature review. You can consider this research as similar to the thesis–antithesis–synthesis process. You start out with a thesis, then along comes an antithesis to contradict it, and eventually some resolution of this contradiction called a synthesis is achieved, which is actually a step forward in the knowledge about that topic. But now the synthesis becomes a thesis, and the process starts all over again.

Hilton Obenzinger of Stanford University in "How to Research, Write, and Survive a Literature Review?" calls this type of literature review a "road map." He identifies several other types, most importantly those that review the methodology of the research as well as or instead the research findings. Obenzinger emphasizes that the literature review is not just a passive summary of research on a topic but an evaluation of the strengths and weaknesses of that research—an effort to see where that research is "incomplete, methodologically flawed, one-sided, or biased." In any case, as the following examples show, a literature review is a discussion of a body of research literature not an annotated bibliography. Notice in the following examples that literature reviews use standard bracketed IEEE textual citation style and end with a bibliography (called "References").

Consider the following excerpt, which shows the beginning of the review of literature, found in "Face Recognition: A Literature Review:"

Face recognition, in additional to having numerous practical applications such as bankcard identification, access control, mug shots searching, security monitoring, and surveillance system, is a fundamental human behavior that is essential for effective communications and interactions among people. A formal method of classifying faces was first proposed in [1]. The author proposed collecting facial profiles as curves, finding their norm, and then classifying other profiles by their deviations from the norm. This classification is multi-modal, i.e., resulting in a vector of independent measures that could be compared with other vectors in a database.

As you can see, the first paragraph establishes the topic and its importance; the second paragraph goes back to the beginning of modern research that provided a foundation for computer-based face recognition. This literature review moves on to the current status of research in this field:

Progress has advanced to the point that face recognition systems are being demonstrated in real-world settings [2]. The rapid development of face recognition is due to a combination of factors: active development of algorithms, the availability of a large databases of facial images, and a method for evaluating the performance of face recognition algorithms.

Notice how this next excerpt describes an important advance in the research on this topic, but then points out its deficiencies:

The literature review of face-recognition research examines many different methods used in computer-based face recognition. For each, it summarizes the method, the results, and the strengths and weaknesses of that method. This example is not so much the thesis-antithesis-synthesis pattern mentioned above but rather a collection of efforts all striving toward a common goal, increased accuracy of computer-based face recognition. Here's how the summary of that process ends in this literature review:

In [83], a combined classifier system consisting of an ensemble of neural networks is based on varying the parameters related to the design and training of classifiers. The boosted algorithm is used to make perturbation of the training set employing MLP as base classifier. The final result is combined by using simple majority vote rule. This system achieved 99.5% on Yale face database and 100% on ORL face database. To the best of our knowledge, these results are the best in the literatures.

References

A. S. Tolba, A.H. El-Baz, and A.A. El-Harby, "Face Recognition: A Literature Review." International Journal of Signal Processing, vol. 2, no. 2, 2005

By: David McMurrey

Objectives

Upon completion of this chapter, readers will be able to do the following:

- Explain the purpose of a business plan.
- Identify and define common sections of business plans.
- Navigate and apply the format of business plans.

Introduction to Business Plans

A *business plan* is a document used to start a new business or get funding for a business that is changing in some significant way. Business plans are important documents for business partners who need to agree upon their plans, government officials who need to approve that plan, and of course potential investors such as banks or private individuals who may fund the business.

A business plan is very much like a proposal, except for at least one big difference. The business plan seeks to start a new business or significantly expand an existing business. A proposal, on the other hand, seeks approval to do a specific project. For example, a business plan might seek funding to start a software company to create computer games. A proposal, on the other hand, might bid to do the development work for some specific computer game.

Caution: In a technical writing course, treat a business-plan project as a *writing* project, not as a real-world business plan. This chapter should *not* be viewed as a definitive guide for writing a real-world business plan.

Common Sections in Business Plans

Many of the elements of the plans resemble those of the proposal—particularly the qualifications and background sections. Remember that these sections are only typical and not necessarily in any required order. For your plan, you'll need to think about the best sequencing of the sections and about other sections that might also be necessary.

3. **Product or service to be offered**: One of the most important sections of the business plan is the description of the actual product or service to be offered. If it is a description of a product—a physical object—you need to use the techniques for technical description. If a service is to be offered, explain it and take readers on a step-by-step tour of how the service will be handled.
4. **Technical background on the product or service**: If your product or service involves technologies or technical processes potentially unfamiliar to your readers, explain these. Remember that business plans often go to nonspecialists who, despite their lack of technical expertise, have the investment funds or the legal understanding to get your business going.
5. **Market for the product or service**: Critical also to any business plan is the exploration of the existing marketplace into which your product or service fits. What other companies exist that offer the same thing you plan to offer? How much business do they do? How are they different from each other? How will your business differ from them?
6. **Process by which the product or services is produced**: If applicable, explain how the product or service will be produced. Explain how the proposed business will operate on a day-to-day basis.
7. **Facilities and personnel needed for the operation**: Plan to discuss the facilities (storefronts, warehouses, production facilities, vehicles) your business will require as well as the personnel that will be needed.
8. **Projected revenues from the operation**: Of obvious importance in any business plan is the discussion of the revenues you project for your business. If you know the estimate of total revenues for the market area in which you plan to operate, what percentage do you expect to win? Obviously, in your first few years, you may operate at a loss-at what point in time do you project to break even?

9. **Funding necessary for the startup and operation**: The plan should also discuss the funding you'll need to get the business started as well as the operating costs—the funding needed to run the business on a daily basis.
10. **Qualifications and background of the personnel**: Important too is the section that presents your qualifications to start and operate the business you are proposing. Of course, "you" can mean a number of people with whom you are working to start the business. This section can be very much like a collection of resumes, although you want to write an introduction in which you describe your group's qualifications as a whole.
11. **Discussion of feasibility and investment potential**: You'll want to include in your plan a discussion of the likelihood of the success of your business. Obviously, you believe that it will be a success, but you must find a way to support this belief with facts and conclusions in order to convince your readers. Also, you must discuss what sort of return on investment readers can expect.
12. **Investment offering**: And finally, you may need to present what kinds of investment apparatus you are actually offering.

In planning your business plan, remember that you try to provide whatever information the audience may need to consider your idea. Your goal is to convince them you have a good idea and to encourage them to invest in it (or to approve it in some way). It's okay to provide marginal information—information you're not quite sure that readers will want. After all, you section off the parts of a business plan with headings; readers can skip over sections they are not interested in.

Format for Business Plans

You can use the format for the formal report, the format for proposals, or some combination of the two.

Business plans, even those for small operations, can run well over 15 pages—in which case you'll want to bind the plan (see the suggestions in the chapter on formal reports). You'll also need a cover letter—examples of this are also in the chapter on report formatting.

As you plan the format of your business plan, think about designing it so that readers can find and read essential information quickly. This means setting up an abstract but calling it "Executive Summary."

Also plan to group similar sections. In the preceding section that lists the various kinds of information to include in a plan, some of suggestions should be combined—for example, the sections on financial aspects of the proposed business.

And finally, make use of appendixes for unwieldy, bulky information. Enable readers to quickly find the main sections of the plan, without having to wade through tables and charts that go on for pages and pages.

Resources for Business Plans

Here are some additional resources on business plans:

1. Starting a Business and Writing a Business Plan. Lots of good detail and links. From DiscoverBusiness.us
2. The Ultimate Guide to Business Plans. Focus on ecommerce. From Ecommerce University.
3. bplans.com. Samples available.
4. Business Plan Guide. Made available by Miller consulting, this site contains good information on business plans plus numerous links to other sites on the same topic.

By: David McMurrey and Jonathan Arnett

Objectives

Upon completion of this chapter, readers will be able to do the following:

- Explain the purpose of a proposal.
- Identify and explain the different types of proposals.
- Navigate and apply the format and structure of a proposal.

What Proposals Do

A proposal is an offer or bid to do a certain project for someone. Proposals may contain other elements—technical background, recommendations, results of surveys, information about feasibility, and so on. But what makes a proposal a proposal is that it is a persuasive document that asks the audience to approve, fund, or grant permission to do the proposed project.

If you plan to be a consultant or run your own business, written proposals may be one of your most important tools for bringing in business. If you work for a government agency, nonprofit organization, or a large corporation, the proposal can be a valuable tool for initiating projects that benefit the organization or you the employee-proposer (and usually both).

A proposal should contain information that would enable the proposal's audience to decide whether to approve the project, to give you money for the project, or to hire you to do the work, and maybe all three. To write a successful proposal, put yourself in the place of your audience—the recipient of the proposal—and think about what sorts of information that person would need to feel confident about you doing the project.

It's easy to get confused about proposals. Imagine that you have a terrific idea for installing some new technology where you work and you write up a document explaining how it works and why it's so great, showing the benefits, and then end by urging management to go for it. Is that a proposal? No, at least not in this context. It's more like a feasibility report, which studies the merits of a project and then recommends for or against it. All it would take to make this document a proposal would be to add elements that ask management for approval for you to go ahead with the project. Certainly, some proposals must sell the projects they offer to do, but in all cases, proposals must sell the writer (or the writer's organization) as the one to do the project.

Types of Proposals

Consider the situations in which proposals occur.

Sometimes proposals originate through a formal process. A company may send out a public announcement requesting proposals for a specific project. This public announcement—called a **request for proposals** (RFP)—could be issued through newspapers, trade journals, Chamber of Commerce channels, or individual letters. Firms or individuals interested in the project would then write proposals in which they summarize their qualifications, describe schedules and costs, and discuss their approaches to the project. The recipient of all these proposals would then evaluate them, select the best candidate, and then work up a contract.

But proposals also come about much less formally. Imagine that you are interested in doing a project at work (for example, investigating the merits of bringing in some new technology to increase productivity). Imagine that you visited with your supervisor and tried to convince her to buy the new technology. She might respond by saying, "I like your idea, but I can't approve a purchase that large. Write me a proposal. I'll present it to upper management." You would then write a proposal in which you describe the problem, explain why it needs to be solved, introduce your intended solution, describe schedules and costs, and ask for permission to bring in the new technology. Your supervisor would then forward the proposal to upper management, who would either deny the request or release funds to make the project happen.

As you can see from these examples, proposals can be divided into several categories:

- **Internal/External**: A proposal to someone within your organization (a business, a government agency, etc.) is an internal proposal. With internal proposals, you might omit certain sections (such as qualifications) or not need to include as much information in them. An external proposal is one written from a separate, independent organization or individual to another such entity. The typical example is an independent consultant proposing to do a project for another firm.
- **Solicited/Unsolicited**: A proposal that comes in response to an RFP is a solicited proposal. Typically, a company will send out RFPs through the mail or publish them in some news source. But proposals can be solicited in person, as well. For example, if you are explaining to your boss what a great thing it would be to install a new technology in the office, your boss might get interested and ask you to write up a proposal that offered to do a formal study of the idea. An unsolicited proposal comes even though the recipient has not requested proposals. With unsolicited proposals, you sometimes must convince the recipient that a problem or need exists before you can begin the main part of the proposal.
- **Research/Goods-and-Services**: A research proposal is one in which the recipient requests permission or funding (and sometimes both) to study something and write a report about the findings. A goods-and-services proposal is a classic business-type proposal, in which one party offers to sell a product or service to another party.

Format of Proposals

You have many options for the format and packaging of your proposal. Two of the most common formats are listed here.

Cover Letter or Memo with Separate Proposal

In this format, you send a cover letter or cover memo along with the proposal, but the letter or memo does not appear inside the proposal's main body. They are distinct documents, and the letter or memo should follow standard professional format. If the proposal is printed in hard copy, the letter or memo is often paper clipped to the front cover.

Consolidated Business-Letter or Memo Proposal

In this format, you consolidate the entire proposal within a standard business letter or memo. You include headings and other special formatting elements as if it were a larger, formal document. (This consolidated memo format is illustrated in the left portion of the following illustration.) Use the memorandum format for internal proposals and the business-letter format for external proposals.

To: Fernando dos Marias, Dir.
            San Marcos Photovoltaic Systems, Inc.

From: Lorenzo Messi, Planner.
            San Marcos Photovoltaic Systems, Inc.

Date: June 6, 2015

Subject: Proposal: to installation of

The following is a proposal to desig
for Empresaa de Distribuicao de El
following is a discussion of the bene
the system-installation process, out
company's qualifications. My consu
cells system in two other provinces

Photovoltaic Systems: Benefits
Like many other areas in Africa, Lui
outlined in this proposal will go a lo

 San Marcos Photovoltaic Systems, Inc.
1124 State Blvd., Suite 300
San Marcos, TX 78666

March 09, 2009

Mr. Fernando dos Marias
EDEL – Luanda
1214 Saldanha
Luanda, Angola 2442 335437

Subject: Proposal to add photovoltaic cells to the EDEL distribution system

Dear Mr. Dos Marias:

The following is a proposal that will guide your staff in the addition of photovoltaic cells to the Empresaa de Distribuicao de Electricidade (EDEL) system. As an electrical engineer working in Lubango, I observed the need for photovoltaic systems. Like many other areas in Africa, Lubango experiences frequent power shortages. The system outlined in this proposal will go a long way toward resolving this problem.

The following proposal describes the benefits of using photovoltaic cells for the production of electricity, the installation process, output projections, and costs. Included is a schedule of completion and my company's qualifications.

Please feel free to contact me at 517-000 0000. I appreciate your time and consideration.

Sincerely,

Helena Genao
Attached: proposal

Figure 1: Proposal that uses the consolidated memo format (left) and a proposal that is separate from its cover letter (right)

Common Proposal Structure

The following is an outline of the internal structure you'll commonly find in proposals. It is not an absolute structure, so you can reorganize, cut, or add sections as necessary, but it is the most common sequence and should serve you well as a basic framework, whether your proposal is a single page or a multi-volume stack of bound paper.

Front Matter

Cover letter: A proposal that is longer than a few pages often contains a brief "cover" letter or memo (depending on if the proposal is external or internal, respectively) that is paper clipped to the proposal itself. This cover letter or memo briefly announces that a proposal follows and outlines its contents. In fact, the contents of the cover letter or memo are pretty much a condensed version of the introduction section. This redundant content is because the letter or memo may get detached from the proposal, or the recipient may not even bother to look at the letter or memo and just dive right into the proposal itself.

Binding, section tabs, cover, label: Consider packaging the document in a professional-looking way, especially if you are preparing an external proposal in hard copy. Use a spiral or comb binding, insert tabs for major sections (on long proposals; short documents are easily navigable without tabs), and prepare a label for the cover that includes at least these four pieces of information:

1. the proposal's formal title

2. the intended recipient
3. the authors (or, often, the authors' organization)
4. the date of submission

Title page: A proposal that is longer than a few pages usually includes a title page. On this page, you should include the same basic information that appears on a cover label. You may also wish to include a descriptive abstract at the bottom. (See the next section, Abstract / Executive summary.)

Do not include a running header or page number on a title page.

Abstract—Executive summary: These two elements are superficially similar, but they serve different purposes. An abstract is a capsule summary of the proposal's high points; it's usually a single paragraph, and its purpose is to clue a reader in to the document's purpose and general contents. An executive summary is a more-detailed summary that includes all the important points in the proposal; it will contain multiple paragraphs and is significantly longer than an abstract, and its purpose is to allow a busy executive to decide whether reading the entire proposal is worthwhile.

Long proposals may contain both an abstract and an executive summary. Short proposals most likely contain an abstract but no executive summary.

There is no hard limit on an executive summary section's length; it can vary from a half-page to as long as needed. On a very long and complex proposal (for example, a proposal written for the federal government about a multi-billion-dollar project), the executive summary can be a short book. However, a good rule of thumb is to limit an executive summary to two pages.

Table of contents: Any technical document of more than a few pages that includes distinct major sections should include a table of contents (ToC), and each major section should start on a new page.

The number of subheading levels you include in the ToC is up to you. A long, complex proposal with multiple subheadings may be more navigable if every subheading has its own ToC entry, but a relatively short proposal may only need its major headings to appear in the ToC.

The ToC should not include the title page or the cover letter/memo. If the proposal includes an abstract and/or executive summary, those sections should appear in the ToC, and it is customary to paginate them with lower-case roman numerals. The ToC should not include itself. Treat it as page zero.

Table of figures: If your proposal contains more than one figure or table, list them in a table of figures (ToF), sometimes called a "list of figures."

Please note that tables and figures are different things. Strictly speaking, figures are illustrations, drawings, photographs, graphs, and charts. Tables are rows and columns of words and numbers; they are not considered figures.

For longer reports that contain multiple figures and tables, create separate lists for each. Put them on a separate page from the ToC, but put them together on the same page if they fit. You can identify the lists separately, as Table of Figures and Table of Tables.

Main Body

Introduction: Plan the introduction to your proposal carefully. Make sure it does all of the following things (but not necessarily in this order) that apply to your particular proposal:

- Indicate that the following document is a proposal.
- Refer to some previous contact with the recipient of the proposal or to your source of information about the project.

- Include one brief motivating statement that will encourage the recipient to read beyond the introduction and to both consider doing your project (if it's an unsolicited or competitive proposal) and consider hiring you to do the project.
- Give an overview of the proposal's contents.

Take a look at the introductions in the first two example proposals listed at the beginning of this chapter and try to identify these elements.

Background on the problem, opportunity, or situation: The background section discusses why the project is necessary or desirable—what problem exists, what opportunity there is for improving things, and/or what the basic situation is. For example, managers of a chain of daycare centers may need to meet state licensing requirements by ensuring that all employees know CPR. An owner of pine timber land in east Texas may want to harvest saleable timber without destroying the local ecosystem.

If your proposal's audience knows the problem very well, this section might not be needed. Writing the background section still might be useful, however, in demonstrating your particular view of the problem. And, if the proposal is unsolicited, a background section is almost a requirement—you will probably need to convince the audience that a problem or opportunity exists and that it should be addressed.

Benefits and feasibility of the proposed project: Most proposals discuss the advantages or benefits of doing the proposed project. This section acts as an argument in favor of approving the project. Also, some proposals discuss the likelihood of the project's success. In the forestry proposal, the proposer recommends that the landowner make an investment; at the end of the proposal, he explores the question of the potential return on that investment. In an unsolicited proposal, this section is particularly important—you are trying to "sell" the audience on the project.

Title: be sure to include
"Proposal"

Introduction:
- Purpose, content
- Context
- Encouragement
- Overview of proposal
  contents

Project background

Statement of the
proposed work

Benefit, advantages of the
work

Procedure for the project

Description of the finished
product or service

If necessary, the likelihood
of the project's success

Schedule, milestones for
the project: dates and
accomplished work

Project Background

Proposed Project

Project Benefits

Procedure for the Proposed Work

Description of the Completed Project

Feasibility of the Project

Schedule for the Proposed Project

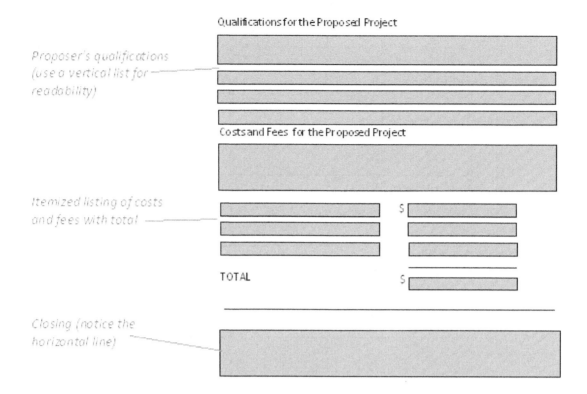

Figure 2: Schematic view of proposals

Description of the deliverable (results of the project): Most proposals need to describe the deliverable—the finished product that the audience will receive after hiring you to complete the project. If you are writing a research proposal, the deliverable will be a report. If you are writing a goods-and-services proposal, the deliverable will be an object or action.

Method, procedure, theory: In some proposals, you'll want to explain how you'll go about doing the proposed work. This section acts as an additional persuasive element; it shows the audience you have a sound, well-thought-out approach to the project. Also, it serves as the other form of background some proposals need. Remember that the background section (the one discussed above) focused on describing the problem or need that brings about the proposal. However, in this section, you discuss the technical background relating to the procedures or technology you plan to use in the proposed work. For example, in the forestry proposal, the writer gives a bit of background on how timber management is done. Once again, this section gives you, the proposal writer, a chance to show that you know what you are talking about and to build confidence in the audience.

Schedule: Most proposals contain a section that shows not only the projected completion date but also key milestones for the project. If you are doing a large project spreading over many months, the timeline would also show dates on which you would deliver progress reports. If you can't cite specific dates, cite amounts of time for each phase of the project.

If you are writing a research proposal about a potential project, you should divide the Schedule section into two separate parts. One subsection should address the schedule for researching and writing the report. The other subsection should address (at least in general terms) the schedule for the major project that you are researching. For example, in the forestry proposal, the timber landowner would have two major questions about time: when would your report arrive, and how long would it take to harvest the pine timber in an ecologically responsible way? You'd need to address both these questions in the Schedule section, but you'd need to keep them in separate subsections.

Costs, resources required: Most proposals also contain a section detailing the costs of the project, whether internal or external. With external projects, you may need to list your hourly rates, projected hours, costs of equipment and supplies, and so forth, and then calculate the total cost of the complete project. For internal projects, you will still need to list the project costs: for example, hours you will need to complete the project, equipment and supplies you'll be using, assistance from other people in the organization, and so on.

If you are writing a research proposal about a potential project, you should divide the costs/resources section into two separate parts, just like the schedule section. One subsection should address the costs for researching and writing the report. The other subsection should list the costs and necessary resources (or at least reasonable estimates of them) for the major project you are researching. Again, with the forestry example, the timber landowner would want to know how much you'd charge to research and write a report about eco-friendly ways of logging his land. Likewise, the land's owner would want to know that he can afford the ecologically-sound logging project. If harvesting the timber in the eco-friendliest way will cause him to go broke, there's no point in hiring you in the first place. You need to address both these issues in the costs-and-resources section but keep them in separate subsections.

Qualifications: Most proposals contain a summary of the proposing individual's or organization's qualifications to do the proposed work. It's like a mini résumé contained in the proposal. The proposal audience uses it to decide whether you are suited for the project. Therefore, this section lists work experience, similar projects, references, training, and education that shows familiarity with the project.

Conclusions: The final major section of the proposal should do two things:

* refocus the audience's attention on the positive aspects of the project
* urge the audience to contact you with their approval

You can also encourage the audience to get in touch to work out the details of the project, remind them of the project's benefits, and put in one last plug for you or your organization as the right choice for the project.

Back Matter

Appendices: An appendix is an "extra" section that appears after the proposal's main body. Any useful content that you feel is too large for the main part of the proposal or that you think would be distracting and interrupt the flow of the proposal should go into an appendix. Common examples of appendix-appropriate material are large tables of data, big chunks of sample code, fold-out maps, background that is too basic or too advanced for the body of the report, or large illustrations that just do not fit in the main body.

Use separate appendices for each item or category of items, and label each one alphabetically, as "Appendix A: (descriptive title of contents)" and so on. If you've got only one appendix, continue the proposal's page numbering scheme. If you have multiple appendices, you can number each appendix's pages separately, as A-1, A-2, and so on.

Glossary: It's always a good idea to define specialized terms in the document's main text, but if your proposal contains a significant number of terms that are unfamiliar to your audience, you may need to include a glossary.

Index: Long, complex proposals may need to include an index so that readers can find the specific word or topic that interests them.

Information sources: If your proposal quotes, paraphrases, or summarizes information that came from outside sources, cite the sources appropriately in the main text and include bibliographic information in a separate section at the proposal's end. Use whatever citation format is appropriate for your audience's profession and field. Common formats include IEEE, MLA, APA, CSE, Chicago, and Turabian.

Proposal Pre-Writing Strategy

When you develop a proposal, go through this checklist and think about these issues. Make a list of your thoughts on them so you (and if you are working in a group, all your coworkers) have a master document you can refer back to.

Audience: Describe the intended audience of the proposal and the proposed report (they may be different) in terms of the organization they work for, their titles and jobs, their technical background, their ability to understand the report you propose to write.

Situation: Describe the situation in which the proposal is written and in which the project is needed: What problems or needs are there? Who has them? Where are they located?

Deliverable type: Describe the deliverable that you are proposing. If you are writing a research proposal, will you give your client a technical background report? A recommendation report? A feasibility report? If you are writing a goods-and-services proposal, what object or service will you provide?

Information sources: If you are writing a research proposal, make sure you know that there is adequate information for your topic. List specific books, articles, reference works, interview subjects, field observations, and other kinds of sources that you think will contribute to your report.

Graphics: List the graphics you think your report will need according to their type and their content. Odds are, you'll need at least one figure or table.

2.5: Progress Reports

By: David McMurrey

Objectives

Upon completion of this chapter, readers will be able to do the following:

- Explain the purpose of a progress report.
- Navigate and apply the format and structure of a proposal.
- Explain common components of a progress report.

Introduction to Progress Reports

You write a progress report to inform a supervisor, associate, or customer about progress you've made on a project over a certain period of time. The project can be the design, construction, or repair of something, the study or research of a problem or question, or the gathering of information on a technical subject. You write progress reports when it takes well over three or four months to complete a project.

Functions and Contents of Progress Reports

In the progress report, you explain any or all of the following:

- How much of the work is complete
- What part of the work is currently in progress
- What work remains to be done
- What problems or unexpected things, if any, have arisen
- How the project is going in general

Progress reports have several important functions:

1. Reassure recipients that you are making progress, that the project is going smoothly, and that it will be complete by the expected date.
2. Provide recipients with a brief look at some of the findings or some of the work of the project.
3. Give recipients a chance to evaluate your work on the project and to request changes.
4. Give you a chance to discuss problems in the project and thus to forewarn recipients.
5. Force you to establish a work schedule so that you'll complete the project on time.
6. Project a sense of professionalism to your work and your organization.

Timing and Format of Progress Reports

In a year-long project, there are customarily three progress reports, one after three, six, and nine months. Depending on the size of the progress report, the length and importance of the project, and the recipient, the progress report can take the following forms:

- Memo—A short, informal report to someone within your organization
- Letter—A short, informal report sent to someone outside your organization
- Formal report—A formal report sent to someone outside your organization

Organizational Patterns for Progress Reports

The recipient of a progress report wants to see what you've accomplished on the project, what you are working on now, what you plan to work on next, and how the project is going in general. To report this information, you combine two of these organizational strategies: time periods, project tasks, or report topics.

Time Periods

A progress report usually summarizes work within each of the following:

- Work accomplished in the preceding period(s)
- Work currently being performed
- Work planned for the next period(s)

Project Tasks

Practically every project breaks down into individual tasks.

Table 1: Project Tasks—One Organizational approach to progress reports

Project	Individual Task
Building municipal ball parks on city-owned land	<ul><li>Measuring community interest</li><li>Locating suitable property</li><li>Designing the bleachers, fences, etc.</li></ul>
Writing a report	<ul><li>Studying the assignment</li><li>Selecting a topic</li><li>Identifying the audience of the report</li><li>Narrowing the topic</li><li>Developing a rough outline</li><li>Gathering information</li><li>Writing one or more rough drafts</li><li>Documenting the report</li><li>Revising and editing the report draft</li><li>Typing and proofreading the report</li><li>Putting the report in its final package</li></ul>

Report Topics

You can also organize your progress report according to the work done on the sections of the final report. In a report project on co-combusting municipal solid waste, you would need information on these topics.

Topics to be covered in the final report:

- The total amount of MSW produced—locally—nationally
- The energy potential of MSW, factors affecting its energy potential
- Costs to modify city utilities in order to change to co-combustion

For each of these topics, you'd explain the work you have done, the work you are currently doing, and the work you have planned.

A progress report is actually a combination of two of these organizational strategies. The following outline excerpts give you an idea of how they can combine.

Table 2: Progress Report Outlines

Progress Report A	Progress Report B	Progress Report C
Task 1 • Work completed • Current work • Planned work Task 2 1. Work completed 2. Current work 3. Planned work Task 3 • Work completed • Current work • Planned work	Work Completed • Task 1 • Task 2 • Task 3 Current Work • Task 1 • Task 2 • Task 3 Future Work • Task 1 • Task 2 • Task 3	Topic 1 • Work completed • Current work • Planned work Topic 2 • Work completed • Current work • Planned work Topic 3 • Work completed • Current work • Planned work

The following illustration shows an example of the project-tasks approach with subheadings for time periods.

Brain Drainage Tube Modifications

During this period, we have continued to work on problems associated with the brine drainage tubes.

Previous period. After minor adjustments during a month of operation, the drainage tubes and the counterwasher have performed better but still not completely satisfactorily. The screen sections of these tubes, as you know, are located at variable distances along the height of the washer.

Current period. The screen portion of the brine drainage tubes have been moved to within 5 feet of the top of the pack. So far, no change in counterwasher performance has been observed. Production statistics at the end of this month (February) should give us a clearer idea of the effect of this modification.

Next period. Depending on the continued performance of the screen in its current position in relation to the top of the pack, we may move the screen to within 3 feet of the top of the pack in the next period of testing. Although the wash ratio was greater with greater screen height, the washing efficiency seems to remain relatively constant; the production vs. compressor KW data for all screen locations so far has seemed to follow the same linear curve.

The following example shows a progress report organized by project tasks.

WORK COMPLETED

As of this time, I have completed almost all of the research work and am putting the sections of the final report together. Here is a breakdown of the work that I have done so far.

Development of the Bottle. In the development section of my report, I have written a technical description of a typical PET soft-drink bottle. It is complete and gives the reader a good idea of what the product should look like and be able to accomplish.

Favorable Properties. The section of the report describing the properties of PET is finished. I have chosen four physical properties that many raw materials containers are tested for, and I have shown how PET withstands these tests.

Manufacturing Processes. For the section on manufacturing processes, I have done research to help me recommend one particular production method for PET bottles. Here, I have described this chosen method and have explained exactly how a plastic bottle is produced on an assembly line.

Economics. I have finished work on half the economics section of this report. So far, I have written an economic comparison of the use of plastic and glass bottles.

Other Parts of Progress Reports

In your progress report, you also need the following.

- an introduction that reviews the purpose and scope of the project
- a detailed description of your project and its history
- an overall appraisal of the project to date, which usually acts as the conclusion.

Introduction

I am now submitting to you a report on the progress that I have made on my research for your company, Ginseng Cola. Immediately following the January 15 acceptance of my firm's bid to study the advantages of bottling your soft-drink product in plastic bottles, I began investigating all areas of the project.

In the following sections of this progress report, you will be informed on the work that I have already accomplished, the work I am now involved in, the work left to do, and finally an overall appraisal of the how the project is going.

Review the details of your project's purpose, scope, and activities. This will aid recipients who are unfamiliar with the project, who do not remember certain details, or who want to doublecheck your approach to the project. The introduction can contain the following:

- Purpose of the project
- Specific objectives of the project
- Scope, or limits, of the project
- Date the project began; date the project is scheduled to be completed
- People or organization working on the project
- People or organization for whom the project is being done
- Overview of the contents of the progress report

Project Description

In most progress reports, include a project description to review the details of your project for the recipients.

Project Description

Here is a review of the purpose and scope of this project.

Purpose. The original investment plan of this corporation included only long-term, low-risk investment in corporate bonds and U.S. securities. This project was designed to answer questions about the potential of short- term, high-dollar investments, particularly those suited to the future expansion of this company's investment plan.

Scope. The report will cover basic definitions of stocks and options as well as reasons for and against these two investment strategies. The report will be broken down into four areas:

1. Mechanics of stocks and options
2. Comparisons of stocks and options
3. Example investment scenarios
4. Recommendations for an investment plan

Conclusion

The final paragraph or section usually reassures audiences that all is going well and on schedule. It can also alert recipients to unexpected changes or problems in the project.

Overall Appraisal

The project to recommend PET production is coming along well. I have not run into any major problems and have found plenty of material on this subject. However, I have not heard from Mr. Simon Juarez of PET Mfg., who is sending information on PET production methods used in several plants in the Southwest.

I can foresee no major problems that will keep me from submitting my report to you on the contract date. In fact, I may be able to get it to you a few days earlier than planned. In general, I am finding that the PET bottle is an even more attractive packaging idea than had seemed in our earlier discussions. Full details on this, however, will appear in the final report.

Sincerely,
Steven C. Crosswell
Process Engineer
C&S Engineering

Revision Checklist for Progress Reports

As you reread and revise your progress report, watch out for problems such as the following:

- Make sure you use the right format. Remember, the memo format is for internal progress reports; the business-letter format is for progress reports written from one external organization to another. (Whether you use a cover memo or cover letter is your choice.)
- Write a good introduction—in it, state that this is a progress report, and provide an overview of the contents of the progress report.
- Make sure to include a description of the final completed project.
- Use one or a combination of the organizational patterns in the discussion of your work.
- Use headings to mark off the different parts of your progress report, particularly the different parts of your summary of work done on the project.
- Use lists as appropriate.
- Provide specifics—avoid relying on vague, overly general statements about the work you've done on the final report project.
- Be sure and address the progress report to the real or realistic audience—not your instructor.
- Assume there will be nonspecialists reading your progress report. But don't avoid discussion of technical aspects of the project—just bring them down to a level that nonspecialists can understand.

By: David McMurrey and Cassandra Race

Objectives

Upon completion of this chapter, readers will be able to do the following:

- Analyze and evaluate a set of technical instructions.
- Write clear and accurate instructions with an introduction and conclusion.
- Develop and design an instruction manual for a specific audience.

The focus for this chapter is one of the most important of all uses of technical writing—*instructions*. As you know, instructions are those step-by-step explanations of how to do something: how to build, operate, repair, or maintain things.

Writing Instructions

One of the most common and one of the most important uses of technical writing is instructions—those step-by-step explanations of how to do things: assemble something, operate something, repair something, or do routine maintenance on something. But for something seemingly so easy and intuitive, instructions are some of the worst-written documents you can find. Like me, you've probably had many infuriating experiences with badly written instructions. What follows in this chapter may not be a fool-proof, goof-proof guide to writing instructions, but it will show you what professionals consider the best techniques.

Ultimately, good instruction writing requires:

- Clear, concise writing
- A thorough understanding of the procedure in all its technical detail
- Your ability to put yourself in the place of the reader, the person trying to use your instructions
- Your ability to visualize the procedure in great detail and to capture that awareness on paper
- Finally, your willingness to go that extra distance and test your instructions on the kind of person you wrote them for.

By now, you've probably studied headings, lists, and special notices—writing a set of instructions with these tools probably seems obvious. Just break the discussion out into numbered vertical lists and throw in some special notices at the obvious points and you're done! Well, not quite, but that's a great start. This chapter explores some of the features of instructions that can make them more complex. You can in turn use these considerations to plan your own instructions.

Some Preliminaries

At the beginning of a project to write instructions, it's important to **determine the structure** or characteristics of the particular procedure you are going to write about. Particularly in technical instructions, your understanding of the procedure could make the difference between success and failure, or at more complex levels, life and death.

Early in the process, **define the audience and situation** of your instructions. Remember that defining an audience means defining its level of familiarity with the topic as well as other details, including age and ability level. See the discussion of audiences and steps to use in defining audiences.

If you are in a writing course, you may need to **write a description of your audience** and attach that to your instructions. This will enable your instructor to assess your instructions in terms of their rightness for the intended audience. And remember too that in a technical-writing course it is preferable to write for non-specialist audiences—much more of a challenge to you as a writer.

Next, examine the procedure you are describing to **determine the number of tasks**. How many tasks are there in the procedure you are writing about? Let's use the term *procedure* to refer to the whole set of activities your instructions are intended to discuss. A *task* is a semi-independent group of actions within the procedure: for example, setting the clock on a microwave oven is one task in the big overall procedure of operating a microwave oven.

A **simple procedure** like changing the oil in a car contains only one task; there are no semi-independent groupings of activities. Within that task are a number of steps, such as removing the plug, draining the old oil, replacing the filter, and adding the new oil. If you were writing instructions on maintaining your car yourself to save money, you would have several tasks, some which are independent, such as rotating the tires, checking the fluids, or replacing the windshield wiper blades.

A **complex procedure** like using a microwave oven is another example of a procedure that contains plenty of such semi-independent tasks: setting the clock; setting the power level; using the timer; and cleaning and maintaining the microwave.

There may be more to your instructions than just tasks. Some instructions have only a single task but have many steps within that single task. For example, imagine a set of instructions for assembling a kids' swing set. In my own experience, there were more than 130 steps! That can be a bit daunting. A good approach is to group similar and related steps into **phases** and start renumbering the steps at each new phase. **A *phase* then is a group of similar steps within a single-task procedure**. In the swing-set example, setting up the frame would be a phase; anchoring the thing in the ground would be another; and assembling the box swing would be still another.

Another consideration, which maybe you can't determine early on, is **how to focus your instructions**. For most instructions, you can focus on **tasks**, or you can focus on **tools** (or features of tools). Your approach will depend on your overall objective in writing the instructions, and you will find that the task approach is one you will probably use most often, with the discussion of the tools included in notes or supplementary sections like a glossary.

Use task orientation. Focus on the tasks your readers want to perform; use how to or -ing phrasing on headings.

In a **task approach** (also known as task orientation) to instructions on using a phone-answering service, you'd have these sections:

1. *recording your greeting*
2. *playing back your messages*
3. *saving your messages*
4. *forwarding your messages*
5. *deleting your messages,* and so on

These are tasks—the typical things we'd want to do with the machine.

On the other hand, in a **tools approach** to instructions on using a photocopier, there would be these unlikely sections:

- *copy button*
- *cancel button*
- *enlarge/reduce button*
- *collate/staple button*
- *copy-size button,* and so on

If you designed a set of instructions on this plan, you'd write steps for using each button or feature of the photocopier. Instructions using this approach are hard to make work. Sometimes, the name of the button doesn't quite match the task it is associated with; sometimes you have to use more than just the one button to accomplish the task. Still, there can be times when the tools/feature approach may be preferable.

Finally, you have to decide how you are going to group tasks if there are more than one. Simply listing tasks may not be all that you need to do. There may be so many tasks that you must group them so that readers can find individual ones more easily. For example, the following are common task groupings in instructions:

- *unpacking and setup tasks*
- *installing and customizing tasks*
- *basic operating tasks*
- *routine maintenance tasks*
- *troubleshooting tasks,* and so on

Common Sections in Instructions

The following is a review of the sections you'll commonly find in instructions.

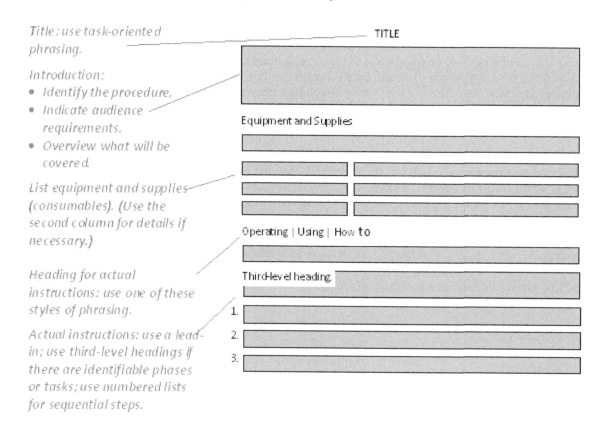

Figure 1: Schematic view of instructions. Remember that this is a typical or common model for the contents and organization—many others are possible.

Title. Naturally you need one, and it should be concise. Avoid awkward noun strings like "Amazing Pizza Rolls Baking Instructions" and instead opt for the "how to", such as "How to Clean Your G.E Microwave" or the gerund, or -ing word phrase, such as "Maintaining Your Apple iPhone."

Date. With technical instructions, the date is crucial. It enables the reader to be certain that these instructions are the most current, and if they are not, where these instructions belong in the line of documents related to this product or procedure.

Table of Contents. If your instructions consist of multiple tasks or have multiple sections, or if they are being presented in the form of a manual, a table of contents is necessary.

Introduction. Plan the introduction to your instructions carefully. Make sure it does any of the following things (but not necessarily in this order) that apply to your particular instructions:

- Indicate the specific tasks or procedure to be explained as well as the scope of coverage (what won't be covered).
- Indicate what the audience needs in terms of knowledge and background to understand the instructions. You may also specify audience age here.
- Give a general idea of the procedure and what it accomplishes. If this is a lengthy set of instructions, indicate how much time may be necessary to complete the task or procedure.
- Indicate the conditions when these instructions should (or should not) be used.
- Give an overview of the contents of the instructions.

General warning, caution, danger notices. Instructions often must alert readers to the possibility of ruining their equipment, screwing up the procedure, and hurting themselves. Also, instructions must often emphasize key points or exceptions. For these situations, you use special notices—note, warning, caution, and danger notices. Typically, danger means that there is a risk of severe bodily harm or death; warning means there is actual risk of bodily harm or major damage to the product; caution means be careful here—there might be a risk; and a note is used to explain details, or tell how to trouble shoot a step within a task.

Technical background or theory. At the beginning of certain kinds of instructions (after the introduction, of course), you may need a discussion of background related to the procedure. For certain instructions, this background is critical—otherwise, the steps in the procedure make no sense. Here is where you get to show your expertise in writing technical definitions and descriptions. For example, you may have had some experience with those software applets in which you define your own colors by nudging red, green, and blue slider bars around. To really understand what you're doing, you need to have some background on color. Similarly, you can imagine that, for certain instructions using cameras, some theory might be needed as well.

Equipment and supplies. Notice that most instructions include a list of the things you need to gather before you start the procedure. This includes equipment, the tools you use in the procedure (such as mixing bowls, spoons, bread pans, hammers, drills, and saws), and supplies, the things that are consumed in the procedure (such as wood, paint, oil, flour, and nails). In instructions, these typically are listed either in a simple vertical list or in a two-column list. Use the two-column list if you need to add some specifications to some or all of the items—for example, brand names, sizes, amounts, types, model numbers, and so on. This may be a good place to use graphics or visuals, especially if a necessary tool is a specialty item.

Discussion of the steps. When you get to the actual writing of the steps, there are several things to keep in mind:

- the structure and format of those steps
- supplementary information that might be needed
- the point of view and general writing style

Structure and format. Normally, we imagine a set of instructions as being formatted as vertical numbered lists. And most are in fact. Normally, you format your actual step-by-step instructions this way. There are some variations, however, as well as some other considerations:

- *Fixed-order steps* are steps that must be performed in the order presented. For example, if you are changing the oil in a car, draining the oil is a step that must come before putting the new oil. These are numbered lists (usually, vertical numbered lists). When in doubt, structure your instructions in this format. You may then use notes to indicate if there is any leeway to perform the steps in another sequence.
- *Variable-order steps* are steps that can be performed in practically any order. Good examples are those troubleshooting guides that tell you to "check this, check that" where you are trying to fix something. You can do these kinds of steps in practically any order. With this type, the bulleted list is the appropriate format.
- *Alternate steps* are those in which two or more ways to accomplish the same thing are presented. Alternate steps are also used when various conditions might exist. Use bulleted lists with this type, with "OR" inserted between the alternatives, or the lead-in indicating that alternatives are about to be presented.
- *Nested steps* are those in which individual steps within a procedure can be rather complex in their own right and need to be broken down into substeps. In this case, you indent further and sequence the sub-steps as a, b, c, and so on.

- *"Stepless" instructions* are those that really cannot use numbered vertical lists and that do little if any straightforward instructional-style directing of the reader. Some situations must be so generalized or so variable that steps cannot be stated.

Supplementary discussion. Often, it is not enough simply to tell readers to do this or to do that. They need additional explanatory information such as how the thing should look before and after the step; why they should care about doing this step; what mechanical principle is behind what they are doing; and even more micro-level explanation of the step—discussion of the specific actions that make up the step.

The problem with supplementary discussion, however, is that it can hide the actual step. You want the actual step—the specific actions the reader is to take—to stand out. You don't want it all buried in a heap of words.

There are at least two techniques to avoid this problem: you can split the instruction from the supplement into separate paragraphs; or you can bold the instruction. The example below shows you a possible technique for including supplementary discussion so that it doesn't obscure the instructions.

How to change engine oil in six steps

When changing engine oil, always check the owner's manual to find the correct amount and type of oil and filter needed.

- **Start the vehicle and allow the engine to warm up for a minute**. This allows the existing oil in the engine to warm up so that it drains out very smoothly.
- **Locate the oil pan drain plug and remove the plug for draining**. Removing the fill cap and pulling the oil dipstick will allow good flow for the oil while draining. If there is more than one plug, drain the oil from both plugs into a container.

Caution: Be careful because the old oil may be hot and could burn you.

Bold text helps distinguish the actual action from the supplementary information.

Avoid telegraphic writing—omitting "understood" articles (the, a, an). True, robots write that way, but we don't have to.

Writing style. The way you actually write instructions, sentence by sentence, may seem contradictory to what previous writing classes have taught you. However, notice how "real-world" instructions are written—they use a lot of imperative (command, or direct-address) kinds of writing; they use a lot of "you." That's entirely appropriate. You want to get in your reader's face, get her or his full attention. For that reason, instruction-style sentences sound like these: "Press the Pause button on the front panel to stop the display temporarily" and a clarifying note might read "You should be careful not to..."

If your instructions have to be more formal, ask your teacher about preferences for using "you." You may find that the direct address isn't appropriate for certain contexts.

For the most effective instructions, **begin each step with an action verb**.

Never **use the passive voice in instructions**. For some weird reason, some instructions sound like this: "The Pause button should be depressed in order to stop the display temporarily." Not only are we worried about the Pause button's mental health, but we wonder who's supposed to depress the thing (are you talkin' to me?). Or consider this example: "The Timer button is then set to 3:00." Again, as the person following these instructions, you might miss this; you might think it is simply a reference to some existing state, or you might wonder, "Are they talking to me?" Almost as bad is using the third person: "The user should then press the Pause button." Again, it's the old double-take: you look around the room and wonder, "Who me?"

Another of the typical problems with writing style in instructions is that people seem to want to leave out articles: "Press Pause button on front panel to stop display of information temporarily" or "Earth person, please provide address of nearest pizza restaurant." Why do we do this? Do we all secretly want to be robots? Anyway, be sure to include all articles (a, an, the) and other such words that we'd normally use in instructions.

Conclusion. You really don't want to just end your instructions with the last step. A conclusion ties the process up neatly; offers trouble shooting information (i.e. what to do if something went wrong); and, if you are writing the instructions as part of your work responsibility, should include contact information.

Other Back Matter. Your set of instructions may include a list of references, a glossary or appendix, an index, or technical specifications. Items placed here are important to the overall instructions because they provide additional information that certain audiences may need, but that are not critical to understanding how to complete the procedure.

Graphics and Images in Instructions

Probably more so than in any other form of writing (except maybe for comic books), graphics are crucial to instructions. Sometimes, words simply cannot explain the step. Illustrations are often critical to readers' ability to visualize what they are supposed to do. Consider the example of car repair manuals which actually use photographs to illustrate procedures, or screen shots that demonstrate the process of using software.

In a technical writing course, instructions may require you to include illustrations or other kinds of graphics—whatever would normally be used in the instructions. Just be sure that the graphics you choose are appropriate and **placed in close proximity to the steps they illustrate**. Don't make your audience flip pages to see the accompanying graphic.

If you don't create your own graphics or images, and find them in other sources, be sure that you cite the source, preferably right below the graphic.

Format of Instructions

Headings. In your instructions, make good use of headings. Normally, you'd want headings for any background section you might have, the equipment and supplies section, a general heading for the actual instructions section, and subheadings for the individual tasks or phases within that section. Take a look at the examples at the beginning of this chapter.

Lists. Similarly, instructions typically make heavy use of lists, particularly numbered vertical lists for the actual step-by-step explanations. Simple vertical lists or two-column lists are usually good for the equipment and supplies section. In-sentence lists are good whenever you give an overview of things to come.

Special notices. In instructions, you must alert readers to possibilities in which they may damage their equipment, waste supplies, cause the entire procedure to fail, or injure themselves or others—even seriously or fatally. Companies have been sued for lack of these special notices, for poorly written special notices, or for special notices that were out of place.

Replace the Guitar Neck

If you've followed the previous steps, your fretboard is now scalloped. The only thing left to do is put your guitar back together. To put it back together, follow these steps:

- Remove the tape from the frets.
- Insert the neck back into the body.
- Put the metal panel back in its place and put in the screws.
  Note: Make sure that you put each screw firmly back in place. The screws keep the neck secure inside the body. If the screws are not installed correctly, the guitar could develop intonation problems.
- Restring the guitar.

Notice how the *note* is indented to the text of the preceding step.

Mounting the NID

Follow these instructions to mount the network interface device (NID) on the wall.

Warning: Always wear safety glasses when using hand tools. Misuse of the tool or ricochet from power tools can result in eye injury.

1. **Select the location for the NID**. This should be close to an electrical ground and located in a place where the ISP's wire will reach the NID. The electrical ground can be identified as a copper wire coming from the electric company's equipment on the exterior of your home.
2. **Drill the NID into place using the screws**. You will need to drill screws into the slots on the top and bottom of the NID.

Notice that the *warning* (more severe than a *note*) is placed at the beginning before any of the steps.

Number, abbreviations, and symbols. Instructions also use plenty of numbers, abbreviations, and symbols. Be sure you are using them correctly. Remember if your instructions pertain to a brand name product to use trademark symbols appropriately.

Revision Checklist for Instructions

As you reread and revise your instructions, watch out for problems such as the following:

1. Make sure you provide real instructions—explanations of how to build, operate, or repair something.
2. Identify where the instructions will be used.
3. Write a good introduction—in it, indicate the exact procedure to be explained, indicate audience requirements, and provide an overview of contents.
4. Make sure that you use the various types of lists wherever appropriate. In particular, use numbered vertical lists for sequential steps.
5. Use headings to mark off all the main sections and subheadings for subsections. (Remember that no heading "Introduction" is needed between the title and the first paragraph. Remember not to use first-level headings in this assignment; start with the second level.)
6. Use special notices as appropriate.
7. Make sure you use the style and format for all headings, lists, special notices, and graphics as specified by your teacher for instruction writing assignments.
8. Use graphics to illustrate any key actions or objects and make certain they are located right beside or beneath the step they illustrate and properly labeled.
9. Provide additional supplementary explanation of the steps as necessary.
10. Remember to create a section listing equipment and supplies, if necessary.

Some final thoughts about writing instructions. As a technical or workplace writer, your ability to write good instructions carries a number of ethical implications. Keep in mind that poorly or carelessly designed instructions leave you or your company liable for damages. They also destroy your credibility and authority. Before you submit any instructions for final review, be sure you get other eyes on them. For small or routine procedures, it may be enough to have a coworker look them over, but more complex instructions should always be tested for usability. Make sure that you have read the chapter on Usability Testing and carried out the necessary testing before your instructions go to publication and distribution.

Exercises and Activities

Exercise 1: Locate a set of instructions for an item you currently own. How effectively do these instructions meet the guidelines presented in this chapter? Analyze each part of the instructions separately and summarize your findings in a memo to your instructor. Be prepared to share examples with the class if you are in a face-to-face classroom.

Exercise 2: For discussion: Identify the ethical issues or concerns you must address in creating instructions for the following: installing a water heater; changing the brakes on a car; preparing an elaborate meal for a large group;

attaching the wing to a fighter jet (okay, I know...this is pretty obvious); office policies and procedures for new employees. Can you think of other situations in which ethical concerns must be addressed?

Exercise 3: Create an instruction manual. This may be completed as a group or individual project: Instructions for this activity may be found here. Your teacher will provide additional information and guidelines.

By: David McMurrey and Tamara Powell

Objectives

Upon completion of this chapter, readers will be able to do the following:

1. Explain the purpose of a user guide.
2. Define the technical writing concepts of this textbook that apply to user guides.
3. Explain and apply the style, format, components, and process for creating user guides.

Introduction to User Guides

A *user guide* is essentially a book-length document containing instructions on installing, using, or troubleshooting a hardware or software product. A user guide can be very brief—for example, only 10 or 20 pages or it can be a full-length book of 200 pages or more. While this definition assumes computers, a user guide can provide operating instructions on practically anything—lawnmowers, microwave ovens, dishwashers, and so on.

The more complex the product, the greater the page count. When this happens, some elements of the user guide get split out into their own separate volumes—especially the installation procedures, troubleshooting procedures, and the commands. A user guide can even contain a brief tutorial—for example, getting users started using the product—but if there is too much tutorial, it too goes into a separate book.

Filepad User Guide
Gimp User Guide
Parallels User Guide

Style and Format of User Guides

A user guide is a combination of many things presented in this online textbook. At its core its instruction writing; you need to be good at the writing style, headings, lists, notices, highlighting, tables, and graphics commonly used in instructions. As a set of instructions, a user guide should use the style and format that is presented elsewhere in this online textbook:

- **Headings.** Use headings to mark off key contents of the information so that readers can find it quickly.
- **Lists.** Use numbered and bulleted lists to help readers scan information quickly.
- **Special notices.** Use special notices such as warnings, cautions, and notes to alert readers to potential problems or emphasize special points.
- **Instructional design.** In general, use the standard design of instructions; primarily, this means task-oriented headings and sections and numbered vertical lists for actual steps that readers are to perform.

Instructions—and therefore user guides—also make abundant use of:

1. **Graphics.** Show readers key components of the objects they will be working with, before and after views, and illustrations of key actions that readers must perform.
2. **Tables.** Provide statistical information and other such details in easy-to-access table form. In user guides, tables are particularly useful whenever reference-type information must be presented.
3. **Highlighting.** Use a consistent and standard scheme of highlighting (bold, italics, alternate fonts, color, caps, and so on).

Components of User Guides

As a book, a user guide must have some combination of the standard book-design components such as the following:

- Front and back covers
- Title page
- Edition notice
- Trademarks
- Disclaimers
- Warranties
- License agreements
- Safety notices
- Preface
- Appendixes
- Glossary
- Index
- Reader comment form

There is no standard combination or sequence of these elements; every company does it differently. Details on the contents, format, and design of these elements can be found in the book design chapter.

Information Included in User Guides

Here's review the common contents of user guides:

Instructions. The most obvious are those step-by-step directions on how to assemble, operate, or troubleshoot the product. Instructions in user guide should generally be task-oriented—that is, written for specific tasks that users must perform. Instructions should generally use vertical numbered lists for actions that must be performed in a required sequence. Similar or closely related instructions in user guides should be grouped into chapters.

Precautionary information. You'll see notes, warning, caution, and even danger notices in user guides. These represent liability concerns for the manufacturer of the product.

Reference information. User guides typically contain plenty of reference information, but only up to a certain point. For example, if there are numerous commands, a separate book for commands is necessary. Reference information in user guides is often presented in tables: columnal lists of settings, descriptions, variables, parameters, flags, and so on.

Getting started information. Some user guides will actually include brief tutorials that will help new users get acquainted with using the product.

About the product. User guides also provide some description of the product, a review of its essential features or its new features. Sometimes this information also gets put into a separate volume, if it is extensive. Typically, the volume will be called something like "Introducing New Product..."

Technical background. Sometimes, user guides will include technical explanations of how the product works, what physical or chemical principles are essential to its operation, and so on. For example, you will see considerable background in user guides for graphic or audio programs—you can't operate them without understanding the concepts of brightness, saturation, and hue; μ law, A law, and other such.

Process and Internal Documents for User Guides

An important part of user guides—in fact, of almost any technical document—is the process that produces it:

- **Initial planning.** Early planning on a user guide involves needs assessment (is any documentation needed at all?), audience analysis (who will be using the user guide? what are their needs?), task analysis (what will users use the product for? what are their common tasks?), library plan (what books and media, in addition to a user guide, are needed to support the product?), and so on.

- **Documentation proposal.** If you are working freelance or as part of an independent documentation firm, you may have to write a documentation proposal in an effort to win a contract to do a certain technical documentation project.
- **Documentation plan.** User guides need documentation plans, which are internal supporting documents that specify content, audience, design, format, production team members, schedule, and other such information about a documentation project and its "deliverables." The documentation plan resembles the documentation proposal in certain ways, but the plan represents an established plan agreed upon by everybody involved in the production process (and that means both the user guide and the product it documents).
- **Prototype and specifications.** Important planning tools, which also serve as useful reference tools during a documentation project, include the prototype of the user guide and the specifications for the user guide. The prototype is a dummy version of the book with all planned components of the book (see the list on book-design components) and all planned elements (see the list under format and style). However, the prototype uses "greeked" text (also known as Lorem ipsum) like the example shown.

Lorem ipsum

Lorem ipsum dolor sit amet, consectetuer adipiscing elit, sed diam nonummy nibh euismod tincidunt ut laoreet dolore magna aliquam erat volutpat. Ut wisi enim ad minim veniam, quis nostrud exerci tation ullam corper suscipit lobortis nisl ut aliquip ex ea commodo consequat. Duis autem vel eum iriure dolor in hendrerit in vulputate velit esse molestie consequat, vel illum dolore eu feugiat nulla facilisis at vero eros et accumsan.

Typically, the prototype of the user guide is very brief: it needs to include only as many pages as it takes to illustrate every unique textual component and textual element that will be used in the user guide. Specifications are descriptions of a book design in table form. Specifications describe every unique component or element of a book, so that it can be recreated by someone who might not have access to the electronic files, templates, or styles of that book.

- *Template and style catalog.* A well-designed user guide, and a well-designed process to produce that user guide, should include templates and style catalogs. A template is an electronic file that defines such aspects of the user guide as page size, headers and footers, page-numbering style, regular and special page layout, and other such detail. A style catalog is also an electronic thing that defines the format and style of textual elements such as headings, headers, footers, lists, paragraphs, tables, and so on. For example, a style for a "heading 1" might specify 24-point Arial bold with 24 picas above and 12 picas below. Styles help you create a user guide more efficiently; styles also help you maintain consistency in the format and style of that user guide.
- *Multiple review drafts & sign-off.* A good process for the production of a user guide also includes several drafts that editors, technical experts, usability testers, and documentation team members can review and provide comments on. You as writer then implement those comments and produce a new draft for these same people to review again. When everybody is satisfied with the draft of the user guide (or worn out or out of time), they sign off on the user guide, and it can then go into "production," which means producing the finished bound copies or the PDF that is made available to users.

As you can see, a user guide brings together many of the topics covered in this online textbook. If you are taking a technical writing course, you probably cannot implement all these features and phases of a user guide. Get with your instructor to see which are required.

2.8: Standard Operating Policies and Procedures

By: David McMurrey and Tamara Powell

Objectives

Upon completion of this chapter, readers will be able to do the following:

- Explain the purpose of standard operating policies and procedures.
- Identify basic structure of standard operating policies and procedures.
- Review examples and apply concepts from them to their writing.

Introduction to Standard Operating Policies and Procedures

This chapter introduces you to policies and procedure documents and to standard operating procedure documents. Click on the links, below, to see samples.

Hand-washing policies for health care personnel
Accounting policies and procedures
Standard operating procedures: pouring dental impressions

Overview

Standard operating procedures and policy-and-procedure documents are roughly the same: they establish standards for doing things and present specific step-by-step procedures for doing those things. Although these distinctions blur in practice, a policy-and-procedure document focuses more often on behavior expected of employees (for example, policies and procedures on smoking, substance abuse, or sexual harassment). Standard operating procedures focus more standard expectations for performing specific procedures such as handwashing by health care professionals or taking a dental implant in a dental lab.

Organizations use policies and procedures documents to record their rules and regulations: attendance policies, substance-abuse policies, work-flow procedures, and so on. Once recorded, the policies and procedures are there for everybody in the organization to refer to, and these documents become the means of settling most disputes within the organization. To distinguish between these two terms, policies are rule statements. Policies are like laws: for example, most organizations have antiharassment policies, which mimic actual government-legislated laws. Procedures, on the other hand, are the step-by-step methods of carrying out those policies. Of course, some policies do not require procedures. If the organization has a no-smoking policy, that's all that needs be said. However, if someone breaks that policy, a procedure is needed for handling that situation.

Writing Projects

If you are enrolled in a course associated with this page, you are in a writing course, not a business management course. Our focus is on good writing; well-designed documents; documents that accomplish their purposes; and documents that meet common expectations as to their content, organization, and format. Standard operating procedure and policy-and-procedure documents are obviously an important application of writing and can contain substantial technical information about an organization's operations. But don't view this chapter as the last word on these topics.

Structure

As you can see from the two standard operating procedures and policy-and-procedure documents in the links above, there are some standard contents and format.

- Decimal numbering system—This feature enables policies or procedures to be "cited." For example, if an employee smokes at a building entryway, you can cite admin policy 23.1.4 (or just give a warning and forget the whole thing this once).
- Heavy use of predicates ("Establish" this, "promote" that).
- Distinction between policies and procedures in the hand-washing example. Policies tell employees what to do; procedures tell them exactly how to do it.
- Tracking numbers to enable ease of reference.
- Ownership and approval names are specified.
- Revision dates, to enable employees to know whether they are looking at the most current version.
- Definitions to establish the precise meanings of key terms.
- Use of "will" to indicate a requirement (older style uses "shall").

Resources

Here is a resource for standard operating procedures:

Guidance for Preparing Standard Operating Procedures (SOPs) from the EPA

Here are some resources for policies and procedures:

Articles about policies and Procedures from Stephen Page
Sample Policies and Procedures from About.com
Management Articles from About.com
Policies and Procedures from Wikipedia
Guide to Writing Policy and Procedure Documents from UC Santa Clara
Policies and Procedures from BusinessDictionary.com

2.9: Recommendation and Feasibility Reports

By: David McMurrey and Jonathan Arnett

Objectives

Upon completion of this chapter, readers will be able to do the following:

1. Explain the differences between recommendation, feasibility, and evaluation reports.
2. Define the common components of recommendation and feasibility reports.
3. Explain and apply organization strategies for reports.

Introduction to Recommendation and Feasibility Reports

This chapter addresses a loosely defined group of report types that examine a situation, evaluate the evidence, and render a judgment.

Some rather fine distinctions...

The reports in this loosely defined category are variously called feasibility reports, recommendation reports, evaluation reports, assessment reports, and who knows what else. They all do roughly the same thing—provide carefully studied opinions and, sometimes, recommendations. There are some subtle differences among some these types.

Feasibility Report

This type of report studies a situation (for example, a problem or opportunity) and a plan for doing something about it and then determines whether that plan is "feasible"—whether it is practical in terms of current technology, economics, social needs, and so on. The feasibility report answers the question "Should we implement Plan X?" by stating "yes" or "no," but more often, "maybe." Not only does it give a recommendation, it also provides the data and the reasoning behind that recommendation.

Recommendation Report

This type of report starts from a stated need, a selection of choices, or both, and then recommends one, some, or none. For example, a company might be looking at grammar-checking software and want a recommendation on which product is the best. As the report writer on this project, you could study the market for this type of application and recommend one particular product, a couple of products (differing perhaps in their strengths and their weaknesses), or none (maybe none of them are any good). The recommendation report answers the question "Which option should we choose?" (or in some cases "Which are the best options?) by recommending Product B, or maybe both Products B and C, or none of the products.

Evaluation Report

This type of report provides an opinion or judgment rather than a yes-no-maybe answer or a recommendation. It provides a studied opinion on the value or worth of something. For example, for over a year the city of Austin had free bus transportation in an attempt to increase ridership and reduce automobile traffic. Did it work? Was it worthwhile? —These are questions an evaluation report would attempt to answer. This type of report compares a thing to a set of requirements (or criteria) and determines how well it meets those requirements. (And of course, there may be a recommendation—continue the project, scrap it, change it, or other possibilities.)

As you can see, these distinctions are rather fine, and they overlap. In real-world writing, these types often combine—you might see elements of the recommendation report combine with the feasibility report, for example. Of course, the writers of these reports don't care which type they are writing—and well they shouldn't! They're trying to get a job done.

Whatever shade of feasibility or recommendation report you write, whatever name people call it—most of the sections and the organization of those sections are roughly the same.

The structural principle that undergirds this type of report is simple: you provide not only your recommendation, choice, or judgment, but also the data and the conclusions leading up to it. That way, readers can check your findings, your logic, and your conclusions and come up with a completely different view. But, more likely, they will be convinced by all your careful research and documentation.

Introduction

As with any technical report, the introduction sets forth the report's purpose (in this case, indicate that it's a recommendation, feasibility, or evaluation report), specifies the report's intended audience, provides a limited description of the report's context and background, forecasts the report's scope, and previews the report's contents and/or organization.

Problem Description/Definition

If the problem is complex, expand on the situation you briefly mentioned in the Introduction, and remind the readers why they are reading your report. What is the problem? Why is it a problem? Why does it need a solution? How will this report help address the problem?

This section's size can vary tremendously. If the audience is deeply familiar with the problem, you may be able to omit this section and summarize the problem in the report's introduction. Or you could include a short problem description section that summarizes the issue's major points. Or you may need to delve into detail in order to prove that the audience should take you and your report seriously. Alternatively, if the audience is grappling with a problem they don't fully understand, then you may need to write a detailed problem description in order to justify your report's existence.

Technical Background

If the readers are not familiar with the issues, objects, or techniques discussed in the report, then you may need to include a separate section in which you explain any information that requires specialized skills or knowledge. This section often goes after the problem description or in an appendix. Alternatively, it may make more sense to fit the technical discussion into the comparison sections where it is relevant.

For example, a discussion of power and speed of tablet computers is going to necessitate some discussion of RAM, megahertz, and processors. Should you put that in a section that compares the tablets according to power and speed? Or should you keep the comparison neat and clean, limited strictly to the comparison and the conclusion, and put the technical discussion into a separate section?

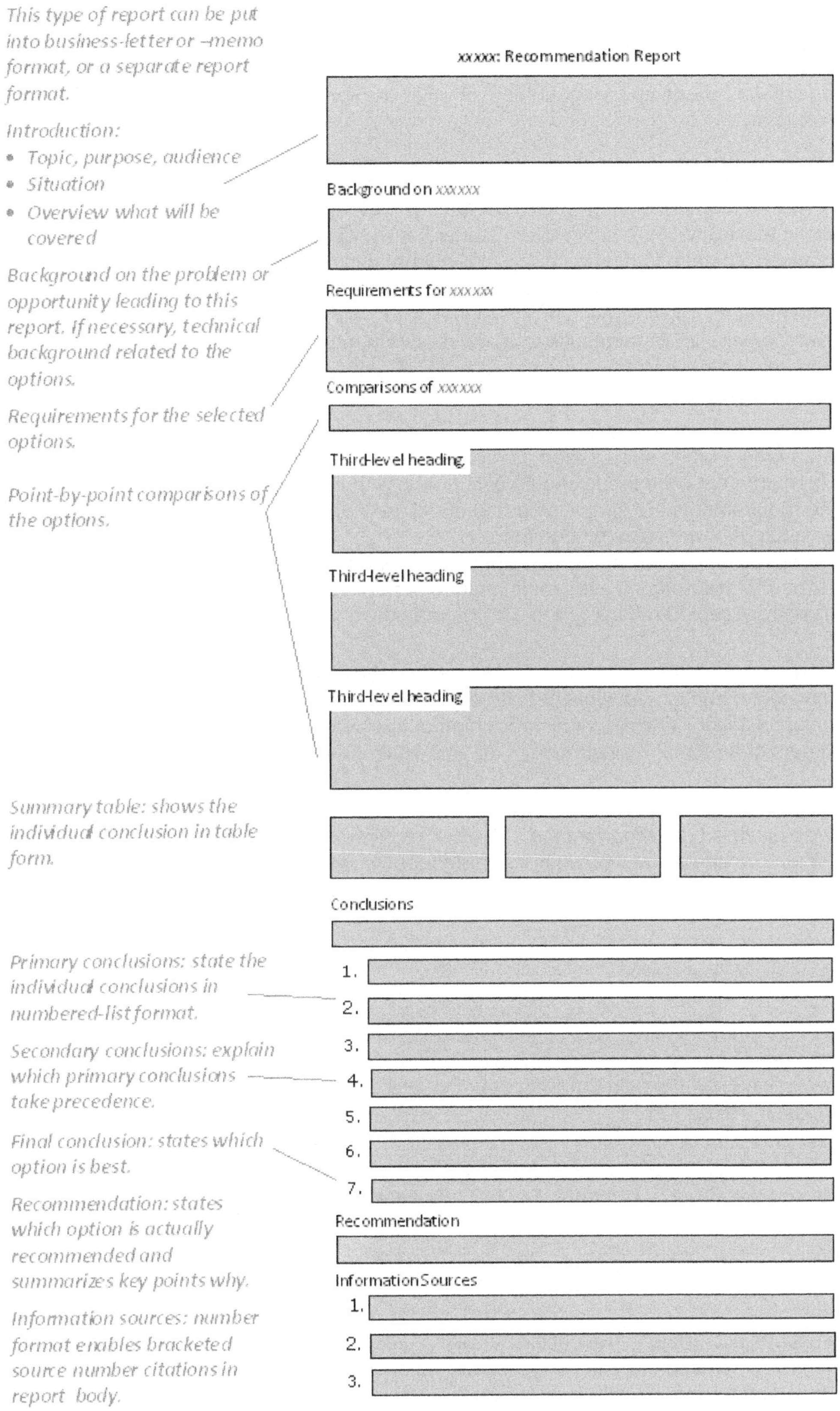

This type of report can be put into business-letter or –memo format, or a separate report format.

Introduction:
- *Topic, purpose, audience*
- *Situation*
- *Overview what will be covered*

Background on the problem or opportunity leading to this report. If necessary, technical background related to the options.

Requirements for the selected options.

Point-by-point comparisons of the options.

Summary table: shows the individual conclusion in table form.

Primary conclusions: state the individual conclusions in numbered-list format.

Secondary conclusions: explain which primary conclusions take precedence.

Final conclusion: states which option is best.

Recommendation: states which option is actually recommended and summarizes key points why.

Information sources: number format enables bracketed source number citations in report body.

xxxxx: Recommendation Report

Background on *xxxxx*

Requirements for *xxxxx*

Comparisons of *xxxxx*

Third-level heading

Third-level heading

Third-level heading

Conclusions

1.
2.
3.
4.
5.
6.
7.

Recommendation

Information Sources
1.
2.
3.

Figure 1: Schematic view of recommendation and feasibility reports

Requirements/Decision-Making Criteria

If your technical report requires you to make a judgment of some sort—is the project feasible? what is the best option? did the item pass or fail a test? —describe and define the factors that guide your decision. Common examples of decision-making criteria include costs, schedules, popular opinions, demonstrated needs, and degrees of quality. Here are some examples:

- If you're trying to recommend a tablet computer for use by employees, your requirements are likely to involve size, cost, hard-disk storage, display quality, durability, and battery function.
- If you're looking into the feasibility of providing every student at Austin Community College with an ID on the ACC computer network, you'd need to define the basic requirements of such a program—what it would be expected to accomplish, problems that it would have to avoid, and so on.
- If you're evaluating the free bus transportation program in Austin, you'd need to know what was expected of the program and then compare its actual results to those requirements.

Requirements can be defined in several basic ways:

1. *Numerical values:* Many requirements are stated as maximum or minimum numerical values. For example, there may be a cost requirement—the tablet should cost no more than $900.
2. *Yes/no values:* Some requirements are simply a yes-no question. Does the tablet come equipped with Bluetooth? Is the car equipped with voice recognition?
3. *Ratings values:* In some cases, key considerations cannot be handled either with numerical values or yes/no values. For example, your organization might want a tablet that has an ease-of-use rating of at least "good" by some nationally accepted ratings group. Or you may have to assign ratings yourself.

Criteria may need to be defined on a fairly granular level. For example, "chocolate flavor" may be a criterion for choosing among brands of chocolate truffles, but what defines a desirable chocolate flavor? Do you want a milk chocolate flavor? A dark chocolate flavor? White chocolate? A high or low percentage of cacao? Sweet, bitter, or spicy? Single-origin cacao beans or a blend? If single origin, do you want Ghanaian, Venezuelan, Honduran, Ecuadorian, or Filipino?

The criteria section should also discuss how important the individual requirements are in relation to each other. Picture the typical situation where no one option is best in all categories of comparison. One option is cheaper; another has more functions; one has better ease-of-use ratings; another is known to be more durable. Set up your criteria so that they dictate a "winner" from situation where there is no obvious winner.

Discussion of the Options

In certain kinds of feasibility or recommendation reports, you'll need to explain how you narrowed the field of choices down to the ones your report focuses on. Often, this section follows right after the discussion of the criteria. Your basic requirements may well narrow the field down for you. But there may be other considerations that disqualify other options—explain these as well.

Additionally, you may need to provide brief descriptions of the options themselves, along with some brief, general specifications on each option you are about to compare. DO NOT, however, actually compare the options in this section. Simply describe them.

Criterion-to-Criterion Comparisons

In this section, evaluate the options according to the decision-making criteria. **Do not** make a list of pros and cons. You can organize the comparison by criteria or by options, depending on what is most appropriate for the subject and your audience, but the best approach is usually to compare the options point-by-point.

For example, if you were comparing tablet computers, you'd have a section that compared them on cost, another section that compared them on battery function, and so on. It would be less effective to have a section that discussed everything about an iPad, another section that discussed everything about a Windows Surface, and so on, because you still need to make the criterion-to-criterion comparisons somewhere.

Table 1: Examples of comparison approaches

Whole-to-Whole Approach	Point-by-Point Approach
Option A • Cost of Option A • Functions of Option A • Ease of use: Option A Option B • Cost of Option B • Functions of Option B • Ease of use: Option B Option C • Cost of Option C • Functions of Option C • Ease of use: Option C	Cost • Option A • Option B • Option C Functions • Option A • Option B • Option C Ease of use • Option A • Option B • Option C

Each of these comparative sections should end with a conclusion that states which option is the best choice in that particular category. Of course, it won't always be easy to state a clear winner—you may have to qualify the conclusions in various ways, providing multiple conclusions for different conditions.

If you were creating an evaluation report, you obviously wouldn't be comparing options. Instead, you'd be comparing the thing being evaluated against the requirements placed upon it, the expectations people had of it. For example, the city of Austin, TX, tested a program in which it provided free bus transportation in order to increase ridership and reduce automobile traffic. What was expected of that program? Did the program meet those expectations?

Equipment price. The price of the highest functioning portable satellite radio/MP3 player offered by XM was $399.99 for the Pioneer Inno [2]. The price for Sirius' highest functioning satellite radio/MP3 player was $259.99 for the Sirius S50 [3]. The price range for the XM plug-and-play radios is $49.99 to $119.99 [2]. The price range for Sirius plug-and play radios is $39.99 to $124.99 [3]. In terms of equipment prices, both XM and Sirius offer similar products from high functioning to low functioning. Because Sirius only offers one portable/MP3 player, it holds a lower average price than XM. **XM has more options for the lower prices plug-and-play radios than Sirius does, so it holds a lower average price than Sirius.**

Summary Table

After the individual comparisons, include a table that summarizes the conclusions from the comparison section. Some readers are prone to pay attention to details in a table rather than in paragraphs. DO NOT just create a summary table and omit the descriptive paragraphs.

Testing Results of XM and Sirius Radio

Category	XM Satellite Radio	Sirius Satellite Radio
Music channels	4	3

Sports channels	4	2.5
Talk and entertainment channels	3.5	4
Subscription price	4	3.5
Portbable radio/MP3 player price	2.5	3.5
Plug-and-Play radio price	4	2.5
Signal	3	4
Portable radio/MP3 player features	4	4
Plug-and-Play radio features	3	4
TOTAL	32	31

Note: 1 – Poor, 2 – Good, 3 – Very Good, 4 – Excellent

Conclusions

The conclusions section of a feasibility or recommendation report summarizes or restates the conclusions you already reached in the comparison sections. In this section, you restate the individual conclusions; for example, which model had the best price, which had the best battery function, and so on.

But this section has to go further. It must untangle all the conflicting conclusions and somehow reach the final conclusion. Thus, the conclusion section first lists the *primary conclusions*—the simple, single-category ones. But then it must state *secondary conclusions*—the ones that balance conflicting primary conclusions. For example, if one tablet computer is the least inexpensive but has poor battery function, but another is the most expensive and has good battery function, which do you choose, and why? The secondary conclusion would state the answer to this dilemma.

And of course, the conclusions section ends with the *final conclusion*—the one that states which option is the best choice, or whether the project is feasible, or whether the program you are evaluating is a success or a failure.

Recommendation or Final Opinion

In a feasibility or recommendation report, the final section states the recommendation. You'd think that that ought to be obvious by now. Ordinarily it is but remember that some readers may skip right to the recommendation section and bypass all your hard work! Also, there will be some cases where there may be a best choice, but you wouldn't want to recommend it. Early in their history, laptop computers were heavy and unreliable; there may have been one model that was better than the rest, but even it was not worth having.

The recommendation section should echo the most important conclusions leading to the recommendation and then state the recommendation emphatically. Ordinarily, you may need to recommend several options based on different possibilities. This situation can be handled, as shown in the examples, with bulleted lists.

Summary

The following is a summary of the comparisons of XM Satellite Radio and Sirius Satellite Radio.
Primary conclusions:

- XM and Sirius are the only two competitors when it comes to satellite radio.
- XM and higher total number of music and sports channels than Sirius.
- XM has overall lower costs for monthly and yearly subscriptions than Sirius.

Secondary conclusions:

- Sirius has the best signal and satellite coverage.

- Although XM offers more than four portable satellite radios/MP3 players, they are all much higher priced than Sirius' one option.
- The price range for the Sirius plug-and-play radios start lower than XM, but XM offers more options of lower priced plug-and-play radios than Sirius.
- The features of the XM and Sirius portable radios/MP3 players are all very similar, but the XM Pioneer Inno is the highest price option at $399.99.
- The features of the XM and Sirius plug-and-play radios are also similar, but the Sirius Streamer Replay is the best. It's also the same price as XM's highest priced radio--Delphi SKYFi2 at $119.99.

Final Conclusion:
The best option for satellite radio is XM radio because it has more options to choose from at lower prices than Sirius.

In an evaluation report, this final section states a final opinion or judgement. Here are some possibilities:

1. Yes, the free-bus-transportation program was successful, or at least it was, based on its initial expectations.
2. No, it was a miserable flop—it lived up to none of its minimal expectations.
3. Or, it was both a success and a flop—it did live up to some of its expectations but did not do so in others. But in this case, you're still on the hook—what's your overall evaluation? Once again, you need to state the basis for that judgment somewhere in the Requirements/Decision-making criteria section.

Organizational Plans for Feasibility and Recommendation Reports

This is a good point to discuss the two basic organizational plans for this type of report.

Traditional Organization

This layout corresponds to the order that the sections have just been presented in this chapter. You start with background and decision-making criteria, define the options, then move to comparisons, and end with conclusions and recommendations.

Abstract

1. Introduction
2. Shiner Facility Background
    1. Energy consumption
    2. Alternative fuel sources
3. Existing Heating System
    1. Heat production
    2. Fuel consumption and costs
    3. Replacement costs
4. Proposed Wood-Fired System
    1. Design Basis
        1. System description
        2. Boiler system
        3. HVAC
    2. Costs
        1. Investment costs
        2. Replacement costs
        3. Operation and maintenance costs
5. Conclusions
6. Recommendations

Executive Plan

This layout moves the conclusions and recommendations to the front of the report and pitches the full discussion of background, criteria, options, and the comparisons into appendices. That way, the "busy executive" can see the most important information right away and turn to the detailed discussion only if there are questions. (In a large report printed in hard copy, there would be tabs for each major section and appendix.)

Introduction
Factual Summary
Conclusions
Recommendations

- Appendixes
    - Shiner Facility Background
    - Energy consumption
    - Alternative fuel sources
- Existing Heating System
    - Heat production
    - Fuel consumption and costs
    - Replacement costs
- Proposed Wood-Fired System
    - Design Basis:
        - System description
        - Boiler system
        - HVAC
    - Costs:
        - Investment costs
        - Replacement costs
        - Operation and maintenance costs

Report Pre-Writing Strategy

When you develop a recommendation, feasibility, or evaluation report, go through this checklist and think about these issues. Make a list of your thoughts on them so you (and if you are working in a group, all your coworkers) have a master document you can refer back to.

Audience. Describe the report's intended audience in terms of the organization they work for, their titles and jobs, their technical background, and their ability to understand the report.

Situation. Describe the situation and subject that the report will address. What problems or needs are there? Who has them? Where are they located? What will the report discuss?

Deliverable type. Describe the report that you are writing. Is it a recommendation, feasibility, or evaluation report?

Research subject. Develop a research question. What, exactly, will you investigate? (Be specific!)

Available options. Identify and describe the things you will be comparing. What are these things? Are you going to determine yes or no? Choose from multiple options? Decide if something is good or bad?

Criteria. Identify specific features, values, or ideas you can use to compare the various options or make an informed decision. Which of those criteria is most important? Least important?

Information sources. Identify places where you can get information about your research subject. List specific books, articles, reference works, interview subjects, field observations, and other kinds of sources that you think will contribute to your report.

Graphics. List the graphics you think your report will need according to their type and their content. Odds are, you'll need at least one table.

By: David McMurrey

Objectives

Upon completion of this chapter, readers will be able to do the following:

A. Explain the three types of information found in handbooks.
B. Explain and apply the guidelines for handbook format and style.

Handbook Basics

A *handbook*, as we are defining it here, is a combination of concept, instruction, and reference information focused on a specific topic for a specific audience's needs.

Concepts

Conceptual information explains how things work, how things are put together. For more complex instructions, you have to know some concepts, theory, background, and principles to perform the instructions. Consider the example of the software function that enables you to modify or create your own color. Using something like Photoshop, Illustration, CorelDraw or Paint Shop Pro to do this—the actual buttons and sliders—is easy. But understanding how hue, intensity, brightness, saturation, density, contrast, and RGB work—that's hard. You have to know computer color theory to create the color you need.

Consider another example: simple Linux file system commands—ls, cd, cp, mv, pwd. To use these commands, you need to understand what files and directories are, and probably what an operating system is as well as wildcards. You really can't understand how to use these commands—follow instructions using them—unless you understand these basic concepts.

Instructions

If you do understand the fundamental concepts, then you can intelligently follow the step-by-step procedures. Instructions are those familiar numbered-list things that carefully walk you through a procedure. Instructions are everywhere, on product packaging, in user guides that come with appliances, and on computers.

Reference

The last category of information involves look-up information, or quick-reference information. If you followed the file system example above, you had to study and learn the concepts of files, directory, and wildcards first. Then you could follow and understand the instructions on changing directories, copying, deleting, or moving files. After a while you no longer need the instructions, but now and then you have special requirements not covered in the instruction section or you can't remember certain procedures that were covered in the instruction section. Now's the time you need basic reference information: you just go to that section and quickly look it up.

And so, after more time, you no longer need the concepts section and the instructions section: you gotten so accustomed to those procedures, you know them by heart. But now and then you forget some little detail, or you have some special task you've never done before —that's when you go to the reference section. You could probably tear off the concepts and instructions sections and throw them away. All you'll ever need is the reference section.

Handbook Format and Style

In creating a handbook, you should adhere to rather specific guidelines for the use of headings, lists, notices, graphics, tables, documentation, and introductions—which of course assumes that you must use these things:

Handbook Prototype

From the link below you can get a dummy version of the handbook. It includes all the required pages in good format. Included in this Word document are paragraph and character styles that will make your work easier and add some professional skills to your repertoire.

Handbook prototype

Contents Prototype

The prototype for the table of contents is particularly useful: it gives you the Word styles to produce a professional-looking TOC. It is tough to get the left- and right-alignments and leader dots right.

Table of contents prototype

Actually, these same prototypes can be used for any formal report.

2.11: Titles, Abstracts, Introductions, and Conclusions

By: David McMurrey

Objectives

Upon completion of this chapter, readers will be able to do the following:

A. Summarize strategies for writing effective document titles.
B. Define abstract and explain the different types of abstracts.
C. Explain the purposes of different types of introductions and summarize the common elements of them.
D. Explain the components and purposes of conclusions.

Title It, Summarize, It, Introduce It, Conclude It

Formal technical reports over eight to ten pages contain several components that deserve their own focus because they are important in technical reports and because people are unfamiliar with them:

1. **Titles** explores strategies for making document titles specific but not paragraphs long.
2. **Abstracts** provide several kinds of summaries of the report contents and conclusions.
3. **Introductions** get readers ready to read reports by indicating the topic, purpose, intended audience, contents, and other such matters.
4. **Conclusions** shape how readers view and understand the report upon leaving it.

Abstracts

Summarize It

An *abstract* is a summary of a body of information. Sometimes, abstracts are in fact called summaries—sometimes, executive summaries or executive abstracts. The business and scientific worlds define different types of abstracts according to their needs. If you are taking a technical writing course based on this online textbook, your technical report (depending on your instructor) may use two types: the descriptive abstract and the informative abstract.

Descriptive Abstracts

The descriptive abstract provides a description of the report's main topic and purpose as well an overview of its contents. As you can see from the example, it is very short—usually a brief one- or two-sentence paragraph. In this report design, it appears on the title page. You may have noticed something similar to this type of abstract at the beginning of journal articles.

In this type of abstract, you don't summarize any of the facts or conclusions of the report. The descriptive abstract does *not* say something like this:

Based on an exhaustive review of currently available products, this report concludes that none of the available grammar-checking software products provides any useful function to writers.

This is the style of summarizing you find in the informative abstract. Instead, the descriptive abstract says something like this:

This report provides conclusions and recommendations on the grammar-checking software that is currently available.

The descriptive abstract is a little like a program teaser. Or, to use a different analogy, it is as if the major first-level headings of the table of contents have been rewritten in paragraph format.

Informative Abstracts

The informative abstract, as its name implies, provides information from the body of the report—specifically, the key facts and conclusions. To put it another way, this type of abstract summarizes the key information from every major section in the body of the report.

It is as if someone had taken a yellow marker and highlighted all the key points in the body of the report then vacuumed them up into a one- or two-page document. (Of course, then some editing and rewriting would be necessary to make the abstract readable.) Specifically, the requirements for the informative abstract are as follows:

1. Summarize the key facts, conclusions, and other important information in the body of the report.
2. Equals about 10 percent of the length of a 10-page report: for example, an informative abstract for a 10-page report would be 1 page. This ratio stops after about 30 pages, however. For 50- or 60-page reports, the abstract should not go over 2 to 3 pages.
3. Summarize the key information from each of the main sections of the report, and proportionately so (a 3-page section of a 10-page report ought to take up about 30 percent of the informative abstract).
4. Phrase information in a very dense, compact way. Sentence are longer than normal and are crammed with information. The abstract tries to compact information down to that 10-percent level (or lower for longer reports). While it's expected that the writing in an informative abstract will be dense and heavily worded, do not omit normal words such as the, a, and an.
5. Omit introductory explanation, unless that is the focus of the main body of the report. Definitions and other background information are omitted if they are not the major focus of the report. The informative abstract is not an introduction to the subject matter of the report—and it is not an introduction!
6. Omit citations for source borrowings. If you summarize information that you borrowed from other writers, you do not have to repeat the citation in the informative abstract (in other words, no brackets with source numbers and page numbers).
7. Include key statistical detail. Don't sacrifice key numerical facts to make the informative abstract brief. One expects to see numerical data in an informative abstract.
8. Omit descriptive-abstract phrasing. You should not see phrasing like this: "This report presents conclusions and recommendations from a survey done on grammar-checking software." Instead, the informative abstract presents the details of those conclusions and recommendations.

This last point is particularly important. People often confuse the kinds of writing expected in descriptive and informative abstracts. Study the difference between the informative and descriptive phrasing in the following examples:

Table 1: Examples of informative and descriptive phrasing

Informative	Descriptive
Based on an exhaustive review of currently available products, this report concludes that none of the available grammar-checking software products provides any useful function to writers.	This report provides conclusions and recommendations on the grammar-checking software that is currently available.

ABSTRACT

Computerized speech recognition takes advantage of the most natural form of communication, the human voice. During speech, sound is generated by the vocal cords and by air rushing from the lungs. If the vocal cords vibrate, a voiced sound is produced; otherwise, the sound is unvoiced. The main problem in speech recognition is that no two voices produce their sounds alike and that an individual voice varies in different conditions. Because voices do vary and because words blend together in a continuous stream in natural speech, most recognition systems require that each speaker train the machine to his or her voice and that words have at least one-tenth of a second pause between them. Such a system is called an isolated word recognition system and consists of three major components that process human speech: (1) the preprocessor which removes irregularities from the speech signal and then breaks it up into parts; (2) the feature extractor which extracts 32 key features from the signal; and (3) the classification phase which identifies the spoken word and includes the training mode and reference pattern memory. Spoken words are identified on the basis of a certain decision algorithm, some of which involve dynamic programming, zero crossing rate, linear predictive coding, and the use of a state diagram.

Voice recognition systems offer many applications including data entry, freedom for mobility, security uses, telephone access, and helpful devices for the handicapped. However, these same systems also face problems such as poor recognition accuracy, loss of privacy among those who use them, and limited vocabulary sizes. The goal of the industry is the development of speaker-independent systems that can recognize continuous human speech regardless of the speaker and that can continually improve their vocabulary size and recognition accuracy.

This type summarizes the key facts and conclusions in the body of the report. (By the way, speech recognition has come a long way since this report was written in 1982!)

Executive Summary

The executive summary is a hybrid of the descriptive and informative summaries. Written for executives whose focus is business decisions and whose background are not necessarily technical, it focuses on conclusions and recommendations but provides little background, theory, results, or other such detail. It doesn't summarize research theory or method; it makes descriptive-summary statements: for example, "theory of heat gain, loss, and storage are also discussed."

To get a sense of the executive summary, study the following example:

EXECUTIVE SUMMARY Rural Health Clinics: Requirements The most important needs of rural health clinics, which require energy resources, are as follows: Refrigeration. Absorption refrigeration, fueled by propane or kerosene and common at unelectrified health clinics, is vulnerable to interruption and is thus inadequate for the vaccines needed in immunization programs for dangerous diseases including polio, diphtheria, tetanus, pertussis, tuberculosis, measles, yellow fever, and Hepatitis B. Instead, compression-type refrigerators powered by 12- or 24-volt storage batteries and recharged by photovoltaic panels or a small wind turbine can meet these needs. Lighting. Instead of kerosene lighting, common in unelectrified communities and a known safety hazard and contributor to poor indoor air quality as well, renewable energy technologies can improve lighting in rural health clinics for such important functions as emergency treatment, birthing, maternity care, surgery, and administrative tasks. Communications. Health care services and emergency medical treatment, in particular, are greatly facilitated with reliable radio and radio-telephone communications to other health clinics and facilities in the region. Rural health clinics can have reliable two-way regional communication via VHF radio with electricity provided by a single 30-W PV module. Medical appliances. Small medical appliances that operate on 120-volt AC electricity require an inverter, which is easily incorporated into wind- or solar-based systems. Although photovoltaic systems can provide the electricity needed for the high temperatures, approximately 120°C (250°F) needed in sterilization, solar thermal collector systems can produce high temperatures at a lower cost, especially in areas with good solar insolation. Water. Solar and wind power can be used to generate high volumes of potable water in tandem with techniques such as ozone treatment, reverse osmosis, photochemical treatment, also known as ultraviolet or UV, disinfection and carbon filters. Ozone treatment is very suitable to solar- or wind-generated power requiring only 0.3 watt-hours per liter. Clean water can also be provided from deep wells but requires an energy source for pumping significant volumes. Solar or wind power (or both) generated on site can economically meet the broad range of these needs.

Revision Checklist for Abstracts

As you re-read and revise your abstracts, watch out for problems such as the following:

- Make sure that the descriptive abstract does *not* include informative abstract phrasing; make sure that the informative abstract does not include descriptive abstract phrasing.
- Make sure the descriptive abstract provides an overview of the topics covered in *all* the major sections of the report.
- Make sure that the informative abstract summarizes *all* the major sections of the report. (And don't forget—the informative abstract is not an introduction!)

- Make sure the informative abstract summarizes *all* key concepts, conclusions, and facts from the body of the report (including key statistical information).
- Make sure that the informative abstract excludes general, obvious, deadwood information and that the phrasing is compact and concentrated.
- Make sure that the informative abstract is neither too brief (less than 10 percent) nor too long (more than 15 percent).

Introductions

Get Readers Ready to Read that Document

The introduction is one of the most important sections of a report—or, for that matter, any document—but introductions are often poorly written. One reason may be that people misunderstand the purpose of introductions. An introduction introduces readers to the report and not necessarily, or only minimally, to the subject matter. "Introduction" does not equal "background"; it may contain some background but only minimally.

Readers have an understandable need to know some basic things about a report before they begin reading it: such as what is it about, why was it written, what's it for, for whom it written, and what are its main contents. Readers need a basic orientation to the topic, purpose, situation, and contents of a report—in other words, an introduction.

Imagine that, years ago, you were writing a recommendation report about CD-ROM computer devices. You might be tempted to use the introduction to discuss the background of compact disc development or its theoretical side. That might be good stuff to include in the report, and it probably belongs in the report—but not in the introduction, or at least not in much detail or length.

For 10-page reports, introductions might average one half to one full page. On that one page, you might have three paragraphs. One of those paragraphs could be devoted to background information—in other words, to introducing the subject matter. But the other two paragraphs must do the job of introducing the report and orienting the reader to the report, as discussed in the following.

Common Elements of Introductions

Each of the following elements is not required in all introductions, and some elements combine into the same sentence. Rather than mechanically applying these elements, write the introduction that seems good to you, then come back and search for these elements in it.

Topic. Early in the introduction, indicate the specific topic of the report. Some introductions seem to want to hold readers in suspense for a while before they indicate the true topic—that's a gamble. Better is to indicate the topic early—such that you could circle the topic words in the first three to four lines.

Purpose and situation. A good introduction needs to indicate why it was written, for whom, and for what purpose. If the report provides recommendations on whether to implement a program, the introduction needs to indicate that purpose. You might also consider indicating something of the scope of the report—what it is *not* intended to accomplish.

Audience. Indicate who are the appropriate or intended readers of the report—for example, "experienced technicians trained on the HAL/6000." Indicate what level of experience or knowledge readers need to understand the report, if any. If none is needed, say that. If the report was prepared for council members of the City of Utopia, Texas, the introduction needs to express that.

Overview of contents. Indicate the main contents of the report. You can do this with an in-sentence list, as the examples illustrate. If you are concerned about readers' exaggerated expectations, indicate what topics the report does *not* cover.

Background on the topic. This is everybody's favorite! Some minimal background is usually in an introduction—for example, key definitions, historical background, theory, the importance of the subject. Information like this gets readers interested, motivated to read, grounded in some fundamental concepts. Watch out, though—this discussion can get away from you and fill up more than page. If it does, that's okay—all is not lost. Move it in to the body of the report, or into an appendix.

Background on the situation. Another kind of background is also a good candidate for introductions—the situation that brought about the need for the report. For example, if there were a lot of conflicting data about some new technology, which brought about the need for the research, this background could be summarized in the introduction. For example, if a company needed new equipment of some kind or if the company had some problem or need and some requirements in relation to that equipment—discussion of these matters should go in the introduction.

Notice in the discussion of these elements the word "indicate" keeps getting used. That's because you'd like to avoid heavy-handed language such as "The topic of this report is..." or "This report has been written for..." Notice how the example introductions generally avoid this kind of phrasing.

Introductions to Brief Documents

If you are writing a brief document of 1 to 2 pages, you don't need all those elements common to report introductions discussed in the preceding section. Here's the subset of what you are likely to need:

Topic. If you can circle the topic words somewhere in the first three to four lines of the introduction, you're good.

Purpose and situation. In instructions, it's enough to tell readers that they are going to see how to do something. In a recommendation report, just mention that readers will be seeing conclusions and recommendations.

Audience. Indicate what level of experience or knowledge readers need to understand the document. If none is needed, say that.

Overview of contents. Indicate the main contents of the document. A simple in-sentence list will do.

Background. Always remember that an introduction is not a background discussion; it may contain some, but only minimally.

Example of a brief introduction with most of the key elements present

Section Introductions

We don't normally think that there is more than one introduction in a report. However, in reports over 8 to 10 or more pages, the individual sections also need some sort of introduction. These can be called *section introductions* because they prepare readers to read a section of a report—they orient readers to its contents and purpose and show some linkage to the preceding section.

Of course, a section introduction need not have all the elements of a report introduction. However, it does have several that, if handled well, can make a lot of difference in the clarity and flow of a report.

Example of a section introduction

Notice that this section introduction not only mentions the preceding and upcoming topics but shows how they are related. (From a report written in 1983.)

Topic indication. As with the report introduction, indicate the topic of the upcoming section. But remember—it doesn't have to be the stodgy, heavy-handed "The topic of this next section of the report is..."

Contents overview. Just as in the report introduction, it is a good idea to list the main contents. The in-sentence list serves this purpose well.

Transition. An element that is very useful in section introductions is transitional phrasing that indicates how the preceding section relates to the one about to start. In reports of any length and complexity, it is a good technique—it guides readers along, showing them how the parts of the report all fit together.

Revision Checklist for Introductions

As you revise your introductions, watch out for problems such as the following:

- Avoid writing an introduction consisting of only background information; avoid allowing background information to overwhelm the key elements of the introduction.
- Make sure to indicate the topic early.
- Be sure to indicate the audience and situation—what the readers should expect from the report; what knowledge or background they need to understand the report; what situation brought about the need for the report.
- Make sure there is an overview of the report contents, plus scope information—what the report doesn't cover.

Conclusions

Get It Over with...Gracefully

We normally use the word "conclusion" to refer to that last section or paragraph of a document. However, the word refers more to a specific type of final section. If we were going to be fussy about it, the current section should be called "Final Sections," which covers all possibilities.

There seem to be at least four ways to end a report: a summary, a true conclusion, an afterword, and nothing. Yes, it is possible to end a document with no conclusion (or "final section") whatsoever. However, in most cases, that's a bit like slamming the phone down without even saying good-bye. More often, the final section is some combination of the first three ways of ending the document.

Summaries

One common way to wrap up a report is to review and summarize the high points. If your report is rather long, complex, heavily detailed, and if you want your readers to come away with the right perspective, a summary is in order. For short reports, summaries can seem absurd—the reader thinks "You've just told me that!" Summaries need to read as if time has passed, things have settled down, and the writer is viewing the subject from higher ground.

VIII. SUMMARY

This report has shown that as the supply of freshwater decreases, desalting water will become a necessity. While a number of different methods are in competition with each other, freezing methods of desalination appear to have the greatest potential for the future.

The three main freezing techniques are the direct method, the indirect method, and the hydrate method. Each has some advantage over the others, but all three freezing methods have distinct advantages over other methods of desalination. Because freezing methods operate at such low temperatures, scaling and corrosion of pipe and other equipment is greatly reduced. In non-freezing methods, corrosion is a great problem that is difficult and expensive to prevent. Freezing processes also allow the use of plastic and other protective coatings on steel equipment to prevent corrosion, a measure that cannot be taken in other methods that require high operating temperatures.

Desalination, as this report has shown, requires much energy, regardless of the method. Therefore, pairing desalination plants with nuclear or solar power resources may be a necessity. Some of the expense of desalination can be offset, however...

"True" Conclusions

A "true" conclusion is a logical thing. For example, in the body of a report, you might present conflicting theories and explored the related data. Or you might have compared different models and brands of some product. In the conclusion, the "true" conclusion, you'd present your resolution of the conflicting theories, your choice of the best model or brand—your final conclusions.

V. CONCLUSIONS

Solar heating can be an aid in fighting high fuel bills if planned carefully, as has been shown in preceding sections. Every home represents a different set of conditions; the best system for one home may not be the best one for next door. A salesman can make any system appear to be profitable on paper, and therefore prospective buyers must have some general knowledge about solar products.

A solar heating system should have as many of the best design features as possible and still be affordable. As explained in this report, the collector should have high transmissivity and yet be durable enough to handle hailstorms. Collector insulation should be at least one inch of fiberglass mat. Liquid circulating coils should be at least one inch in diameter if an open loop system is used. The control module should perform all the required functions with no added circuits. Any hot water circulating pumps should be isolated from the electric drive motor by a non-transmitting coupler of some kind.

Homeowners should follow the recommendations in the guidelines section carefully. In particular, they should decide how much money they are willing to spend and then arrange their components in their order of importance. Control module designs vary the most in quality and therefore should have first priority. The collector is the second in importance, and care should be taken to ensure compatibility. Careful attention to the details of the design and selection of solar heating devices discussed in this report will enable homeowners to install efficient, productive solar heating systems.

Afterwords

One last possibility for ending a report involves turning to some related topic but discussing it at a very general level. Imagine that you had written a background report on some exciting new technology. In the final section, you might broaden your focus and discuss how that technology might be used, or the problems it might bring about. But the key is to keep it general—don't force yourself into a whole new detailed section.

VII. CONCLUSION: FUTURE TRENDS

Everyone seems to agree that the car of the future must weigh even less than today's down-sized models. According to a recent forecast by the Arthur Anderson Company, the typical car will have lost about 1,000 pounds between 1978 and 1990 [2:40]. The National Highway Traffic Safety Administration estimates the loss of another 350 pounds by 1995. To obtain these reductions, automobile manufacturers will have found or develop composites such as fiber-reinforced plastics for the major load-bearing components, particularly the frame and drivetrain components.

Ford Motor Company believes that if it is to achieve further growth in the late 1980's, it must achieve breakthroughs in structural and semi structural load-bearing applications. Some of the breakthroughs Ford sees as needed include improvements in the use of continuous fibers, especially hybridized reinforced materials containing glass and graphite fibers. In addition, Ford hopes to develop a high-speed production system for continuous fiber preforms. In the related area of composite technology, researchers at Owens Corning and Hercules are seeking the best combination of hybrid fibers for structural automotive components such as engine and transmission supports, drive shafts, and leaf springs. Tests thus far have led the vice president of Owen Corning's Composites and Equipment Marketing Division, John B. Jenks, to predict that hybrid composites can compete with metal by the mid-1980's for both automotive leaf springs and transmission supports.

With development in these areas of plastics for automobiles, we can look forward to lighter, less expensive, and more economical cars in the next decade. Such developments might well provide the needed spark to rejuvenate America's auto industry and to further decrease our rate of petroleum consumption.

Combinations

In practice, the preceding ways of ending reports often combine. You can analyze final sections of reports and identify elements that summarize, elements that conclude, and elements that discuss something related but at a general level (afterwords).

Here are some possibilities for afterword-type final sections:

- Provide a brief, general look to the future; speculate on future developments.
- Explore solutions to problems that were discussed in the main body of the report.
- Discuss the operation of a mechanism or technology that was described in the main body of the report.
- Provide some cautions, guidelines, tips, or preview of advanced functions.
- Explore the economics, social implications, problems, legal aspects, advantages, disadvantages, benefits, or applications of the report subject (but only generally and briefly).

Revision Checklist for Conclusions

As you reread and revise your conclusions, watch out for problems such as the following:

- If you use an afterword-type last section, make sure you write it at a general enough level that it doesn't seem like yet another body section of the report.
- Avoid conclusions for which there is no basis (discussion, support) in the body of report.
- Keep final sections brief and general. □

2.12: Oral Presentations

By: David McMurrey and Cassandra Race

Objectives

Upon completion of this chapter, readers will be able to do the following:

- Plan and prepare a talk or presentation.
- Deliver the presentation.
- Create presentation materials that reflect standards of effective presentation.
- Evaluate presentations delivered by others, including classmates.

Introduction to Oral Presentations

A common assignment in technical writing courses—not to mention in the workplace—is to prepare and deliver an oral presentation, a task most of us would be happy to avoid. However, while employers look for coursework and experience in preparing written documents, they also look for experience in oral presentations as well. Look back at the first chapter. Remember how important interpersonal communication skills are in the workplace.

The following was written for a standard face-to-face classroom setting. If you are taking an online technical writing course, oral reports can be sent in as "scripts," or audio versions can be transmitted live or recorded. In any case, students may evaluate each other's oral reports by filling out a form like the one provided at the end of this chapter or responding through the discussion board.

If you can believe the research, most people would rather have root canal surgery without Novocain than stand up in front of a group and speak. It truly is one of the great stressors. But with some help from the resources that follow, you can be a champion presenter.

For additional information on oral presentations and public speaking in general, see Effective Presentations. This is part of an online tutorial series provided by Kansas University Medical Center. This section has many resources that will be helpful to you.

Topic and Situation for the Oral Presentation

For the oral report in a technical writing course, imagine that you are formally handing over your final *written* report to the people with whom you set up the hypothetical contract or agreement. For example, imagine that you had contracted with a software company to write its user guide. Once you had completed it, you'd have a meeting with chief officers to formally deliver the guide. You'd spend some time orienting them to the guide, showing them how it is organized and written, and discussing some of its highlights. Your goal is to get them acquainted with the guide and to prompt them for any concerns or questions. (Your class will gladly pretend to be whomever you tell them to be during your talk.)

As you can see, you shouldn't have to do any research to prepare for this assignment—just plan the details of your talk and get at least one visual ready. If you have a report topic that you'd prefer not to present orally, discuss other possibilities with your instructor. Here are some brainstorming possibilities in case you want to present something else:

- **Purpose:** One way to find a topic is to think about the purpose of your talk. Is it to instruct (for example, to explain how to run a text editing program on a computer), to persuade (to vote for or against a certain technically oriented bond issue), or simply to inform (to report on citizen participation in the new recycling program)?
  - *Informative purpose:* An oral report can be primarily informative. For example, as a member of a committee involved in a project to relocate the plant, your job might be to give an oral report on the condition of the building and grounds at one of the sites proposed for purchase. Or, you might be

required to go before the city council and report on the success of the new city-sponsored recycling project.

- o *Instructional purpose:* An oral report can be instructional. Your task might be to train new employees to use certain equipment or to perform certain routine tasks.
- o *Persuasive purpose:* An oral report can be persuasive. You might want to convince members of local civic organizations to support a city-wide recycling program. You might appear before city council to persuade its members to reserve certain city-owned lands for park areas, softball and baseball parks, or community gardens.
- **Topics:** You can start by thinking of a technical subject, for example, solar panels, microprocessors, drip irrigation, or laser surgery. For your oral report, think of a subject you'd be interested in talking about, but find a reason why an audience would want to hear your oral report.
- **Place or situation:** You can find topics for oral reports or make more detailed plans for them by thinking about the place or the situation in which your oral report might naturally be given: at a neighborhood association? at the parent–teachers' association meeting? at a church meeting? at the gardening club? at a city council meeting? at a meeting of the board of directors or high-level executives of a company? Thinking about an oral report this way makes you focus on the audience, their reasons for listening to you, and their interests and background. As in all technical writing situations, identifying and understanding your audience is of the utmost importance.

Contents and Requirements for the Oral Presentation

The focus for your oral presentation is clear, understandable presentation; well-organized, well-planned, well-timed discussion. You don't need to be Mr. or Ms. Slick-Operator—just present the essentials of what you have to say in a calm, organized, well-planned manner.

When you give your oral presentation, we'll all be listening for the same things. Use the following as a requirements list, as a way of focusing your preparations:

1. **Situation:** Plan to explain to the class what the situation of your oral report is, who you are, and who they should imagine they are. Make sure that there is a clean break between this brief explanation and the beginning of your actual oral report.
2. **Timing:** Make sure your oral report lasts no longer than the time allotted. Your instructor will work out some signals to indicate when the mark is approaching, has arrived, or has passed.
3. **Introduction:** Pay special attention to the introduction to your talk. Here's where you tell your audience what you are going to tell them.
    1. Indicate the *purpose* of your oral report
    2. Give an *overview* of its contents
    3. Find some way to *interest* the audience
4. **Visuals:** Use at least one visual—preferably slides using presentation software (such as PowerPoint) or transparencies for the overhead projector. Flip charts and objects for display are okay but avoid scribbling stuff on the chalkboard or whiteboard or relying strictly on handouts. Make sure you discuss key elements of your visuals. Don't just throw them up there and ignore them. Point out things about them; explain them to the audience.
5. **Explanation:** Plan to explain any technical aspect of your topic clearly and understandably. Don't race through complex, technical stuff—slow down and explain it carefully so that we understand it.
6. **Transitions:** Use "verbal headings"—by now, you've gotten used to using headings in your written work. There is a corollary in oral reports. With these, you give your audience a very clear signal you are moving from one topic or part of your talk to the next. Your presentation visual can signal your headings.
7. **Planning:** Plan your report in advance and practice it so that it is organized. Make sure that listeners know what you are talking about and why, which part of the talk you are in, and what's coming next. Overviews and verbal headings greatly contribute to this sense of organization.
8. **Closing:** End with a real conclusion. People sometimes forget to plan how to end an oral report and end by just trailing off into a mumble. Remember that in conclusions, you can:
    1. *Summarize* (go back over high points of what you've discussed
    2. *Conclude* (state some logical conclusion based on what you have presented
    3. Provide some last *thought* (end with some final interesting point but general enough not to require elaboration)
    4. Or some combination of these three

9. **Questions:** And certainly, you'll want to prompt the audience for questions and concerns.
10. **Timing (again):** As mentioned above, be sure your oral report is carefully timed. Some ideas on how to work within an allotted time frame are presented in the next section.

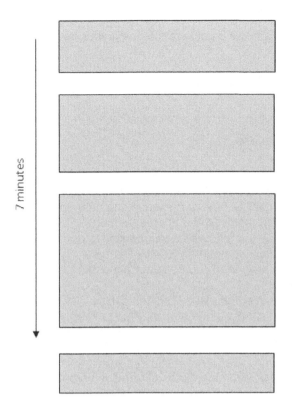

Context: Explain who the intended audience is, what the situation is—before you begin your actual talk.

Introduction: At the beginning of your actual oral report, tell who you are, indicate its topic and purpose, provide an overview of its main contents, get the audience interested.

Body of the report:
- Use verbal headings.
- Explain technical details clearly.
- Use visuals—explain them.
- Speak clearly, not fast. Avoid nervous mannerisms.
- Stay organized.
- Be aware of the 7-minute time limit.

Conclusion: Have a planned way to end your report: summarize, conclude, provide one last general thought. Invite questions.

Figure 1: Diagram of the 7-minute oral presentation

Preparing for the Oral Presentation

Pick the method of preparing for the talk that best suits your comfort level with public speaking and with your topic. However, plan to do ample preparation and rehearsal—some people assume that they can just jump up there and ad lib for so many minutes and be relaxed and informal. It doesn't often work that way—drawing a mental blank is the more common experience. A well delivered presentation is the result of a lot of work and a lot of practice.

Here are the obvious possibilities for preparation and delivery:

- Write a script, practice it; keep it around for quick reference during your talk.
- Set up an outline of your talk; practice with it, bring it for reference.
- Set up cue cards, practice with them, and use them during your talk.
- Write a script and read from it.

Of course, the extemporaneous or impromptu methods are also out there for the brave and the adventurous. However, please bear in mind that up to 25 people will be listening to you—you owe them a good presentation, one that is clear, understandable, well-planned, organized, and on target with your purpose and audience.

It doesn't matter which method you use to prepare for the talk, but you want to make sure that you know your material. The head-down style of reading your report directly from a script has problems. There is little or no eye contact or interaction with the audience. The delivery tends toward a dull, boring monotone that either puts listeners off or is hard to understand. And, most of us cannot stand to have reports read to us!

For many reasons, most people get nervous when they have to give oral presentations. Being well prepared is your best defense against the nerves. Try to remember that your classmates and instructor are a very forgiving, supportive group. You don't have to be a slick entertainer—just be clear, organized, and understandable. The nerves will wear off someday, the more oral presenting you do. In the meantime, breathe deeply and enjoy.

The following is an example of an introduction to an oral presentation. Use it as a guide for planning your own.

Introductory remarks in an oral presentation

Delivering an Oral Presentation

When you give an oral report, focus on common problem areas such as these:

- **Timing:** Make sure you keep within the time limit. Finishing more than a minute under the time limit is also a problem. Rehearse, rehearse, rehearse until you get the timing just right.
- **Volume:** Obviously, you must be sure to speak loud enough so that all of your audience can hear you. You might find some way to practice speaking a little louder in the days before the oral presentation.
- **Pacing, speed:** Sometimes, oral presenters who are nervous talk too fast. All that adrenaline causes them to speed through their talk, making it hard for the audience to follow. In general, it helps listeners understand you better if you speak a bit more slowly and deliberately than you do in normal conversation. Slow down, take it easy, be clear...and breathe.
- **Gestures and postures:** Watch out for nervous hands flying all over the place. This too can be distracting—and a bit comical. At the same time, don't turn yourself into a mannequin. Plan to keep your hands clasped together or holding onto the podium and only occasionally making some gesture. Definitely keep your hands out of your pockets or waistband. As for posture, avoid slouching at the podium or leaning against the wall. Stand up straight and keep your head up.
- **Verbal crutches:** Watch out for too much "uh," "you know," "okay" and other kinds of nervous verbal habits. Instead of saying "uh" or "you know" every three seconds, just don't say anything at all. In the days before your oral presentation, practice speaking without these verbal crutches. The silence that replaces them is not a bad thing—it gives listeners time to process what you are saying.

The following is an example of how topic headings can make your presentation easy for your listeners to follow.

Examples of verbal headings in an oral presentation

Planning and Preparing Visuals for Oral Presentations

Prepare at least one visual for this report. Here are some ideas for the "medium" to use for your visuals:

- **Presentation software slides:** Projecting images ("slides") using software such as PowerPoint has become the standard, even though maligned by some. One common problem with the construction of these slides is cramming too much information on individual slides. A quick search on terms like PowerPoint presentation will enable you to read about creating these slides and designing them intelligently. Of course, the room in which you use these slides has to have a computer projector.
- **Transparencies for overhead projector:** The overhead projector used with transparencies seems to have been relegated to antiquity—but not entirely. If you have to use this method, you will design your visual on a sheet of blank paper, then photocopy it, and create a transparency of it.
- **Poster board-size charts:** Another possibility is to get some poster board and draw and letter what you want your audience to see. Of course, it's not easy making charts look neat and professional.
- **Handouts:** You can run off copies of what you want your listeners to see and hand them out before or during your talk. This option is even less effective than the first two because you can't point to what you want your listeners to see and because handouts distract listeners' attention away from you. Still, for certain visual needs, handouts are the only choice. Keep in mind that if you are not well prepared, the handouts become a place for your distracted audience to doodle.

- **Objects:** If you need to demonstrate certain procedures, you may need to bring in actual physical objects. Rehearse what you are going to do with these objects; sometimes they can take up a lot more time than you expect.

Avoid just scribbling your visual on the chalkboard or whiteboard. Whatever you scribble can be neatly prepared and made into a presentation slide, transparency, or poster board-size chart. Take some time to make your visuals look sharp and professional—do your best to ensure that they are legible to the entire audience.

As for the content of your visuals, consider these ideas:

- **Drawing or diagram of key objects:** If you describe or refer to any objects during your talk, try to get visuals of them so that you can point to different components or features.
- **Tables, charts, graphs:** If you discuss statistical data, present it in some form or table, chart, or graph. Many members of your audience may be less comfortable "hearing" such data as opposed to seeing it.
- **Outline of your talk, report, or both:** If you are at a loss for visuals to use in your oral presentation, or if your presentation is complex, have an outline of it that you can show at various points during your talk.
- **Key terms and definitions:** A good idea for visuals (especially when you can't think of any others) is to set up a two-column list of key terms you use during your oral presentation with their definitions in the second column.
- **Key concepts or points:** Similarly, you can list your key points and show them in visuals. (Outlines, key terms, and main points are all good, legitimate ways of incorporating visuals into oral presentations when you can't think of any others.)

During your actual oral report, make sure to discuss your visuals, refer to them, guide your listeners through the key points in your visuals. It's a big problem just to throw a visual up on the screen and never even refer to it.

As you prepare your visuals, look at resources that will help you. There are many rules for using PowerPoint, down to the font size and how many words to put on a single slide, but you will have to choose the style that best suits your subject and your presentation style.

The two videos that follow will provide some pointers. As you watch them, make some notes to help you remember what you learn from them. The first one is funny: Life After Death by PowerPoint by Don McMillan, an engineer turned comedian.

Life After Death by PowerPoint

You may also have heard about the presentation skills of Steve Jobs. The video that follows is the introduction of the iPhone...and as you watch, take notes on how Jobs sets up his talk and his visuals. Observe how he connects with the audience...and then see if you can work some of his strategies into your own presentation skills. This is a long video...you don't need to watch it all but do take enough time to form some good impressions.

Steve Jobs iPhone Presentation

Now you are ready! Go to the exercises on the next page as warmups to help you start working towards that big day!

Activities and Exercises

- Ready to get started? Think of a topic that interests you and develop an introduction to a talk about it that follows the guidelines in the chapter for writing an introduction. Try it out on a classmate. Then, take turns asking each other questions about your topic.
- Design 3 visuals for your topic, including a title page. Use the Styles and Themes feature in PowerPoint to create a consistent theme for a presentation.

- Find a YouTube video or a tutorial online on how to make good presentations. Share it with classmates by teaching some of the main points in group discussion.
- In small groups, develop a list of "rules" to follow when you have to give an oral presentation...then create a class list!
- In a memo to your teacher (or in an online discussion forum) share some of your" best practices" ideas for getting through a presentation. Also, share some details from the most horrible presentations you've ever seen...or given...maybe you can help a classmate avoid making the same mistakes! (I once had a friend who introduced his talk on gun control by firing a pistol loaded with blanks right beside his ear...it wasn't actually funny, but yes, yes it was...oh well!)

Oral Evaluation Sheet

By: Tamara Powell and Tiffani Reardon

Objectives

Upon completion of this chapter, readers will be able to do the following:

- Identify basic memo and email formats.
- Describe the key differences between basic memo and basic email formats.
- Explain cc, bcc, and attachment functions and when to use them.

Introduction to Memos and Emails

If you like movies, especially ones set in historical periods, you might enjoy finding anachronisms, or things in the wrong time period. You might see something from the present, such as a mobile phone, that is not supposed to be in a movie set in the past, such as 1850.

Anachronism: "a person or a thing that is chronologically out of place; especially: one from a former age that is incongruous in the present" (Merriam-Webster)

For example, a well-known anachronism is in the first Indiana Jones movie, Raiders of the Lost Ark. In the movie, we see a plane flying over a map to show us Indy's route to adventure in Nepal. But while the movie was set in the 1930s, the map is from the 1980s. For example, viewers see the plane fly over Thailand, but the country was called Siam until 1939.

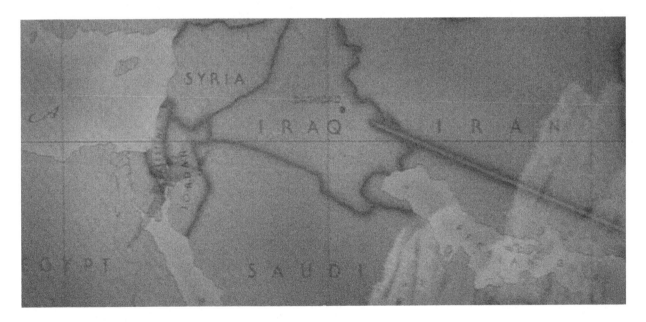

Maybe no one has ever confused the writing of an email or memo with an action movie. But if you enjoy finding anachronisms, there are a few hiding out in your everyday email form. It has anachronisms embedded in it from the old days before computers. Can you think of any right now? As we cover the basics of email and memos, I'll point out a few—let's see if I can tell you about any that you might not know about.

Figure 1: An email form

If you have ever written an email, you may have noticed that you have to provide the name of the person you are sending the email to and the subject. The email automatically provides the name of the sender and the date.

Email formats are based on memo formats—that is, they are set up to provide the four key pieces of introductory information that a memo states in the heading: to, from, subject, and date.

Memos and emails have the to, from, subject, date heading format in common. For this reason, emails are often considered to be synonymous with memos. Also, much of the information that is shared via email is the information categorized into types of memos, for example, meeting minutes, lab reports, progress reports, directives, and other types of business and professional correspondence.

In fact, the main difference, if one is said to exist, between emails and memos, is that non-email memos exist on paper. The key format difference, then, is the signature.

That's right—it is common in email for persons to "sign" the email like a letter. In an informal email, the person might just sign his or her first name. In a more formal email, the person might have a closing like in a letter—"Sincerely," for example, along with his or her full name and title. In this way, emails can be more like letters.

Paper memos NEVER have a closing and signature. Instead, the writer would indicate that he or she really wrote the memo by initialing by his or her name in the paper heading using blue or black ink. Historically, memos were typed up by stenographers and taken back to a boss for approval. Thus, the stenos would put their lower-case initials after a backslash at page bottom, like so:

To: Martha Garner
From: Greg Brown
Subject: Server Outage
Date: December 1, 2015

We will be performing several software updates on our servers this Friday at 7pm EST. The maintenance is required in order to keep our servers secure and up to date.

Our lms, email, and support forum may be momentarily unavailable around that time. We expect only a very short interruption of services (i.e. a few seconds while the web server software is restarting).

/gb

However, since people write their own messages on their own computers, the /ab now indicates authorship as long as they match the From line.

Of course, in email, the reader feels pretty confident that the email really came from the sender because, presumably, the sender had to log in to a secure email account.

Figure 2: The cc/carbon copy line

If you take a look at your email when you are about to send one, you will notice some other options you have that are related to the olden days of memo writing and letter writing. You have the options of cc. CC stands for carbon copy. You may not be old enough to remember that before copy machines and computers that could print off multiple copies of a document, people used carbon paper to make copies. When a person would write or type, he or she would slip a piece of carbon paper underneath the document, and the striking of the pen or typewriter key would make a duplicate mark on a second piece of paper underneath the carbon paper, hence the term carbon copy. So, the "cc" in the email heading stands for carbon copy, even though we don't use carbon anymore. In fact, sometimes, the cc is just changed to c for copy.

When do you use the cc option? When you want someone to have a copy of the email, but only for reference purposes. Or to put it more casually, to keep someone in the loop. For example, you manage a team, and you recently had a meeting. You send the meeting minutes to the team members who attended the meeting. You also want your supervisor to know that 1) you had a meeting and 2) you covered important topics and some decisions are made. Your supervisor isn't necessarily going to respond to the email and isn't directly involved in the meeting or projects. This is a good time to use a cc. When you cc someone on the email, everyone who gets the email can see who is cc-ed.

Figure 3: The bcc/blind carbon copy line

Your email has a bcc or bc option. Bcc stands for blind carbon copy, and bc is blind copy, but they are the same thing. When you use the bc option, only the person bc-ed can see who gets the email. The person in the "to" box or anyone cc-ed cannot see that a bc copy was sent or who received it. Some people consider the bc option to be unethical. Persons who disagree say that it is appropriate to use the bc option when emailing a subordinate about a difficult matter—a disagreement regarding policy, for example—and you want to make sure your supervisor knows what you wrote. You would bc your supervisor. You don't want your subordinate to think you are "tattling" on him or her, but you do want your supervisor to know what you did in case the matter ends up in his or her office, he or she is not caught unawares.

People generally agree that using the bc option is appropriate for privacy reasons. For example, perhaps you are an attorney, and you email an insurance company a copy of a client's claim. You might bc the client to ensure the client knows you sent the document and to keep his or her email address private from the insurance company. The insurance company likely assumes that the client will get a copy of the claim, or already has one. In another example, as a professor, I might send out an email to my entire class but bc all the students to keep their emails private from each other. With the bc, every student will receive the email, but each student can only see my name as the sender. Or, you might use bc for courtesy. For example, perhaps you have received an email with the hundreds of email addresses that were cc-ed on the original email, and you have to scroll through them to get to the message. It's annoying. If it's not necessary for the recipients to know who received the email—maybe it's just a reminder that the office is closing early today--and you want to avoid the scroll through the cc's, then you can bc all the recipients. That way, there's no cc scroll, and when someone replies, there's no chance that he or she will accidentally hit "reply all."

Something you may not know about is the "through" or "via" line on paper memos. In the military or in especially hierarchical companies, it may be frowned upon for a person to send an email to someone at a level above his or her direct supervisor. At such organizations, any correspondence to a person above the writer's direct supervisor must go through the supervisor. The memo must go first to the direct supervisor, indicated with a "through" or "via" line. The direct supervisor initials by his or her name to show he or she has read and approved the memo, and then sends it to the next level until it arrives at its destination. When the final recipient receives it, he or she is assured that your memo has been read and approved all the way up the chain of command.

To: Martha Garner
Through: Allison Hall
From: Greg Brown GB
Subject: Server outage
Date: December 1, 2015

We will be performing several software updates on our servers this Friday at 7pm EST. The maintenance is required in order to keep our servers secure and up to date.

Our lms, email, and support forum may be momentarily unavailable around that time. We expect only a very short interruption of services (i.e. a few seconds while the web server software is restarting).

/ah

In an email-only culture, this same process would be achieved by sending the email to your direct supervisor and allowing him or her to forward the email up the chain of command.

Regardless of how hierarchical you believe your organization to be, it is not generally a good practice to send correspondence—paper or electronic—to persons at levels above your supervisor without talking to your supervisor about the matter first and perhaps asking him or her to unofficially review and approve your memo or email.

Figure 4: The add attachment button

Finally, in the days of paper, memos also indicated attachments. If a memo arrived on a desk with the notation "Attachment" it meant that there was supposed to be something paper clipped to the memo with additional information. And the recipient saw nothing paper clipped; something was missing. It is for this reason that you often see in an email a paper clip icon for the attachment button or notification. And because enclosures/attachments are often indicated by paper clip symbols in an email feed, the "Attachment" note is not used in emails.

What impression do you want to make on readers in your email/memo correspondence?

Do you want readers to respect your writing, read it with ease, and come away with a clear sense of what you intended to communicate and a positive impression of you as a co-worker or team member?

If so, knowing the memo format and a bit of the reason why memos look as they do will help you in structuring your memo/email properly. As we move through this lesson, you will learn more about what types of content go in the main types of emails/memos, and how to write clearly and effectively.

One last thing. As you can see, memos and emails are not exactly the same thing. But memos evolved into emails, although paper memos are still created, and often then scanned and distributed electronically. In this chapter, we will usually refer to emails and memos as the same thing, and then clarify if we are referring to one or the other specifically.

Five Types of Memos

When this content for this chapter was first being developed, a helpful colleague imparted this wisdom to me: "Just show them a memo, have the participants write one, and boom, success!" Wouldn't it be GREAT if that were how it worked? The high interest in this topic shows how important memos and emails are, and yet at the same time, how much people want to improve their memo and writing skills. And if the problem were that you just hadn't ever seen a memo or email before, well, this chapter would be a lot shorter. It would be great if there were "one memo to rule them all," so to speak, that once you saw it and copied it, all your future memo and email writing endeavors would flow effortlessly from your fingertips.

The truth is, as you well know, there are lots of different occasions to write emails and memos. And emails and memos have been classified into over 10 different types. In this chapter, we will look at the five most common types—progress report, meeting minutes, incident report, directive, and response to an inquiry. With these five types of memos/emails in your writing arsenal, you should be ready to tackle most memo/email writing tasks.

First, note that progress reports, meeting minutes, incident reports, directives, and responses to inquiry can be created in many formats—as memos, emails, informal reports, and even formal reports. We will look at these types of documents as memos or emails.

As memos or emails, you will want to start by putting the documents in the correct format. For a memo, you will open up a word processing program, such as Microsoft Word, and you will type the memo header at the top of the document: to, from, subject, and date. You will fill in the information, and then you will begin your memo. If it is a longer memo (longer than a paragraph), you may wish to use section headers. But you do not start the memo with "Dear Mr. Carter," or any other type of salutation.

Note that you also do not sign the memo or end it with any type of closing. After you print the memo, you then initial by your name, and then, if you are sending the memo format by email (this is not uncommon), then you scan it (unless directed otherwise, it is recommended that you save it as a pdf), and you attach it to the email. The email should alert readers to the contents of the attachment.

If you are sending the progress report by email, then you fill in the email headings—the "to" and "subject" lines. Make sure the subject line is clear: "Progress Report for ABC Project." You may also have readers to include in the cc lines—persons who need to be aware that you sent the progress report but who may not need to act on it, or persons involved in the project who will not respond directly to the progress report but who requested a copy. After you have filled in the headings, you start your email with a greeting and a note letting the readers know what they are receiving. You might write something like the example shown to the right.

Dear Mr. Carter,

I hope this email finds you well. I have attached the progress report for the ABC project. Please let me know if you have any problems accessing it, or if you have any questions.

Thank you for the opportunity to be involved in this project.

Sincerely,
Mary Lewis, ABC Project Manager

It is assumed that you wrote your progress report in MS Word or another word processing program so that you could run spell check and save the document on your own computer. So, when you are ready to send it via email, you copy it into the open email form. Proofread it to make sure the copy happened correctly, and then hit "submit."

Progress Reports

A progress report is much like what it sounds like. It lets your supervisor know the status of an ongoing project. Let's say you work for a company that serves clients by creating web pages for middle school sports teams. But because you are very good at writing and designing documents, you have been put in charge of an annual project—the company newsletter. This newsletter comes out once a year around the holidays, and it's really a feel-good piece sharing the wonderful things your company has done all year. It's important, but maybe not a high stress or high dollar task that you are in charge of. Nevertheless, you are expected to work on it with your team all year and submit quarterly progress reports to your supervisor. Therefore, each quarter you will prepare your progress report on the team meetings, what is planned, what has been done, and what will be done. You also list any problems you are having or any you foresee. This last part is very important. While on the one hand, you don't want a progress report that reads like a disaster report, on the other hand you do want to prepare the reader for any upcoming problems. This preparation is especially important if something really might be delayed or over budget. You don't want to submit perfect progress reports and then suddenly your supervisor finds out the project is behind schedule!

Of course, the stakes become higher if a progress report is about a high-pressure task. If, for example, your team is in charge of the new renovations on the parking deck, and those renovations are behind, you want to let your supervisor know as soon as possible in the progress report so that he or she can prepare for things like, letting his or her supervisor know that there is a delay, extending the rental on the parking lot that has been used while the deck is built, and moving the cleanup crew's scheduled work dates back until they are actually needed, and a host of other things that will be impacted by a change in timeline.

Something related to a progress report is a status report or status update. While a progress report reports upon the progress of a single project, a status report is a report on the status of your entire unit or department—it can encompass a range of projects and activities, and it is usually submitted at regular intervals—monthly or quarterly— regardless of what projects are underway.

Meeting Minutes

For most meetings, notes are kept regarding what important topics were brought up in the meeting and what important decisions were made. These notes are often kept on file so that people can look back through them if questions arise about, for example, important votes or discussions about topics. These notes are called meeting minutes. Sometimes a secretary is appointed to always take minutes. And sometimes the duty rotates among attendees. The minutes are then "written up," which is a common term for preparing them to share with the group. Meeting minutes take a particular form, whether they are distributed via memo or email. The header includes the organization's name, the date and location of the meeting, who was present, and the meeting leader and the person taking the minutes. They also include the time the meeting started and the time the meeting ended.

Meetings have an agenda that is usually distributed before the meeting. Many times, people taking minutes for a meeting like to pull up the agenda on their word processing program and take the minutes right on that agenda so that they know they are using the original wording of the topics, as they are presented to the group.

Most importantly, as mentioned above, minutes include what happened during the meeting, including who presented on main topics and who brought forth and seconded votes, and what decisions were made. It's important not to make the minutes a "play by play" of conversations, and especially don't get bogged down in the details. Just make sure to take down the main points. If a heated discussion breaks out, don't put that in the minutes. Just note that the topic was discussed and note the resolution, if any, or if the topic was tabled (that is, put on hold for another time). You want to portray the organization positively, and for that reason, avoid recording squabbling or other human behavior that is normal, but that is not beneficial to preserve in meeting minutes.

More information about meeting minutes

Incident Reports

Incident reports are written by police officers, security personnel, and anyone who was involved in an incident or accident. As you can see from the story of Police Constable/Police Dog Peach, incident reports (here in the form of a witness statement) often are forms one fills out. Even so, it is important to secure the correct form and make sure that you fill in the requested information. Usually there is a portion of the form where you are asked to tell what happened—provide the narrative of the event. You will want to double check all information before you commit it to the incident report, which is a legal document. You may have to look up the names and titles of persons also involved. You also want to make sure the date is correct, and any equipment names or room numbers are correct. Do not write what you THINK happened. Write where you were and what happened to you or what you saw. Explain what happened after the incident, as well. How did you handle it? What did you do? Also, be very clear and avoid any language that might not be understood by people outside your field. Instead of saying you reached for the bandages, but they were "86" (slang for "out of"), say there were no bandages in the first aid kit. Be honest. Dishonest information can put your job in jeopardy or inhibit your ability to receive medical treatment or compensation for an incident/accident.

You do not (and likely should not) make judgments about who is at fault, and I would advise you not to admit that you were at fault or did something wrong. After all, that judgment is better made by someone who can see a bigger picture than you can. Instead, report the facts as clearly as possible.

If there is no form to fill out, then organize your narrative chronologically. Use paragraph breaks at logical points to make it easier to read your report. In incident reports, because perhaps a person was hurt or property was damaged, it's very important to make sure your grammar and spelling are correct. As you probably know, problems in language clarity can create legal problems that again, might impede your ability to receive medical treatment or compensation for an incident/accident.

More information on incident reports

Directives

You send out emails and memos for a variety of reasons—usually to distribute information. Sometimes, you want to let people know that tomorrow is doughnut day, and so you might send out a short email such as "Hello Everyone! Just a quick reminder that tomorrow is doughnut day!" Such an email is appropriate because everyone knows what doughnut day means—Joan in marketing will be bringing in some yummy doughnuts to share. And it's probably okay to be that informal because it's also not an official event that requires action on the employees' parts. But what if tomorrow is the annual blood drive? That event may require more explanation, especially since new employees (hired since the last blood drive) may not be aware of the company's long-standing support of the local blood bank. It may also be nice to remind everyone of the positive impact this event has on the local community and how Roger, from Accounts, has a daughter who has a health condition that frequently requires blood transfusions (assuming Roger is okay with sharing that personal information). On more than one occasion, the local blood bank has been able to provide that blood because the company's support helps to make sure they have the resources they need on hand.

Such an email or memo would first start with the announcement of this year's blood drive, a reminder to drink a lot of water and eat a meal before donating, and then name the date, time, and place. Then the memo/email might move into some of the history of the blood drive at the company and present the facts about last year's effort—the number of participants and pints collected. And then end with "I encourage everyone who is able to show up to support the blood drive."

This common type of email/memo is an informational email/memo. A directive is a little different, and it has a little different organization. The directive is not a piece of general information but, as its title makes clear, directions that direct readers to follow a particular procedure or policy.

Unlike the general information memo, a directive generally starts with the rationale behind the directive so that people feel that it is a reasonable request, and also to help people remember it. It then ends by stating the policy or procedure that readers are directed to follow. For example, let's say that for security reasons, the janitorial staff will no longer be allowed access to employee offices. Instead, employees will put their trash cans outside their offices on Mondays, Wednesdays, and Fridays for the janitorial staff to empty. Employees will then put their trash cans back in their offices the following morning. This is a new practice, so you want to issue a directive.

First, you explain the situation. You don't want to give too many details because you don't want to encourage similar incidents, and you don't want to cast suspicion on any particular employees, but you do want to provide enough details so that employees understand the rationale behind this policy. You might write that in the past two weeks, a few employees have entered their offices in the mornings to find their computers on. A forensic investigation confirms that the computers were tampered with. As an extra precaution, the janitorial staff will no longer have access to the employee offices. This step is taken to help narrow down who might be responsible for these incidents. At this point, it is not clear if any sensitive information was stolen, but you will let the employees know as soon as any information becomes available. You might also ask everyone to change his or her passwords now for extra security and remember not to leave passwords written down and lying around their computers.

You end with the directive: effective immediately, employees are directed to place their trash bins outside their office doors on Mondays, Wednesdays, and Fridays at 5pm. The bins are to be put back in the offices on the following business morning. The janitorial staff will no longer enter your offices to empty your trash.

So that's it. A directive is different from a general information memo in that it involves a policy or procedure, and it generally starts by providing an explanation and ending with the new policy or procedure that is being implemented.

Response to an Inquiry

Our final type of memo/email is the response to an inquiry. Most of the memos/emails you send will be informational or response to an inquiry.

Response to an inquiry memos/emails address a question or series of questions—perhaps about an action, a product, or a policy. Perhaps a customer wants to know why something doesn't work. Perhaps your supervisor wants to know his computer has not yet been updated. Perhaps your team member wants to know what the policy is on splitting up vacation days into half days. Whatever the case, you are responding to an inquiry.

To begin your response, especially if you are responding to a client, you might thank the writer for purchasing your product or for being a loyal customer or client. Keep in mind, this person took time out of his or her day to write you, so it was important. And the person may be out of patience if the inquiry is in relation to a malfunction. If the inquiry is from a colleague, you might begin with "It's nice to hear from you," or another polite phrase to be your response.

Next, provide the answer to the question. If there are multiple questions, and if they are numbered, number your responses the same way for clarity. For example, if question 3 is "The directions say to put tab A into slot B, but I can only see tab A and slot C," then you might answer, "3. Please turn the paper doll over. Slot B is on the side opposite slot C." Also, if there is a website that provides information that you think might be helpful, mention the website and provide the link. Be sure to double check the link to make sure it is correct.

If you cannot answer the question, either because you don't know the answers or because you are not allowed to divulge the requested information (perhaps it is a company secret, or proprietary), let the reader know. Close the email/memo with an offer to assist with other requests or answer further questions.

Please keep in mind that if it is your job to answer questions on the topic of x, then it doesn't look good if you say, "I don't know the answer to that question on the topic of x," and end the email/memo. Such a response will sour a customer on your brand very quickly. Just yesterday, I heard a story of a person to whom all responses to inquiries were met with "I don't know." It certainly is easier to do business that way—and it is a real time saver to just have one, standard response. But when you don't answer people's questions, they turn to other people. And they quickly learn that the person with no answers really isn't serving any purpose in the office. The person mentioned above lost her job right before Christmas. The moral of this story is that if it is your job to answer questions on the topic of x, then you should find the answer. Ask a colleague or supervisor to assist you. And if it is someone else's job to answer the question on the topic of x, privately (in person, by phone, or in a separate email) ask that person if it is okay if you forward the question to him/her. You don't want to just automatically shove your emails off on other people—such actions may also cost you your job. Finally, if it is not your job to answer the question on the topic of x, and you have permission to forward the inquiry to the person whose job it is, then ask the person making the inquiry if it is okay if you forward his/her correspondence to the correct person. Then, if you have permission, do so. It is never okay to just forward email without permission.

Finally, always be polite and practice the "you" attitude. Think about how it must feel to need information—and to perhaps be frustrated. It's true, you might be frustrated, too, at the questions that you feel are silly or repetitive, but still. Have empathy, be polite, and offer to assist with other questions or requests.

2.14: Technical Definitions and Descriptions

By: Jonathan Arnett

Objectives

Upon completion of this chapter, readers will be able to do the following:

1. Explain and apply the 5 primary characteristics of technical definitions.
2. Write a definition using appropriate content, descriptors, details, length, placement, and audience analysis.
3. Avoid common technical definition problems.
4. Explain and apply the 5 primary characteristics of technical descriptions.
5. Write a description using the 6 common parts.
6. Organize a description according to the 3 common organizational patterns.

Technical Definitions

When you think of the word "definition," what comes to mind? If you're like most people, you think of a dictionary's contents. What, then, does a dictionary definition contain?

Typically, dictionary definitions include a word's

1. Standard spelling
2. Syllable breaks
3. Pronunciation
4. Part of speech
5. Meaning
6. Current and archaic usage
7. Etymology
8. Synonyms/antonyms
9. Variant spellings
10. Variants including suffixes

If you've used a dictionary before, then none of these items should surprise you. Think, though... Are all dictionaries the same? And do they contain the same types of thing?

Not really. All dictionaries contain lists of words, but their contents are otherwise markedly different. A children's dictionary, for example, is much simpler and shorter than a "collegiate" dictionary, which is shorter and simpler than an unabridged dictionary, which pales in comparison to the Oxford English Dictionary, a two-volume monster that comes with a reinforced bookstand and its own magnifying glass.

All these different dictionaries share several characteristics, though, which are characteristics of any technical definition:

1. their authors focus on a particular audience;
2. their contents describe the object of attention;
3. their contents clarify ambiguity;
4. readers can use the contents to communicate across expertise levels; and
5. readers can use the contents to solve problems.

At least one of these ideas should sound familiar. For example, focusing on a particular audience...haven't we mentioned that sometime before, in this very class?

As far as the other four elements go, the temptation is to say, "Well, yeah, of course. That's what a definition does." The trick, though, is to include the right information, structure it the right way, and build a good definition. That's what we'll talk about next.

As the name might suggest, a technical definition should explain what a thing is. But what does "explain what a thing is" actually mean? How long does the explanation have to be? And where does the explanation go?

The answers to these questions depend on the characteristics listed above and the noun (person, place, thing, idea, or process) you're defining, and we see the answers expressed in terms of content, length, and placement.

Descriptors

Let's talk descriptors that can be used in writing a definition. Here's a partial list of possible items you can use to define a noun:

- physical characteristics (a thing's color, shape, size, material, smell, taste, texture, and so on)
- uses
- functions
- operation (how it works, but not how to work it--that's what goes in instructions)
- effects
- origins
- analogies ("It tastes like chicken," for example)
- specific examples
- pictures
- diagrams

More possible descriptors exist, but these are the usual suspects. You'll choose appropriate ones based on the situation at hand.

Details

The kind of detail you'd include in a technical definition will vary. As with everything you write—and quite literally *everything*, whether you're writing it for this class, in future classes, or over the rest of your life—you need to consider your audience very carefully. For example, who is your audience? What is s/he like? What kind of language would you use? What medium would the audience respond to best? What kind of words will the audience respond to best? *Et cetera*... In short, analyze your audience carefully and tailor the content to that audience.

As an illustration of the kind of details you'd choose for a particular audience, let's think about defining the special steel used in the crumple zone of a car's frame. (If you don't know what a crumple zone is, it's an area of a car that's designed to get squished in a crash and absorb all the kinetic energy, thereby making the passengers safer.)

We're going to define the steel in this part of the car for three different audiences: you, a car manufacturer, and a car buyer.

For you, if I defined the steel as *boron-doped high-austenite steel that undergoes a martensitic transformation in a crash*, that would probably mean nothing because the information is too detailed. However, if I defined the steel in a modern car's crumple zone as *relatively soft steel that suddenly stiffens up when it's put under stress*, then you'd probably understand just fine.

For a modern car manufacturer, though, neither of those definitions would be detailed enough. The manufacturer would need to know specifics about how much boron went into the steel, how ductile (bendable) the steel is, how much stress the steel can take before it stiffens or breaks, and how quickly the steel stiffens when it's put under stress. For this audience, you'd need to write a highly detailed, highly technical definition.

A car buyer, on the other hand, simply doesn't care what kind of steel goes into a car's crumple zone. The only thing a car buyer wants to know is if the car's NTSA crash test ratings are good.

Another thing to consider is what sort of object/process/thing it is you're documenting. Some nouns just don't require certain types of descriptors.

As an illustration of necessary details for a particular subject, let's consider the same example again: the steel used in a car's crumple zone.

High-austenite steel is relatively ductile; its manufacturing process includes cold rolling, annealing, and quenching; and car manufacturers use high-austenite steel in crumple zones because this steel gets harder and stiffer under pressure, thus protecting drivers.

All of these properties make sense when we're talking about metal. In contrast, saying that a certain piece of high-austenite steel has a mottled gray appearance, makes a clang in the key of C-sharp, or tastes like chocolate chip cookies probably isn't relevant to anybody.

Length

As we've already mentioned, the audience's need for information will drive how much information you provide. If the audience both needs and can handle a lot of information, then get super-detailed. On the other hand, if the audience only needs or only can handle the basics for whatever reason, then keep the definition short and include just the absolutely necessary information.

As an illustration of length, let's consider a dictionary definition.

A person who consults the Oxford English Dictionary probably wants detailed information about the many ways a particular word has been used over the centuries. Accordingly, the OED definition should be very long and full of examples.

In contrast, a middle-school student who just wants to know how to pronounce a word or find out a word's meaning won't want to read pages upon pages of etymology and usage. That student just wants the basic information and nothing more.

Placement

The audience's need for information and the type of information you're defining will also drive where you place definitions. Four major options include placing definitions in

- independent sentences
- dependent clauses
- parenthetical asides
- separate sections

If you're using relatively simple terms and have a knowledgeable audience, use simple, short definitions that fit within an ordinary sentence. If the definition is a bit more complex and/or your audience needs a bit more information, use a parenthetical statement. If you're defining complicated or detailed information, even to a knowledgeable audience, insert full paragraphs or subsections.

Sometimes, depending on the nature of the document that contains a definition, you'll refer readers to entire sections, such as footnotes, a glossary in the back of a textbook, or appendices at the end of formal proposals and reports (*hint, hint* on this last part).

In a separate sentence: *Peanut butter is a paste made from ground peanuts.*

In a dependent clause: *Jim's Steakhouse uses wide-mouth Mason jars, like those used for preserving homemade jam, as water glasses.*

In a parenthetical statement: *Siamese cats—easily identifiable by their blue eyes, triangular-shaped heads, incessant yowling, and self-entitled attitudes—come from Southeast Asia.*

Problems

When you write technical definitions, pay special attention to avoiding these three problems:

- audience-inappropriate content/language
- circular definitions
- synonymous definitions

Audience-Inappropriate Material

We've already discussed this, so I'll keep my rap short: Analyze your audience and give your audience members what they need, in a way they can understand it.

Circular Definitions

Some bad definitions depend on the reader already knowing what the defined thing is/does.

Here's an example:

Super chlorination is a swimming pool chemistry technique that enables operators to achieve breakpoint chlorination.

Okay...but what is breakpoint chlorination?

Breakpoint chlorination is an elevated level of chlorine that swimming pool operators reach by super chlorinating the water.

sigh

Synonymous Definitions

Other bad definitions substitute one synonym for another. Here's an example:

Chloramines are another name for combined chlorine.

Okay...but what is combined chlorine? Oops. I've just defined a thing as itself.

Here's a revised version:

Chloramines are molecules of 'free chlorine' (the chemically active form of chlorine that sanitizes, oxidizes, and disinfects pool water) that met an organic substance, chemically bonded to the organic substance, became chemically neutral, and began to give off a foul odor.

This version is much better, yes?

Technical Descriptions

Technical descriptions are similar to technical definitions. but technical descriptions can be stand-alone documents, whereas technical definitions are always components of a larger document. Furthermore, technical descriptions

- are usually longer than technical definitions,
- contain more detail,
- focus on functionality,
- often describe complicated subjects with multiple parts, and

- contain technical definitions.

Since technical descriptions are longer and more detailed than technical definitions, descriptions contain two major sections: Introductions and Body sections.

Introduction

The contents of a technical description's introduction are very similar to the contents of a formal letter. In the first paragraph, you need to

- identify the thing to be described;
- provide some basic background information (purpose of writing, context of writing);
- give a brief overview of the thing to be described (what is it like, what is its purpose); and
- preview the rest of the document.

Body

After the Introduction, a technical description's content will vary, depending on your audience and the thing being described. However, there are a few common themes in any technical description's body paragraphs.

Background

The body paragraphs flesh out the background information in more detail. Again, like the body of a formal letter contains details about the letter's subject, the body of a technical description contains details about the background of the thing being documented. Of course, tailor the content based on your audience and the subject at hand.

Parts/Characteristics

The body paragraphs also include details about the various parts that make up the thing being described. If the thing is a physical object, you'll want to list and describe the various parts that make up the whole. If the thing is a place, then what makes it different from or similar to other places? If the thing is a process, then what are its necessary conditions and its various stages/steps?

Visuals

A technical description's body can also include visual materials (and, conceivably, audio materials if the description is multimedia). These can be pictures, tables, diagrams, charts, graphs...if it's appropriate, put it in. One particular kind of visual material that we need to address under its own heading, though, is the specification.

Specifications

The word "specifications" has two definitions. One of the definitions refers to a list (often a table) of technical details about the object or process you're documenting. These can be part of a technical definition and are often necessary in a technical description.

The second meaning, which we'll address here, refers to images that depict the subject of a description and include callouts (lines or arrows with text attached) to highlight that object's constituent parts.

Please note: *Specifications are not descriptions*. They may be part of descriptions, but specifications cannot stand alone.

Here's why: Imagine that you bought a new, top-of-the-line TV. You're quite excited, as it's a technologically advanced TV, with one bazillion features that you can program and customize for the world's most amazing TV experience.

You unpack the box and, instead of an owner's manual, all you find is a single piece of paper that pictures the TV's remote control, with labeled arrows to each button. One button is labeled "Skip."

- What will the TV do if you press the button?
- What will be skipped?
- Can you undo a skip?
- What if you press the button twice? Three times?
- Can "Skip" be used while watching regular TV, or just during DVR replay?
- Does "Skip" have meaning for programming your DVR?

All these questions need answering before you dare press the "Skip" button. You'd be very unhappy if you missed recording this week's episode of *Game of Thrones* or somehow recorded over the *Jersey Shore* marathon...

Organization

Long technical definitions need their own organization strategies, just as any piece of writing does, but technical descriptions usually rely on one of three organization schemes:

- general-to-specific
- spatial
- chronological

Your choice of an organization strategy will depend on the kind of thing you're describing. In general, you'll always want to go from general to specific, for you need to begin by defining the thing and then proceed by breaking it down thematically. What that theme is, though, depends on the nature of the thing being described.

General-to-Specific

For example, let's say you're documenting a bicycle. Would it do any good to just start naming pieces?

Okay...here's the front wheel, and here's the seat, and here's the handlebars...ooh! My favorite part, the chain guard!

Of course not; you need some sort of internal logic to the parts list. A logical scheme might be to begin with major systems—frame, wheels, gears, brakes—and then describe how the systems work together or go into more detail about the parts that compose each of these systems.

Spatial

What about describing the construction of a four-barrel carburetor? You'd likely want to describe how the parts fit together, so a spatial organization scheme would make sense, complete with an exploded-view diagram of the parts. (As a completely irrelevant side note, in the year 2000, I met the inventor of the four-barrel carburetor; he was in his early nineties, and he was volunteering as a math tutor at a community college in Arizona. He was a very nice fellow.)

Chronological

But what about describing a process, like smelting iron? Giving a tour of the factory wouldn't make much sense, would it?

Here's the blast furnace, and over here is the rock crusher. And then on this side, we've got the mold-making shop and a pile of spare wheelbarrow tires.

No... you'd want to proceed chronologically, step-by-step, through the process.

First, dump trucks haul in raw ore and pour it into this bin. Then we use a bucket loader to transfer the ore into this machine, where we pulverize it. Then we load the crushed ore into these crucibles and roast the ore until the iron melts out. From that point, we...

You get the idea.

Chapter 3: Ethics in Technical Communication

By: Tamara Powell

Objectives

Upon completion of this chapter, readers will be able to do the following:

- Define ethics.
- Analyze a situation with regard to utility, rights, justice, and care.
- Explain the importance of ethical behavior.
- Explain copyright law, why it is important, and how to make ethical decisions regarding it.
- Explain how to ethically analyze data.
- Explain how biases can lead to unethical decisions/behavior in technical communication.

Introduction to Ethics

Virtue, then, is a state of character concerned with choice, lying in a mean, i.e. the mean relative to us, this being determined by a rational principle, and by that principle by which the man of practical wisdom would determine it. Now it is a mean between two vices, that which depends on excess and that which depends on defect; and again it is a mean because the vices respectively fall short of or exceed what is right in both passions and actions, while virtue both finds and chooses that which is intermediate. Hence in respect of its substance and the definition which states its essence virtue is a mean, with regard to what is best and right an extreme.

Aristotle, Nicomachean Ethics, Book II

Ethics is one of the most important topics in technical communication. When you can communicate clearly and effectively, and when it is your task to help others to understand an object, process, or procedure, it is your responsibility to do so in an ethical fashion.

After all, good writing isn't just grammatically correct, or even functional. As Zuidema and Bush state, "If we define *good writing* simply as writing that gets the audience to do or think what the writer wants, we fail to take into consideration the needs or well-being of the audience, and we ignore the ways in which writing may hurt others or cause harm" (Zuidema and Bush 95). But what does it mean to communicate ethically with regard to technical communication? There is a lot of confusion regarding what "ethics" means, and when you drill down to what ethical technical communication means, the answer becomes very complicated.

We might think asking someone if he or she is an ethical person is the same as asking someone if he or she is a good person. Certainly, my Aunt Maudie, who always held herself to be the definitive judge of whether someone was a good person or not, would tell you that a good person does what he or she feels is right in his or her heart. But the human heart can be very complicated. If you find a dollar on the floor, what is the right thing to do?

- run around asking anyone if he or she lost a dollar? What if the person who says "yes" is lying and didn't lose the dollar? Was it right, then, to give the dollar to him or her? What about the person who really lost the dollar? How do you know?
- turn the dollar into lost and found?
- keep the dollar, with the rationalization that you probably lost a dollar in the past, and this is just karma returning that dollar to you?
- give the dollar to charity with the rationalization that by doing so, at least you know it will do some good?

Any of these potential answers might feel right in your heart. Such a criterion really isn't the best to use to judge more complex ethical problems such as you might find in technical communication situations.

Also, note all of these potential answers are legal. Just because something is legal doesn't make it ethical. In the past, in the United States, it was legal for health care insurance companies to deny coverage to persons who had health problems. That is, if a person had a heart attack and did not have insurance, then he or she would not be able to purchase insurance afterward, even though it was clear that he or she would not be able to afford health care without health insurance. Such a practice was common and legal, but it was not at all ethical to deny sick persons the ability to afford the health care they needed.

Key Concepts: Utility, Rights, Justice, and Caring

According to ethicist Manuel G. Velasquez, there are four basic kinds of moral standards: "utility" (61), "rights, justice, and caring" (59). While each of these categories is complex, at the basic level, these categories can be explained as follows:

1. Utility: "The inclusive term used to refer to the net benefits of any sort produced by an action" (61). This standard favors the solution that yields "the greatest net benefits to society or impose[s] the lowest net costs" (61).
2. Rights: This standard "look[s] at individual entitlements to freedom of choice and well-being" (68).
3. Justice: This standard "look[s] at how the benefits and burdens are distributed among people" (68).
4. Care: With regard to the "ethic of care,....the moral task is not to follow universal and impartial moral principles, but instead to attend and respond to the good of particular concrete persons with whom we are in a valuable and close relationship. Compassion, concern, love, friendship, and kindness are all sentiments or virtues that normally manifest this dimension of morality" (102).

You may have noticed that these standards can quite easily contradict each other. Let's think through a rather silly example.

Let's say you have a face to face technical communication class at a local college or university. It meets twice a week, and you attend the scheduled class periods. One of your classmates, let's call him Percival, likes to sleep in class. More than that, he snores loudly while the professor is trying to teach.

The first class period this problem manifests itself, the professor first tries calling on Percival to keep his attention, and then the professor nicely suggests he go get a drink of water to wake himself up. Percival, however, is having none of this. He evidently prefers to spend classtime sleeping—and snoring. The snoring is really distracting, and everyone is finding it hard to learn in this environment. The second class period, the drama repeats itself, but the professor has come prepared. At the first loud, earsplitting snore, the professor pulls out a water gun at Percival. She aims, fires, and SPLAT! Percival is awake! The class laughs uproariously, and every time Percival snores, he gets water in the face. It's still kind of hard to concentrate, with the professor watergunning Percival every 15 minutes or so, but it's very entertaining.

This scenario is a little off the wall, but let's evaluate it, anyway. The professor's solution to the problem is effective, at least in this one instance. But how does it stack up to an ethical evaluation?

- Rights—people in contemporary societies have a wide variety of rights. For example, students have the right to a conducive learning environment. So on the one hand, students have the right to attend class and not have to fight through Percival's snoring to hear the professor's lecture.On the other hand, students have the right to attend class and not be shot at with a water gun.

- Justice—the benefit to the professor's solution to the problem is that it is effective. It stops Percival's plan to snore through class and make learning difficult for the other students. It also seems, at first, to bring the class together against a common distraction and provide some temporary amusement. Everyone is having fun at Percival's expense. But let's think. Students have a right to attend class and not be subjected to abuse. Shooting a student with a water gun is abuse. It's very much outside of the appropriate treatment a student might expect from a professor. And it is humiliating. Kant's categorical imperative has been translated thus: "Act only on that maxim through which you can at the same time will that it should become a universal law," (Kant 24). Granted, all sleeping students will be attacked with a water gun would be a pretty silly maxim. Reasonable people wouldn't even consider such a rule. But if they were to, it would be clear that we wouldn't want to be attacked with a water gun if we accidentally fell asleep and started snoring, and we wouldn't want our loved ones subjected to such treatment, either. Certainly, Percival never consented to be attacked with a water gun. His rights are being violated in this example. With regard to justice, sure, at first the water gun accomplishes the goal, but it is also distracting. And how long will it take for students to wonder, who else will get watergunned? Suddenly, the professor's blatant disrespect for Percival can easily move to disrespect for anyone. Morale can drop. The students can lose respect for the professor, and then the learning environment is compromised. The entire class suffers, and the learning outcomes also suffer, because the professor made the decision to employ a water gun.

- Utility: One of the ways to look at utility is to ask the question, "Is there a better solution that helps everyone achieve the desired outcomes?" Or at least, is there a solution that minimizes the disadvantages to the larger population? In this case, yes. At most institutions, the professor has a variety of ways to deal with a disruptive student. After informing the student of the consequences of repeating his or her disruptive actions, the professor may call campus security to remove the student. The professor may also contact the student's academic advisor to discuss a solution, and at some institutions, the professor can have the student removed from the class roster. While official solutions may not be as dramatic, as fun, and as quickly effective as watergunning as student, they do protect all students' dignity and right to a safe environment conducive to learning.

- Care: At the end of the day, a professor is a human being, too. And he or she may be at wit's end trying to deal with students do not want to be in the class are actively working against the professor's efforts to do his or her job. It is frustrating. And it might even be understandable that he or she wants to pull out a water gun and just solve the problem and blow off a little steam. But the professor has a job, and that job brings in income. It's highly likely that the professor has a family to support. Watergunning a student will bring in negative publicity to the professor, the class, the academic department, and the institution that he or she teaches in. With public scrutiny, the professor might earn a reprimand or, at worst, lose his or her job. How will he or she help to support his or her family?

As we analyze this situation, we quickly see that watergunning the student is unethical. It violates the rights of the student and can impede upon the professor's ability to care for his or her family. Furthermore, it may lower morale in the classroom, which may rob all students in the class of an environment conducive to learning. And finally, there are better, accepted channels to use to deal with this situation.

Such a simple scenario, but so many ways to look at the situation. Analyzing any situation with regard to ethics should take time and care so that the best evaluation can be produced. And here, we have only invoked some of the ethical aspects of Aristotle, Kant, and Velasquez. In this short introduction to ethics, we are only scratching the surface of a much larger and very complicated and fascinating field.

Here are some sample scenarios that you can analyze with regard to rights, justice, utility, and care.

Sample ethical dilemmas

Faulty Communication and Real Consequences

Let's move to a real example of an ethical situation in technical communication.

In 1986, the spaceship Challenger exploded. What you may not know is that a failure of communication was partially responsible for that disaster. There was an "O-ring problem," or "the failure of a rubber seal in the solid rocket booster" with regard to the shuttle's construction (Winsor 336). From early 1984 until July 1985, the O-ring problems were noticed but not taken seriously. Or dismissed. On July 22, 1985, MIT engineer Roger Boisjoly sent a memo to R.K. Lund, who was MIT's Vice President of Engineering. In the memo, Boisjoly stated that the O-ring problem was serious, and concluded, "It is my honest and very real fear that if we do not take immediate action . . .

to solve the problem . . . then we stand in jeopardy of losing a flight along with all the launch pad facilities" (Winsor 341). MIT engineer Brian Russell wrote an August 9 letter in response to Boisjoly's memo. Russell's letter stated the facts very plainly. For example, he writes, "If the primary seal were to fail from . . . 330-660 milliseconds the chance of the second seal holding is small. This is a direct result of the o-ring's slow response compared to the metal case segments as the joint rotates" (Winsor 343). Russell's memo does not provide any interpretation of the situation, and as such, "did not communicate its intent [as] is shown by the fact that the people who read it were uncertain about what it meant" (343). The important information in the Russell memo, which was quoted above, was buried deep in the letter after such reassurances as "MIT has no reason to suspect that the primary seal would ever fail after pressure equilibrium is reached" (343). While it might seem prudent in the face of bad news to report "just the facts," if lives are at stake, it is important to communicate clearly. Do not hide or bury the information that there is a problem. Make a clear recommendation to solve the problem, if appropriate and possible. Make clear the perceived consequences if the problem is not dealt with. Of course, no one wants to be wrong or to be perceived as overly dramatic. But at the same time, ethical communication is clear and appropriately detailed so as to prevent disasters such as the Challenger explosion. The Challenger launch was delayed because of the O-ring problem, but on January 28, 1986, the shuttle launched. And exploded.

Of course, no one wants to be the bearer of bad news. And no one wants to point the finger. We all are concerned about how we are perceived by others. And we don't want to jeopardize our position within a company or organization. Also, we might be asked by someone above us to "fudge the data" a little bit in order to keep a grant or contract. Our working relationships or even our jobs might be on the line. Perhaps a grant might not get funded if certain data are not reported. Or perhaps our company won't get a contract if we don't promise that our construction plan can hold the number of cars the client desires. When the pressure is on, the consequences may not seem so dire. But as Kant reminds us, if we don't wish others to lie about the maximum amount of cars that can use the parking deck safely while we are in the parking deck, then we certainly should not do it, either.

Appropriate Language in Technical Communication

From Kueffer and Larsen:

Factual Correctness

Every metaphor simplifies by illustrating certain aspects of a scientific object while neglecting others. Scientific metaphors can nonetheless, be interpreted in terms of their factual content, and, in this respect, they can be considered wrong. At the start of the genomic era, for instance, Avise (2001) proposed alternative genetic metaphors to replace prior mechanistic ones (e.g., the blueprint metaphor) that he felt misrepresented new insights about the nature of the genome . . . . Metaphors should be consistent with the state of knowledge to the degree of scientific accuracy required in a particular context (e.g., research, popular science writing, science-based decision making).

Socially acceptable language

The same rules that apply to everyday life concerning socially acceptable language also apply to science. Metaphors that are racist, sexist, or in other ways offensive should be avoided. Herbers (2007) for example, condemns references to slavemaking and negro ants and reference to rape in animal behavior studies.

Neutrality

It is often difficult to assess the neutrality of a metaphor. Scientists should, nonetheless, seek in their communication to avoid language that is generally recognized to be loaded with emotion, such as apocalyptic warnings and dramatic hyperbole. This language can distract from the perceived neutrality of a scientist, who is expected to present research results that invite open and critical discussion. One rhetorical function of such metaphors is to convince when evidence is missing or ambiguous; however, this is inadvisable, insofar as it leads to scientific statements' being supported with rhetoric instead of facts.

Transparency

When a metaphor is used, it should be introduce das such and its connection with specific aspects of scientific concepts should be illustrated. At least in longer texts, authors should explicitly reflect on the connotations and

To get started, let's watch a video on using appropriate language in technical writing. Appropriate language becomes an ethical concern if inappropriate languages is imprecise or disrespectful.

Appropriate Language in Technical Communication

To continue to address some specific aspects of ethics in technical communication, Kueffer and Larson remind us that sometimes writers use inappropriate metaphors in technical communication that reduce the credibility of the scientific writing or research that they are trying to communicate to the public. We live in a time when, especially in advertising and popular culture, dramatic language is pervasive. It may be tempting to overstate or dramatize a scientific finding to garner public attention to something very important such as climate change. For example, a letter with the title, " 'Alien species: Monster fern makes [International Union for Conservation of Nature] invader list' " really grabs the attention. But Kueffer and Larson explain, "We consider this choice of words to be undesirable, because it merely expresses a value judgment of the authors (i.e., that the species is like a monster because it is bad) rather than illustrating the science. The metaphor devalues this plant species in its entirety (like a monster that is always bad) rather than specifying which aspects of its behavior are problematic" (721). Kueffer and Larson continue, "It is better to communicate precisely, and to use appropriate metaphors so that if, for example, later contradictory information becomes available, the public does not dismiss scientific findings. Responsible technical communicators understand that scientific research involves a level of uncertainty which must be made clear to readers" (721).

Ethics and Copyright Law

Another important aspect of ethics involves awareness of and respect for copyright law.

The information found here is based on materials developed by Jean T. Kreamer and Georgia Harper for the LaCADE (Louisiana Consortium for the Advancement of Distance Education) program.

Copyright has become a widely discussed topic with the advent of the Internet. Images and designs are everywhere. It is so easy to click and save a background, a photograph, even a cartoon from a web site. Many ask "what are the rules?" Here are the answers to some frequently asked questions about copyright laws.

Why do we have copyright laws?

The purpose behind copyright law is the protection of the creator's creation. If you come up with a fantastic new design for Kennesaw State University, for example, you would want credit and compensation for your genius. You would copyright the design and offer it to KSU. KSU might then decide to use it. You might grant KSU exclusive rights for free, or you might require a one time fee for KSU to buy the rights of the design, or you might request a sum of money every time the design is used. All of these negotiations would require you to waive, protect or sell your copyright. However, think about a situation where you sold your design to KSU for a fee each time the design was used or for a percentage of the sales. Then, a large discount chain began marketing shirts with your logo, but without your permission? What if buyers could get your great new design at half the price because you were no longer getting your cut? It's great for the consumer and the discount chain, but you and KSU have been cheated. To prevent such theft and unethical use, there are copyright laws.

What does copyright protect?

Copyright does not protect facts, ideas, or descriptions. To use another's facts, ideas, or descriptions in your work you will need to cite properly using an acceptable form of documentation (APA or MLA, for example). Copyright protects creative expression. Creative expression is found in designs (such as Web page designs or layouts, portfolio designs, etc), logos, pictures, icons, and other creative ways to express information. A religious group recently used a cartoon character to deliver their message in a religious tract. Using a well-recognized cartoon character made the tract very popular, and the religious organization was very pleased with the results. However, the religious organization had not contacted the artist and negotiated any agreement for use of the image. The religious organization was stunned when they were sued for copyright infringement. To use an image, photograph, icon, logo, graph, chart, or layout that was not created by the user and for which the user has no agreement or authorization is an infringement of copyright. It does not matter how benign you believe the use is or how beneficial you feel the use might be to the creator. It is an infringement of copyright to use creations that are not your own if you do not have permission from the creator or his or her agent.

Is it okay to take an image if I can save it to my desktop?

No. It is a mistake to think that an image is only copyright protected if the web page designer has made it so that the image cannot be copied onto the computer. Just because an image can be taken doesn't mean it is not copyright protected. If you need copyright free images, Bing is a great searchable database. You can enter a term into the search box, and then you can narrow your search by license, depending upon what you plan to do with the image.

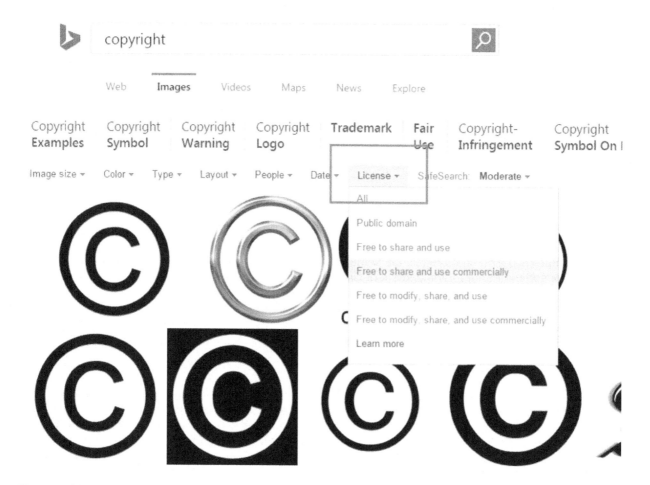

Figure 1: License tools on Bing Images

Google images has a similar feature. After you have searched for an image, click on "Search tools" to see more tools. One will be "Usage rights." Use that tool to filter by license.

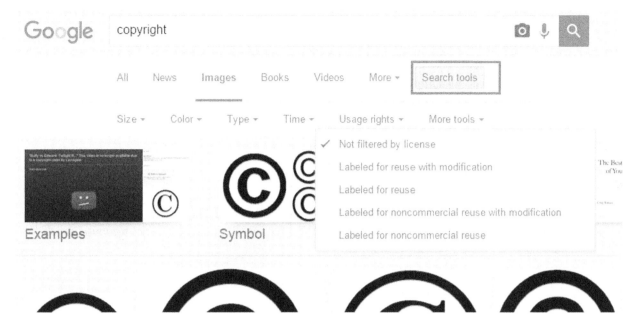

Figure 2: Usage rights tools on Google Images

Isn't using images, such as a popular fast food chain logo, actually free advertising?

It may be free advertising, but it is also a violation of copyright. It is a popular myth that linking the image back to the original bypasses copyright laws. The designer can still sue you. Always get written permission to use a design. Some designers announce that designs may be used if the designer is credited and/or if a link is provided back to the home page. In this case, you are given permission to use the graphic as long as you abide by the designer's stipulations.

What about fair use laws? Can't I use a graphic if I follow the fair use laws?

Unfortunately, graphics are not covered under fair use laws that apply to students. The limits of copyright exist mainly for libraries and government use. For example, a designer's copyright protection does not prohibit libraries from making copies for interlibrary loan purposes or archiving; does not prohibit book owners from throwing away or reselling books; does not prohibit educational uses in face-to-face teaching and in distance learning; and does not prohibit making copies of a work or altering it to make it available to disabled persons.

Fair use does allow people other than the copyright holder to use part of a copyrighted work in certain circumstances even without permission. To learn more, read about it here.

If I am a student, does that mean I can use another's design in my own papers and presentations?

Because your papers and presentations are an educational use for a restricted audience, you are allowed to use copyrighted designs, under certain conditions. If a chart or graph or logo conveys the message that you want to convey in your paper or presentation, you may use it provided you cite it just as you would any other information that you used. Consult your documentation guide for proper documentation of graphs, charts, graphics, drawings, photographs, icons, symbols, or logos. In addition, if you take the information from a chart but create the chart yourself, you do not need to cite the chart in your paper, but you will still need to cite the information and document it properly in your paper. If you take information from a source and create a graphic explaining that information, you still need to document your use properly. The Conference on Fair Use (CONFU) Educational Fair Use Guidelines for Digital Images decided that "[s]tudents may download, transmit and print out images for personal study and for use in the preparation of academic course assignments and other requirements for degrees" (9). If you are creating work that will be put on the open web—such as in a publicly accessible blog for a class assignment—you will need to search for images that are copyright free or labeled for reuse.

What if there's no trademark or copyright symbol on the design?

Stealing another's design is unethical. It is also important to note that an absence of trademark does not mean the design is not copyrighted. Designs that are in the process of copyright approval can win damage awards if an infringement occurs while the design is awaiting an official copyright. And today, copyrighted works are no longer obligated to carry notice of copyright. For works created after March 1, 1989, absence of copyright is no indication of copyright status.

Will an international company such as Sony really catch me putting a few of their song lyrics up on my personal web page?

Large companies employ lawyers to surf the web searching for infringements of their copyrights. Many humble college students have been surprised by letters from big-name firms threatening lawsuits if lyrics or logos aren't removed from a personal web page. There are additional penalties if materials in question are not removed quickly enough to suit the offended party.

Some of this seems very silly. So what if I use a fast food logo on my web page or in my research paper and don't get permission or proper credit. What does it really matter?

First, if you were the artist, wouldn't you want proper credit for your creative expression? It's just good manners. And it is not difficult to request permission to use designs. Second, copyright laws are in flux right now. There is a lot of debate about what is or is not fair use regarding the Internet (how can you write a movie review on the Internet without making a few movie clips available, for example? Is that fair use? Is that copyright infringement? These issues are being debated). There is debate regarding whether a university can be sued along with a student if a student misuses a corporate logo on a university website. Obviously, everyone is very interested in who is liable. To keep yourself as safe as possible, err on the side of caution and respect copyrights.

What about copyright-free images, such as clip art?

If you go to a site that has copyright-free clip art, then that clip art is yours to use as you please. There are no restrictions or royalties involved regarding copyright-free images. But the site must say copyright free clipart. Wikipedia is not copyright free, unless you look at the image and see that it is in the Creative Commons. See the tips in #3 for how to obtain copyright-free clip art.

How well do you understand basic copyright law?

Ethical Analysis of Data

As you analyze data, avoid cooking, trimming, and cherry picking data.

Cooking data is the practice of falsifying data. It can also be the practice of deleting data that does not prove a hypothesis in order to present a stronger argument that proves the hypothesis. For example, what if you were ordering pizza for an event, and you really wanted every pizza to have bacon on it. You LOVE bacon. If you surveyed 100 people about whether or not they liked bacon, and 50 people said yes, and 50 people said no, but 25 of the "no's" were vegetarians, then you could report the data truthfully, that half of the people surveyed like bacon. Perhaps half of the pizzas should have bacon on them. Or, you could "cook" the data by excluding the vegetarians from the survey because, as you reason, it's not that they don't like bacon but that they don't EAT bacon, which is completely different from liking it. You could then say that 2/3 of the people surveyed like bacon, or 67%, and therefore you have a rationale to order bacon on all the pizzas.

Trimming data is a method used to lessen the effect of statistical outliers on the results of a study. If you trim data, then you must tell your reader that you trimmed the data, and to what percent you trimmed it. For example, if you were ordering pizza for an event, and you really wanted every pizza to have bacon on it, then you could survey 100 people about whether or not they liked bacon. Your survey also includes a question about what planet people are from (this is a ridiculous example, but I just wanted it to be simple). When you look at the results, you see that 55 people really like bacon. You notice that 45 people say they don't like bacon, but that there are irregularities in that data. For example, 10 of those respondents say that they are from the planet Mercury, so they can't eat any human food at all. So, you will trim the data to omit these irregularities. That means 55 people really like bacon and 35 don't. And you would tell your readers that 10% of the responses were culled for irregularities. You can also state what the irregularities were. It's fine to trim data that is outside the realm of possibility--as long as you tell your readers. It is not okay to trim data simply because it makes it easier for you or supports your argument better.

Cherry picking data is the practice of only using data that supports your hypothesis. A good example, with graphs and humor, of cherry picking is here.

We see these methods used so often in the presentation of data in the media, that we might come to believe it's okay to cook, trim, and cherry pick data for analysis. It is not.

How well do you understand ethics in data analysis?

Biases and Technical Communication (An Activity)

As a final discussion of ethics and technical communication, let's look at ways one can "translate" a document to a different audience. The sample document linked below is *The First Citizens' Report*, a document created in India by India's Centre for Science and Environment. Click on the link to see a sample item from that document. The sample item, "The Killer Still at Large," explains the impact that baby formula is having on the health of India's children.

The Killer Still at Large

The question for you is, how does one "translate" an informative piece written to a certain audience (in this case, Indian) with a certain perspective (concern for the environment and public health) and a certain bias (that commercial formula is inferior to breast milk) into a human interest piece for readers of a small newspaper in the Southern United States? Four writers, below, take on the task.

After reading the original article, linked to the cover, above, read through the four revisions, linked below. Each one was revised to serve as a human interest newspaper story for a small town newspaper the American South.

Article revised by Fenton Harcourt
Article revised by Chandra Mistry
Article revised by Lisa Reed
Article revised by Jerry Rouche

Which writer did the best job of revising the original article to serve the needs of the new audience? Why do you think so? Register your vote here:

If you were the editor of this newspaper, what feedback would you provide to the writers? Using your best, professional technical communication skills, provide feedback to the writers in the appropriate boxes on the Padlet. Keep in mind that what you post is publicly available. Adhere to these netiquette guidelines.

Made with **padlet**

Access the Padlet

Works Cited

Aristotle, Nicomachean Ethics Book 2. Translated by W.D. Ross. 350 B.C. E.
http://classics.mit.edu/Aristotle/nicomachaen.2.ii.html

Avise, J.C. 2001. Evolving genomic metaphors: A new look at the language of DNA. Science 294: 86-87.

Carolan MS. 2006. The values and vulnerabilities of metaphors within the environmental sciences. Society and Natural Resources 19: 921-930.

Herbers, JM. 2007. Watch your language! Racially loaded metaphors in scientific research. BioScience 57: 104-105.

Kant, Immanuel. Groundwork for the Metaphysics of Morals. Translated by Jonathan Bennett. 1785. http://www.earlymoderntexts.com/assets/pdfs/kant1785.pdf

Keuffer, Christoph and Brendon M. H. Larson. "Responsible Use of Language in Scientific Writing and Science Communication." BioScience. 64.8 (2014): 719-724.

Velasquez, Manuel G. Business Ethics: Concepts and Cases. 6th Edition. Pearson/Prentice Hall: Upper Saddle River, NJ, 2006.

Zuidema, Leah A. and Jonathan Bush. "Professional Writing in the English Classroom." English Journal. 100.6 (2011): 95-98.

Chapter 4: Document Design

4.1: Report Design

By: David McMurrey and Jonathan Arnett

Objectives

Upon completion of this chapter, readers will be able to do the following:

- Explain the importance of effective report design.
- Explain the purpose of a letter of transmittal.
- Define when covers and labels are appropriate for reports.
- Explain the purposes of and write a descriptive abstract and executive summary for a report.
- Apply design principles of tables of contents and figures.
- Apply basic design considerations on the body of a report.
- Define the appropriateness of a conclusion, appendix, and information sources.

Report Design

Technical reports (including handbooks and guides) have various designs depending on the industry, profession, or organization. This chapter shows you one traditional design. If you are taking a technical writing course, make sure the design presented in this chapter is acceptable. The same is true if you are writing a technical report in a science, business, or government context.

Technical reports have specifications as do any other kind of project. Specifications for reports involve layout, organization and content, format of headings and lists, the design of the graphics, and so on. The advantage of a required structure and format for reports is that you or anyone else can expect them to be designed in a familiar way—you know what to look for and where to look for it. Reports are usually read in a hurry—people are in a hurry to get to the information they need, the key facts, the conclusions, and other essentials. A standard report format is like a familiar neighborhood.

When you analyze the design of a technical report, notice how repetitive some sections are. This duplication has to do with how people read reports. They don't read reports straight through: they may start with the executive summary, skip around, and probably do not read every page. Your challenge is to design reports so that these readers encounter your key facts and conclusions, no matter how much of the report they read or in what order they read it.

The standard components of the typical technical report are discussed in this chapter. The following sections guide you through each of these components, pointing out the key features. As you read and use these guidelines, remember that these are guidelines, not commandments. Different companies, professions, and organizations have their own varied guidelines for reports—you'll need to adapt your practice to those as well as the ones presented here.

Letter of Transmittal

The transmittal letter is a cover letter. It is usually attached to the outside of the report with a paper clip, but it can be bound within the report, as a kind of author's preface. It is a communication from you—the report writer—to the recipient, the person who requested the report and who may even be paying you for your expert consultation. Essentially, it says "Okay, here's the report that we agreed I'd complete by such-and-such date. Briefly, it contains this and that, but does not cover this or that. Let me know if it meets your needs." The transmittal letter explains the context—the events that brought the report about. It contains information about the report that does not belong in the report.

Use the standard business-letter format for cover letters. If you write an internal report, use the memorandum format instead; in either case, the contents and organization are the same:

- **First paragraph.** Cites the name of the report, putting it in italics. It also mentions the date of the agreement to write the report.
- **Middle paragraph(s).** Focuses on the purpose of the report and gives a brief overview of the report's contents.
- **Final paragraph.** Encourages the reader to get in touch if there are questions, comments, or concerns. It closes with a gesture of good will, expressing hope that the reader finds the report satisfactory.

As with any other element in a report, you may have to modify the contents of this letter (or memo) for specific situations. For example, you might want to add a paragraph that lists questions you'd like readers to consider as they review the report.

Cover and Label

If your report is over ten pages, bind it in some way and create a label for the cover.

Covers

Covers give reports a solid, professional look as well as protection. You can choose from many types of covers. Keep these tips in mind:

1. The best covers use either a spiral (best) or plastic "comb" (second-best) binding and thick, card-stock paper for the covers. These bindings allow reports to lie open by themselves, are inexpensive, and add to the professionalism of your work. Any copy shop can make one for you.
2. Three-ring binders (also called loose-leaf notebooks) are a decent second choice. They allow your report to lie flat, but they are often too bulky for short reports, and the page holes tend to tear. However, if the audience will want to remove or replace pages, then a three-ring binder is an appropriate choice.
3. Three-hole binders that use brads to hold the pages together are a distant third choice. They are less bulky than three-ring binders, but they prevent the pages from lying flat, and readers must either weigh down or crease the pages. If you do use one of these, add an extra half-inch to the left margin to account for the "gutter" between pages.
4. Clear (or colored) plastic slip cases with the plastic sleeve on the left edge are never appropriate for a professional report. These are like something out of grade school, and they are aggravating to use. They won't lay flat, so readers must struggle to keep them open, and they generate static electricity, which makes pages stick together.

Labels

Be sure to devise a label for the cover of your report. It's a step that some report writers forget. Without a label, a report is anonymous; it gets ignored.

The best way to create a label is to use your word-processing software to design one on a standard page with a graphic box around the label information. Print it out, then go to a copy shop and have it photocopied directly onto the report cover.

There are no standard requirements for the label, although your company or organization should have its own requirements. Common elements to include are

- the report's formal title
- the intended recipient
- the authors (or, often, the author's organization)
- a report tracking number
- the date of submission

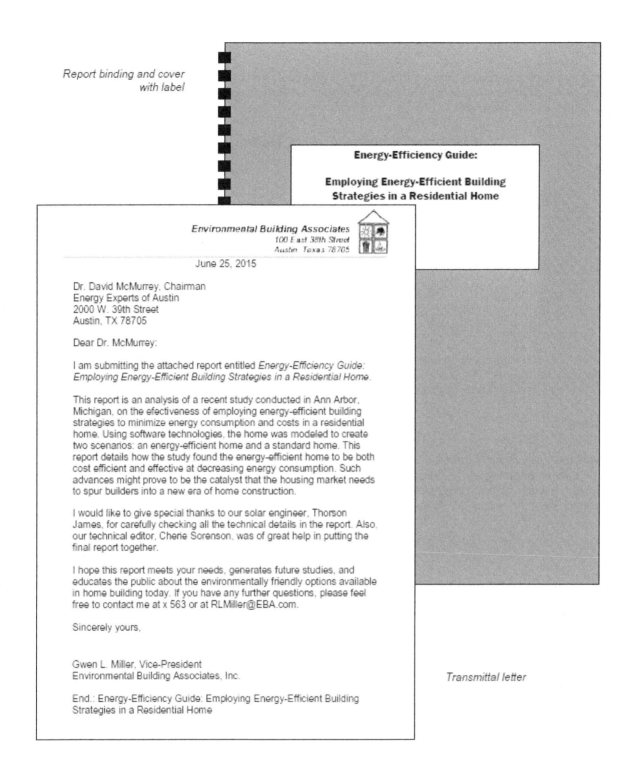

Report binding and cover with label

Energy-Efficiency Guide:

Employing Energy-Efficient Building Strategies in a Residential Home

Environmental Building Associates
100 East 38th Street
Austin, Texas 78705

June 25, 2015

Dr. David McMurrey, Chairman
Energy Experts of Austin
2000 W. 39th Street
Austin, TX 78705

Dear Dr. McMurrey:

I am submitting the attached report entitled *Energy-Efficiency Guide: Employing Energy-Efficient Building Strategies in a Residential Home.*

This report is an analysis of a recent study conducted in Ann Arbor, Michigan, on the effectiveness of employing energy-efficient building strategies to minimize energy consumption and costs in a residential home. Using software technologies, the home was modeled to create two scenarios: an energy-efficient home and a standard home. This report details how the study found the energy-efficient home to be both cost efficient and effective at decreasing energy consumption. Such advances might prove to be the catalyst that the housing market needs to spur builders into a new era of home construction.

I would like to give special thanks to our solar engineer, Thorson James, for carefully checking all the technical details in the report. Also, our technical editor, Cherie Sorenson, was of great help in putting the final report together.

I hope this report meets your needs, generates future studies, and educates the public about the environmentally friendly options available in home building today. If you have any further questions, please feel free to contact me at x 563 or at RLMiller@EBA.com.

Sincerely yours,

Gwen L. Miller, Vice-President
Environmental Building Associates, Inc.

Encl.: Energy-Efficiency Guide: Employing Energy-Efficient Building Strategies in a Residential Home

Transmittal letter

Figure 1: Transmittal letter and report cover (with cover label)

Abstract and Executive Summary

Most technical reports contain a descriptive abstract or an executive summary, and sometimes both. Each element summarizes a report's contents, but they do so in different ways and for different purposes.

Descriptive Abstract

This brief paragraph provides a capsule overview of the report's purpose and contents. It's usually a single paragraph. In many report designs, the descriptive abstract appears at the bottom of the title page (not the cover page), as shown in the following example.

LIGHTWATER NUCLEAR REACTORS

submitted to

Mr. David A. McMurrey
Energy Research Consultants, Inc.
Austin, Texas

April 27, 19XX

by Jeffrey D. Lacruz

This report examines light water reactors as a possible alternative source of energy for Luckenbach, Texas. Both types of light water reactors are described, and an explanation of how each reactor produces electricity is presented. Safety systems and economic aspects conclude the main discussion of the report.

Executive Summary

Another common element in a report's front matter is an executive summary, which also summarizes the key facts and conclusions contained in the report. Its purpose is to allow a busy executive to absorb the report's major findings without having to wade through pages of details. A typical executive summary runs from a half-page to two pages, but it can be longer if the report is very long.

Table of Contents and Table of Figures

Table of Contents

Any technical document of more than a few pages that includes distinct major sections should include a table of contents (ToC), and each major section should start on a new page.

The ToC should not include the title page or the cover letter/memo. If the proposal includes an abstract and/or executive summary, those sections should appear in the ToC, and it is customary to paginate them with lower-case roman numerals. The ToC should not include itself. Treat it as page zero.

Always include at least the top two levels of headings, but how many subheading levels you include in a ToC is up to you. A long, complex report with multiple subheadings may need a ToC entry for each subheading, but this approach may result in an extremely long and confusing ToC. A potential solution is to create two ToCs, one listing just the top two levels of headings and one listing all levels of headings.

One final note: Make sure the words in the ToC are the same as they are in the text. As you write and revise, you might change some of the headings—don't forget to update the ToC accordingly. See Figure 3 for an example of a ToC and executive summary:

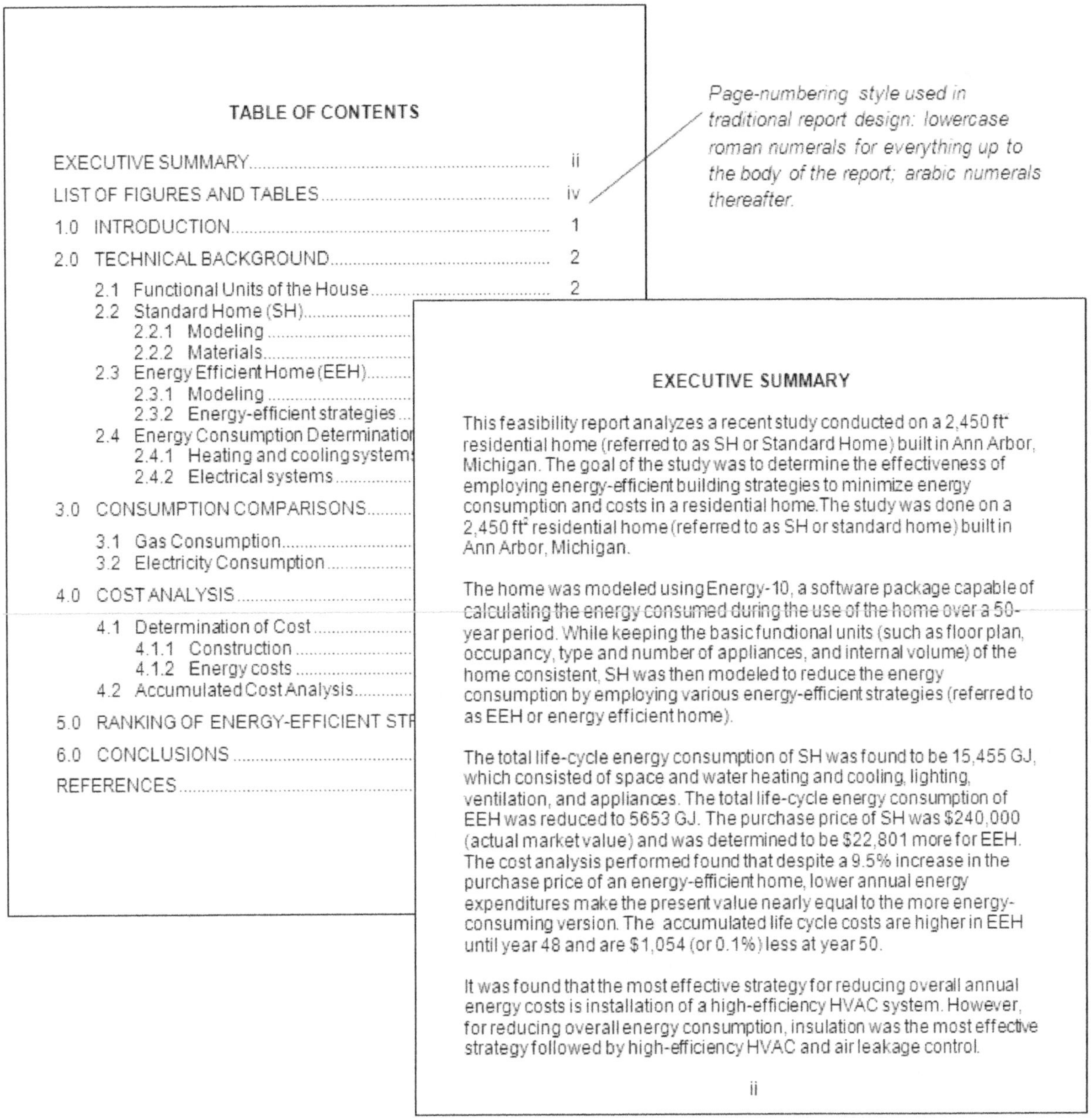

TABLE OF CONTENTS

EXECUTIVE SUMMARY ii
LIST OF FIGURES AND TABLES iv
1.0 INTRODUCTION 1
2.0 TECHNICAL BACKGROUND 2
2.1 Functional Units of the House 2
2.2 Standard Home (SH) ....
2.2.1 Modeling ....
2.2.2 Materials ....
2.3 Energy Efficient Home (EEH) ....
2.3.1 Modeling ....
2.3.2 Energy-efficient strategies ...
2.4 Energy Consumption Determinatio
2.4.1 Heating and cooling system
2.4.2 Electrical systems ....
3.0 CONSUMPTION COMPARISONS ....
3.1 Gas Consumption ....
3.2 Electricity Consumption ....
4.0 COST ANALYSIS ....
4.1 Determination of Cost ....
4.1.1 Construction ....
4.1.2 Energy costs ....
4.2 Accumulated Cost Analysis ....
5.0 RANKING OF ENERGY-EFFICIENT STF
6.0 CONCLUSIONS ....
REFERENCES ....

EXECUTIVE SUMMARY

This feasibility report analyzes a recent study conducted on a 2,450 ft² residential home (referred to as SH or Standard Home) built in Ann Arbor, Michigan. The goal of the study was to determine the effectiveness of employing energy-efficient building strategies to minimize energy consumption and costs in a residential home.The study was done on a 2,450 ft² residential home (referred to as SH or standard home) built in Ann Arbor, Michigan.

The home was modeled using Energy-10, a software package capable of calculating the energy consumed during the use of the home over a 50-year period. While keeping the basic functional units (such as floor plan, occupancy, type and number of appliances, and internal volume) of the home consistent, SH was then modeled to reduce the energy consumption by employing various energy-efficient strategies (referred to as EEH or energy efficient home).

The total life-cycle energy consumption of SH was found to be 15,455 GJ, which consisted of space and water heating and cooling, lighting, ventilation, and appliances. The total life-cycle energy consumption of EEH was reduced to 5653 GJ. The purchase price of SH was $240,000 (actual market value) and was determined to be $22,801 more for EEH. The cost analysis performed found that despite a 9.5% increase in the purchase price of an energy-efficient home, lower annual energy expenditures make the present value nearly equal to the more energy-consuming version. The accumulated life cycle costs are higher in EEH until year 48 and are $1,054 (or 0.1%) less at year 50.

It was found that the most effective strategy for reducing overall annual energy costs is installation of a high-efficiency HVAC system. However, for reducing overall energy consumption, insulation was the most effective strategy followed by high-efficiency HVAC and air leakage control.

ii

Page-numbering style used in traditional report design: lowercase roman numerals for everything up to the body of the report; arabic numerals thereafter.

Figure 2: Table of contents and executive summary

Downloadable example of executive summary

Table of Figures

The table of figures (ToF), sometimes called the "list of figures," has many of the same design considerations as the table of contents. Readers use the ToF to find the illustrations, diagrams, tables, and charts in your report.

Please note that tables and figures are different things. Strictly speaking, figures are illustrations, drawings, photographs, graphs, and charts. Tables are rows and columns of words and numbers; they are not considered figures.

For longer reports that contain multiple figures and tables, create separate lists of figures and tables. Put them on a separate page from the ToC, but put them together on the same page if they fit. You can identify the lists separately, as Table of Figures and Table of Tables.

Introduction

In a technical report, the introduction prepares the reader to read the main body of the report. It introduces the report's purpose, specifies the report's intended audience, provides a limited description of the report's context and background, forecasts the report's scope, and previews the report's contents and/or organization.

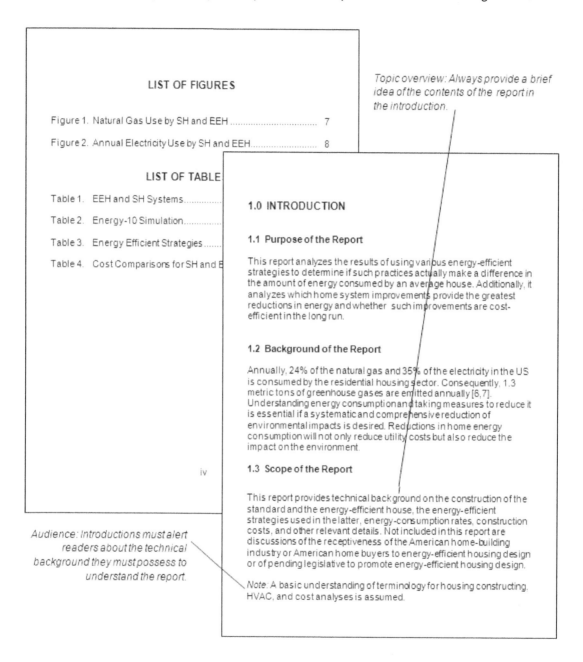

Figure 3: Table of figures, followed by the introduction

Downloadable example of introduction

If the introduction, executive summary, and letter of transmittal strike you as repetitive, remember that readers don't necessarily start at the beginning of a report and read page by page to the end. They skip around: they may scan the table of contents; they usually skim the executive summary for key facts and conclusions. They may read carefully only a section or two from the body of the report, and then skip the rest. For these reasons, reports are designed with massive duplication so that readers will be sure to see the important information no matter where they dip into the report.

Major Design Considerations

This part of the chapter describes several design-related issues that you will likely need to consider when creating a report.

Headings. In all but the shortest reports (two pages or less), use headings to mark off the different topics and subtopics covered. Headings enable readers to skim your report and dip down at those points where you present information that they want.

Bulleted and numbered lists. In the body of a report, also use bulleted, numbered, and two-column lists where appropriate. Lists help by emphasizing key points, by making information easier to follow, and by breaking up solid walls of text.

Symbols, numbers, and abbreviations. Technical discussions ordinarily contain lots of symbols, numbers, and abbreviations. Remember that the rules for using numerals as opposed to words are different in the technical world. The old rule of thumb about writing out all numbers below 10 does not always apply in technical reports.

Graphics and figure titles. In a technical report, you're likely to need drawings, diagrams, tables, and charts. These not only convey certain kinds of information more efficiently but also give your report an added look of professionalism and authority. If you've never put these kinds of graphics into a report, there are some relatively easy ways to do so—you don't need to be a professional graphic artist.

Wall design was given particularly careful consideration. Pierquet, et al., compares the annual energy savings of 12 different wall systems based on varying R-values [5]. Using a standard 2 x 4 stud wall with fiberglass insulation as the base case, Pierquet, et al., compared it with wall sections made of strawbale, structural insulated panels (SIPs), I-beam studs, autoclaved cellular concrete, and varying combinations of 2 x 4 construction and rigid foam insulation. Both the strawbale and the double 2 x 4 walls had very high R-values. Appliances were selected that conserve energy by being more efficient. The range and clothes dryer were switched to run on natural gas [1].

2.4 Energy Consumption Determination

For the purposes of the study, energy consumption was divided into two main home systems: heating and cooling, and electrical.

2.4.1 Heating and cooling systems. Heating and cooling energy were determined with Energy-10 for SH as well as for EEH. The program calculates the heat required to maintain the internal temperature based on the following fac...

- Average conductivity of the therma values of the walls, ceiling, floor, fo

- Internal temperature (includes adju seasonal/daily temperature chang

- Outside air infiltration through gaps forced-air ventilation systems

- Furnace and A/C efficiencies were

- Solar heat gains through windows

2.4.2 Electrical systems. Electrical e determined independently from Energ in the house was determined, which c

IEEE citation using brackets: The borrowed information comes from source 5 listed in References.

Acronym: On this first use, it is spelled out with the acronym shown in parentheses. The spelled-out version does not use initial caps because it is not a proper noun.

Second- and third-level headings: Notice how the system adds a decimal number to each lower-level section heading.

3.0 CONSUMPTION COMPARISONS

For energy consumption comparison, resources were broken down into total annual gas and electricity consumption, and then compared for the two homes.

3.1 Gas Consumption

Figure 1 shows annual natural gas use for both SH and EEH. The dramatic decrease in natural gas consumption is due to the greatly improved thermal envelope and a much more efficient HVAC system, causing a decrease in heating natural gas consumption of 91.8%.

While EEH uses natural gas for the stove and dryer (which is not the case for SH), EEH total annual natural gas use is only 21% that of SH [1].

Informal overview of the contents of this section: gas consumption; electricity consumption.

Chart depicting comparative natural gas usage. Notice this chart is treated as a figure and that the figure title appears below the chart.

Figure 1: Comparison of Annual Natural Gas Use by SH and EEH. [1, p. 8-9]

7

Figure 4: Excerpt from the body of a technical report

Cross-references. You may need to point readers to closely related information within your report, or to other books and reports that have useful information. These are called cross-references. For example, you can point readers from the discussion of a mechanism to an illustration of it. You can point readers to an appendix where background on a topic appears (background that just does not fit in the text). And you can point readers outside your report to other information—to articles, reports, and books that contain information related to yours.

Page numbering. All pages in the report (excluding the front and back covers, title page, and ToC) are numbered. Use lower-case roman numerals to paginate material that appears before the ToC. Don't number the ToC; it's page zero. Use arabic numerals to paginate material that appears after the ToC.

Longer reports often use the page-numbering style known as folio-by-chapter or double-enumeration (for example, pages in Chapter 2 would be numbered 2-1, 2-2, 2-3, and so on, and pages in Appendix B would be numbered B-1, B-2, and so on). Similarly, tables and figures would use this numbering style. This style eases the process of adding and deleting pages.

If page numbers appear in a running header, don't display numbers on pages where a heading or title is at the top of the page (such as chapter or section openers).

Conclusions

For most reports, you'll need to include a final section in which you sum up the report's contents and provide a "takeaway" for the reader. When you plan this final section of your report, think about the functions it can perform in relation to the rest of the report.

Appendices

An appendix is an "extra" section that appears after the proposal's main body. Any useful content that you feel is too large for the main part of the proposal or that you think would be distracting and interrupt the flow of the proposal should go into an appendix. Common examples of appendix-appropriate material are large tables of data, big chunks of sample code, fold-out maps, background that is too basic or too advanced for the body of the report, or large illustrations that just do not fit in the main body.

Use separate appendices for each item or category of items, and label each one alphabetically, as "Appendix A: (descriptive title of contents)" and so on. If you've got only one appendix, continue the proposal's page numbering scheme. If you have multiple appendices, you can number each appendix's pages separately, as A-1, A-2, and so on.

Information Sources

If your proposal quotes, paraphrases, or summarizes information that came from outside sources, cite the sources appropriately in the main text and include bibliographic information in a separate section at the proposal's end. Use whatever citation format is appropriate for your audience's profession and field. Common formats include IEEE, MLA, APA, CSE, Chicago, and Turabian.

4.2: Book Design

By: David McMurrey

Objectives

Upon completion of this chapter, readers will be able to do the following:

- Recognize the standard components of a front cover, back cover, and title page.
- Recognize the common front matter of a book including edition notices, disclaimers, trademarks, warranties, safety notices, and communication statements.
- Recognize the common organization strategies of books including tables of contents, tables of figures, a preface, and body chapters.
- Explain and apply typical book layout and design.

Book Design Overview

The following provides an overview of the typical components of a printed technical book and the typical content, format, style, and sequence of those components. Certainly, no single user guide, technical reference manual, quick-reference document, or other such document would actually have all of these components designed and sequenced in precisely the way you are about to read. Instead, this review will give an overview of the possibilities—let's say the range of possibilities.

Before you begin reading the following, grab a number of hardware and software books so that you can compare their content, style, format, and sequencing to what is discussed here.

For even more detail than you see here, consult these two standard industry resources:

- Sun Technical Pubs. *Read Me First!* Any recent edition. Prentice Hall.
- Microsoft Corporation. *Microsoft Manual of Style for Technical Publications.* Any recent edition. Microsoft Press.

Front and Back Covers

Product documents for paying customers usually have nicely designed front covers even if, on the inside, the book is bargain basement in terms of its quality. On the front cover, you will typically see some or all of the following:

1. Company name
2. Product name
3. Product platform or operating system
4. Product version and release numbers
5. Book title
6. Company or product logos
7. Trademark symbols
8. Artwork
9. Book order number
10. Company or product slogan

It can be challenging to figure out a good format for the company name, product name, and book title. Sometimes, these can amount to a whole paragraph of text! Companies are quite divided on whether to indicate version and release numbers on front covers—some do; some don't. Almost always, however, you'll see the platform indicated—whether the product is for the Macintosh, the PC, UNIX, and so on.

The back cover of hardcopy user guides and manuals is usually very simple. Typically, it contains the book order number, the name of the company with appropriate trademark symbols, a copyright symbol and phrasing as to the ownership of the book, and a statement as to which country the book was printed in. You'll also find bar codes on the back cover. See if your software can generate a bar code—you just access the bar code utility and type in the book order number, and the utility generates the bar code.

Title Page

The title page is typically a duplicate of the front cover, but with certain elements omitted. Typically omitted are the artwork, company or product logos, and slogans. Some technical publications omit the title page altogether because of the seemingly needless duplication. (And in a print run of 20,000 copies, a single page means a lot!)

Edition Notice

The edition notice is typically the first instance of regular text in a technical publication, although it is typically in smaller type. It occurs on the backside of the title page. If the technical publisher is taking the lean-and-green approach and eliminating the title page, the edition notice will appear on the backside of the front cover.

No one likes to read fine print, but take a look at the statements typically included in an edition notice:

- **Date of publication:** included not only is the year but sometimes even the month that the book was published.
- **Edition number:** whether the book is a first, second, or third edition.
- **Product applicability:** the edition notice typically indicates which platform, version, and release number of the product the book applies to.
- **Full title of the book:** shown in italics.
- **Disclaimers:** shockingly, product manufacturers will make statements to the effect that they do not guarantee the book is technically correct, complete, or free from writing problems or that the product is free from minor flaws or that it meets the needs of the customer. You'll be able to find additional disclaimers beyond these as well.
- **Copyright symbol and statement:** you'll see the circle-C copyright symbol © and some statement warning readers not to copy the book without permission.
- **Copyright permissions:** the high-tech world often moves so rapidly that instead of creating their own versions of a product component and its corresponding documentation, companies will simply buy the code or design and the rights to reprint the documentation as well. This usually entails copyright acknowledgement in the edition notice (although if a lot of borrowing has happened, publishers must get creative about where to put all these acknowledgements).
- **Reader responses:** sometimes, the edition notice will include some encouragement to customers to contact the company about product or documentation concerns. Instructions on how to contact the company are sometimes included in the edition notice. Included also is often a rather unfriendly statement that any customer communication becomes the property of the company.
- **Trademarks:** some technical publications list known trademarks in the edition notice. This includes both the company's own trademarks and the trademarks of other companies referenced in the book. With the explosion of new products in the high-tech world, and thus the explosion of trademarks, some publications essentially throw up their hands and insert a simple statement that any references to trademarked product names are owned by their respective companies.

Disclaimers

See the previous section on edition notices, where disclaimers are usually tucked away. If a product or its publication needs a whole separate page for its disclaimers, I'm not buying it!

Trademarks

Although many companies do list their own and other companies' trademarks in the edition notice, some prefer to list them on a separate page, just after the edition notice. These placement decisions are almost strictly the province of company attorneys; as a writer, you may have to comply no matter how bad the the decision is in terms of book design or writing style. Remember, you list only those trademarked product names that occur in that particular book.

You'll notice that some publications go to extreme measures with trademarks: they'll asterisk or footnote the first, or even every occurrence of a trademarked product name. But again, these are directives of company attorneys unto which technical writers must resign themselves, however sadly.

Warranties

These are the "guarantees" that the company will support concerning its product. Sometimes these are published in the front matter of the book; but, more appropriately from a book-design standpoint, they are printed on a separate card and inserted in the shrinkwrap of the book or the product. Again, as with edition notices, this is text you simply bring in as "boilerplate" and position in the right place within the book.

However, you should be aware that companies sometimes maintain multiple versions of edition notices, safety notices, warranties, communication statements, and other such. As a writer, you must make sure that you are using the right version (and, in finding out which is correct, you'll have a chance to get out and meet lots of new people in the company!). And whatever you do, don't change the text of these boilerplate items, however horribly they are written. Changes typically must be approved by company attorneys (who typically do so begrudgingly and only after many efforts on your part and after much time has passed).

Safety Notices

Hardware products typically have a section of safety notices at the front of their books. These may occur as a subsection of the preface, for example, or as a separate section in their own right. These sections typically bring together all of the danger, warning, and caution notices that occur throughout the book and arrange them in some sort of logical way. But even with this up-front alert, hardware books still place the individual notices at the points where they apply.

Communication Statements

Hardware books also require communications statements as stipulated by the governments of the countries to which these products are shipped. In the U.S., the FCC requires certain communications statements depending on the "class" of the hardware product. As a writer, you must be careful to use the right communication statement for the product you are documenting—and not to edit the statement in any way (holy legal words!).

Table of Contents

The table of contents (TOC) usually contains at least a second level of detail (the first-level headings in the actual text) so that readers can find what they need more precisely. Writers, editors, and book designers typically argue about the sequencing of the TOC. In terms of usability, it's much better to have the TOC as close to the front of the book as possible, if not at the very first of the book. In terms of legalities, however, people worry that all those communication statements, warranties, copyrights, trademarks, and safety notices should come first. In those places where usability wins out, books use every tactic they can to get this legalistic material out of the front matter: warranties are put on separate cards and shrink-wrapped with the book or product; warranties, communication statements, trademarks, and other such may be dumped in appendixes.

List of Figures

Technical manuals for ordinary users typically don't have lists of figures. In fact, the figures themselves typically do not have full-blown figure titles. But this isn't to say that a list of figures has no place in technical manuals. It all depends on the reader and the reader's needs—and the content of the book as well. If the book contains tables, illustrations, charts, graphs, and other such that readers will want to find directly, the figure list is in order.

Preface

The function of the preface is to get readers ready to read the book. It does so by:

- characterizing the content and purpose of the book
- identifying or even briefly describing the product the book supports
- explaining the type of reader for whom the book is meant
- outlining the main contents of the book
- showing any special conventions or terminology used in the book
- providing support and marketing numbers, and other such

In traditional book publishing, the preface comes before the table of contents; but as discussed previously in the table of contentssection, technical publishing people want the TOC to come earlier in the book for usability reasons.

Body Chapters

Oh yes, and there is actual text in these books—it isn't all front matter! Little else to say here other than most technical books have chapters or sections, and, in some cases, parts.

Appendixes

As you know, appendixes are for material that just doesn't seem to fit in the main part of a book but can't be left out of the book either. Appendixes are often the place for big unwieldy tables. Some technical publications have things like warranties in the appendixes. In terms of format, an appendix is just like a chapter—except that it is named "Appendix A" or some such, and the headers and footers match that different numbering and naming convention (A-1, A-2, and so on for pages in Appendix A).

Glossary

Some technical publications include a section of specialized terms and their definitions. Notice that most glossaries use a two-column layout. Typically, each term and its definition make up a separate paragraph with the term lowercased (unless it is a proper name) and in bold, followed by a period and then the definition in regular roman. Notice too that definitions are typically not complete sentences. Multiple definitions are typically identified by arabic numbers in parentheses. Glossary paragraphs also contain *See* references to preferred terms and *See also* references to related terms.

Index

Indexes are also typically two-column and also contain *See* references to preferred terms and *See also* references to related terms.

Reader-Response Form

Before the rise of the Internet and social media, some technical publications contained a hardcopy form to enable readers to send in comments, questions, and evaluation of the book. Of course, it turns out that these forms more often elicit complaints about faulty function in the product that the book documents. With the rise of the Internet, these forms have gone online, and books merely point to their location online.

Book Design and Layout

Typically, user guides and manuals produced by hardware and software manufacturers are designed in a rather austere and spartan way. High-tech companies develop new versions and releases of their product sometimes every nine months. In this context, sophisticated design is just not practical. Here are some of the typical layout and design features you'll see:

- Page size is often determined by packaging considerations as well as by standard page sizes available with printing companies. When page size is not a constraint, some companies will use the 8.5 × 11-inch page size—this makes production much easier for writers.
- Pages are typically designed with alternating right and left pages. The footer for the left (even) page starts with the page number and ends with the title of the book. The footer for the right (odd) page starts with the title of the chapter and ends with the page number.
- Practice is mixed on whether page numbering is consecutive throughout the book or by-chapter.
- Unless pages are rather small, the hanging-head design of headings in relation to pages is quite common in technical manuals. The hanging indent is usually one inch to one-and-a-half inches.
- Fonts are often 12-point Times New Roman for body text and Arial for headings. Standard line spacing and word spacing are used.
- Margins are fairly standard, one to two inches all the way around. Typically, an extra half-inch is used on inside margins to allow for binding.
- Typically, color is *not* used in these manuals and guides, usually out of cost and efficiency considerations.

4.3: Page Design

By: David McMurrey and Jonathan Arnett

Objectives

Upon completion of this chapter, readers will be able to do the following:

- Explain and apply design guidelines for heading and list use in technical documents.
- Explain and apply design guidelines for including notices in technical documents.
- Explain and apply design guidelines for table and figure use in technical documents.
- Explain and apply design guidelines for text highlighting and alignment in technical documents.
- Explain and apply design guidelines for font and color in technical documents.

Common Page Design

Page design means different things to different people, but here it will mean the use of typography and formatting such as you see in professionally-designed documents.

Our focus here is technical documentation, which implies modest, functional design.

For even more detail than you see here, consult these two standard industry resources:

- Sun Technical Pubs. *Read Me First!* Any recent edition. Prentice Hall.
- Microsoft Corporation. *Microsoft Manual of Style for Technical Publications.* Any recent edition. Microsoft Press.

Headings

The following presents some of the standard guidelines on headings.

1. Insert plenty of headings, perhaps one heading for every two to three paragraphs. Avoid overkill, though: lots of headings with only one or two sentences per heading does not work.
2. Indicate a heading's level through design. Use type size, type style, color, boldness, italicization, and alignment to make a heading's level obvious. ("Levels" of headings are like levels in an outline: Level 1 corresponds to the large, capitalized roman numerals; Level 2 to the capital letters; Level 3 to the arabic numerals; Level 4 to the lower-case roman numerals; and so on.)
3. Limit the levels of heading. Most documents only need three or fewer levels of heading; more levels can confuse your readers.
4. Describe the sections' contents with specific language. Vague headings like "Technical Background" don't tell anybody anything.
5. Use parallel phrasing. Parallel headings tell readers if the sections are similar to each other.
6. Avoid "lone headings." If you have one heading, you should use a second. It's the same concept as having an "A" without a "B" or a "1" without a "2" in outlines.
7. Avoid "stacked headings" (two or more consecutive headings without text in between).
8. Don't use a pronoun to refer to a heading. If you have a heading like "Configuring the Software," don't follow it with a sentence like "This next phase..."
9. Consider the "hanging-head" format for major headings. In this design, some or all of the headings are on the left margin, while all text is indented one to two inches. This format will make headings stand out more and reduce the main text's line length.
10. Consider using "run-in" headings for your lowest-level headings. In this design, the heading "runs into" the beginning of a paragraph and ends with a period. You can use some combination of boldness, italics, or color for these headings. This format avoids the problem of lower-level headings blending in with each other.

Lists

Lists are useful tools for emphasizing important points, enabling readers to scan text rapidly, and providing more white space. The following presents some of the standard guidelines on lists.

- Use numbered lists to show sequence, order, or hierarchy. Use bulleted lists for items that can appear in any order.
- Use standard numbered- and bulleted-list formats. They are built into word-processing programs, and HTML has ordered- and unordered-list tags.
- Use parallel phrasing for lists' contents.
- Introduce all lists with lead-in text; don't start a list immediately after a heading.
- Unless your organization's style overrides, punctuate list items with a period only if they are complete sentences or have embedded dependent clauses.
- Be consistent with using initial caps or lower-case letters on the first words of list items.
- Use different symbols for the second levels of nested lists. For numbered lists, use lowercase letters. For bulleted lists, use bolded en dashes or empty-centered circles. In either case, make sure that nested items align to the *text* of the previous level.
- Avoid using too many lists or overstuffing lists. Seven to ten items is generally about the maximum number of items.

Notices

Notices are specially-formatted chunks of text that alert readers to special points, exceptions, potential problems, or danger. The following presents some of the standard guidelines for notices.

- Make notices more prominent and noticeable as they become more severe. Consider using this standard hierarchy:
    o "Danger" for situations that could involve severe injury or death
    o "Warning" for situations that could involve minor injury
    o "Caution" for situations that could involve equipment damage, data loss, or a threat to a procedure's success
    o "Note" for exceptions or situations that do not require the preceding tags
- Whatever notice design you use, avoid using long strings of bold text, italics, capital letters, or combinations of these. In addition to telling readers to do or not do something, explain three things:
    o under what conditions they should use the notice
    o what will happen if they ignore the notice
    o how to recover if they ignore the notice
- Make notices' text succinct, but not at the expense of clear writing. Avoid telegraphic writing style (omitting articles like *a, an, the*) in notices.
- In numbered lists, align notices to the *text* of the list items they apply to. Put notices in two places:
    o *before* the step in which the potential problem exists
    o at the beginning of the entire procedure

Figures

Figures are illustrations, drawings, schematics, photos, and other visual materials. The following presents some of the standard guidelines on figures.

- In the text before each figure appears, provide a cross-reference to the figure.
- If you include a label and caption, place them *below* each figure.
- Omit labels and captions if they have no vital function and are not needed (for example, in instructions when the figures are closely related to the individual steps).

Tables

Tables are like lists, which were discussed previously, but are more structured and formal. In your text, look for repeating pairs, triplets, or quadruplets of items that can be formatted as tables. For example, a series of terms and definitions is a classic use for tables. The following presents some of the standard guidelines for tables.

- Look for repeating groups of items in your text that you can format as tables.
- In the text before each table appears, provide a cross-reference to the table.
- Include a table title unless the content of the table is utterly obvious and the table contains few items. Place the table title *above* the table, or make it the top row of the table.
- Use column and row headings (or both) to define the contents of the columns and rows. Consider highlighting these headings.
- Left-align text columns (unless the contents are simple alphabetic characters). Left-align text columns with their headings.
- Right-align or decimal-align numerical data, and center it under its heading.
- Put standard measurement units (*ft, mm, gal.*) in the column or row heading rather than with each item in the column or row.
- Briefly discuss the main trend in the table—what you want readers to notice.

Highlighting

Software documentation typically uses a lot of highlighting. Highlighting here refers to bold text, italics, alternate fonts, capital letters, quotation marks, and other typographical tricks used to call attention to text. The following presents some standard guidelines for highlighting.

- Establish a plan for using highlighting, and apply it consistently.
- Use highlighting for specific, functional reasons. Avoid too much highlighting, and avoid complicated highlighting schemes.
- Consider using this fairly standard highlighting scheme:
  - For simple emphasis, use italics.
  - Use bold for commands, on-screen buttons and menu options.
  - Use italics for variables for which users must supply their own words.
  - Use an alternate font for text displayed on screen or text that users must type in.
  - For screen and field names, use the capitalization style shown on the screen but no other highlighting.
  - Use an initial cap for key names but no other highlighting.
  - For extended emphasis, use the notice format.

Margins, Indentation, and Alignment

As mentioned in the section on headings, you may wish to indent main text one to two inches while leaving headings on the left margins. This style does two things: it makes the headings stand out, and it shortens the main text's line length.

Fonts & Color

Here are some suggestions concerning fonts and color:

- Limit the number of main fonts that appear in a document to two. For example, you might use Arial for headings and Times New Roman for body text.
- Use only one alternate font, at most two. For example, you might use Arial for headings, Times New Roman for body text, and Courier New for text that users will see onscreen or that users must type in.
- If you use color, use it minimally and consistently. For example, if you have black text on a white background, you might select another color for headings. You might use that same color for figure and table titles as well as the tags for notices (the actual "Note," "Warning," "Caution," and "Danger" labels on notices).

- Avoid unusual combinations of background and text colors. For example, purple or red text on a black background is unreadable. Stick with black text on a white or gray background unless there is a strong, functional reason for some other color combination.

4.4: Headings

By: David McMurrey and Cassandra Race

Objectives

Upon completion of this chapter, readers will be able to do the following:

- Identify the uses of headings.
- Distinguish between the different levels of headings.
- Evaluate the use of headings in technical documents.
- Use the Styles tool in Microsoft Word to create custom headings.
- Create and use headings in your own documents.

Headings Overview

One of the most useful characteristics of technical writing is the use of headings.

Headings are the titles and subtitles you see within the actual text of much scientific, technical, and business writing. Headings are like the parts of an outline that have been pasted into the actual pages of the document.

Headings are an important feature of technical writing: they alert readers to upcoming topics and subtopics, help readers find their way around in long reports and skip what they are not interested in, and break up long stretches of straight text. They make text easy to navigate and enable the reader to find information they need quickly.

Headings are also useful for you, the writer. They keep you organized and focused on the topic. When you begin using headings, your impulse may be to slap in the headings *after* you've written the rough draft. Instead, visualize the headings before you start the rough draft, and plug them in as you write.

Take a look at this page from Healthy People.gov: Environmental Health

Examine the page, and observe how the use of headings makes the document readable and accessible. Its easy to see what each section is about, and you can quickly jump to sections that interest you.

"Well-designed headings can help not only readers but also writers understand the organization of a document."

General Guidelines for Headings

In this chapter, you are encouraged to use a specific style of headings. If you want to use a different style, contact your instructor. Here are some specific guidelines on headings (see the figures at the end of this chapter for illustrations of these guidelines):

- Use headings to mark off the boundaries of the major sections and subsections of a report
- Until you become confident in the use of heading styles, use exactly the design for headings described here and shown in the illustrations in this chapter. Use the same spacing (vertical and horizontal location), capitalization, punctuation, and typography (bold, italics, etc.)
- Try for 2 to 3 headings per regular page of text. Don't overdo headings: for example, a heading for each of a series of one- or two-sentence paragraphs. (Also, you don't need a heading per paragraph; normally, an individual heading can apply to multiple paragraphs.)
- For short documents, begin with the second-level heading; skip the first-level.
- Make the phrasing of headings parallel. In the following illustration, notice that the second-level headings use the *how, what, when, where, why* style of phrasing. The third-levels use noun phrases. (Check out this tutorial on Parallel Structure from the Purdue OWL)
- Make the phrasing of headings self-explanatory: instead of "Background" or "Technical Information," make it more specific, such as "Physics of Fiber Optics."

- Make headings indicate the range of topic coverage in the section. For example, if the section covers the *design* and *operation* of a pressurized water reactor, the heading "Pressurized Water Reactor Design" would be incomplete and misleading.
- Avoid "lone" headings—any heading by itself within a section without another like it in that same section. For example, avoid having a second-level heading followed by only one third-level and then by another second-level. (The third-level heading would be the lone heading.)
- Avoid "stacked" headings—any two consecutive headings without intervening text.
- Avoid pronoun reference to headings. For example, if you have a third-level heading "Torque," don't begin the sentence following it with something like this: "This is a physics principle....."
- When possible, omit articles from the beginning of headings. For example, "The Pressurized Water Reactor" can easily be changed to "Pressurized Water Reactor" or, better yet, "Pressurized Water Reactors."
- Don't use headings as lead-ins to lists or as figure titles.
- Avoid "widowed" headings: that's where a heading occurs at the bottom of a page and the text it introduces starts at the top of the next page. Keep at least two lines of body text with the heading, or force it to start the new page.

II. PROCESS OF PHOTOSYNTHESIS

First-level heading (always begins a new page)

Photosynthesis is the process by which green plants use the energy of light to convert carbon dioxide and water into the simple sugar glucose. Plants use much of this glucose as an energy source to build leaves, flowers, fruits, and seeds. A byproduct of photosynthesis is oxygen, which is created during the process of converting carbon dioxide and water into glucose.

Where Photosynthesis Occurs

Second-level heading

Photosynthesis occurs in leaves and green stems within specialized cell structures called chloroplasts. A plant leaf is composed of tens of thousands of cells; each cell contains forty to fifty chloroplasts. Embedded in the membranes of leaves are hundreds of molecules of chlorophyll, a light-trapping pigment required for photosynthesis. Each chloroplast will contain millions of the chlorophyll pigment molecules.

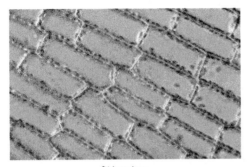

Chloroplasts.
Source: Microsoft Encarta Online Encyclopedia, 2001.

Second-level heading

How Photosynthesis Works

Photosynthesis can be divided into two stages: first, the light-dependent reaction, in which chloroplasts trap light energy and convert it into glucose; second, the light-independent reaction, which provides the energy used to synthesize glucose into the leaf structure. These two stages reflect the literal meaning of the term photosynthesis: to build with light.

Third-level heading

Light-dependent reaction. Photosynthesis relies on flows of energy and electrons initiated by light energy. Electrons are minute particles that travel in a specific orbit around the nuclei of atoms and carry a small electrical charge. Light energy causes the electrons in chlorophyll to boost up and out of their orbit, releasing vibrating energy as they go, all in millionths of a second. The vibrating energy passes rapidly from one chlorophyll to the next, like the transfer of energy in billiard balls.

Third-level heading

Light-independent reaction. The light-independent reaction requires the presence of carbon dioxide molecules, which enter the plant through pores in the leaf called stomata.

Figure 1: Heading style and format standard for courses using this online textbook. If you want to use a different format, contact your instructor.

Specific Format and Style

The style and format for headings shown in this chapter is not the "right" or the "only" one, just one among many. Many technical writers must write according to a "house" style. Most organizations expect their documents to look a certain way. Using the style and format for headings described here gives you some experience with one of the key requirements in technical writing—writing according to "specifications."

To see the "house style" for headings—the style and format for headings you will use—see the illustrations in this chapter. Pay close attention to formatting details such as vertical and horizontal spacing, capitalization, use of bold, italics, or underlining, and punctuation. Notice that you can substitute bold for underlining.

Headings occur *within* the body of a document. Don't confuse headings with document titles. Although titles may look like first-level headings in smaller documents, think of them as separate things. Now, here are the specifications for headings in this chapter.

Note: To make things less complicated, consider the document title as a *title* not as a *first-level heading*. They certainly look the same, except that the title could be prefaced by a roman numeral. In short documents such as those you write for technical writing classes, use a centered title and then start with second-level headings in the body of the document.

II. PRESURIZED WATER REACTOR

This section of the report describes the key components of the pressurized light water reactor and explains their operation in the production of electricity.

Description of the Major Parts

In a pressurized water reactor (see Figure 1), the reactor cooling water entering the core is highly pressurized so that it remains below the boiling point. The water leaves the reactor to pass through steam generators where a secondary coolant is allowed to boil and produce steam to drive the turbine.

Headings are like individual outline items inserted into the text where they apply.

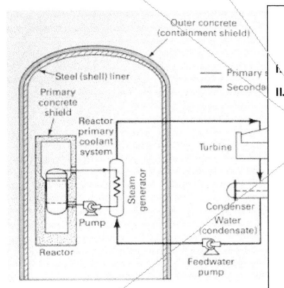

Figure 1. Schematic of a Pressurized Water Reactor. Sou V. *A Guidebook to Nuclear Reactors*, p. 78.

The key components in this process are the core, the cor reactor vessel, the steam generators, and the pressurizel

Core. The core is the active portion of the reactor provid system. The core contains fuel assemblies that contain fu fuel pellets.

Fuel. The fuel in the pressurized water reactor consists of slightly enriched uranium dioxide with a diameter of 0.325 in by 0.55 in. The pellets are dished at the ends to allow for thermal expansion [12:2004].

Fuel rod. A fuel rod consists of a cylindrical tube made of Zircalloy, a steel-gray alloy that highly resistant to corrosion. This tube is 13 ft long with an outer diameter of 0.39 in and a 0.025-in thich wall. The tube is filled with fuel pellets and is sealed [10:122].

OUTLINE

I. INTRODUCTION

II. PRESSURIZED WATER REACTORS

  A. Description of the Major Parts

    1. Core
        a. Fuel
        b. Fuel rod
        c. Fuel assembly
    2. Control Rods
    3. Reactor Vessel
    4. Steam Generators
    5. Heat Exchangers
    6. Steam Drum
    7. Pressurizer

  B. Production of Electricity

    1. Circulating of water
    2. Separating steam
    3. Drying steam
    4. Producing electricity

Figure 2: Headings and outlines: headings function like outline elements inserted into the text at those points where they apply.

First-Level Headings

First-level headings are for formal reports with multiple sections (or "chapters"). If you are writing a brief document, start with second-level headings in the body of the document. Follow these guidelines for first-level headings:

1. Make first-levels all-caps.
2. Use Roman numerals with first-levels.
3. Bold the entire heading including the Roman numeral.
4. Make first-levels centered on the page.
5. Start a new page whenever you have a first-level heading.
6. Begin first-levels on the standard first text line of a page.

Note: In short documents such as those you write for technical writing classes, use a centered title and then start with second-level headings in the body of the document.

Second-Level Headings

In smaller documents (such as a two-page set of instructions), first-level headings are too much. Start with second-level headings in the body of these smaller documents. Follow these guidelines for second-level headings:

- Make second-levels headline-style caps (every main word).
- Use bold on second-levels.
- Do not include outlining apparatus such as "A." or "B." or "1." or "2." with second-levels.
- Make second-levels flush left.
- Leave the equivalent of 2 blank lines between previous text and second-levels.
- Leave the equivalent of 1 blank line between second-levels and the following text.

Note: If you prefer to make third-level headings standalone like second-levels, they may not be visually distinct enough from second-levels. If so, put a top border on second-levels, as you can see in this chapter.

Third-Level Headings

Third-level headings are "run in to" the paragraph they introduce. Follow these guidelines for third-level headings:

- Make third-levels sentence-style caps.
- Use bold for third-levels including the period.
- End third-levels with a period, which is also bold.
- Do not include outlining apparatus such as "A." or "B." or "1." or "2." with third-levels.
- Either indent third-levels standard paragraph indentation, or just start third-levels flush left.
- Do not make third-levels a grammatical part of sentences that follow.
- Whether third-levels are indented or not, start all following lines flush left. Don't indent the entire paragraph.
- Use the standard spacing between paragraphs for paragraphs that contain third-levels.

Note: If you need a fourth level of heading, consider using italics instead of bold on the run-in heading format.

Using Word-Processing Styles for Headings

If you manually format each individual heading using the guidelines presented in the preceding, you'll find you're doing quite a lot of repetitive work. The styles provided by Microsoft Word, OpenOffice Writer, and other software save you this work. You simply select Heading 1, Heading 2, Heading 3, and so on. You'll notice the format and style are different from what is presented here. However, you can design your own styles for headings. Here's a video tutorial that will show you quickly how to use the Styles feature in MicroSoft Word.

Common Problems with Headings

When you design your own heading style, be careful about going overboard with fancy typographical elements. Also, continue to use the guidelines presented in this chapter; they apply to practically any design. And finally, use your heading design consistently throughout your document.

I.   THE NATURAL WEATHER PATTERNS

II. THE MECHANISMS OF THE GREENHOUSE EFFECT

    A.   Natural Greenhouse Effect
    B.   Radiation Absorption by Carbon Dioxide and Water Vapor
    C.   Positive Feedback Mechanisms

III. HOW THE CARBON CYCLE WORKS

    A. CO_2 from Fossil Fuel
    B.   Carbon Dioxide Produced by
    C.   Future Levels of Carbon Dio

IV. CLIMATIC EFFECTS OF INCREAS

    A.   Changes in Local Weather P
    B.   1930s as Climate Analog
    C.   Drought
    D.   Increased Tropical Storm A
    E.   Sea Level Increase

V.   REDUCING THE GREENHOUSE

Unnecessary introductory articles

Two items not parallel in phrasing

I.   NATURAL WEATHER PATTERNS

II. MECHANISMS OF THE GREENHOUSE EFFECT

    A.   Natural Greenhouse Effect
    B.   Radiation Absorption by Carbon Dioxide and Water Vapor
    C.   Positive Feedback Mechanisms

III. CARBON CYCLE

    A. CO_2 from Fossil Fuel
    B.   Carbon Dioxide Produced by Different Fuels
    C.   Future Levels of Carbon Dioxide

IV. CLIMATIC EFFECTS OF INCREASED CO_2 CONCENTRATIONS

    A.   Changes in Local Weather Patterns
    B.   1930s as Climate Analog
    C.   Drought
    D.   Increased Tropical Storm Activity
    E.   Sea Level Increase

V.   WAYS TO REDUCE THE GREENHOUSE EFFECT

Types of Thunderstorms

Single cell thunderstorms. A single cell thunderstorm is a storm that contains only one updraft and one downdraft. A single cell storm is actually not a common occurrence, because one cell usually triggers the formation of another cell.

Multicell thunderstorms. A multicell is a line of thunderstorms with a gust front at the head of the storm. A *gust front* is a boundary of cool dry air that forms in front of a cold front. When the cold dry ai air, the cold dry air forces the warmer air multicell storm has multiple updrafts and different stage of the thunderstorm cycle.

Supercell thunderstorms. This is the m thunderstorm, capable of producing deva heavy precipitation, and tornadoes. A sup other types of thunderstorms can be seve destructive is the presence of a rotating u

The mesocyclone funnels the warm moist rather than creating several individual up strength, and size of a thunderstorm and weather.

Benefits of thunderstorms. Though the destructive forces, they have a beneficial

Stacked headings: intervening text needed.

Pronoun referring to a heading from following text

Heading at wrong level: it should be a 2nd level like "Types of Thunderstorms"

Types of Thunderstorms

Thunderstorms are classified in three categories based upon the storm's severity. Storms can have physical traits that cross the boundaries of these categories, and a storm may change its category during its existence. Storms can form as one isolated cell, a group of cells, or a supercell.

Single cell thunderstorms. A single cell thunderstorm is a storm that contains only one updraft and one downdraft. A single cell storm is actually not a common occurrence, because one cell usually triggers the formation of another cell.

Multicell thunderstorms. A multicell is a line of thunderstorms with a gust front at the head of the storm. A *gust front* is a boundary of cool dry air that forms in front of a cold front. When the cold dry air of the gust front meets warm moist air, the cold dry air forces the warmer air up with thunderstorms as a result. A multicell storm has multiple updrafts and downdrafts with each cell operating in a different stage of the thunderstorm cycle.

Supercell thunderstorms. The supercell is the most powerful and longest lasting thunderstorm, capable of producing devastating weather, such as high winds, heavy precipitation, and tornadoes. A supercell is always severe weather; the other types of thunderstorms can be severe or not. What makes a supercell so destructive is the presence of a rotating updraft, called a *mesocyclone*.

The mesocyclone funnels the warm moist air into one large spiraling updraft, rather than creating several individual updrafts. This increases the longevity, strength, and size of a thunderstorm and heightens the chances for severe weather.

Benefits of Thunderstorms

Though thunderstorms are frequently viewed as destructive forces, they have a beneficial side as well....

A few more common heading problems: nonstandard capitalization, incorrect subordination, and "stacked" heads. There's nothing "wrong" about the caps style used in the first version; it's just not the "house" style. Subordination refers to the level of headings. "Stacked" headings occur when there is no text between two consecutive headings.

Want some more information on using headings? The Purdue OWL has a great guide on using APA style to create your headings. This style is also compatible with the styles noted for scientific journals. Check out the APA Headings page!

Practice what you've learned!

Complete the following activities to reinforce what you have learned about headings.

Activity 2: In that same journal (you may have to actually visit the library...or use the university's data base) examine the use of headings. Can you explain in your own words how the headings work to organize the article? See if you can find examples of headings that don't reflect the guidelines in this chapter.

By: David McMurrey

Objectives

Upon completion of this chapter, readers will be able to do the following:

- Distinguish between different types of lists in technical documents and explain appropriate situations for using each.
- Explain and apply general guidelines for formatting different types of lists.
- Use Microsoft Word to style lists appropriately.

Introduction to Lists

Lists are useful because they emphasize selected information in regular text. When you see a list of three or four items strung out vertically on the page rather than in normal paragraph format, you are likely to pay more attention to it. Certain types of lists also make for easier reading. For example, in instructions, it is a big help for each step to be numbered and separate from the preceding and following steps. Lists also create more white space and spread out the text so that pages don't seem like solid walls of words.

Like headings, the various types of lists are an important feature of professional technical writing: they help readers understand, remember, and review key points; they help readers follow a sequence of actions or events; and they break up long stretches of straight text.

Your task for this chapter is to learn about the different types and uses of lists and to learn their specific format and style.

"Lists emphasize important points and help readers follow a sequence."

General Guidelines

In technical-writing contexts, you must use a specific style of lists, like the one presented here.

- Use lists to highlight or emphasize text or to enumerate sequential items.
- Use exactly the spacing, indentation, punctuation, and caps style shown in the following discussion and illustrations.
- Make list items parallel in phrasing. See this tutorial from commnet.edu's Guide to Grammar and Writing on Parallel Structures.
- Make sure that each item in the list reads grammatically with the lead-in.
- Use a lead-in to introduce the list items and to indicate the meaning or purpose of the list (and punctuate it with a colon).
- When two items are alternatives, use a bulleted list (with or between). Do not use numbered lists for OR-ed items. For three or more alternatives, indicate that in the list lead-in.
- When a separate notice or explanatory paragraph follows a item, indent that separate material to the text of the parent list item.

> 5. Select the **Save preview picture** check box.
> 6. Click **OK** to close the dialogue box.
>
> **Note:** Keep the properties window open for the next exercise.

Notice that this note is indented to the *text* of the parent list item.

Figure 1: Indented material that elaborates on the parent list item.

- Avoid using headings as lead-ins for lists.
- Avoid overusing lists; using too many lists destroys their effectiveness.
- Use similar types of lists consistently in similar text in the same document.
- Use the "styles" function in your software to create vertical lists rather than constructing them manually.

Note: In-sentence lists could be called "horizontal" lists. All the other lists types presented here are "vertical" lists in that they format the items vertically rather than in paragraph format.

Specific Types of Lists

It's difficult to state guidelines on choosing between the various kinds of lists, but here's a stab at it:

1. Most importantly, use numbered lists for items that are in a required order (such as step-by-step instructions) or for items that must be referred to by item number. Use bulleted lists for items that are in no required order.
2. With in-sentence lists, there are no conventions when to use letters (a), (b), and so on, as opposed to numbers (1), (2), and so on. If you are in a numbered list and need a sublist, use lowercase letters, to contrast with the numbers. Otherwise, there seem to be no widely agreed-upon guidelines—just be consistent!
3. Use vertical lists as opposed to in-sentence lists when you want the emphasis provided by the vertical presentation. In-sentence lists provide only minimal emphasis; vertical lists provide much more.
4. Within an individual report, use in-sentence lists and vertical lists consistently for similar situations. For example, if you have topic overviews for each section of a report, use in-sentence or vertical lists for the overview—but don't mix them for that particular use.

Common Problems with Lists

Problems with lists usually include the following:

- Mix-up between numbered and bulleted lists
- Lack of parallel phrasing in the list items
- Use of single parentheses on the list-item number or letter
- Run-over lines not aligned with the text of list items
- Lack of a strong lead-in sentence introducing list items, and lack of a colon to punctuate lead-ins
- Inconsistent caps style in list items
- Unnecessary punctuation of list items
- Inconsistent use of lists in similar text
- Lists that have too many items and need to be subdivided or consolidated

Format for Lists

Use the following for specific details on the capitalization, typography (bold, underlining, different fonts, different types sizes), and spacing for each type of list.

In-Sentence Lists

Use these guidelines for in-sentence lists:

- Use a colon to introduce the list items *only* if a complete sentence precedes the list. In this problem version, the colon breaks right into the middle of a sentence (how dare it!):

    Problem: For this project, you need: tape, scissors, and white-out.

    Revision: For this project, you need tape, scissors, and white-out.

- Use both opening and closing parentheses on the list item numbers or letters: (a) item, (b) item, etc.
- Use either regular Arabic numbers or lowercase letters within the parentheses, but use them consistently. (Do not punctuate either with periods.) Use lowercase for the text of in-sentence lists items, except when regular capitalization rules require caps.
- Punctuate the in-sentence list items with commas if they are not complete sentences; punctuate with semicolons if they are complete sentences.
- Use the same spacing for in-sentence lists as in regular non-list text.
- Make the in-sentence list occur at the *end* of the sentence. *Never* place an in-sentence list introduced by a colon anywhere but at the end of the sentence, as in this example:

Problem: The following items: tape, scissors, and white-out are needed for this project.

Revision: The following items are needed for this project: tape, scissors, and white-out.

The purpose of the *How to Collect Minerals Guide* is to get you started without overwhelming you with too much information. You can begin mineral collecting after you have learned (1) how to identify the difference between minerals and rocks, (2) how to select mineral collecting tools, (3) how to identify different types of minerals, (4) how to identify a good mineral-collecting location, and (5) how to collect minerals.

No colon after "learned"—the sentence is completed by the list items.

Both sides of the parenthesis are used.

List items are parallel in phrasing. (They could have been "identifying..., selecting...," and so on.)

Figure 2: Examples of in-sentence lists.

Simple Vertical Lists

Use these guidelines for simple vertical lists:

- Introduce the list with a lead-in phrase or clause (the lead-in need not be a complete sentence; the list items can complete the grammar started by the lead-in). Punctuate the lead-in with a colon.
- Use simple vertical lists when the list items do not need to be emphasized and are listed vertically merely for ease of reading.
- Use sentence-style capitalization on list items.
- Begin run-over lines under the text of the list item, not the regular left margin. This format is called the *hanging-indent* style.
- Use the equivalent of a blank line above and below vertical lists.
- Either start list items flush left or indent them no more than half an inch.
- Use "compact" list format if you have just a few list items only a single line each. In the compact format, there is no vertical space between list items. Use a "loose" format—vertical space between list items—if the list items are multiple lines long.
- Punctuate list items only if they are complete sentences or verb phrases that complete the sentence begun by the lead-in (and use periods in these two cases).
- Watch out for lists with more than 6 or 8 list items; for long lists, look for ways to subdivide or consolidate.
- When possible, omit articles (*a, an, the*) from the beginning of non-sentence list items.

Now that you know the three types of rocks to look for, it's time to gather or purchase the necessary tools:

Collecting bag
Gloves
Handheld rock pick
Hand trowel
Hard hat
Safety goggles
Rock chisel

Lead-in to the list punctuated with a colon

No bullets—Items require no emphasis

Example of a simple vertical list. No numbers or bullets.

Bulleted Lists

Use these guidelines for bulleted lists:

1. Introduce the list with a lead-in phrase or clause (the lead-in need not be a complete sentence; the list items can complete the grammar started by the lead-in). Punctuate the lead-in with a colon.
2. Use bulleted lists when the list items are in no necessary order but you want to emphasize the items in the list.
3. Use asterisks or hyphens if you have no access to an actual bullet. Use your software's list styles for these vertical lists.
4. Use sentence-style capitalization on list items.
5. Begin run-over lines under the text of the list item, not the bullet. This format is called the the *hanging-indent* style.
6. Use 0.25 inches for the hanging-indent (between the bullet and the text of the list item).
7. Use the equivalent of a blank line above and below vertical lists.
8. Either start list items flush left or indent them no more than half an inch.
9. Use "compact" list format if you have just a few list items only a single line each. In the compact format, there is no vertical space between list items. Use a "loose" format—vertical space between list items—if the list items are multiple lines long.
10. If you have sublist items in a bulleted list, use a less prominent symbol for a bullet (such as a dash or clear disc), and indent the sublist items to the *text* of the higher-level list items. (It is certainly possible to have subnumbered items within a bulleted list, in which case indent them the same as subbulleted items.)
11. Punctuate bulleted list items only if they are complete sentences or verb phrases that complete the sentence begun by the lead-in (and use periods in these two cases).
12. Watch out for bulleted lists with more than 6 or 8 list items; for long bulleted lists, look for ways to subdivide or consolidate.
13. Avoid single-item lists. It's just like traditional outlines: if you have a 1 or an a, you need a 2 or a b.
14. When possible, omit articles (*a, an, the*) from the beginning of list items.

Two of the utility-scale wind turbines sponsored by DOE are commercially available:

Lead-in to the list punctuated with a colon

- Advanced Wind Turbines AWT-26
- Zoned Systems Z-40.
- New World Power Technology Company
- New World Grid Power
- Flowind Corporation

Vertical space between regular text and the list

No punctuation on list items unless they are complete sentences

Figure 4: Example of a bulleted list. Items not in any required order.

Numbered Lists

Use these guidelines for numbered lists:

1. Introduce the list with a lead-in phrase or clause (the lead-in need not be a complete sentence; the list items can complete the grammar started by the lead-in). Punctuate the lead-in with a colon.
2. Use numbered lists when the list items are in a required order (for example, chronological) or must be referenced from somewhere else in the text.
3. Type the number followed by a period; do not use parentheses on the number. Use your software's list styles for these vertical lists.
4. Use sentence-style capitalization on list items.
5. Use "compact" list format if you have just a few list items only a single line each. In the compact format, there is no vertical space between list items. Use a "loose" format—vertical space between list items—if the list items are multiple lines long.
6. Begin run-over lines under the text of the list item, not the number. This format is called the *hanging-indent* style.
7. Use 0.25 inches for the hanging-indent (between the number and the text of the list item).
8. Use the equivalent of a blank line above and below vertical lists.
9. Either start list items flush left or indent them no more than half an inch.
10. If you have sublist items in a numbered list, use lowercase letters, and indent the sublist items to the *text* of the higher-level list items. (It is certainly possible to have subbullet items within a numbered list, in which case indent them the same as subnumbered items.)
11. If you have sublist items, use a less prominent symbol for a bullet (such as a dash or clear disc) or a lowercase letter for subnumbered items, and indent the sublist items to the text of the higher-level list items.
12. Punctuate numbered list items only if they are complete sentences or verb phrases that complete the sentence begun by the lead-in (and use periods in these two cases).
13. Watch out for numbered lists with more than 8 or 10 list items; for long numbered lists, look for ways to subdivide or consolidate.
14. Avoid single-item lists. If you have a 1 or an a, you need a 2 or a b.
15. When possible, omit articles (*a, an, the*) from the beginning of list items.

Beginning a Basic Scan

Lead-in to the list punctuated with a colon

After accepting the default options for ScanDisk, begin your scan by doing the following:

1. Select the drive you want to check for errors by clicking once on the drive.

2. Select the type of test you want to run.

3. Click the **Start** button.

ScanDisk will begin checking your hard drive for errors and upon completion will display the results of your hard drive scan.

ScanDisk Results – (C:)

ScanDisk found errors on this drive and fixed them all.

6,237,052 KB total disk space
0 bytes in bad sectors
6,049,792 bytes in 1,299 folders
9,560,064 bytes in 220 hidden files
2,544,607,232 bytes in 23,120 user files
3,826,524,160 bytes available on disk
4,096 bytes in each allocation unit
1,559,263 total allocation units on disk
934,210 available allocation units

Close

Vertical space above and below the list

List items end with periods; they are complete sentences

Example of a numbered vertical List. Items are in a required order.

Two-Column Lists

Use these guidelines for two-column lists:

1. Use two-column lists when you have a series of paired items, for example, terms and definitions.

2. Introduce the list with a lead-in sentence that is a complete sentence. Punctuate the lead-in sentence with a colon.
3. Column headings are optional; if used, align them to the left margin of the text of the columns.
4. Either start list items flush left or indent them no more than half an inch.
5. Use "compact" list format if you have just a few list items only a single line each. In the compact format, there is no vertical space between list items. Use a "loose" format—vertical space between list items—if the list items are multiple lines long.
6. Use sentence-style capitalization for both columns.
7. Punctuate items in the columns only if they are complete sentences.
8. Left-align the items in both columns.
9. When possible, omit articles (*a, an, the*) from the beginning of list items.

Note: The best way to create a two-column list is to use a table and hide the grid lines. If you use tabs between the columns, you are in for a mess if the text changes at all.

VTS components. For professional-quality video teleconferencing systems (VTS), a number of equipment components, including the following, are usually required:

Broadband modem	Connects an office to a high-speed internet service. A standard modem is insufficient; a great deal of bandwidth is required for a VTC.
Router	Manages the connectivity and traffic that occurs when VTC participants in an office connect to a broadband modem.
Webcam	Records the video signal that is sent to participants during a live session. Incorporates autofocus capability.
CODEC	Translates video and audio signals for transmission.
Monitors	High-quality displays are necessary for conducting professional-level conferencing.
Speakers and microphones	Good quality speakers and microphones are necessary, both for room-based systems and personal computers.

Lead-in to the list punctuated with a colon

Secretly, this two-column list is a table with the grid lines turned off.

The two-column items are a mix of predicates and complete sentences—all starting with an initial capital and punctuated with a period.

Figure 6: Example of a two-column list (pairs of list items). Not illustrated here, column headings are often used to indicate the contents of the two columns (for example, here it might be "Term" as the heading for the column 1 and "Definition" for column 2).

Lists with Run-In Headings

One last little variation on lists is the vertical list with run-in headings or labels at the beginning of the items. This format is used extensively in this book. It's like another way of doing a two-column list.

You can use bold or italics for the actual run-in heading (italics is used in the figure).

Stem Cell Development

Stem cells are simply "primitive" cells occurring in an organism's early developmental stages that give rise to other types of cells. There are three primary stem cell types:

- *Totipotent* – cells with the potential to form a complete organism or differentiate into any of its tissues or cells

- *Pluripotent* – cells with the potential to form many types of cells but not all needed for fetal development

- *Multipotent* – cells with the potential to develop into specialized cell types

Lead-in to the list punctuated with a colon

Labels for the list items can be bold; a period or semicolon can be used to punctuate the labels.

Figure 7: Example of a vertical list with run-in headings. Very useful for indicating the contents of each item in a lengthy vertical list when a two-column list is not quite right for the situation.

Nested Lists

A *nested* list contains two or more level of list items. Nested lists can contain every combination of list type: numbered list items (123...) with lowercase-letter sublist items (abc...), filled-disc bulleted list items with clear-disc or hyphenated sublist items; and other combinations of these.

7. Optionally, click **Delivery Options** and select one of the following delivery options:

   - Define the importance of a message
   - Confirm delivery of a message
   - Change the delivery priority of a mail message
   - Prevent copying or forwarding of a mail message
   - Spell check the message
   - Prevent receipt of out-of-office messages from others
   - Add a mood stamp to a mail message

8. Click **Send**.

Notice the the bullets align to *the text* of the parent item (the numbered items).

This is a *bulleted* sublist because the items are in no necessary order.

Figure 8: Example of a nested list. If the sublist items were in a required order, they would be abc....

Now here's another example of a nested list:

Basic manicure steps. Once you have these items at your workstation, you are ready to begin the manicure by following these steps:

Note: Unlike professional nail salons, MMD specialists do not cut the client's cuticles during the manicure process. MMD abstains from this process for health and safety reasons, as it can cause the client pain as well as run the risk of infection or inflammation.

1. Remove old polish:
   a. Check to see if your client has any old polish on her nails; you need to remove this polish before you can begin the manicure process.
   b. Pour about 7 drops of acetone (from the acetone bottle) onto a cotton ball.
   c. Beginning at the base of the nail (the part that is farthest from you and closest to the client), press down with the cotton ball and pull it down to the tip of the nail. Repeat until you remove all polish from the nail

Figure 9: Another example of a nested list. Standard is to use lowercase letters for sublist items that are in a required order.

Now that you are an expert on the types of lists you can use in your documents, check out this tutorial video for using features in your word processing program to create lists that are attractive and formatted appropriately.

Lists in MS Word

4.6: Special Notices

By: David McMurrey and Tamara Powell

Objectives

Upon completion of this chapter, readers will be able to do the following:

1. Distinguish between the four most common types of special notices.
2. Explain and apply the appropriate use for each type of special notice.
3. Explain and apply standard format guidelines for each type of special notice.

Introduction to Special Notices

Special notices are an important feature of professional technical writing: they highlight special information readers need to know to understand what they are reading, to accomplish what they want to do, to prevent damage to equipment, and to keep from hurting themselves or others.

Your task in this section is to learn the different types of special notices, their uses, and formats.

"Notices alert readers to the possibility of error, damage, or injury. They can also provide extra emphasis."

Specific Types of Special Notices

In this section, and in this course, you use a specific style of notices. If you want to use a different style, get with your instructor. Otherwise, follow these guidelines in planning and designing special notices—they are your "specs"!

1. Use special notices to emphasize key points or warn or caution readers about damage or injury.
2. Be careful to use the types of special notices precisely for their defined purposes. Use the four types of special notices in the following ways:

   Note—To emphasize points or remind readers of something, or to indicate minor problems in the outcome of what they are doing.

   Warning—To warn readers about the possibility of minor injury to themselves or others.

   Caution—To warn readers about possible damage to equipment or data or about potential problems in the outcome of what they are doing.

   Dangers—To warn readers about the possibility of serious or fatal injury to themselves or others.

   Deciding on which type of notice to use is not an exact science. Don't use a danger notice when a warning is more appropriate (the same as "crying wolf"). Also, use notices in a consistent way throughout a report. Do not create your own notices, such as putting "Important" in place of "Warning."
3. Place special notices at the point in text where they are needed. For example, place a caution or danger notice before discussing a step in which readers might hurt themselves.
4. Avoid having too many special notices at any one point in the text. Otherwise, the effectiveness of their special format will be lost. (If you have too many, combine them.)
5. Explain the consequences of not paying attention to the notice. State what will happen if the reader does not heed the notice.
6. Avoid all-caps for the text of any special notice. The examples in this section use bold or italics.

Note: Take a look around your garage or kitchen, and look at the special notices you see on products. You will see some variation, but these are likely to be dependent on specific industry standards.

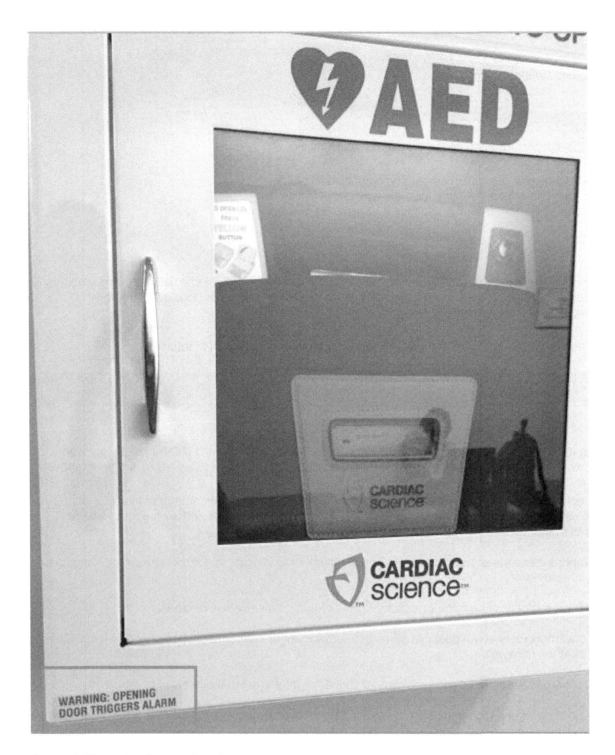

Figure 1: Example of a warning sign.

Activity

Take pictures of the special notices around you and share them on the Padlet, below. Please remember that everything you share on the Padlet is public.

Made with **padlet**

Access the Padlet

Format for Special Notices

Use the following for specific details on the capitalization, typography (bold, underlining, different fonts, different types sizes), and spacing for each type of special notice.

Note

Use the following format for simple notes:

1. Type the word "Note" followed by a colon. (Although the following examples use bold, consider using italics instead to prevent visual confusion with headings.)
2. Begin typing the text of the note one space after the colon. (But don't put the text of the note in bold or italics.)
3. Single space within the text of the note; skip one line above and below the note.
4. Start run-over lines on the regular left margin.
5. Align the note with the text to which it refers (as illustrated in the second example).

Testing the Drive

To test your new drive by reading a data CD:

1. Open the drive tray and place a CD on the tray.
2. Close the drive and wait a moment for the drive and CD to spin.
3. Click **My Computer** on your Windows desktop to view the available drives. You should see your new drive and drive letter.
4. Click the new drive to access the files on the CD.

Note: The drive letter you see as your new drive may vary depending on the number of hard drives installed on your system.

Notice that an infinitive phrase is used as a lead-in to the list (legal!).

Since this note pertains to the entire task, it is not indented the way the note in the next example is.

Figure 2: Example of a simple note.

SEO Note Settings

To make general settings before you start working with SEO Note:

1. Open **Settings > Settings** from the menu. The General tab opens.
2. Define the standard format for your new notes: HTML, text, or RTF (Rich Text Format).

   Note: Because most word processors are able to read and write RTF documents, select **RTF** as standard note format. It allows you to insert html formatted text, web links and plain text.

3. Enable the three Auto save options. Your notes will automatically be saved when you switch to another application, minimize the window, or exit the application.
4. Enable **Start with Windows** if you want SEO Note to always start with Windows.

Notice that an infinitive phrase is used as a lead-in to the list (legal!).

Notice that this note is indented to the text of the parent item (a numbered-list item).

Figure 3: Example of a note within a bulleted list (not regular running text). This same principle (that special notices align to the text they refer to) applies to the other types of special notices as well.

Notes

Use the following format for multiple notes:

1. Use this format when you have so many notes that they would distracting to present individually.
2. Type the word "Notes" followed by a colon. Italicize the word "Notes," if possible.
3. Use a numbered list for the individual notes; in it, follow the rules for numbered lists. (Do not use bold or italics for the individual notes.)
4. Align the notes with the text to which they refer; skip the equivalent of one line above and below the notes.

---

5. Place the stage monitors center stage and facing the violinist.

6. Set up your microphones and microphone stands in front of the monitors where the vocalists will be standing.

Notes:

1. Avoid problems with the feedback by ensuring the vocalist is not placed in front of the speakers.

2. Consider the length of your microphone cables and the location of your electrical outlets in the room.

This list and the multiple notes occur at the end of a section entitled "Building the Stage."

This multiple note uses numbered-list format, which for many goes against the rule about using numbered lists. Some prefer to use bullets.

Always make sure your lists are parallel.

Figure 4: Example of a multiple note. Use this format if you have lots of notes and want to collect them all in one place to prevent distraction.

Warning

Use the following format for warnings:

1. Type the word "Warning," italicize it, and follow it with a colon.
2. Either tab to beginning of the text of the warning, or use the hanging-indent format (which is much better). Try for 0.25 to 0.5 inches of space between the end of the warning label and the beginning of the text.
3. Use regular body font for the text of the warning notice (no bold, no italics, no all-caps, no color).
4. Align the warning notice with the text it refers to.
5. Skip the equivalent of one line above and below the warning notice.

Prepare for New Brake Shoes. To prepare the rear wheel assembly for the new brake shoes, perform the following tasks:

Warning: Wear a dust mask when cleaning brake components. Brake dust may contain hazardous materials and should not be inhaled.

1. Clean dirt and brake dust from backing plate and brake parts with aerosol brake cleaner.

2. Apply grease to the six flat friction points where the brake shoes touch the backing plate.

Pay attention to these formatting details:

- The notice only italicizes the word "Warning."
- The notice uses the "hanging head" style.
- The notice is indented to the text of the preceding text.

Figure 5: Example of notices.

Caution

Use the following format for caution notices:

1. Type the word "Caution," follow it with a colon, and bold both the label and the colon.
2. Skip one line and begin the text of the caution aligned with the start of the caution label.
3. Singlespace the text of the caution; skip one line above and below the notice.
4. Align the caution notice with the text it refers to (in the preceding, the warning notice occurs within a numbered list and is indented accordingly).

1. Pump the brake pedal until firm.

2. Check that the brake fluid level is between the maximum and minimum lines on the reservoir. Add or remove fluid accordingly.

   Caution:
   Keep brake fluid from getting on painted surfaces as it can cause damage to the paint.

3. Perform test drive.

Caution notice: Alerts people to problems with the procedure or damage to equipment

Format: notice the following:
- Only the word "Caution" is bold and is displayed on a line separate from the text of the notice.
- The notice is indented to the *text* of the preceding step.

Figure 6: Example of a caution notice. Use this one to alert readers of possible damage to equipment or problems with the procedure.

Danger

Use the following format for danger notices:

1. Type the word "DANGER" in all-caps. (Underline it, or use bold.)
2. Align the danger notice with the text it refers to.
3. Singlespace the text of the danger notice; skip one line above and below the danger notice.
4. Use bold on the text of the danger notice if you have it (but never all-caps).
5. If you have graphics capability, draw a box around the danger notice (including the label).

Lower the Vehicle. To lower the vehicle, perform the following:

1. Jack up rear of car with a hydraulic jack on a solid part of frame, remove the jack stands, and lower the car to ground.

   > **DANGER: Never work underneath a car that is only supported by a jack. Failure to support vehicle may result in death or severe injury if the vehicle falls from the jack.**

2. Pump the brake pedal until firm.

3. Check that the brake fluid level is between the maximum and minimum lines on the reservoir. Add or remove fluid accordingly.

Danger notice: Some standards require that this type of notice *precede* the step in which the danger occurs.

Format: notice the following:
- The danger notice is enclosed within a box
- Only the word "DANGER" is all-caps. All-caps for the entire notice would decrease redability.
- The notice is indented to the *text* of the preceding step.

Figure 7: Danger notice. Use this one to alert readers of the possibility of serious injury or fatality.

Other Formatting Issues

Here are some additional points to consider concerning special notices:

1. **Special alignment**. Special notices must align to the text to which they refer. For example, if you have a note that adds some special detail to something in a bulleted list item, you must align that note to the *text* of the bulleted item. Of course, if the note follows a bulleted list but refers to the whole list, then you can use the regular left margin.

2. **Single spaced text**. All of the examples and discussion in this unit are based on double spaced text. For single spaced text, use your document-design "eye" to decide on spacing. Leave either one blank lines between running text and special notices—depending on what looks best to you. (And of course both running text and the text of the special notices would be singlespaced.)

3. **Placement of special notices**. The standard rule is to place special notices before the point at which they are relevant. For example, you warn readers to back up all data before you tell them to reformat their hard drive. However, in practice this applies to serious special notices where great harm to data, equipment, or people is likely to ensue.

   One technique used by very cautious writers (maybe those who have been burned) is to place all serious notices (warnings, cautions, and dangers) somewhere at the beginning of the document, and then repeat them individually where they apply.

4. **Multiple special notices**. You run into situations where you have three or four special notices, all jammed together in the same part of the text, each one following another. This is a problem because the whole point of the special formatting of the notices is lost: something is special because it is different from the surrounding. The solution to this problem is to create one identifying heading (for example, "Notes and Warnings"), and then list the notices (either bulleted or numbered) below it.

5. **Other important things to remember**. In any list, make sure your list is parallel. If you use bullets or numbers, make sure you have more than one bullet or number. That is, if you only need one bullet or one number in a bulleted or numbered list, you don't actually need a bulleted or numbered list.

By: David McMurrey and Tamara Powell

Objectives

Upon completion of this chapter, readers will be able to do the following:

1. Distinguish between tables, charts, and graphs.
2. Identify chief characteristics of tables, charts, and graphs.
3. Identify and apply best practices in creating tables, charts, and graphs in technical communication.

Introduction to Tables, Charts, and Graphs

One of the nice things about technical writing courses is that most of the papers have graphics in them—or at least they should. A lot of professional, technical writing contains graphics—drawings, diagrams, photographs, illustrations of all sorts, tables, pie charts, bar charts, line graphs, flow charts, and so on. Graphics are important in technical communication. We learn more from a document when graphics are included (Gatlin, 1988). In fact, people learn about 1/3 more from a document with graphics than without (Levie and Lentz, 1982). A recent study found that readers learn faster and are better able to use the information they learn when the text includes graphics (Große,Jungmann, and Drechsler, 2015). That does not, of course, mean that one should place graphics willy-nilly into every spot possible. On the contrary, graphics should be used carefully and correctly. The information below will help you to make informed decisions regarding graphic creation and placement that will help to make your documents more effective for your readers.

Tables

Tables, of course, are those rows and columns of numbers and words, mostly numbers. They permit rapid access to and relatively easy comparison of information. If the data is arranged chronologically (for example, sales figures over a ten-year period), the table can show trends—patterns of rising or falling activity. Of course, tables are not necessarily the most vivid or dramatic means of showing such trends or relationships between data—that's why we have charts and graphs (discussed in the next section).

Uses for Tables

The biggest use of tables is for numerical data. Imagine that you are comparing different models of laser printers in terms of physical characteristics such as height, depth, length, weight, and so on. Perfect for a table.

However, don't get locked into the notion that tables are strictly for numerical data. Whenever you have situations where you discuss several things about which you provide the same categories of detail, you've got a possibility for a table. For example, imagine that you were comparing several models of a laser printer: you'd be saying the same category of thing about each printer (its cost, print speed, supply costs, warranty terms, and so on). This is ideal stuff for a table, and it would be mostly words rather than numbers (and in this case, you'd probably want to leave the textual discussion where it is and "re-present" the information in table form).

Table Format

In its simplest form, a table is a group of rows and columns of data. At the top of each column is a column heading, which defines or identifies the contents of that column (and often it indicates the unit of measurement). On the left edge of the table may be row headings, which define or identify the contents of that row. Things get tricky when rows or columns must be grouped or subdivided. In such cases, you have to create row or column subheadings. This situation is illustrated here:

Table 3. Energy production by major source from 1960 to 1980[1]					
Year	Total production (quad Btu)	Percent production			
		Coal	Petroleum	Natural gas	Other[2]
1960	41.5	26.1	36.0	34.0	3.9
1970	62.1	23.5	32.9	38.9	4.7
1980	64.8	28.7	28.2	34.2	8.9

[1] *Source:* U.S. Energy Information Administration, *Annual Energy Review*

[2] Includes hydropower, nuclear power, geothermal power, and others.

Figure 1: Format for tables with grouped or subdivided rows and columns. Notice that the table title goes above the table.

Traditionally, the title of a table is placed on top of the table or is the first row of the table. If the contents of the table are obvious and there is no need to cross-reference the table from anywhere else in the report, you can omit the title.

As for specific style and formatting guidelines for tables, keep these in mind:

- Refer to the table in the text just preceding the table. Explain the general significance of the data in the table; don't expect readers to figure it out entirely for themselves.
- Don't overwhelm readers with monster 11-column, 30-row tables! Simplify the table data down to just that amount of data that illustrates your point—without of course distorting that data.
- Don't put the word or abbreviation for the unit of measurement in every cell of a column. For example, in a column of measurements all in millimeters, don't put "mm" after every number. Put the abbreviation in parentheses in the column or row heading.
- Right- or decimal-align numbers in the columns. If the 123 and 4 were in a column, the 4 would be right below the 3, not the 1.
- Normally, words in columns are left-justified (although you will occasionally see columns of words all centered).
- Column headings are centered over the columns of numerical data (forming a T-shape); left-aligned with columns of text. The alignment of column headings to the actual columnar data is variable. If you have a column of two- or three-letter words, you'd probably want to center the column heading over that data, even those it is words not numbers. (Doing so, avoids an odd-looking L-shaped column.)
- When there is some special point you need to make about one or more of the items in the table, use a footnote instead of clogging up the table with the information.

Producing Tables

Normally, you'll be borrowing information in which a good table occurs. If it's a simple table without too many rows and columns, retype it yourself into your own document (but remember to document where you borrowed it from in the figure title). However, if it is a big table with lots of data, you're justified in scanning, screen-capturing, or photocopying it and bringing it into your report that way.

If you use OpenOffice, Word, or WordPerfect, get used to using the table-generating tools. You don't have to draw the lines and other formatting details.

Occasionally, in rough-draft technical reports, information is presented in regular running-text form that could be better presented in table (or tabular) form. Be sure and look back over your rough drafts for material that can transformed into tables.

It's startling how many earthquakes are located worldwide per year—between 12,000 and 14,000. However, the magnitude and intensity, as measured on the Richter scale, is such that most don't make the front page of your local newspaper. The monster earthquakes, those 8.5 and higher, occur only 0.3 times per year—but that's certainly more than enough! Earthquakes measuring 8.0 to 8.4 are slightly more frequent at 1.1 occurrences per year. Any earthquake 8.0 or over is considered a "great" earthquake. "Major" earthquakes are those between 7.0 and 7.9. In the upper half of that range, 3.1 occur per year, while 15 occur in the 7.0 to 7.4 range. The frequency is considerably higher in the 6.5 to 6.9 range: an average of 56 per year, while 210 occur in the 6.0-6.4 range per year. See wwwneic.cr.usgs.gov/neis/general/handouts/mag_vs_int.html the U.S.

Notice how much text is needed to explain how many earth-quakes occur on average per year in the different magnitude ranges.

...cated worldwide per ...ver, the magnitude and ...le, is such that most don't ...per. As the following table ...5 and higher, occur only 0.3 times per year—but that's certainly more than enough! As the magnitude decrease, the average per year increases. Earthquakes 8.0 and above are referred to as "great" earthquakes; those in the 7.0-7.9 range are referred to as "major" earthquakes. See the U.S. Geological Survey's web page on magnitude and intensity comparisons at:wwwneic.cr.usgs.gov/neis/general/handouts/mag_vs_int.html.

Notice that the writer refers readers to the table and gives them a start interpreting it. Since the writer doesn't refer to this table elsewhere in the document, numbering it is unnecessary.

Earthquakes Worldwide per Year	
Magnitude	EQ/year
8.5 - 8.9	0.3
8.0 - 8.4	1.1
7.5 - 7.9	3.1
7.0 - 7.4	15
6.5 - 6.9	56

Figure 2: Example of information included in text that would be better represented in a table.

Charts and Graphs

Charts and graphs are actually just another way of presenting the same data that is presented in tables—although a more dramatic and interesting one. At the same time, however, you get less detail or less precision in a chart or graph than you do in the table. Imagine the difference between a table of sales figures for a ten-year period and a line graph for that same data. You get a better sense of the overall trend in the graph but not the precise dollar amount.

More information on creating charts in MS Word

Formatting Requirements

When you create charts and graphs, keep these requirements in mind (most of these elements are illustrated below):

1. Axis labels—In bar charts and line graphs, don't forget to indicate what the x and y axes represent. One axis might indicate millions of dollars; the other, five-year segments from 1960 to the present.

2. Keys (legends)—Bar charts, line graphs, and pie charts often use special color, shading, or line style (solid or dashed). Be sure to indicate what these mean; translate them in a key (a box) in some unused place in the chart or graph.

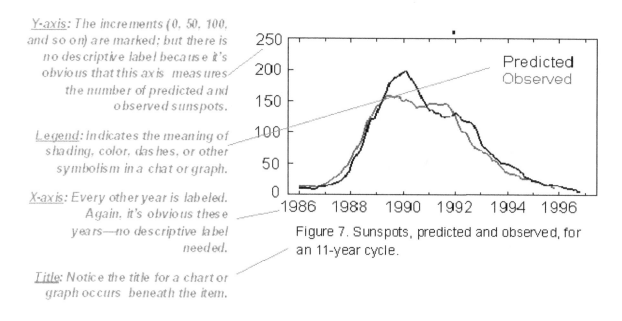

Y-axis: The increments (0, 50, 100, and so on) are marked; but there is no descriptive label because it's obvious that this axis measures the number of predicted and observed sunspots.

Legend: Indicates the meaning of shading, color, dashes, or other symbolism in a chat or graph.

X-axis: Every other year is labeled. Again, it's obvious these years—no descriptive label needed.

Title: Notice the title for a chart or graph occurs beneath the item.

Figure 7. Sunspots, predicted and observed, for an 11-year cycle.

Figure 3: Example of a line graph.

Example of a Graph

Notice that a *figure* title is placed beneath the graph.

- Figure titles—For most charts and graphs, you'll want to include a title, in many cases, a numbered title. Readers need some way of knowing what they are looking at. And don't forget to cite the source of any information you borrowed in order to create the graphic. The standard rule for when to number figures or tables is this: if you cross-reference the figure or table elsewhere in the text.
- Cross-references—Whenever you use a chart or graph, don't forget to put a cross-reference to it from the related text. With that cross-reference, provide some explanation of what is going on in the graphic, how to

interpret it, what its basic trends are, and so on.

In recent benchmark tests performed by *PC Magazine*, all three of the systems compared here performed at or near the same levels [1: 116-118]. The Micron system comes out on top with slightly better average scores, as shown in Figure 5.

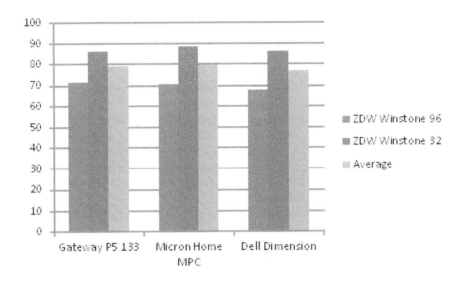

Figure 5. Benchmark ratings of system performance [1:116-118]

It is important to note that the Gateway P5 system used in these tests was equipped with 256K Pipeline Burst cache—a feature not present in the basic configuration noted above (Figure 5). The lack of secondary cache in Pentium systems is widely regarded to result in a decrease in system performance of up to 30%.

Figure 4: Example of a chart. Notice that text above and below the chart calls attention to the chart and briefly indicates its significance.

- Documentation—When you borrow information to create a graphic, be sure to use the standard format to indicate the source. It does not matter how you import the graphic into your report—it is *all* borrowed information, which some brave and noble soul worked hard to develop and who deserves credit for that effort.

Producing Charts and Graphs

As with illustrations, you have these options for creating charts and graphs: screen-capturing, scanning, photocopying, generating your own with software, and drawing your own.

Helpful information regarding choosing what type of graph to use

Helpful downloads to jumpstart your graph creation

Documenting Tables, Charts, and Graphs: Indicating Sources

As mentioned earlier, it's perfectly legal to borrow tables—to copy, photocopy, scan, or extract subsets of data from them. But you're obligated to cite your sources for tables, charts, and graphs just as you are for the words you borrow. Normally, this is done in either the table title or in a footnote just below the table. Check the example in the table shown previously.

General Guidelines for Tables, Charts, and Graphs

The preceding sections state a number of common guidelines that need to be stated all in one place. These are important!

- Watch out for areas in your text where you discuss lots of numeric data in relation to two or more things—that's ideal for tables or even charts or graphs.
- Watch out for areas in your text where you define a series of terms—that's ideal for tables.
- Always discuss tables in preceding text. Don't just throw a table, graph, or chart out there unexplained. Orient readers to it; explain its basic significance.
- Make sure your tables, charts, and graphs are appropriate to your audience, subject matter, and purpose—don't zap beginners with massive, highly technical constructions they can't understand.
- Use a title unless the table, chart, and graph is very informal. Remember that the title goes *just above* the table; for charts and graphs, below.
- Left-align words and phrases in table columns (including the column heading). Right-align numeric data in table columns (but center the column heading). A nice touch to put a bit of right margin on this right-aligned data so that it moves out into the center of the column rather than remaining jammed to the right edge.
- Some believe that it is easier for readers to compare vertically rather than horizontally. If you believe that, format your tables so that your *columns* contain the information to be compared. For example, if you were comparing cars, you'd have *columns* for MPG, price, and so on.
- Indicate the source of tables, charts, and graphs you have borrowed either part of or entirely. This can be done in the title or in a footnote.
- Indicate identifying measurement values in column or row headings—not in each cell.
- Cross-reference all tables, charts, and graphs from the preceding text. In the cross-reference, give the number (if it is a formal table with title), indicate the subject matter of the table, and provide explanatory information as necessary.

Best Practices for Creating Graphics in Technical Writing: Examples

What are best practices for creating graphics? How can one mess up when adding a graphic to technical communication? This video will show you how to do things correctly and incorrectly.

Graphics in Technical Writing

For more information and examples on how NOT to create graphs, please look at C.J. Schwarz' "A Short Tour of Bad Graphs." Shared with permission.

References

Gatlin, P. L. (1988). Visuals and prose in manuals: The effective combination. In *Proceedings of the 35th International Technical Communication Conference* (pp. RET 113-115). Arlington, VA: Society for Technical Communication.

Große, C. S., Jungmann, L., & Drechsler, R. (2015). Benefits of illustrations and videos for technical documentations. *Computers In Human Behavior*, 45109-120. doi:10.1016/j.chb.2014.11.095

Levie, W.H., and Lentz, R. (1982). Effects of text illustrations: A review of research. *Journal of Educational Psychology*, 73, 195-232.

By: David McMurrey

Objectives

Upon completion of this chapter, readers will be able to do the following:

- Explain and apply the various uses of graphics in technical documents.
- Create and format appropriate graphics for technical documents.

Introduction to Graphics

One of the nice things about technical writing courses is that most of the papers have graphics in them—or at least they should. A lot of professional, technical writing contains graphics—drawings, diagrams, photographs, illustrations of all sorts, tables, pie charts, bar charts, line graphs, flow charts, and so on. Once you get the hang of putting graphics like these into your writing, you should consider yourself obligated to use graphics whenever the situation naturally would call for them.

Unlike what you might fear, producing graphics is not such a terrible task—in fact, it's fun. You don't have to be a professional graphics artist or technical draftsperson to get graphics into your technical writing. The Internet has advanced our sources for graphics immensely. And, if you are still living the 1970s, you can produce professional-looking graphics with tape, scissors, white-out, and a decent photocopying machine.

Overview

Before getting into details on creating, formatting, and incorporating graphics, consider the types and their functions. You can use graphics to represent the following elements in your technical writing:

- Objects—If you're describing a fuel-injection system, you'll probably need a drawing or diagram of the thing. If you are explaining how to graft a fruit tree, you'll need some illustrations of how that task is done. Photographs, drawings, diagrams, and schematics are the types of graphics that show objects.
- Numbers—If you're discussing the rising cost of housing in Austin, you could use a table with the columns marking off five-year periods since 1970; the rows could be for different types of housing. You could show the same data in the form of bar charts, pie charts, or line graphs. Tables, bar charts, pie charts, and line graphs are some of the principal ways to show numerical data.
- Concepts—If you want to show how your company is organized, the relationships of the different departments and officials, you could set up an organization chart—boxes and circles connected with lines that show how everything is hierarchically arranged and related. A concept graphic shows nonphysical, conceptual things and their relationships. In the figure below, see how Apple Computer illustrated the difference between 32-bit processors and 64-bit processors (these days, these are called infographics).
- Words—And finally graphics are used to depict words. You've probably noticed how textbooks put key definitions in a box, maybe with a different color. The same can be done with key points or extended examples. Not the sexiest form of graphics, but it still qualifies, and it's good to keep in mind as a useful technique.

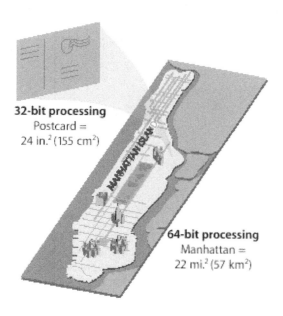

32-bit processing
Postcard =
24 in.^{2} (155 cm^2)

64-bit processing
Manhattan =
22 mi.^{2} (57 km^2)

Figure 1: Graphic of the difference between 32-bit processors and 64-bit processors from Apple Computer

Drawings, Diagrams, Photos

To depict objects, places, people, and relationships between them, you can use photos, drawings, diagrams, and schematics.

Uses of Illustrations and Photos

In the realm of illustrations and photographs, the types run from minimal detail to maximal. A simple line drawing of how to graft a fruit tree reduces the detail to simple lines representing the hands, the tools, the graft stock, and graft. Diagrams are a more abstract, schematic view of things, for example, a wiring diagram of a clock radio; it hardly resembles the actual physical thing at all. And of course photographs provide the most detail of all. These graphics, supplying gradations of detail as they do, have their varying uses. Here are some examples:

1. In instructions, simple drawings (often called line drawings) are the most common. They simplify the situation and the objects so that the reader can focus on the key details. In the examples below, you can see a fully detailed photograph and a simplified, labeled diagram. Which would you prefer?

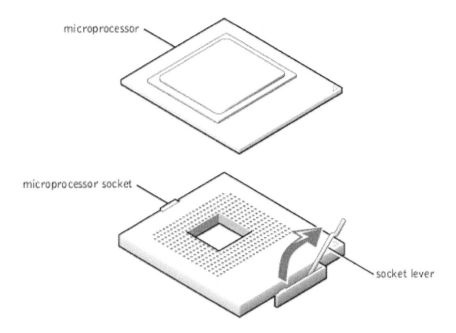

microprocessor

microprocessor socket

socket lever

Figure 3: Simplified, labeled diagram

2. In descriptions, you would want to use drawings, but in this case drawings with more detail, such as shading and depth perspectives.
3. In feasibility, recommendation, and evaluation reports, photographs are often used. For example, if you are recommending a photocopier, you might want to include photos of the leading contenders.

Formatting Requirements

When you use an illustration in a report, there are several requirements to keep in mind (most of these are shown in this illustration):

The ionization chamber is a sealed unit with vents on the casing to allow air circulation. Inside the case are two metal plates separated by an air gap. A radiation source sits behind one of the plates, which has a hole in it to allow the radiation into the air gap (see Figure 2). A voltage is applied across the two plates, giving one a positive and the other a negative electrical charge. The radiation source used is usually a small amount (approximately 0.2 mg)

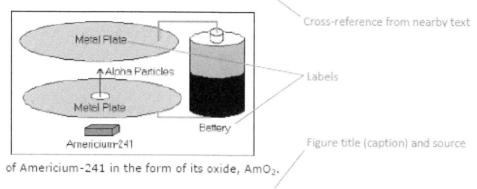

Cross-reference from nearby text

Labels

Figure title (caption) and source

of Americium-241 in the form of its oxide, AmO_2.

Figure 2. Ionization chamber of a smoke detector. *Source:* "Ionization chamber." http://en.wikipedia.org/wiki/Ionization_chamber. Accessed June 6, 2014.

Figure 4: Formatting requirements

- Labels—Just about any illustration should contain labels—words and phrases—with pointers to the parts of the things being depicted.
- Keys—If the illustration has certain shadings, colors, line styles, or other such details that have a special meaning in the illustration, these should be indicated in a key—an area in an unused corner of the illustration that deciphers their meaning.
- Titles—Except in special cases, illustrations should have titles, and these titles should be numbered (Figure 1, Figure 2, and so on). The exceptions are these: if you have lots of illustrations (for example, in certain instructions, there are illustrations practically after every paragraph) and if there is no benefit from the titles; if you only have one or two illustrations and they are not cross-referenced; and/or if you do not cross-reference your illustrations. In some of these cases, you might want to keep the title but discard the word "Figure" and the number following it.
- Cross-references—Almost all illustrations should be referred to from the relevant point in the discussion. And, do more than just tossing in a "(See Figure 2)"; discuss the illustration a bit—focus readers' attention on the key details of the illustration.
- Location within the report—Ideally, you place illustrations just after the point where they are needed. However, sometimes because of the pagination (the way the text falls on the pages) and the size of the illustrations, this close placement is not possible. No problem—just put the illustration at the top of the next page; that is what the figure-numbering system is for.
- Size of illustrations—Again, ideally, you want illustrations to be between one-half to one-quarter of the vertical size of the page. You want them to fit on the page with other text. In fact, that's what you really want—to interperse text and graphics in a report. What you do *not* want is to append the illustration to the back of the report! When you have a large illustration, use your software or a photocopier to reduce it.
- Placement within margins—Make sure that your illustrations fit neatly and comfortably within standard margins. You don't want the illustration spilling over into the right or left margins. You want to allow the equivalent of at least one blank line above and below the illustration.
- Level of technical detail—And, rather obviously, you want illustrations to be at the right technical level for your readers. No chip circuitry diagrams for computer beginners!

Producing Illustrations

Now for the question we're all waiting to ask—how to create graphics? There are several options: scanning, photocopying, using computer graphics, and hand-drawing. In all of these production methods, don't forget that you must indicate the source of the borrowed graphic.

- Scanning is the best way to pull graphics into your document files. Scanners are quite affordable now, especially those that include printing and faxing capabilities. Universities and colleges usually make scanners available to students and faculty. Print shops will scan for a fee. You copy your graphics to graphic-format files (such as .jpg or .png) then copy them into your document files.

  Note: When you scan a graphic, trim off the title (caption) and other material from the original. Replace this material with words of your own.
- Photocopying used to be the method. You photocopied graphics from print sources, trimmed them, left room for them as you typed text (yes, with a typewriter), taped in the photocopies, and photocopied the whole document. Done well, the result could look almost professional.
- Using computer graphics With a little practice, you can create graphics like the ones show in the figure here in OpenOffice Writer or Microsoft Word (and of course GIMP and Illustrator). With a computer-graphics drawing like the keylock mechanism to the right, you are at the very edge of what OpenOffice Writer or Microsoft Word can do.
- Hand-drawing may not be as out of the question as you might think. Take a blank sheet of paper and start sketching lightly with a soft-leaded pencil. Keep working until you have the drawing the way you like. Then use a black marker to ink in the lines that you want, and erase the stray pencil markings. Now, scan this drawing and follow the method described above.

Figure 8: Illustrated graphic

Documenting Graphics: Indicating Sources

As mentioned earlier, it's perfectly legal to borrow graphics—to trace, photocopy, scan, or extract subsets of data from them. But you're obligated to cite your sources for graphics just as you are for the words you borrow. Normally, this is done in the figure title of the graphics.

Guidelines for Graphics: A Review

The preceding sections state a number of common guidelines that need to be stated all in one place. These are important!

- Use graphics *whenever* they would normally be necessary—don't wimp out because it seems like too much trouble! But at the same time, don't get hung up about creating perfect graphics (scans and photocopies work just fine for our purposes as long as you cite your source). This course is a writing course, not a graphic-arts course.
- Always discuss graphics in nearby text preceding the graphic. Don't just throw a graphic out there unexplained. Orient readers to the graphic; explain its basic meaning.
- If a certain graphic is difficult to produce, discuss the problem with your instructor (you might be able to leave a blank with a descriptive note in the middle).
- Make sure your graphics are appropriate to your audience, subject matter, and purpose—don't zap beginners with advanced, highly technical graphics they can't understand.
- Intersperse graphics and text on the same page. Don't put graphics on pages by themselves; don't attach them to the end of documents.
- Use figure titles for graphics (see the exceptions to this rule in the preceding).
- Indicate the source of any graphic you have borrowed—this includes tables, illustrations, charts, and graphs. Whenever you borrow a graphic from some other source, document that fact in the figure title.
- Include identifying detail such as illustration labels, axis labels, keys, and so on. For labels, use text boxes and turn off the borders.
- Make sure graphics fit within normal margins—if they don't, enlarge or reduce the copies. Leave at least one blank line above and below graphics.
- This guideline is for folks still operating in the 1970s. When you tape graphics in to your report, photocopy your *entire* report, not just the pages on which the tape-ins occur. Hand in the entire photocopied document, *not* the original and *not* a mixture of original and photocopied pages. Don't manually add color or

other detail on the pages of the final copy that you intend to submit—in other words, don't draw on the final copy. Any details like these should be added before photocopying. If you must have color, use color photocopying equipment.

- Place graphics as near to the point in the text where they are relevant as is reasonable. However, if a graphic does not fit properly on one page, put it at the top of the next, and continue with regular text on the preceding page. Don't leave half a page blank just to keep a graphic near the text it is associated with.
- Cross-reference all graphics from the appropriate text. In the cross-reference, give the figure number (if one is used), indicate the subject matter of the graphic, and provide explanatory information as necessary.

4.9: Indexing

By: Cassandra Race

Objectives

Upon completion of this chapter, readers will be able to create an index using Microsoft Word.

Help Desk: Creating an Index

In long technical documents, an index, or a list of almost everything in the document, is found at the end of the document. The index is a helpful tool for quickly locating information, and many readers expect it. There are several techniques for creating an index, but the most efficient and up to date is right at your fingertips.

Microsoft Word allows you to create an index for a single word, a phrase, or even a symbol. You can also create an index item for a topic that covers several pages or paragraphs, or one that refers to another entry, such as "Chihuahua. See Dogs."

After you have completed your document, consider what you think needs to be referenced in the index so the reader can find it quickly. You may need to brainstorm to make some decisions here, especially as to how detailed you want the index to be.

Then, get started! Open the References tab on your Word toolbar (see below).

Figure 1: The references tab on the Word toolbar

In your text, go to the first word you want to go into the index and highlight it. Then, go to the Index tool in the References tab and click on "Mark Entry." The dialog box below will pop up, with your highlighted word in the main entry field. You may then choose to insert a subentry and then click "Mark" if you just want only this reference to the term listed, or "Mark All" if you want every instance the term appears in your document listed in your index.

After you mark all the index entries you want, you can choose an index design and build the finished index. Word collects the index entries for you, sorts them in alphabetical order, lists page numbers, finds and removes duplicate entries, and puts the index in the document.

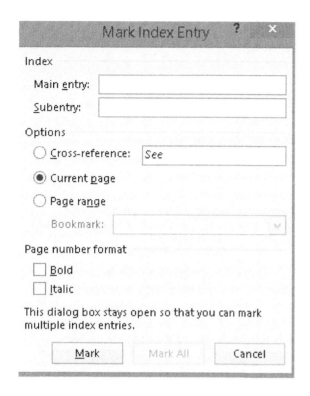

Figure 2: Mark index entry window in Word

Don't panic when your document begins to look strange. When you select text and mark it for an index entry, Microsoft Word adds a special XE (Index Entry) field that includes the marked main entry and any cross-reference information that you choose to include. The example below is from Support.Office.com.

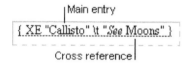

Figure 3: Index Entry (XE) field

When you are satisfied that you've gotten all the important stuff (and you can even include topic headings and illustrations in the index) its time to create the actual index!

Back to the Indexing tool...

Click where you want to add the index to your document. Now, click on "Insert Index." You will see a dialogue box like the one below. Unfortuntely, it won't show your index in the preview page, but you can get an idea of how it works.

The preview will scroll so you can see how the whole thing will look, and under Formats just below the preview screen, you can choose from 4 different styles. You can also create your own style by selecting "From template" and choosing "Modify" in the bottom right corner of the box.

Click okay. Don't worry...you can always go back and update or edit if you need to by going to the Update Index button in the Index tool. If your document still has all the crazy looking markups, just go to to the Paragraph tool in the Home tab and click on the little show/hide icon (¶)in the upper right hand corner.

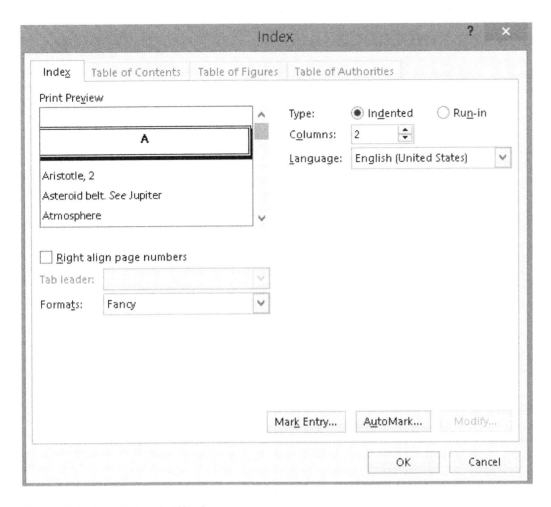

Figure 4: Index window in Word

Chapter 5: Processes and Guidelines in Technical Writing

5.1: Writing Processes: From Audience to Rough Draft

By: David McMurrey

Objectives

Upon completion of this chapter, readers will be able to:

- Brainstorm and narrow down topics for a report.
- Create an outline for a report.

Introduction to the Writing Process

The writing process takes you from the very beginning of a writing project—finding topics and analyzing audience and purpose—all the way to the end—writing and revising the rough draft. The following chapters focus on some of the key phases of that process:

- Strategies for team-writing
- Audience analysis
- Brainstorming and invention
- Narrowing
- Outlining
- Note-taking
- Libraries, documentation, cross-referencing
- Strategies for peer-reviewing
- Power-revision techniques

Find Report Topics

As a writer in a technical writing course, you may need some strategies for finding topics for writing projects, which are provided in this section.

By definition, technical-writing courses are opportunities to focus on practical uses of your writing skills. In the ideal technical-writing course, you would have a work-related writing project every two to three weeks: for example, instructions for that pesky fax machine down the hall or recommendations on home alarm systems. However, technical-writing courses are also great opportunities for exploring science and technology: latest advances in nanotechnology, latest theories about the origin of the universe, latest methods for hydroponic gardening.

Brainstorm Topics for Writing Projects

If you have a topic for your writing project , the next step is to think about subtopics related to it. Here is an excerpt of a brainstorming session in which these questions were used:

How does a wind-powered electrical system (WPES) work? What are the steps in its operation? Savings: discuss the amount of money that can be saved using WPES. Relationship between average windspeeds and electrical output: what happens when there's no wind, only very light breezes? Too much wind? Basic parts: rotor, generator, tail assembly, tower. Different manufacturers of WPES: how to get a good system and avoid being ripped off. Dimensions, materials, construction of common models of WPES; sensitivity to low wind speeds. Historical background on WPES: the time when more WPES were being used, just before rural electrification in the 1930s; who were the first developers? When has interest in WPES reappeared? Why? Two general class of wind machines: lift and drag machines. Lightning protection of WPES. Aerodynamic principles as they apply to WPES. Understanding weather patterns and seasonal and geographical factors affecting wind. Principles of electricity: circuits, generators, types of current, meanings of terminology. Local, state, federal tax credits and research support in wind systems research, and WPES purchase by consumers.

Narrow That Report Topic

For a writing project in a technical-writing course, the ideal starting place is a workplace problem requiring some writing as part or all of the solution. With such a project, the audience and problem are there to help you narrow the topic. However, if you begin with a topic, it's harder to narrow. You are likely to end up trying to write a ten-pound textbook on automotive plastics, residential solar energy in the home, or La Niña. Narrow the topic and do some careful research—the result will be a practical, useful document that doesn't go on forever.

Narrowing means selecting a portion of a larger topic: for example, selecting a specific time period, event, place, people, type, component, use or application, cause or effect, and so on. Narrowing also means deciding on the amount of detail to use in discussing those topics.

Note: In the following example of the narrowing process, you may wonder how all those subtopics seem to come to mind so effortlessly. If that's not the way it is for you, try some brainstorming and invention first.

Following the Narrowing Process

Let's walk through a typical narrowing exercise to see how it works. This particular example works "backward" from a topic to a realistic audience and purpose. In a "real world" situation, you'd begin with a workplace situation.

1. Imagine that you want to write something about **gardening**. You have a backyard vegetable garden that you grow as a hobby, and of course for the vegetables it produces.
2. What can you do with a topic like gardening? You know you want to focus on **vegetable gardening**, but that's only a first timid step at narrowing. There are still dozens and dozens of topics related to vegetable gardening.
3. What are the **possibilities related to vegetable gardening**? Obviously, there are topics like planting techniques, pest control, fertilization and irrigation topics, perhaps even special-focus reports on individual vegetables—tomatoes, onions, butter beans, peppers. Among these, you lean more to gardening methods or techniques—such as drip irrigation, raised-bed gardening, organic pest control, and so on.
4. Now you are getting somewhere! But you can't write on all those techniques—**pick one**! Recently, you were reading about how NASA's plans for the human exploration of Mars includes growing food there on the planet—specifically by using hydroponic methods. This sparks your curiosity; it's the right topic for a technical document of some kind.
5. You're all done with narrowing, right? Sorry, you're barely half-way there. Hydroponics, the science and craft of growing plants without soil, is a big topic in its own right. What specifically interests you about hydroponics: Interested in setting up a hydroponics system in your garage? Curious whether the claims about hydroponically grown foods are true? Wondering what it takes to run a hydroponics system? Interested in finding a commercially available hydroponic system that meets your needs and price range? Yes—something about practical realities of hydroponics! Your real interest here is the **feasibility of hydroponic gardening, recommendations, or both**.
6. Now you have a choice: (a) focus on the feasibility of hydroponics or (b) focus on commercially available systems to determine which is best and which will fit in your garage. At this stage, you are not ready to pick a system; instead, you must convince yourself that the whole concept is practical. Therefore, let's focus on the **general feasibility**.
7. Another chapter in this book presents several kinds of feasibility: practical feasibility, whether it works; economic feasibility, whether it's too expensive and whether it pays for itself or offers economic advantages; implementation feasibility, whether it's too much trouble, whether you have to remodel your entire garage; and feasibility in terms of the yield and quality— whether hydroponically grown vegetables are any good.
8. So what's it going to be? You know that you want **answers to these questions**: does hydroponic gardening work? What's the yield? Is it any good? How much of a hassle is it? How expensive and how difficult is it to build your own system? And what do you need—in general terms—to build a system? Is this too much for a semester report in a technical-writing course?

You've come a long way from "gardening," but you may still need to keep going. Actually, you've done one other narrowing operation without noticing: the focus is small-time, hobbyist, or "home" hydroponic gardening—not commercial hydroponic gardening. In any case, you have four main questions: (a) how does it work, (b) how well does it work, (c) how much work is it, and (d) and what are the costs? These translate into the subtopics you see at the very bottom of this flow chart.

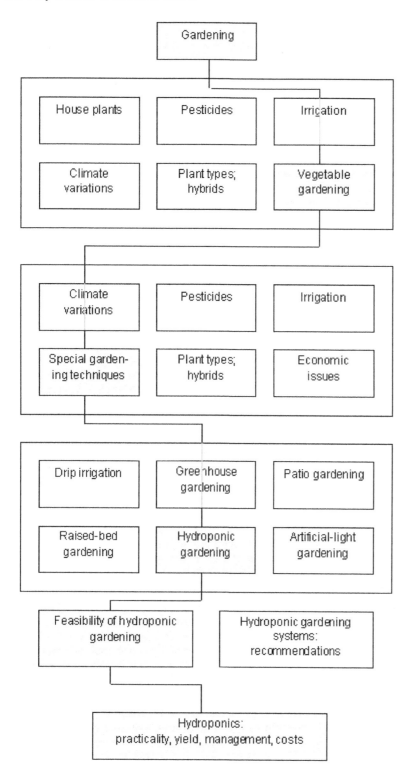

Figure 1: Diagram of narrowing down your topic

To this point, you've been operating in a vacuum, not considering audience and situation, focusing instead on *your interests* in this topic. Now it's time to get real—to define a real or realistic audience and situation. Who wants this document? Who would hire you (hydroponics expert) to write it? How would people obtain this document? Imagine that a hydroponics association, club, or special-interest group sends out a request for proposals (RFP). Its members want a technical writer to develop an overview guide on hydroponics: not a how-to, not a parts list—just an introduction answering people's questions and concerns. The organization will ship your overview to anybody who inquires about the topic—and the organization will pay you for all of this great work.

Are we there yet? Not quite. Narrowing means two things: zooming in on progressively smaller and smaller subtopics. And deciding on level and amount of detail. In this hydroponics overview, must you cover the four subtopics in excruciating detail? No, at most you'll want to cover practicality in moderate detail: readers need enough detail to see that the method actually works. Use the same amount of detail for yield, perhaps citing some comparative studies. But use only light detail for management and costs. You must keep this overview relatively brief and readable.

Finishing the Process

In the end, try to produce something that is integrated with a real or realistic situation.

Outlining-Generating Items and Sequencing Them

When you write a technical report, not only must you think of the right information to include (or exclude); you must also find a good way to arrange it. This is a two-part chapter: this part focuses on generating outline items and sequencing them; the second part focuses on turning a rough outine into a good, polished outline.

Outlines for technical reports are usually hard to handle solely in your mind; it's a little like trying to add a list of large numbers mentally. You must get report outlines in print in order to think about the arrangement of the topics within them. A good working outline serves you in at least four important ways:

- It shows you which areas of information to investigate and gather information on.
- It shows you which areas you can safely ignore (thus saving you plenty of time).
- It enables you to schedule your work into manageable units of time.
- It gives you a "global" view of your report project, an overall sense of the contents, parts and organization of the report.

Generating Outline Elements

If you go through a brainstorming process, you have generated a rough list of topics that you can start working with. The topic list below concerns cocombustion, which is the incineration of municipal solid waste (MSW) with conventional fuels to reduce conventional fuel consumption costs and related MSW disposal problems. Imagine that you had developed a topic list on this subject and then had narrowed the list to these topics:

1. Advantages of cocombustion
2. Steps in cocombusting MSW
3. Disadvantages of cocombustion
4. Historical background on cocombustion
5. Economics of cocombustion
6. Special components for cocombustion
7. Composition of MSW
8. Cocombustion power plant construction costs
9. Cocombustion power plant operating costs
10. Economic advantages of cocombustion
11. Environmental advantages of cocombustion
12. Characteristics of municipal solid waste (MSW)
13. Environmental disadvantages of cocombustion
14. Methods of MSW disposal

You can tell that the list above needs serious help:

- You can see that a number of topics involve advantages and disadvantages; these might be combined in a more general outline called Advantages and Disadvantages of Cocombustion. The specific related topics would be *subordinated* beneath this more general topic: Advantages and Disadvantages of Cocombustion
  - Advantages of cocombustion
  - Disadvantages of cocombustion
- But wait a minute! One of the advantages has to do with economics. So we could create another group: Economics of cocombustion
  - Economic advantages of cocombustion
  - Cocombustion power plant construction costs
  - Cocombustion power plant operating costs
- So what do we do with environmental advantages of cocombustion and environmental disadvantages of cocombustion? It might be best to create a higher-level heading environmental aspects of cocombustion and subordinate those other two beneath it. And so that means we no longer need Advantages and Disadvantages of Cocombustion. It has been split into an economics group and an environment group.
- Looking further at the rough list of topics, you can probably see that Steps in cocombusting MSW, Special components for cocombustion, Composition of MSW, Characteristics of municipal solid waste (MSW) are related to each other and should exist in their own area of the outline.

So this is how the business of generating, grouping, combining and subordinating works early in the outlining process. Outlining is a messy process so you'll probably come back to this phase again.

Sequencing Outline Elements

The next step in outlining is to sequence the items appropriately. There are so many different patterns of sequencing that only most common ones can be reviewed here. And, frankly, these are all pretty obvious. If they are obvious to you, skip to Elaborating the rough outline.

Chronological sequencing. One of the most common patterns in outlining is the chronological one. In a historical background section of an outline, the chronological approach is just about the only one you can use. Here is an outline excerpt concerning the historical background of nuclear research:

- Historical background of nuclear research
  - Becquerel's theory of radition in uranium (1896)
  - The work of the Curies (*far*)
  - The work of Rutherford (*past*)
    - Demonstration of the internal structure of the atom (1911)
    - Transmutation of atoms (1919)
  - Development of technology to study atomic structure
    - Cascade transformer (1928)
    - Linear accelerator (1931)
    - Cyclotron (1932)
    - Betatron (1940)
  - Hahn-Strassmann discovery of uranium fission (1938
  - Oppenheimer work on nuclea chain reactions (*near* (1940s) *past*)
  - Explosion of the first atomic bomb (1945)

In some outlines, however, you almost don't notice the chronological pattern. For example, effects come after causes; solutions, after problems; or findings, after research method. The chronological pattern is most important in a research proposal outline:

- Introduction
  - Historical background on caffeine studies (*past*)
  - Objectives of the study

- o Limitations of the study
- o Plan of development
- Review of the literature on caffeine
- Experimental method to be used
- Results of the tests
- Discussion of the results
- Summary and conclusions
- Implications for further research (*future*)

Chronologically, the researcher first defines the problem, the reviews the literature on the problem, plans a research method, conducts the research and gathers data, analyzes the data and draws conclusions from it. Afterward, she may consider areas for further research on the problem. At-rest to in-motion sequence. Another common outlining pattern is to start with an object at rest, motionless as if in a photograph, and then to move to a discussion of it in operation, in action as if in a motion picture.

II.   Basic Components of Wind-Powered Electrical Systems
    A.   Rotor (*motionless*)
    B.   Generator
    C.   Tower
III. Basic Operation of Wind-Powered Electrical Systems
    A.   Wind energy into mechanical energy
    B.   Mechanical energy into electrical (*in motion*) energy
    C.   Stabilization of electrical energy
    D.   Conversion to household current

Specific to general sequence. Some outlines move from a specific, close-up focus to a more general, panoramic focus. They seem to start with a microscope, examining the minute details of a subject, and end with a telescope, considering the subject from a distance in relation to other things. (This pattern can also be reversed.)

I.   Introduction
II.   Characteristics of municipal solid waste (MSW)
III. Methods of disposal of MSW (*microscrope*)
IV.   Processing municipa solid waste
V.   Plant modifications for cocombustion
VI.   Advantages of cocombusting MSW
    A.   Environmental advantages
    B.   Economic advantages (*telescope*)
VII. Case studies of three cocombustion plants

In this next outline, the focus broadens after part III, changing to aspects related to computerized voice recognition technology:

II.   Introduction
III. Human voice production
    A.   The generation of sound
    B.   Factors affecting the human (*microscope*) voice
IV.   Components of the isolated word recognition system
    A.   The preprocessor
    B.   The feature extractor
    C.   Components in the classification phase
    D.   Decision algorithms
V.   Problems with computerized speech recognition
    A.   Accuracy
    B.   Limited vocabulary size
    C.   Privacy
VI.   Applications of voice recognition systems
    A.   Data entry
    B.   Mobility

C. Security
D. Telephone access
E. Devices for the handicapped (*telescope*)
VII. Current availability of speech recognition systems
VIII. The future of the computerized speech recognition industry

Rhetorical sequence. Elements in outlines can also be arranged rhetorically, in other words, according to what is most effective for the reader. Here are some examples of rhetorical patterns:

I. Simple to complex
II. Least important to most important (or vice versa)
III. Least controversial to most controversial
IV. Most convincing to least convincing (or vice versa)
V. Most interesting to least interesting

This list is by no means complete, but you can see that elements in it are arranged according to impact on the reader—that is, the impact the writer would like to have. Here are some excerpts of outlines where these patterns are used.

If you have ever studied computer programming, you know that commands like PRINT are simple; variable assignment commands (like LET A = 30), less simple; and FOR-NEXT loop statements, rather complex. If you were outlining a report on fundamental BASIC commands for the beginner, you'd probably start with the simple ones and work your way to the complex:

Simple-to-Complex Order

I. USEFUL BASIC COMMANDS
A. PRINT
B. LET
C. IF-THEN
D. FOR-NEXT
E. DIM

An obvious outlining principle is to avoid creating interruptions within an outline sequence. Here's an example:

Outline Excerpt with Interruption

- Municipal solid waste generated in the US
  - Total amounts of MSW
    - Increases since 1950
    - Projected increases to the year 2000
  - Processing MSW for cocombustion
    - Primary storage
    - Grinding
    - Air sorting
    - Magnetic separating
    - Screening
    - Secondary storage
  - Characteristics of MSW
    - Composition of MSW
      - food waste
      - paper and other rubbish
      - noncombustibles
    - Factors affecting energy content
      - moisture content
      - areas of MSW origination
- Power plant modifications for cocombustion

III.   Municipal solid waste generated in the US
    A.   Total amounts of MSW
       I.   Increases since 1950
       II.   Projected increases to the year 2000
    B.   Characteristics of MSW
       I.   Composition of MSW
          I.   food waste
          II.   paper and other rubbish
          III.   noncombustibles
       II.   Factors affecting energy content
          I.   moisture content
          II.   areas of MSW origination
IV.   Processing MSW for cocombustion
    A.   Primary storage
    B.   Grinding
    C.   Air sorting
    D.   Magnetic separating
    E.   Screening
    F.   Secondary storage
V.   Power plant modifications for cocombustion

In the problem version, the municipal solid waste discussion is interrupted by the MSW-processing discussion. A better arrangement would be to discuss MSW fully before going on to the discussion of how it is processed. Use these common arrangement principles to get your topic list into an initial rough order. The rearranged version of the topic list shown previously might look this way:

I.   Historical background
    A.   Rising energy, utility costs
    B.   Search for alternatives (review)
II.   Composition of MSW
III.   Special components of the cocombustion plant
IV.   Steps in the cocombustion of MSW
V.   Economics
    A.   Cost to build or convert
    B.   Cost to operate
    C.   Cost of produced electricity
VI.   Advantages
    A.   Less coal used
    B.   Reduction of utility rates
    C.   Less landfill used
    D.   Reduction of landfill costs and needs
VII.   Disadvantages
    A.   Expense of converting existing facilities
    B.   Handling MSW
    C.   Increased emissions

Electronic Note-Taking Methods

As of 2015, the writing-teaching world—at least at the college level and in terms of textbooks—is seriously behind in terms of what it knows and what it teaches about note-taking for major writing projects. Strangely, the very best writing resource on the Internet, the Purdue OWL, has nothing on note-taking. Read the following section Traditional Note-Taking Methods for a review of just what good *any* note-taking system is.

Until we get our act together, consider how the traditional note-taking system is implemented in software applications.

A number of software applications are available that support note-taking and related tasks: Evernote, EasyBib, NoodleTools, and more. Their basic functions are similar so let's use NoodleTools. It has a nice set of YouTube videos that walk you through the main phases of its use:

How do I create a new project? This video takes you from the very start!

NoodleTools—Creating Outlines. If you've created good notecards, creating the outline from them is easy, as this video shows.

NoodleTools-Works Cited. If you've created good notecards, creating the bibliography from them is also easy.

Traditional Note-Taking Methods

When you've located the right sources of information for your report, it's time to start gathering the right information from them and developing it into a report. In other words, it's time to start reading, summarizing, paraphrasing, interviewing, measuring, calculating, and developing information any other way your report project requires. The technical report may be one of the largest writing projects that you've ever tackled: you may wonder how you are going to do all that reading and remember all that information. Concerning the reading, here are several suggestions:

I. Develop as specific an outline as you can: it shows you what information you must gather and, as importantly, what information you can ignore.
II. Use the indexes, tables of contents, and headings within chapters to read books selectively for just the information you need.
III. Divide your work into manageable, hour-long chunks (make progress rather than relying on big blocks of weekend or vacation time).

As for remembering the information you gather for your report, the most practical suggestion is to use some form of note-taking. Note-taking refers to any system for collecting and storing information until you can use it in the report. Note-taking involves the skills of summarizing, paraphrasing, or quoting. A good system of note-taking is one that enables you to gather a large amount of information over a long period of time and to be able to use that information without having forgotten it or lost it in the meantime.

Traditional Note-Taking Process: An Overview

In the traditional system of taking notes for a long report, you:

I. Develop a rough outline.
II. Do any preliminary reading necessary to construct a rough outline.
III. Locate your information sources, and make bibliography cards for each source.
IV. Take the actual notes on index cards.
V. Label each notecard according to its place in the outline.
VI. Provide bibliographic information on each notecard.
VII. Change or add extra detail to the outline as the note-taking process continues.
VIII. Check off the areas of the outline for which sufficient notes have been taken.

When you have taken sufficient notes to cover all parts of an outline, you transcribe the information from the notecards into a rough draft, filling in details, adding transitions, and providing your own acquired understanding of the subject as you write. Naturally, you may discover gaps in your notes and have to go back and take more notes.

Developing the Rough Outline

As the section on outlining emphasizes, you must have a working outline before you begin gathering information. The rough outline shows you which specific topics to gather information on and which ones to ignore. Think of the outline as a series of questions.

If you don't have a good, specific outline, the sky is the limit on how many notes you can take. Think of the outline as a set of boxes that you fill up with the information you collect as you do your research for the report:

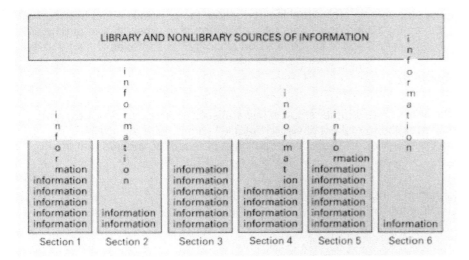

Figure 2: Gathering information and taking notes: you continue gathering information from the various sources until all the boxes are filled.

Information on the Bibliography Cards

On the bibliography cards you should record information that enables you or your readers to locate the books, articles, reports, and other sources. Remember that you'll use this information to create the bibliography or list of references for your report. The section on documentation shows you details on the information to record on many different types of sources, but remember these general guidelines:

- For books, record the "facts of publication": the city of publication, the publisher, and the date of publication.
- For magazines, record the title of the magazine, the date of issue of the specific magazine, and the beginning and ending page numbers of the article.
- For encyclopedia articles, record the edition number and date of the encyclopedia, and look up the authors' initials.
- For government documents, disregard the authors' names, use the department, administration, or agency name as the author, and copy the cataloguing number.
- For any private sources of information you use, for example, interviews or letters, record the date of the communication, the source's full name, title, and organization with which he or she is affiliated.

Information on the Notecards

In the traditional note-taking system, a notecard typically looks like this:

BWR—fuel rod (III,A,1,b) fuel rod material—Zircaloy (same as PWR fuel rod) 148 in. long X 0.493 in. diam. slightly longer >' PWR fuel rod 16 D, 749

This notecard has the following features:

1. A word, phrase, or number that indicates where it fits into the outline (the "locator").
2. Bibliographic information: that is, an abbreviation for the source of the note (book, article, etc.) and a page number.
3. The note itself, the information that will go into the report.
4. A number that indicates the notecard's place in the final arrangement of all the notecards.

Locator. The "locator" phrase or number tells you where the note fits into the outline, that is, when and where you'll use this information in the report. Locaters must be updated regularly. As you read, take notes, and learn more about your subject, you can flesh out, or "elaborate," your outline more and more, subdividing it into third, fourth, and even fifth levels.

Bibliographic information. Each notecard must also contain bibliographic information, those details about the source of the note: the author, title, page number, and so on. Rather than write all such information on each notecard, use abbreviations: assign a letter to each source, and keep track of the sources on bibliography cards, as shown above.

Methods of Recording Information on Notecards

The actual information that you record on the index card is rather small: a few statistics or a sentence or two, and not much else. You take such small bits of information to make it easier to "shuffle" your notecards into the sequence in which you'll use them in writing the rough draft. There are three ways of recording the information on notecards:

- Directly quoting it, copying the information directly from the source word-for-word
- Paraphrasing it, retaining the full detail of the information but in your own words
- Summarizing it, condensing the main points in the information in your own words

See what the Purdue OWL has to say about these methods.

Direct quotation. In most technical reports, direct quotation is needed only for the following situations:

- Statements by important or well-known authorities or leaders
- Controversial statements you do not want attributed to you
- Statements expressed in unusual, vivid, or memorable language

Here is an example notecard with a direct quotation:

Myers, author of *The Nuclear Power Debate* and somewhat of a supporter of nuclear, emphs heavy inspect and penalties: During the period between July 1, 1975 and September 30, 1976 the NRC listed 1,611 items of noncompliance. Only six of these were considered serious violations, 923 were classi- fied as infractions, and 682 were noted as deficiencies. The NRC issued fines to ten utilities totaling $172,250 between July 1, 1975 and December 15, 1976. NRC officials report that the limited use of fines and the efforts to get industry to regulate itself have worked. "By and large," one NRC offi- cial told IRRC, "I think our enforcement program is working." H, 46

When you copy a direct quotation onto a notecard, remember to do a few extra things that will save time and frustration later on:

- Write a lead-in to introduce the quotation, citing the author's name and any other important information about the author.
- Write a brief explanation, interpretation, or comment on the quotation you've just copied.

There are essentially two types of direct quotation: "block" quotations and "running" quotations. Here is an example of a block quotation (any quotation over 3 lines long, which is indented):

In Myers' view, the nuclear power industry has every reason to comply with the NRC's regulations to the very letter: The NRC issues an order to shut down or imposes civil fines only after repeated violations have in- dicated what the NRC considers "a pattern of non- compliance." The NRC argues that, particularly with power plants, civil penalties are unnecessary for the most part. "The greatest penalty," one official said, "is to require the plant to shut down, forcing it to buy replacement power (often at a cost of $100,000 to $200,000 per day) elsewhere. A civil penalty's largest cost—the NRC is limited to a $5,000-per-violation ceiling per 30 days—is the stigma attached to it." (8:46) The "stigma" refers to the fact that, once a nuclear power plant is fined, it will likely be the target of public con- cern and even more stringent and frequent NRC inspection.

"Running" quotations are direct quotations that are trimmed down and worked into the regular sentences of a report. Notice how much smoother and more efficient the running quotation is in the revised version below:

Ineffective direct quotation: There are two types of light water reactors: the pressurized water reactor and the boiling water reactor. LWRs of both types convert heat to electricity with an efficiency of about 32 percent—significantly less than the best fossil-fueled plants, although about equal to the national average for all thermal electricity generation [13:438]. As for harnessing the energy potential of uranium, LWRs are estimated to average only between 0.5 and 1.0 percent.

Revision with running quotation: There are two types of light water reactors: the pressurized water reactor and the boiling water reactor. According to Paul Ehrlich, who has been a consistent critic of nuclear power, both these types of LWRs "convert heat to electricity with an efficiency of about 32 percent—significantly less than the best fossil-fueled plants, although about equal to the national average for all thermal electricity generation" (13:438). As for harnessing the energy potential of uranium, LWRs are estimated to average only between 0.5 and 1.0 percent.

When you use direct quotations in your report, keep these guidelines in mind.

- Using ellipsis in direct quotations. The three dots "..." show that words are omitted from the sentence. The brackets "[ ]" indicate changes made by the writer using the quotation so that it would read as good English and make sense.
- Never use "free-floating" quotations in reports. Always "attribute" direct quotations; that is, explain who made the quoted statement. Notice how this is done in Figure 6.
- Always provide adequate introduction for direct quotations and explain their meaning and importance to your readers. Notice how the block quotation above on NRC penalties (a) prepares the reader for the quotation, and, afterwards, (b) provides interpretive comment, on the meaning of the word "stigma" in particular.
- Use indented or "block" quotations whenever a direct quotation goes over three lines long. With any lengthy quotation, make sure that it is important enough to merit direct quotation.
- Whenever possible, "trim" the quotation so that it will fit into your own writing.
- Punctuate direct quotations correctly. You can see the rules for punctuating direct quotations.
- Use ellipses to shorten direct quotations. When you do, however, make sure that the resulting quotation reads as good English.
- Use direct quotations only when necessary: if the passage doesn't fit one of the reasons for direct quotation cited at the beginning of this section, paraphrase or summarize it instead.

Paraphrasing. In technical-report writing, usually the better approach to note-taking is to paraphrase. When you paraphrase, you convey the information fact-by-fact, idea-by-idea, and point-by-point in your own words. The writer of the original passage ought to be able to read your paraphrase and say that it is precisely what she or he had meant. Here are some example paraphrased notecards:

BWR—fuel assembly (III,A,1,3) fuel assembly—63 f rods spaced, supported in a sq (8 x 8) arrangement by upper + lower plate 3 kinds: (a) tie rods; (b) water rod); (c) stand f rods 3rd, 6th f rods on a bundle's outer edge act as tie rods the 8 tie rods screw into castg of lower tie plate water rod: acts as spacer support rod, as source of moderator material close to the center of f bundle K, 2001

BWR—fuel assem (III,A,1,3) fuel channel—enclosure for f bundle; f bundle + f channel make up fuel assem is a tube with a square shape, made of Zircaloy dimensions: 5.518 in. X 5.518 in. X 166.9 in. function: channel core coolt thru f bundle and guide control rods K, 2001

Paraphrases are necessary and preferable for a number of reasons:

- You paraphrase because the content of the passage is so important to your report that you need every bit of it.
- When you paraphrase, you adjust the wording of the original to meet the needs of your audience, the purpose of your report, and your own writing style. In other words, you "translate" other writers' material into your own.

- A report of mostly direct quotations would be hard to read.
- Readers tend to skip over direct quotations, particularly long ones.
- One final reason for paraphrasing: you are actually writing bits of the rough draft of your report as you paraphrase.

Here is an example of an original passage and its paraphrases, with the unique wording of the original (which must be changed in the paraphrase) underlined.

Original passage: About a third of light-water reactors operating or under construction in the United States are boiling-water reactors. The distinguishing characteristic of a BWR is that the reactor vessel itself serves as the boiler of the nuclear steam supply system. This vessel is by far the major component in the reactor building, and the steam it produces passes directly to the turbogenerator. The reactor building also contains emergency core cooling equipment, a major part of which is the pressure suppression pool which is an integral part of the containment structure. . . . . earlier BWRs utilized a somewhat different containment and pressure suppression system. All the commercial BWRs sold in the United States have been designed and built by General Electric. Several types of reactors that use boiling water in pressure tubes have been considered, designed, or built. In a sense, they are similar to the CANDU, described in Chapter 7, which uses pressure tubes and separates the coolant and moderator. The CANDU itself can be designed to use boiling light water as its coolant. The British steam-generating heavy-water reactor has such a system. Finally, the principal reactor type now being constructed in the Soviet Union uses a boiling-water pressure tube design, but with carbon moderator. Anthony V. Nero, *A Guidebook to Nuclear Reactors*, Berkeley: University of California Press, 1979.

Paraphrased version: Boiling water reactors, according to Anthony V. Nero in his *Guidebook to Nuclear Reactors*, either completed or constructed, make up about one third of the light-water reactors in the U.S. The most important design feature of the BWR is that the reactor vessel itself acts as the nuclear steam supply system. The steam this important component generates goes directly to the turbogenerator. Important, too, in this de- sign is the emergency core cooling equipment, which is housed with the reactor vessel in the reactor building. One of the main components of this equipment is the pressure suppression pool. The containment and pressure suppression system currently used in BWRs has evolved since the early BWR designs. General Electric is the sole designer and builder of these BWRs in the U.S. The different kinds of reactors that use boiling water in pressure tubes are similar to the CANDU, which separates coolant and moderator and uses pressure tubes, also. CANDU can also use boiling light water as a coolant. The British have designed a reactor generated steam from heavy water that uses just such a system. Also, the Soviets have developed and are now building as their main type of reactor a boiling pressure tube design that uses carbon as the moderator. [12:232]

Guide for writing and using paraphrases

Here are some guidelines to remember when paraphrasing:

- In most cases, paraphrase rather than use direct quotation.
- Avoid the distinctive wording of the original passage.
- Do not interpret, criticize, or select from the original passage.
- Include bibliographic information on the author, source, and page numbers.
- In the rough draft, cite the author's name and other important details about her or him just as you would if were quoting directly. In Figure 9, notice how the paraphrased author's name is given early.
- Refer to the paraphrased author in such a way to make it clear where the paraphrase begins and ends. (See Figure 9.)
- Document a paraphrase just as you would a direct quotation. Mark the area of the paraphrase by citing the paraphrased author's name at the beginning of the paraphrase and by inserting a footnote or parenthetical reference at the end. (Again, see Figure 9.)
- See what the Purdue OWL has to say about paraphrasing.

Summary. Summaries are usually much shorter than their originals. A summary concentrates on only those points or ideas in a passage that are important. Unlike in a paraphrase, the information in a summary can be rearranged. Here is a passage from which summaries below will be taken:

Numerous systems are available for controlling abnormalities [in boiling water reactors]. In the event that control rods cannot be inserted, liquid neutron absorber (containing a boron compound) may be injected into the reactor to shut down the chain reaction. Heat removal systems are available for cooling the core in the event the drywell is isolated from the main cooling systems. Closely related to the heat removal systems are injection systems for coping with decreases in coolant inventory.

Both abnormalities associated with the turbine system and actual loss of coolant accidents can lead closing of the steam and feedwater lines, effectively isolating the reactor vessel within the drywell. Whenever the vessel is isolated, and indeed whenever feedwater is lost, a reactor core isolation cooling system is available to maintain coolant inventory by pumping water into the reactor via connections in the pressure vessel head. This system operates at normal pressures and initially draws water from tanks that store condensate from the turbine, from condensate from the residual heat removal system, or if necessary, from the suppression pool.

A network of systems performs specific ECC [emergency core cooling] functions to cope with LOCAs [loss-of-coolant accidents]. (See Figure 6.) These all depend on signals indicating low water level in the pressure vessel or high pressure in the drywell, or both.

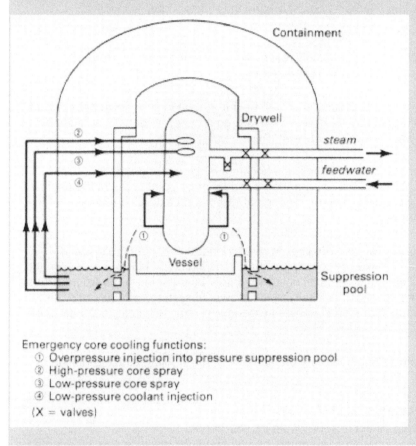

Emergency core cooling functions:
① Overpressure injection into pressure suppression pool
② High-pressure core spray
③ Low-pressure core spray
④ Low-pressure coolant injection
(X = valves)

BWR emergency core cooling systems

The systems include low-pressure injection, utilization of the RHR system, and high- and low-pressure core spray systems. The high-pressure core spray in intended to lower the pressure within the pressure vessel and provide makeup water in the event of a LOCA. In the event the core is uncovered, the spray can directly cool the fuel assemblies. Water is taken from the condensate tanks and from the suppression pool. On the other hand, should it become necessary to use low-pressure systems, the vessel must be depressurized. This depressurization can be accomplished by opening relief valves to blow down the vessel contents into the drywell (and hence the suppression pool). Once this action is completed, the low-pressure core spray may be used to cool the fuel assemblies (drawing water from the suppression pool) or RHR low-pressure injection (again from the sup- pression pool) may be initiated, or both. The RHR system may also be used simply to cool the suppression pool. (Two other functions of the RHR are to provide decay heat removal under ordinary shutdown conditions and, when necessary, to supplement the cooling system for the spent fuel pool and the upper containment pool.)

Anthony V. Nero, *A Guidebook to Nuclear Reactors*, Berkeley: Univ. of California Press, 1979, pp. 104-107.

Sentence-length summaries. Often summaries are only a sentence long. To create sentence-length summaries, use one or a combination of the following methods:

Locate a sentence or two in the original passage that summarizes the information that you want, and simply rewrite it in your own words. Find the sentence in the third paragraph of the original that is the basis for this summary:

BWR—safety sys (IV,B,2) The systems that perform emergency core cooling functions in loss-of-coolant accidents include low-pressure injection, utilization of the RHR system, and high- and low-pressure core spray systems. I, 104

If no individual sentence will work, locate several sentences that contain the right information, and combine them. (This summary sentence is built from paragraphs 1 and 2 of Figure 10.)

BWR—safety sys (IV,B,2) In case of problems with control rods or loss of coolant, BWRs use an absorber to stop the reaction or emergency systems to replenish and maintain coolant around the reactor core, respectively. I, 104-107

Sometimes, the summary sentence is like a new sentence, scarcely resembling any in the original. Here is a different summary sentence on the passage above; notice how new it seems:

BWR—safety sys (IV,B,2) If the control rods malfunction, a substance can be introduced to shut down the reaction altogether, and if water is prevented from reaching the reactor core, BWRs are equipped with backup sources of coolant that can be sprayed or injected into the pressure vessel. I, 104-107

Extended summaries. A summary can be longer than a single sentence because of the important information contained in the original passage. (Remember, however, that a paraphrase is a point-by-point recap of the original, while the summary is a selection, reordering and condensation of the original.) Here's an extended summary of the passage above on BWR emergency safety systems:

Boiling water reactors use numerous systems to control abnormalities in reactor operations. If a problem with control rods occurs, a liquid neutron absorber can be injected to halt the chain reaction. If coolant is cut off from the reactor core, a reactor core isolation cooling system can maintain coolant inventory by pumping water from various storage areas. This system includes low-pressure injection, the residual heat removal system, and the high- and low-pressure core spray systems. The water supply for these various emergency systems ultimately come from the suppression pool.

Whenever you summarize, you must handle the resulting summary the same way you would a direct quotation or paraphrase.

- Cite the name of the author and other important information about that author.
- Document that summary using whichever system is appropriate for your report.
- If it is an extended summary, make it clear where that summary begins and ends, for example, by referring to the author's name at the beginning and placing a footnote or parenthetical reference at the end.

Plagiarism. If you follow the guidelines presented in the preceding, plagiarism should not be a problem at all, but make sure you understand what it is. Plagiarism refers to two kinds of theft:

Reports with plagiarized information are often easy to spot for several reasons:

- Plagiarism is the practice—whether deliberate or not—in which a writer borrows other people's facts, ideas, or concepts and presents them as if they were her or his own.
- Plagiarism is also the practice—again whether deliberate or not—in which a writer uses other writers' exact words without quotation marks.
- In all cases, plagiarism is the lack of proper documentation: documentation refers to any system of footnoting or reference that indicates the author and source of the borrowed information.

- A reader may recognize the ideas or facts in the report as those of someone else. An expert in a field of knowledge can spot this theft of information right away.
- A reader may realize that the report writer could not possibly have developed certain information in the report. If a writer who is at the beginning of his studies sounds like an advanced physicist, something is fishy.
- Most readers can also spot a sudden change in the style or tone of the language of a report. Most people's writing style is as readily identifiable as their voices over the telephone.

Plagiarism is bad business: the plagiarizer can fail an academic course or lose his or her reputation among business and professional associates. It only takes simple documentation to transform a report with plagiarized material in it into one with legally borrowed material. The section on documentation explains these procedures in detail.

Updating the Outline

As you take notes, you must regularly update the locators on all your notecards because as you read, take notes, and learn more about your technical subject, your outline may either change or become more specific. Imagine that you started with this excerpt of a rough outline and had taken these notecards:

Rough Sketch Outline

- Safety Measures
    - Pressurized Water Reactor Safety Measures
    - Boiling Water Reactor Safety Systems
    - Role of the Nuclear Regulatory Commision

Corresponding Notecards

BWR—safety sys. (IV,B) safety sys incl control rods, containmt bldg, resid heat removl sys there work like those in PWR unique to BWR: drywell, emergency core coolg sys 1 I, 100

BWR—safety sys (IV,B) drywell—encloses react vess + assoc equip (includes recirc sys, press relief valves on main steam lines) 2 I, 100

BWR—safety sys (IV,B) emergency core coolg sys—handles loss-of-coolt accidents; includes reactor core iso sys, hi- press core spray sys, lo-press core spray sys (figure for this, p.106) 3 I, 105-6

BWR—safety sys (IV,B) react core iso coolg sys: if loss-of-coolt accidt (causg closing of steam lines,feedwtr lines to react vessel), RCICS activated (maintains coolt inventory by pumpg water to reactor via connex in press vess head 4 I, 104

BWR—safety sys (IV,B) hi-press core spray: lowers press w/in press vessel, provides suppl water in loss-of-coolt accidt. with uncovered cores, spray directly cools fuel assemblies (wtr fr condensed wtr storge tanks + suppress pool 5 I, 104

Revised Outline

- Safety Measures
    - Pressurized Water Reactor Safety Measures
    - Boiling Water Reactor Safety Systems
        - The Drywell
        - Emergency Core Cooling Systems
            - Reactor core isolation cooling system

- High-pressure core spray

Notice that all five of these notecards are about "IV. B. Boiling Water Reactor Safety Systems." Notecard 1 divides this safety system into the drywell and the emergency core cooling systems. This division produces "1" and "2" under "B." Notecards 3 through 5, about the subsystems making up the emergency systems, produce "a," "b," and "c" under "2."

If you had taken these notes and updated your outline, you would revise the locators on the individual notecards like this:

Notecard Original Updated Alternate no. locators locators locators 1 IV. B same Safety/Boil.Wtr.React. 2 IV. B IV. B. 1 Safety/BWR/drywell 3 IV. B IV. B. 2 Safety/BWR/Em.Cor.Cool. 4 IV. B IV. B. 2. a Saf./BWR/Em.Cor.Cool/ React.Cor.Cool. 5 IV. B IV. B. 2. b Saf./BWR/Em.Cor.Cool./ Hi.Pres.Cor.Spray

Remember that if you don't like the number-combinations as locators, you can substitute short phrases, as is shown in the alternate locators above.

Final Stages in the Notetaking Process

As you take notes, check off sections of your outline for which you gather sufficient information, as is done in this outline excerpt. In this example, the writer has taken sufficient notes for much of IV.B. but still needs information for the rest of the outline.

IV.   Boiling Water Reactors
    A.   Description of the Basic Components
        I.   Core
            I.   core
            II.   fuel
            III.   fuel rod
            IV.   fuel assembly
        II.   Control Rods
        III.   Core Shrouds and Reactor Vessel
        IV.   Recirculation System
        V.   Steam Separators
        VI.   Steam Dryers
    B.   Production of Electricity
        I.   Circulating Water
        II.   Separating Steam
        III.   Drying the Steam
        IV.   Producing Electricity
V.   Safety Measures
    A.   Pressurized Water Reactor Safety Measures
        I.   Residual Heat Removal System
        II.   Emergency Core Cooling Systems
            I.   passive system
            II.   low-pressure injection systems
            III.   high-pressure injection systems
        III.   Containment Building
    B.   Boiling Water Reactor Safety Systems
        I.   The Drywell
        II.   Emergency Core Cooling Systems
            I.   reactor core isolation cooling system
            II.   high-pressure core spray
            III.   low-pressure core spray
        III.   Role of the Nuclear Regulatory Commission
    C.   Role of the Nuclear Regulatory Commission
VI.   Economic Aspects of Light Water Reactors
    A.   Busbar Cost

I.	Construction Cost	
II.	Operation and Maintenance Costs	
III.	Fuel Costs	
B.	Operating Capacity	
	I.	Availability Factor
	II.	Capacity Factor

In the final step in notetaking, you arrange the notecards in the order that you'll use them as you write the rough draft. Read through your cards several times to make sure the sequence is right and that there are no gaps in the information you've gathered. When you're sure that the order is right, write sequence numbers on each of the cards to preserve the order (see the sequence numbers on the notecards in the next section). With the notecards in the right order and numbered, you are ready to write the first draft, which is discussed in the section on rough drafting.

Other Systems of Notetaking

There are plenty of other ways to take notes. The main point of any form of note-taking of course is to make your report work easier and less time-consuming. You may prefer some other note-taking system because of your own work style or because of your report project. Or, you may end up using some other system in combination with the traditional one. Any system that enables you to get your work done efficiently is a good one.

IV. Mental notetaking. With short reports, it is possible to remember all the information and not writing any of it down is possible. But few of us are able to remember all of the information for long, highly technical reports.

V. Book marks. If you use only a few articles or books, you can mark the important passages with slips of paper and write the rough draft with them. If you have many books and articles, this approach can get to be quite chaotic.

VI. Photocopying. You can also photocopy everything you think you need in your report. With the photocopied pages, you highlight the important passages, or cut out the important passages and paste them on notecards. Two problems with this approach are that (a) you may photocopy many unnecessary pages and waste money and (b) you still have the job of paraphrasing and summarizing ahead of you. Still, this is a system some report writers use occasionally to supplement their more traditional note-taking procedures.

VII. Exploratory drafts. If you are already familiar with your report subject, you can try writing a rough skeletal draft to show you what information you need. You may discover that all you lack is specific names, statistics, or terminology. You can take notes and plug the information into the draft. Writing the exploratory draft shows you what you know and don't know.

VIII. Notetaking by the source. If you have only a few sources, you can also use one other fairly common system of notetaking:

    A. You take notes from individual sources onto long sheets of paper rather than onto notecards.

    B. You take all the information you need from the source onto as many sheets of paper as necessary; you don't split it up into bits of information on separate notecards.

    C. At the top of each notesheet, you give full bibliographic information on the book or article.

    D. Throughout each notesheet, you indicate the exact pages the information comes from.

    E. Also, you label these pages of notes with locators, the letter-number combinations from the outline.

    F. You mark off sections of the outline as you gather sufficient information for them.

    G. In some cases, you can cut up these full-page notes and actually handle them as if they were notecards. Here is an example sheet of notes using this approach:

In this system, the source (book, article, report, etc.) is indicated at the top of the page; the page numbers are indicated down the right margin in parentheses; and the sheet of notes is keyed to the outline down the left margin in parentheses.

By: David McMurrey

Objectives

Upon completion of this chapter, readers will be able to:

III. Identify the four common categories of audience and explain the differences between them.
IV. Analyze your audience and explain how to tailor your writing to that audience.

Introduction to the Audience Analysis

The audience of a technical report—or any piece of writing for that matter—is the intended or potential reader or readers. For most technical writers, this is the most important consideration in planning, writing, and reviewing a document. You "adapt" your writing to meet the needs, interests, and background of the readers who will be reading your writing.

The principle seems absurdly simple and obvious. It's much the same as telling someone, "Talk so the person in front of you can understand what you're saying." It's like saying, "Don't talk rocket science to your six-year-old." Do we need a course in that? Doesn't seem like it. But, in fact, lack of audience analysis and adaptation is one of the root causes of most of the problems you find in professional, technical documents—particularly instructions where it surfaces most glaringly.

Note: Once you've read this chapter on audience analysis, try using the audience planner below. You fill in blanks with answers to questions about your audience and then e-mail it to yourself. Use the audience planner for any writing project as a way of getting yourself to think about your audience in detail.

Audience Planner

Types of Audiences

One of the first things to do when you analyze an audience is to identify its type (or types—it's rarely just one type). The common division of audiences into categories is as follows:

- **Experts**: These are the people who know the theory and the product inside and out. They designed it, they tested it, they know everything about it. Often, they have advanced degrees and operate in academic settings or in research and development areas of the government and technology worlds. The nonspecialist reader is least likely to understand what these people are saying—but also has the least reason to try. More often, the communication challenge faced by the expert is communicating to the technician and the executive.
- **Technicians**: These are the people who build, operate, maintain, and repair the stuff that the experts design and theorize about. Theirs is a highly technical knowledge as well, but of a more practical nature.
- **Executives**: These are the people who make business, economic, administrative, legal, governmental, and/or political decisions on the stuff that the experts and technicians work with. If it's a new product, they decide whether to produce and market it. If it's a new power technology, they decide whether the city should implement it. Executives are likely to have as little technical knowledge about the subject as nonspecialists.
- **Nonspecialists**: These readers have the least technical knowledge of all. Their interest may be as practical as technicians', but in a different way. They want to use the new product to accomplish their tasks; they want to understand the new power technology enough to know whether to vote for or against it in the upcoming bond election. Or, they may just be curious about a specific technical matter and want to learn about it—but for no specific, practical reason.

Audience Analysis

It's important to determine which of the four categories just discussed the potential readers of your document belong to, but that's not the end of it. Audiences, regardless of category, must also be analyzed in terms of characteristics such as the following:

1. **Background—knowledge, experience, training**: One of your most important concerns is just how much knowledge, experience, or training you can expect in your readers. If you expect some of your readers to lack certain background, do you automatically supply it in your document? Consider an example: imagine you're writing a guide to using a software product that runs under Microsoft Windows. How much can you expect your readers to know about Windows? If some are likely to know little about Windows, should you provide that information? If you say no, then you run the risk of customers' getting frustrated with your product. If you say yes to adding background information on Windows, you increase your work effort and add to the page count of the document (and thus to the cost). Obviously, there's no easy answer to this question—part of the answer may involve just how small a segment of the audience needs that background information.

2. **Needs and interests**: To plan your document, you need to know what your audience is going to expect from that document. Imagine how readers will want to use your document and what will they demand from it. For example, imagine you are writing a manual on how to use a new smart phone—what are your readers going to expect to find in it? Imagine you're under contract to write a background report on global warming for a national real estate association—what do they want to read about; and, equally important, what do they not want to read about?

3. **Other demographic characteristics**: And of course there are many other characteristics about your readers that might have an influence on how you should design and write your document—for example, age groups, type of residence, area of residence, gender, political preferences, and so on.

Audience analysis can get complicated by at least three other factors: mixed audience types for one document, wide variability within audience, and unknown audiences.

- **More than one audience**. You're likely to find that your report is for more than one audience. For example, it may be seen by technical people (experts and technicians) and administrative people (executives). What do you do? You can either write all the sections so that all the audiences of your document can understand them (good luck!). Or you can write each section strictly for the audience that would be interested in it, then use headings and section introductions to alert your audience about where to go and what to avoid in your report.

- **Wide variability in an audience**. You may realize that, although you have an audience that fits into only one category, there is a wide variability in its background. This is a tough one—if you write to the lowest common denominator of reader, you're likely to end up with a cumbersome, tedious book-like thing that will turn off the majority of readers. But if you don't write to that lowest level, you lose that segment of your readers. What to do? Most writers go for the majority of readers and sacrifice that minority that needs more help. Others put the supplemental information in appendixes or insert cross-references to beginners' books.

Audience Adaptation

Okay! So you've analyzed your audience until you know them better than you know yourself. What good is it? How do you use this information? How do you keep from writing something that will still be incomprehensible or useless to your readers?

The business of writing to your audience may have a lot to do with in-born talent, intuition, and even mystery. But there are some controls you can use to have a better chance to connect with your readers. The following "controls" have mostly to do with making technical information more understandable for nonspecialist audiences:

- **Add information readers need to understand your document**. Check to see whether certain key information is missing—for example, a critical series of steps from a set of instructions, important background that helps beginners understand the main discussion, or definition of key terms.

- **Omit information your readers do not need**. Unnecessary information can also confuse and frustrate readers—after all, it's there so they feel obligated to read it. For example, you can probably chop theoretical discussion from basic instructions.

- **Change the level of the information you currently have**. You may have the right information but it may be "pitched" at too high or too low a technical level. It may be pitched at the wrong kind of audience—for example, at an expert audience rather than a technician audience. This happens most often when product-design notes are passed off as instructions.

- **Add examples to help readers understand**. Examples are one of the most powerful ways to connect with audiences, particularly in instructions. Even in noninstructional text, for example, when you are trying to explain a technical concept, examples are a major help—analogies in particular.

- **Change the level of your examples**. You may be using examples but the technical content or level may not be appropriate to your readers. Homespun examples may not be useful to experts; highly technical ones may totally miss your nonspecialist readers.

- **Change the organization of your information**. Sometimes, you can have all the right information but arrange it in the wrong way. For example, there can be too much (or too little) background information up front such that certain readers get lost. Sometimes, background information needs to be consolidated into the main information—for example, in instructions it's sometimes better to feed in chunks of background at the points where they are immediately needed.

- **Strengthen transitions**. It may be difficult for readers, particularly nonspecialists, to see the connections between the main sections of your report, between individual paragraphs, and sometimes even between individual sentences. You can make these connections much clearer by adding transition words and by echoing key words more accurately. Words like "therefore," "for example," "however" are transition words—they indicate the logic connecting the previous thought to the upcoming thought. You can also strengthen transitions by carefully echoing the same key words. In technical prose, it's not a good idea to vary word choice—use the same words so that people don't get any more confused than they may already be.

- **Write stronger introductions—both for the whole document and for major sections**. People seem to read with more confidence and understanding when they have the "big picture"—a view of what's coming, and how it relates to what they've just read. Therefore, make sure you have a strong introduction to the entire document—one that makes clear the topic, purpose, audience, and contents of that document. And for each major section within your document, use mini-introductions that indicate at least the topic of the section and give an overview of the subtopics to be covered in that section.

- **Create topic sentences for paragraphs and paragraph groups**. It can help readers immensely to give them an idea of the topic and purpose of a section (a group of paragraphs) and in particular to give them an overview of the subtopics about to be covered. Roadmaps help when you're in a different state!

- **Change sentence style and length**. How you write—down at the individual sentence level—can make a big difference too. In instructions, for example, using imperative voice and "you" phrasing is vastly more understandable than the passive voice or third-personal phrasing. For some reason, personalizing your writing style and making it more relaxed and informal can make it more accessible and understandable. Passive, person-less writing is harder to read—put people and action in your writing. Similarly, go for active verbs as opposed to be verb phrasing. All of this makes your writing more direct and immediate—readers don't have to dig for it. And obviously, sentence length matters as well. An average of somewhere between 15 and 25 words per sentence is about right; sentences over 30 words are to be mistrusted.

- **Work on sentence clarity and economy**. This is closely related to the previous "control" but deserves its own spot. Often, writing style can be so wordy that it is hard or frustrating to read. When you revise your rough drafts, put them on a diet—go through a draft line by line trying to reduce the overall word, page, or line count by 20 percent. Try it as an experiment and see how you do. You'll find a lot of fussy, unnecessary detail and inflated phrasing you can chop out.

- **Use more or different graphics**. For nonspecialist audiences, you may want to use more graphics—and simpler ones at that. Graphics for specialists are more detailed, more technical. In technical documents for nonspecialists, there also tend to be more "decorative" graphics—ones that are attractive but serve no strict informative or persuasive purpose at all.

- **Break text up or consolidate text into meaningful, usable chunks**. For nonspecialist readers, you may need to have shorter paragraphs. Maybe a 6- to 8-line paragraph is the usual maximum. Notice how much longer paragraphs are in technical documents written for specialists.

- **Add cross-references to important information**. In technical information, you can help nonspecialist readers by pointing them to background sources. If you can't fully explain a topic on the spot, point to a section or chapter where it is.

- **Use headings and lists**. Readers can be intimidated by big dense paragraphs of writing, uncut by anything other than a blank line now and then. Search your rough drafts for ways to incorporate headings—look for changes in topic or subtopic. Search your writing for listings of things—these can be made into vertical lists. Look for paired listings such as terms and their definitions—these can be made into two-column lists. Of course, be careful not to force this special formatting—don't overdo it.

- **Use special typography, and work with margins, line length, line spacing, type size, and type style**. For nonspecialist readers, you can do things like making the lines shorter (bringing in the margins), using larger type sizes, and other such tactics. Certain type styles are believed to be friendlier and more readable than others. (Try to find someone involved with publishing to get some insights on fonts.)

These are the kinds of "controls" that professional technical writers use to finetune their work and make it as readily understandable as possible. And in contrast, it's the accumulation of lots of problems in these areas—even seemingly trivial ones—that add up to a document being difficult to read and understand. Nonprofessionals often question why professional writers and editors insist on bothering with such seemingly picky, trivial, petty details in writing—but they all add up! It reminds me of the ancient Chinese execution method called "death by a thousand cuts." However, in this case, it would be "perplexity by a thousand minor problems."

By: David McMurrey and Tamara Powell

Objectives

Upon completion of this chapter, readers will be able to:

- Define documentation.
- Identify and analyze tasks in order to create documentation.
- Differentiate between function and task orientation and explain the pros and cons of each approach.
- Explain how to begin writing documentation.

Task Analysis and Task-Oriented Documentation

When you write instructions, procedures, and "guide" or user-guide information (generally called documentation), you normally must use a task approach. That means providing steps and explanations for all the major tasks that users may need to perform.

Of course, some instructions involve only one task—for example, changing the oil in a car. But we are concerned here with more complex procedures. While this chapter uses computer software as an example, these techniques can apply to any multi-task procedure—for example, operating a microwave oven.

Identifying Tasks

To write in a task-oriented manner, you first have to do some task analysis. That means studying how users use the product or do the task, interviewing them, and watching them. It can also mean interviewing marketing and product development people. If you can get your hands on the kinds of questions that help-desk people receive, that helps too.

But sometimes, you may not be in a position to do a thorough task analysis. Typically, product developers don't think about documentation until rather late. In these circumstances, it's often difficult to get marketing, development, engineering, and programming people to spend enough time with you to explain the product thoroughly. And so you end up doing a certain amount of educated guesswork. The developer is more likely to review your draft and let you know if your guesswork is right.

To develop your own task analysis, you can study the user interface (buttons, menus, options, etc.) of the product. This process goes for both hardware and software. Consider the interface for an icon editing tool shown below:

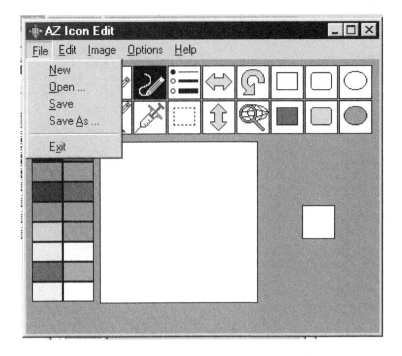

Figure 1: Icon editing tool interface

From just this snippet of the interface, you can identify several obvious tasks:

- Start a new icon project
- Open an existing icon project for editing
- Rename an icon project (Save As)
- Exit AZ Icon Edit

Now, look at the menu options for the next parts of the menu. You can see that when people are using this icon editor, they'll also most likely be doing these tasks:

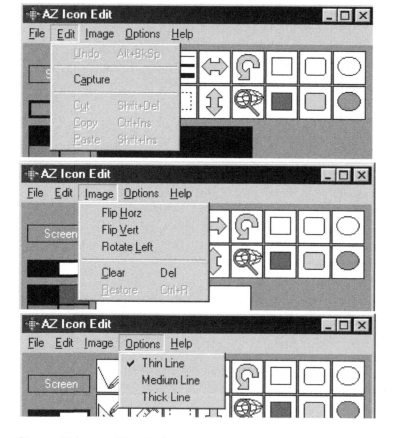

Figure 2" Icon editing tasks

1. Undo a mistake
2. Capture an image or some part of it
3. Cut something out of an icon project
4. Copy something out of an icon project
5. Paste something into an icon project
6. Flip the entire image horizontaly or vertically
7. Rotate the image left
8. Clear the project, which probably means start over
9. Restore, which you'll have to ask around, experiment with, or dig into the programming spec to find out about
10. Draw with a thick, medium, or thin line.

But now look at the interface without the menu options hanging down. What additional tasks can you see? As with a lot of graphical user interfaces, some of the icons duplicate the menu options. For example, the bulleted-list icon enables you to select a thin, medium, or thick line the same way clicking on **Options** does. However, there are some new tools here, not available elsewhere in the interface:

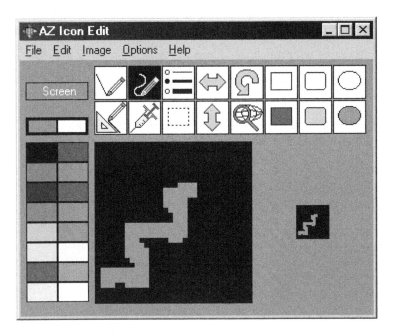

Figure 3: Icon editing tools

- Draw straight lines (you'll have to experiment to see the difference between the two pencil icons)
- Draw freehand lines (the wavy-line icon)
- Draw unfilled rectangles (sharp edges) and unfilled rectangles (rounded edges)
- Draw unfilled ovals and filled ovals
- Fill with color (the hypodermic needle)
- Select portions of the image to move, cut, or rotate (the dotted-line icon)
- Capture images—or parts of images— (the net, but how does it work?)
- Draw filled rectangles (sharp edges) and filled rectangles (rounded edges)
- Select background color (the Screen button)
- Select line or fill color (the double-box icon)

There's a lot you still don't know about this software, but you've already done a lot of guesswork toward defining the major tasks. You'd want to group and consolidate things much more tightly than above, perhaps like the following:

- Creating, editing, renaming, and saving icons
- Selecting foreground and background color
- Drawing lines, rectangles, and ovals
- Cutting, pasting, and copying objects
- Moving, flipping, and rotating objects

You can see that in this rough task list, there is no trace of tasks such as filling an object with color, capturing images, clearing the workspace, undoing a mistake, or restoring. But as you work, these details will begin to find their place in your scheme. Now, stand back from the details of the interface and put yourself in the place of an icon software user. What questions is that individual likely to ask? How do I change the color of the background? We've got that covered. How do I change the thickness of the lines I draw? Got that one covered too. How do I make the background transparent? Hmmm . . . that will be an issue for the color section, but it will take some research.

Different Approaches to Documentation

When you write for users, you have a choice of two approaches, function orientation and task orientation, the latter of which is by far the better choice. A function orientation lists buttons or icons and then lets readers know what the function of each item is. For example, "The **save** button allows you to save your project for later use." This information is helpful for a user (although probably most users know what the save button does). While it is helpful to quickly list major buttons and what they do, it's not sufficient to help readers truly use the software or appliance.

Task-oriented documentation, created for specific goals that you anticipate users will want to achieve (such as, "Capturing Images") allows users to begin using the product quickly and achieving their goals satisfactorily (which hopefully leads to a high level of satisfaction with the product and your documentation).

Writing with a Function Orientation

It ought to be obvious how to proceed after a task analysis, but apparently not. Computer publications—if not technical publications in general—often seem to stray into a non-task-oriented style of writing. But, no! That just doesn't work!

Another reason why some user guide instructions are not task oriented can be blamed on product specifications. Product specifications, which are written by and for programmers, engineers, developers, are written in terms of required function:

Button	Function
File menu button	Enables user to create a new file, open an existing file, rename a file, etc.
Crop icon	Enables user to cut selected segment of image.

You might call this approach *function-oriented* writing because it systematically explains each function, feature, or interface element of a product. Unfortunately, this approach shows up in user guides meant for nontechnical readers—perhaps because the writers are inexperienced, untrained, or untechnical; or else the writers have been called in too late to do much else but polish the developers' spec.

The function-oriented approach almost works sometimes. But "almost" and "sometimes" are not good enough. It almost works because the names of interface elements and functions sometimes match the tasks they support. For example, the **Open** menu option is pretty intuitive: open an existing file. Others are not. For example, what do you suppose is restored by the **Restore** button in the AZ Icon Edit interface? Also, some interface elements don't accomplish tasks all by themselves. In Photoshop, for example, you can't crop text by pressing the **Crop** menu option. You have to first click the text-selection button, then draw a selection box around the part of the image you want to keep, then press the **Crop** button.

Writing with a Task Orientation

Instead of the function-oriented approach, use the task-oriented approach. Identify the tasks users will need to perform with the product, and then structure your document accordingly. Make your headings and subheadings *task-oriented* in their phrasing. Task-oriented phrasing means phrasing like "How to adjust the volume, "Adjusting the volume," or "Adjust the volume." It does not mean phrasing like "Volume" or "Volume Adjustment." Here are some additional examples:

Problem phrasing	Task-oriented phrasing
Capture	Capturing images
Screen button	Selecting background or foreground objects
Rectangles	Drawing rectangles
Oval icon	Drawing ovals and circles

When you have defined user tasks, organized them into logical groups, and have defined task-oriented headings, you're ready to write! Here's an excerpt:

Drawing Rectangles and Ovals

You can use the icon editor to draw squares, rectangles, ovals, and circles.

Draw a rectangle. To draw a rectangle:

- Ensure that you have selected the foreground color you want. (See "Selecting foreground color.")
- Click the rectangle icon.
- Position the mouse pointer in the drawing area where you want the rectangle to appear, hold down the left mouse button, and drag to create the rectangle.

Draw an oval. To draw an oval:

- Ensure that...

In this excerpt, you can see that an overall task-oriented approach is taken and that task-oriented phrasing is used for the headings (Drawing). Notice too that numbered lists are used to guide readers step by step through the actions involved in the task.

View sample documentation on creating checklists with Desire2Learn (D2L). D2L is a learning management system that university faculty might use to share class materials with students. The checklist function helps university faculty to let students know what tasks need to be completed within a course module or unit of time.

By: David McMurrey, Jonathan Arnett, and Tamara Powell

Objectives

Upon completion of this chapter, readers will be able to:

1. Explain and apply strategies for articulating technical discussions to nonspecialist readers.
2. Use audience analysis to decide what information to include or exclude from a document and how to discuss that information.

Articulating Technical Discussions

The ability to explain complex, technical matters with ease, grace, and simplicity so that nonspecialist readers understand almost effortlessly is one of the most important skills you can develop as a technical writer. This ability to "translate" or articulate difficult-to-read technical discussions is important because so much of technical writing is aimed at nonspecialist audiences. These audiences include important people such as supervisors, executives, investors, financial officers, government officials, and, of course, customers.

This chapter provides you with some strategies for articulating technical discussions, that is, specific strategies you can use to make difficult technical discussions easier for nonspecialist readers to understand.

You use your understanding of your audience to decide

1. What information to include in the document
2. What information to exclude from the document
3. How to discuss the information you do include in the document

Articulating is particularly important because it means supplying the right kinds of information to make up for the reader's lack of knowledge or capability. Articulating thus enables readers to understand and use your document.

Some combination of the techniques discussed in this chapter should help you create a readable, understandable translation:

1. Defining unfamiliar terms
2. Comparing to familiar things
3. Elaborating the process
4. Providing description
5. Reviewing theoretical background
6. Providing examples and applications
7. Shorter sentences and paragraphs
8. The "in-other-words" technique
9. Posing rhetorical questions
10. Explaining the importance or significance
11. Providing illustration
12. Providing historical background
13. Providing the human perspective
14. Stronger transitions

This list by no means exhausts the possibilities. Other techniques include

- *Headings.* See the section on using headings that break up text and emphasize points and on how to construct headings that guide readers from section to section.
- *Lists.* See the section on constructing lists that break up text and emphasize points and on how to construct headings that guide readers from section to section.

Definitions of Unfamiliar Terms

Defining potentially unfamiliar terms in a report is one of the most important ways to make up for readers' lack of knowledge in the report subject.

Facial Characteristics of FAS

Taken as a whole, the face of patients of fetal alcohol syndrom (FAS) is very distinctive. Structural deficiencies are thought to be the result of reduced cellular proliferation in the developing stages of the embryo because of the direct action of the alcohol. The face has a drawn-out appearance with characteristics that include short **palpebral fissures**, **epicanthic folds**, low nasal bridge, a short upturned nose, indistinct **philtrum**, small midface, and a thinned upper **vermilion**.

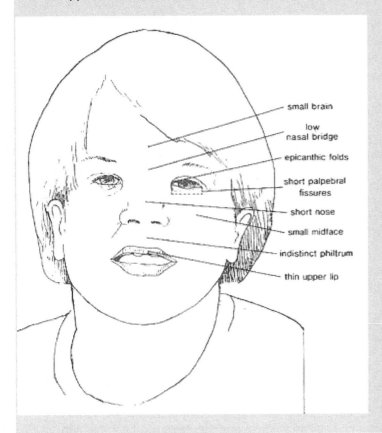

- small brain
- low nasal bridge
- epicanthic folds
- short palpebral fissures
- short nose
- small midface
- indistinct philtrum
- thin upper lip

Facial features characteristic of FAS

Comparisons to Familiar Things

Comparing technical concepts to ordinary and familiar things in our daily lives makes them easier to understand. For example, things in the world of electronics and computer—a downright intimidating area for many people—can be compared to channels of water, the five senses of the human body, gates and pathways, or other common things. Notice how comparison (highlighted) is used in these passages:

The helical configuration of the DNA strands is not haphazard. The nitrogen bases on each strang align themselves to form nitrogen base pairs. The pairs are T-A and C-G. Each pair is held together by hydrogen bonds. The pairing of the bases serves **to fasten the two helical nucleotide strands together much the same way as the teeth of a zipper hold the zipper together**. The existence of the complementary base pairs explain the constant ratios of T/A and C/G. For every T there must be a conplementary A and for every G there must be a complementary C.

David S. Newman, *An Invitation to Chemistry* (New York: Norton, 1978), pp. 380-381.

All the death and all the misery from a virus so small that 2-1/2 million of them in a line would take up one inch. Flu viruses fall into three types: A, B, and C. Type A, the most variables, causes pandemics as well as regular seasonal outbreaks; type B causes smaller outbreaks and is just now receiving greater attention; type C rarely causes serious health problems. **In appearance, a flu virus somewhat resembles the medieval mace--a ball of iron studded with spikes. Hemagglutinin is the substance that in effect bashes into a cell during infection and allows the virus access to the cell interior where it can replicate**.

Stephen S. Hall, "The Flu," *Science* 83, (November 1983), pages 56-57.

Elaborating the Process

Explaining in detail the processes involved in the report subject can also help readers. Consider a paragraph like this one, containing only a sketchy reference to the process:

The Video Alert and Control dashboard system, a newly developed system to help drivers avoid accidents, graphically projects an image of hazards in the road.

This brief reference can be converted into a more complete explanation as is illustrated here:

The Video Alert and Control dashboard systems uses a number of components to help drivers avoid accidents. The infrared detector is the key detecting device in that it searches for warm objects in or near the path ahead of the car. The infrared detector senses the upcoming trouble well before the driver by sensing warm-bloodedness and then alerts the driver. The infrared detector also senses the heat of oncoming traffic. All of these objects are shown draphically on the video screen. To differentiate wildlife from other cars, the x-ray unit is used to check for metal in the object ahead. Thus, if a warm object is detected with metal in it, the computer reads it as a car and shows it on the screen as a yellow dot. On the other hand, if no metal is detected in the warm object, it is read as an animaland plotted as a red dot...

Providing Descriptive Detail

Descriptions also help nonspecialist readers by making the report discussion more concrete and down-to-earth:

Jarvik and his colleagues have been working on other designs, such as a portable artificial heart, which they think will be ready for a patient within the next two years. Electrohydraulic Heart Jarvik has been developing electric-energy converters and blood pumps during the past year. The electrohydraulic energy converter has only one moving part. The impeller of an axial-flow pump is attached to the rotor of a brushless direct-current motor, with the impeller and the rotor supported by a single hydrodynamic bearing. Reversing the rotation of the pump reverses the direction of the hydraulic flow. The hydraulic fluid (silicone oil of low viscosity) actuates the diaphragm of a blood pump just as compressed air does in the Jarvik-7 heart design. This hydraulic fluid is pumped back and forth between the right and left ventricles. The energy converter is small and simple and therefore can be implanted without damaging vital structures. It weighs nearly 85 grams and occupies nearly 30 cubic centimeters. The converter requires an external battery and an electronics package, which is connected to the heart by a small cable through the patient's chest. The batteries weigh 2 to 5 pounds and can be worn on a vest or belt. The battery unit requires new or recharged batteries once or twice a day. The cable through which the power is transmitted from the battery to the heart also carries control signals from the microcomputer controller.

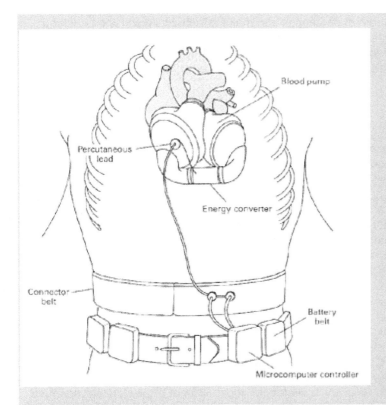

Electrically driven artificial heart system. Source: Jarvik, Robert K. "The Total Artificial Heart," Scientific American, January 1981, p. 80. Jacqueline R. Mudd, Report on Artificial Methods of Combating Heart Disease, University of Texas at Austin, May 6, 1983.

Providing Illustrations

Illustrations—typically, simple diagrams—can help readers understand technical descriptions and explanations of processes. You can see the use of illustration in the FAS example above: epicanthic folds and the philtrum are defined under the diagram.

Providing Examples and Applications

Equally useful in articulating complex or abstract technical discussions are examples or explanations of how a thing can be used. For example, if you are trying to explain a LINUX command, showing how it is used in an example program helps readers greatly. If you are explaining a new design for a solar heating and cooling system, showing its application in a specific home can help also.

Continuous Speech Continuous speech causes many problems in computerized speech recognition. For example: "plea" and "please," while some words have similar acoustics, such as "what" and "watt."

Heidi E. Cootes, *Report on Computers that Recognize Speech*, University of Texas at Austin, May 6, 1983.

Now here is a passage with a longer, extended example:

...The user "scrolls" the worksheet right and left or up and down to bring different parts of it into view. Each position (that is, each intersection of a column and a row) on a screen corresponds to a record in memory. The user sets up his own matrix by assigning to each record either a label, an item of data or a formula; the corresponding position on the screen displays the assigned the label, the entered datum or the result of applying the formula.

Hoo-Mi D. Toong and Amar Gupta, "Personal Computers," *Scientific American*, (December 1982), pp. 99-100.

Shorter Sentences and Paragraphs

As simple a technique as it may seem, reducing the length of sentences can make a technical discussion easier to understand. Consider the following pairs of example passages, the second versions of which contain shorter sentences. (The passage still needs other translating techniques, particularly definitions, but the shorter sentences do make it more readable.) Notice, too, that shorter paragraphs can help in the articulating process, not only in the example below but throughout this chapter.

Original Version: Longer Sentences

UV-flourescence was determined on aliquots of the hexane extracts of subsurface water using the Perkin-Elmer MPF-44A dual-scanning flourescence spectrophotometer upon mousse sample NOAA-16, considered the best representative of cargo oil. Every day that samples were processed, a new calibration curve was developed from serial dilutions of the reference mousse (NOAA-16) at an emission wavelength of ca. 360 nm, and other samples were compared to it as the standard. Emission was scanned from 275-500 nm, offset 25 nm from the excitation wavelength, with the major peak occurring at 360 nm for the reference mousse solutions. In each sample, the concentration of flourescent material, a total oil estimate, was calculated from its respective flourescence, using the linear relationship of flourescence vs. concentration of the reference mousse "standard," with a correction factor applied to account for the reference mousse containing only about 30 percent.

Revised Version: Shorter Sentences

UV-flourescence was determined on aliquots of the hexane extracts of the subsurface water. These measurements were performed using a Perkin-Elmer MPF-44A dual-scanning flourescence spectrophotometer. Mousse sample NOAA-16 was used as the best representative of cargo sample. Other samples were compared to it as the standard. Every day that samples were processed, a new calibration curve was developed from serial dilutions of the reference mousse (NOAA-16). Tests were run at an emission wavelength of ca. 360 nm. Emission was scanned from 275-500 nm, offset 25 nm from the excitation wavelength. The major peak occurred at 360 nm for the reference mousse solutions. In each sample, the concentration of flourescent material, a total estimate, was calculated from its respective flourescence. The linear relationship of flourescence vs. concentration of the reference mousse "standard." A correction factor was applied to account for the reference mousse containing only about 30 percent oil.

Stronger Transitions and Overviews

Transitions and overviews guide readers through text. In difficult technical material, transitions and overviews are important. (For in-depth discussion, see transitions.)

- *Repetition of key words.* As unlikely as it may seem, using the same words for same ideas is a critical technique for comprehension in technical discussions. In other words, don't refer to the hard drive as a "fixed-disk drive" one place and as "DASD" (an old IBM term meaning direct access stationary drive) in another. Same goes for verbs: stick with either "boot up" or "system reset," and don't vary.
- *Arrangement of key words.* Equally important is how you introduce keywords in sentences. If your focus stays on the topic in each sentence of a paragraph, place the keyword at or near the beginning of the second and following sentences. However, if the topic focus shifts from one sentence to the next, use the old-to-new pattern: start the following sentrnce with the old topic and end the sentence with the new topic.
- *Transition words and phrases.* Examples of transition words and phrases are "for example," "however," and so on. When the discussion is particularly difficult and when repetition and arrangement of keywords is not enough, use transition words and phrases.
- *Reviews of topics covered and topics to be covered.* At certain critical moments within and between paragraph (or groups of paragraphs) occurs a transitional device that either captures what has been discussed in a short phrase, previews what is to be discussed in the following paragraphs, or both. The latter device is also called a topic sentence.

The "In-Other-Words" Technique

In technical writing, you occasionally see questions posed to the readers. Such questions are not there for readers to answer; they are meant to stimulate readers' curiosity, renew their interest, introduce a new section of the discussion, or allow for a pause:

When an animal runs, its legs swing back and forth through large angles to provide balance and forward drive. We have found that such swinging motions of the leg do not have to be explicitly programmed for a machine but are a natural outcome of the interactions between the controllers for balance and attitude. Suppose the vehicle is traveling at a constant horizontal rate and is landing with its body upright. What must the attitude controller do during the stance to maintain the upright attitude? It must make sure that no torques are generated at the hip. Since the foot is fixed on the ground during stance, the leg must sweep back through an angle in order to guarantee that the torque on the hip will be zero while the body moves forward.

On the other hand, what must the balance servo do during flight to maintain balance? Since the foot must spend about as much time in front of the vehicle's center of gravity as behind it, the rate of travel and the duration of stance dictate a forward foot position for landing that will place the foot in a suitable spot for the next stance period. Thus during each flight the leg must swing forward under the direction of the balance servo, and during each stance it must sweep backward under the control of the attitude servo; the forward and back sweeping motions required for running are obtained automatically from the interplay of the servo-control loops for balance and attitude.

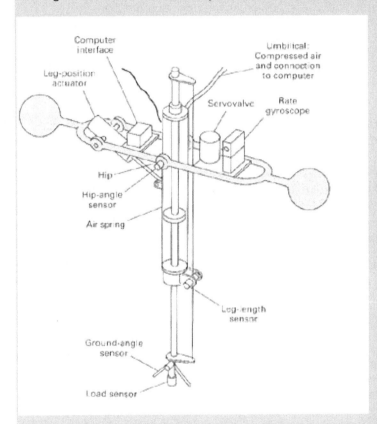

Two-Dimensional Hopping Machine. Source: Marc H. Raibert and Ivan E. Sutherland, "Machines that Walk," Scientific American, (January 1983), p. 50.

Explaining the Importance

Some translating articulating work because they motivate readers. Sometimes readers need to be talked into concentrating on difficult technical discussion: one way is to explain to them or to remind them of the importance of what is being discussed. In this example, the last paragraph emphasizes the importance):

It was Linus Pauling and his coworkers who discovered that sickle cell anemia was a molecular disease. This disease affects a very high percentage of black Africans, as high as 40 percent in some regions. About 9 percent of black Americans are heterozygous for the gene that causes the disease. People who are heterozygous for sickle cell anemia contain one normal gene and one sickle cell gene. Since neither gene in this case is dominant, half the hemoglobin molecules will be normal and half sickled. The characteristic feature of this disease is a sickling of the normally round, or platelike, red blood cells under conditions of slight oxygen deprivation. The sickled red blood cells clog small blood vessels and capillaries. The body's response is to send out white blood cells to destroy the sickled red blood cells, thus causing a shortage of red blood cells, or anemia. The sickle cell gene originated from a mistake in information. A DNA molecule somehow misplaced a base, which in turn caused an RNA molecule to direct the cell to make hemoglobin with just one different amino acid unit among the nearly 600 normally constituting a hemoglobin molecule. So finely tuned is the human organism that this tiny difference is enough to cause death. Since the disease is nearly always fatal before puberty, how can a gene for a fatal childhood disease get so widespread in a population? The answer to this question gives some fascinating insight into the mechanism and purposes of evolution, or natural selection. The distribution of sickle cell anemia very closely parallels the distribution of a particularly deadly malaria-causing protozoan by the name of Plasmodium falciparum, and it turns out that there is a close connection between sickle cell anemia and malaria. Those people who are heterozygous for the sickle cell gene are relatively immune to malaria and, except under reasonably severe oxygen deprivation such as that found at high altitudes, they experience no noticeable effects due to the sickle cell gene they carry. Half the hemoglobin molecules in the red cells of heterozygous people are normal and half are sickled. Thus, under ordinary circumstances the normal hemoglobin carries on the usual respiratory functions of blood cells and there is little discomfort. On the other hand, the sickled hemoglobin molecules precipitate, in effect, when the malaria-causing protozoan enters the blood. The precipitated hemoglobin seems to crush the malaria protozoan, thus keeping the malaria from being fatal. **The significance of all this should be pondered**.

David S. Newman, *An Invitation to Chemistry*, pages 387-388.

Providing Historical Background

Discussion of the historical background of a technical subject helps readers because it gives them less technical, more general, and sometimes more familiar information. It gives them a base of understanding from which to launch into the more difficult sections of the discussion:

Now that alcohol is being used in more and more social settings, it extremely important to recognize its teratogenic effects. Teratogenic, or malforming, agents produce an abnormal presence or absence of a substance that is required in physical development. Although Sullivan first reported on the effects of maternal drinking during pregnancy in 1899, the serious implications of his findings were virtually ignored for the next 50 years. It was not until the dramatic identification of a pattern of malformations, termed the fetal alcohol syndrome (FAS) by Jones et al in 1973, that the scientific community acknowledged the potential dangers of heavy maternal alcohol use. Since then, there has been increasing recognition that alcohol may be the most common drug in causing problems of malformations in humans.

Each morning in the soft, coral flush of daybreak, a laser dawns on Mars. Forty miles above frigid deserts of red stone and dust, it flares in an atmosphere of carbon dioxide. Infrared sunlight kindles in this gas a self-intensifying radiance that continuously generates as much energy as a thousand nuclear reactors. Our eyes are blind to it, but from sunrise to sunset Mars bathes in dazzling lasershine.The red planet may have lased in the sun for eons before astronomers identified its sky-high natural laser in 1980. The wonder is that its existence was unknown for so long. In 1898, in The War of the Worlds, H.G. Wells scourged earth with Martian invaders and a laserlike death ray. Pitiless, this "ghost of a beam of light" blasted brick, fired trees, and pierced iron as if it were paper.

In 1917 Albert Einstein speculated that under certain conditions atoms or molecules could absorb light or other radiation and then be stimulated to shed their borrowed energy. In the 1950s Soviet and American physicists independently theorized how this borrowed energy could be multiplied and repaid with prodigious interest. In 1960 Theodore H. Maiman invested the glare of a flash lamp in a rod of synthetic ruby; from that first laser on earth he extorted a burst of crimson light so brilliant it outshone the sun.

Allen A. Boraiko, "The Laser: 'A Splendid Light,'" *National Geographic*, (March 1984), p.335.

Reviewing Theoretical Background

To understand some phenomena, technologies, or their applications, readers must first understand the principle or theory behind them. Theoretical discussions need not be over the heads of nonspecialist readers. Discussion of theory is often little more than explanation of the root causes and effects at work in a phenomenon or mechanism. In this example, the writer establishes the theory and then can go on to discuss the findings that have come about through the use of NMR on living tissue.

To the extent that objections persist about the validity of modern biochemistry, they continue to be about reducing the processes of life to sequences of chemical reactions. "The reactions may take place in the test tube," one hears, "but do they really happen that way inside the living cell? And what happens in multicellular organisms?" One technique is beginning to answer these questions by detecting chemical reactions as they occur inside cells, tissues and organisms including those of human beings. The technique is nuclear-magnetic-resonance (NMR) spectroscopy. It relies on the fact that atomic nuclei with an odd number of nucleons (protons and neutrons) have an intrinsic magnetism that makes each such nucleus a magnetic dipole: in essence a bar magnet. Such nuclei include the proton (H-1), which is the nucleus of 99.98 percent of all hydrogen atoms occurring in nature, the carbon-13 nucleus (C-13), which is the nucleus of 1.1 percent of all carbon atoms, and the phosphorus-31 nucleus (P-31), which is the nucleus of all phosphorus atoms.

Combining the Articulating Techniques

This last section concludes the techniques for articulating difficult technical prose to be presented here. However, take a look at writing in fields you know about, and look for other kinds of articulating techniques used there. Now, here are several extended passages of technical writing that combine several of these strategies.

Fine-tuning the spectrum To know lasers, one must first know the electromagnetic spectrum, which ranges from long radio waves to short, powerful gamma rays. The narrow band of the spectrum we know as visible, or white, light is made up of red, orange, yellow, green, blue, and violet light. These frequencies, as well as all radiation waves, are jumbled or diffused, much as noise is a collection of overlapping, interfering sounds. Laser light is organized and concentrated, like a single, clear musical note. In lasers, nature's disorder is given coherence, and photons—the basic units of all radiation—are sent out in regular ranks of one frequency. Because the waves coincide, the photons enhance one another, increasing their power to pass on energy and infomation. The first devices to emit concentrated radiation operated in the low-energy microwave frequencies. Today, laser technology is extending beyond ultraviolet toward the high-energy realms of x-rays. Each wavelength boasts its own capacities as a tool for man. A laser's beam can be modulated into an infinite number of wavelengths using flourescent dyes like those produced at Exciton Chemical Company in Ohio. At Hughes Research Laboratories in California, a blue-green laser reflected at an acute angle aneals silicon microchips, while a low-energy red laser monitors the process. Harnessing light As a bow stores energy and releases it to drive an arrow so lasers store energy in atoms and molecules, concentrate it, and release it in powerful waves. When an atom expands the orbits of its electrons, they instantly snap back, shedding energy in the form of a photon. When a molecule vibrates or changes its geometry, it also snaps back to emit a photon. In most lasers a medium of crystal, gas, or liquid is energized by high-intensity light, an electric discharge, or even nuclear radiation. When a photon reaches an atom, the energy exchange stimulates the emission of another photon in the same wavelength and direction, and so on, until a cascade of growing energy sweeps through the medium. The photons travel the length of the laser and bounce off mirrors—one a full mirror, one partially silvered—at either end. Photons, reflected back and forth, finally gain so much energy that they exit the partially silvered end, emerging as powerful beam. Out of the darkness: laser eye surgery Sight-saving shafts of light able to enter the eye without injuring it, lasers are revolutionizing eye surgery. Using techniques of New York opthalmologist Frances L'Esperance, eye surgeons employ four levels of laser energy. Exposure time ranges from 30 minutes for low-energy photoradiation to several billionths of a second for photodisruption. With microscopic focus, beams weld breaks in the retina or seal leaking blood vessels by photocoagulation. A painless 20-minute operation call an irridectomy relieves this excess fluid buildup of glaucoma. When an artificial lens is placed behind the iris, the supportive membrane often grows milky. A laser beam is pinpointed on the taut tissue in a series of minute explosions. This photodisruption causes the tissue to unzip and part like a curtain. Bloodless scalpels, lasers can make extremely delicate incisions, cauterize blood vessels, and leave tissue unaffected only a few cell widths away. Beams that heal Surgical trauma, the jarring aftermath of the surgeon's knife, may one day be consigned to the annals of primitive medicine—thanks to a procedure called "least invasive surgery" by its growing number of practitioners. Using an endoscope, surgeons can view the interior of the body and operate with the least amount of damage. An end view of the flexible tube ... shows a large optical fiber to light the way. Smaller openings facilitate fluid suction and gas suction. A forceps, controlled by a cable near the microscope viewing lens, extracts tissue for analysis. A laser, controlled by dials to the left of the eyepiece, streams from another tube, ready to perform wherever the doctor directs it. Twisting and probing wit the end of the scope, he can identify and coagulate a bleeding ulcer in the stomach or blast tumors in the esophagus. The beam is fed through the scope by an optical fiber from a laser machine ... that might cost the hospital from $20,000 to $150,000.

Allen A. Boraiko, "Lasers: A Splendid Light," *National Geographic*, (March 1984), pp. 338-346.

5.5: Power-Revision Techniques

By: David McMurrey and Jonathan Arnett

Objectives

Upon completion of this chapter, readers will be able to:

- Revise common structure-level problems in technical writing.
- Revise common sentence-level problems in technical writing.

Power-Revision Techniques

The linked chapters here cover some of the most important aspects of writing—what's more important than the information you put in a document, how you organize it, how you link it all up together?

When you look at all these powerful ways you can review (look for potential problems) and then revise (fix those problems), you might think they're tedious and time-consuming. They do take some time, but don't worry...this stuff becomes second nature rather quickly. If you spend some time analyzing writing in the ways outlined in this chapter, the way you write and the way you review what you write will change. You'll start operating—even if you don't consciously realize it—with these ideas in mind.

This chapter covers two major categories of problems you can revise: **structure-level problems** and **sentence-level problems**.

The section on **structure-level problems** includes tips for checking your documents.

- informational value
- internal organization
- topic sentences and overviews
- transitions
- paragraph lengths

The section on **sentence-level problems** includes tips for how to revise

1. nominalizations
2. noun stacks
3. redundant phrasing
4. expletives
5. weak use of passive voice verbs
6. subject-verb mismatches
7. readability, sentence lengths, and sentence structures

Structure-Level Problems

Informational Value

One of the most important ways you can review a rough draft is to check its contents for informational value. All the good transitions, good organization, and clear sentence structure in the world can't help a technical document that doesn't have the right information for its audience.

- **Information is missing.** For example, imagine that somebody wrote a technical report on "virtual communities" but never bothered to define what "virtual community" means. The reader would be utterly lost.

- **Information is there, but not enough.** Take the same example, and imagine that the writer only made a few vague statements about virtual communities. The reader (unless she is an expert on virtual communities) needed at least a paragraph on the subject, if not a full-blown three- or four-page section.
- **Information is there, but at the wrong level for the audience.** Imagine that the report's writer included a two-page explanation of virtual communities but included highly technical information and phrased it in language that only a sociologist (an "expert" academic audience) would understand, when the document was really intended for high-school students. The writer failed to match the readers' knowledge, background, and needs.

If you can get a sense of how information does or doesn't match your audience, you should be well on your way to knowing what specifically to do to revise. One useful brainstorming tool is to think in terms of *types* of content.

Internal Organization

If you have the necessary and audience-appropriate information in a technical document, you're on the right track. However, that information may still not be sufficiently organized—like when you've just moved and everything is a mess or still in boxes—and you need to consider the rough draft's internal organization. Always consider these two aspects of internal organization, on both an individual-paragraph and whole-document level:

- the levels of information
- the sequence of information

Levels of Information

Some paragraphs and sentences contain general information or broader statements about the topic being discussed. Others contain more specific information, or go into greater depth. The first elements form a "framework" that supports the second, "subordinate" elements.

When you revise, check if the document's framework is easy to follow. The most common and effective way to arrange general and specific information is to introduce the framework first, then follow it with specifics. This overarching pattern holds for sentences inside paragraphs and paragraphs inside longer documents, even if the paragraph or document uses a different sequence of information.

Sequence of Information

Match a technical document's internal sequence of information to the document's audience, context, and purpose. Here are some examples of common informational sequences:

- **General > specific.** Arrange chunks of information from general to specific. For example, defining *all* solar collectors is a more general discussion than discussing the different types of solar collectors. And describing the operation of a specific type of solar collector is even less general. This pattern is illustrated here:

Problem version:

There are various types of solar collectors; however the flat-plate solar collector is currently the most common and will be the focus of discussion here. *The most important part of a solar heating system is the solar collector whose function is to heat circulating water necessary for space heating.* A typical solar collector has layers of glass with intervening air spaces to produce a heat-trapping effect. Most solar collectors consist of a black absorber plate covered by one or more of these transparent cover plates made either of glass or plastic with the sides and the bottom of the collector insulated.

Revised version:

The most important part of a solar heating system is the solar collector whose function is to heat circulating water necessary for space heating. There are various types of solar collectors; however, the flat-plate solar collector is currently the most common and will be the focus of discussion here. A typical flat-plate solar collector has layers of glass with intervening air spaces to produce a heat-trapping effect. Most solar collectors consist of a black absorber plate covered by one or more of these transparent cover plates made either of glass or plastic with the sides and the bottom of the collector insulated.

- **simple > complex.** Begin with the simple, basic, fundamental concepts and then move on to the more complex and technical.
- **thing-at-rest > thing-in-motion.** Describe the thing (as if in a photograph), then discuss its operation or process (as if in a video).
- **spatial movement.** Describe a pattern of physical movement; for example, top to bottom, left to right, or outside to inside.
- **temporal movement.** Describe events in relation to what happens first, second, and so on.
- **concept > application of the concept / examples.** Discuss a concept in general terms, then discuss the concept's application and/or examples of the concept.
- **data > conclusions.** Present data (observations, experimental data, survey results) then move on to the conclusions that can be drawn from that data. (This pattern is sometimes reversed: present the conclusion first, then the data that supports it.)
- **problem / question > solution / answer.** Introduce a problem or raise a question, then move on to the solution or answer.
- **simplified version > detailed version.** Discuss a simplified version of the thing, establish a solid understanding of it, then explain it all again, but this time laying on the technical detail. (This approach is especially useful for explaining technical matters to nonspecialists.)
- **most important > least important.** Begin with the most important, eye-catching, dramatic information, and move on to information that is progressively less so. (This pattern can be reversed: you can build up to a climax, rather than start with it.)
- **strongest > weakest.** Start with the most strongest argument for your position—to get everybody's attention—then move on to less and less strong ones. (This pattern can also be reversed: you can build up to your strongest arguments, but the weakest → strongest pattern is often less persuasive.)

These are just a few possibilities. Whichever sequence you choose, be consistent with it, and avoid mixing these approaches randomly. For example, presenting some data, stating a few conclusions, and then switching back and forth between data and conclusions haphazardly will only confuse your reader.

Topic Sentences

One of the best structural revision techniques you can use is to backtrack through a rough draft and insert topic sentences at key points.

A topic sentence is a sentence occurring toward the beginning of a paragraph that in some way tips the reader off as to the focus, purpose, and contents of that paragraph (and perhaps one or more paragraphs following). At its best, it focuses the reader's attention; it says, "Hey, here's what we're talking about!"

Often, when authors create technical documents, they don't consciously think about each paragraph's contents and logic; instead, authors focus on getting words onto the page, and they figure out what they mean while they're writing. Sometimes the results can seem disjointed. Accordingly, authors should go back and insert topic sentences that can help readers understand where they are going, what's coming up next, (often) where they've just been, and how what they are reading connects to the document as a whole.

Types of Topic Sentences

Your best guide for deciding when to use topic sentences and which type to use is probably your own instincts and intuition. But here are some ideas and examples:

- **keyword topic sentence.** This type of topic sentence contains a keyword that hints about the content and organization of the upcoming material. Use one if your section (one or more paragraphs) discusses multiple similar things (for example, problems, solutions, causes, consequences, reasons, aspects, factors).

During Samhain there are a number of activities the Celts took part in that resemble some customs we observe on Halloween today.

- **overview topic sentence.** This type of topic sentence names all the subtopics in the upcoming material. Use one if you want to specify all the subtopics you will address.

Most brains exhibit a visible distinction between gray matter and white matter.

- **thesis-statement topic sentence.** This type of topic sentence makes an assertion—an argument—that the rest of paragraph must support. Use one if your section proves a point and includes multiple supporting statements.

Although Babbage's machines were mechanical monsters, their basic architecture was astonishingly similar to a modern computer.

- **topic definition.** This type of topic sentence names the term being defined, identifies the class it belongs to, and describes its distinguishing characteristics. It must contain highly specific information. Use one if your section introduces an unfamiliar term.

Stress is a measure of the internal reaction between elementary particles of a material in resisting separation, compacting, or sliding that tend to be induced by external forces.

- **topic reference.** This type of topic sentence simply mentions the general subject at hand. It does not forecast what will be said about the subject. Use one to remind your reader about the general subject.

The surface of Mars is thought to be primarily composed of basalt, based upon the Martian meteorite collection and orbital observations.

- **no topic sentence.** Sometimes, you may not need or want a topic sentence. If your materials contain a story that leads to a point, or are part of a popular-science or -technology writing project, a topic sentence up front may be heavy, stodgy, and inappropriate.

Transitions

You may have audience-appropriate information in your technical document, and you may have organized that information well, but you also need to integrate those various pieces of information into a unified whole. If you don't make the document's "flow" of ideas clear, the document will read like a random assortment of ideas, and the reader will not understand how the chunks of information relate or connect to each other.

Use "transitions"—various devices that help readers connect the different sections of a document—to guide your reader from one idea to the next. You need to make clear the logic that connects every sentence in a document.

Here are some common types of transitional words and phrases:

- **additive.** Use these words to demonstrate that one idea is added to another. Examples include *moreover, as well as, too, in addition to, furthermore, also, additionally*.
- **narrative / chronological / temporal.** Use these words to demonstrate that one idea can follow, precede, or occur simultaneously with another. Examples include *then, next, after, before, since, subsequently, following, later, as soon as, as, when, while, during, until, once*.
- **contrastive / comparative.**Use these words to demonstrate differences or similarities. Examples include *but, on the other hand, unlike, as opposed to, than, although, though, instead, similarly*.
- **alternative.**Use these words to demonstrate that two ideas can act as alternatives or substitutes for each other. Examples include *either, or, nor, on the other hand, however, neither, otherwise*.
- **causal.** Use these words to demonstrate that one idea can be the cause or the result (effect, consequence, etc.) of another. Examples include *thus, then, unless, subsequently, therefore, because, consequently, as a result, if, in order to/that, for, so*.

- **illustrative.** Use these words to demonstrate that one idea can be an example or an illustration of another. Examples include *for example, for instance, to illustrate, as an example.*
- **repetitive / reiterative.** Use these words to rephrase an idea using other, perhaps more familiar, terms. Examples include *in other words, in short, that is, stated simply, to put it another way.*
- **spatial / physical.** Use these words to emphasize spatial relationships between things. Examples include prepositions such as *under, beside, on top of, next to, behind*, and many others.

Here are some more advanced types of transitions:

- **summary transitions**. Use a brief phrase (sometimes even a single word) to summarize the concepts in the preceding material. Then, in the same sentence, make a statement about that summary phrase, introduce the upcoming materials, and demonstrate their conceptual link. This technique is especially useful for establishing logical links between short sections. In the following sample paragraph, the words in green summarize the concepts, and dark red words perform the other functions.

> The simplest semiconductor is called a diode. A diode serves as a rectifier to conduct alternating current (ac) to direct current (dc). While the usual current in the U.S. is ac with a frequency of 60 Hz, many electronic devices require dc for at least part of their function. ***The diode solves*** *this* *mismatch* ***of current types by its basic design in which a p- and an n-type semiconductor are joined together.***

- **review-preview transitions.** Use a relatively short phrase or sentence to summarize the topic of the preceding material, use another relatively short phrase or sentence to summarize the upcoming material, and tie them together using transitional words. In the following sample paragraph, the words in green summarize the previous ideas. The words in dark red summarize the following materials. The word in purple is the transitional word.

> **Coring and core analysis techniques are adequate only to a certain extent, as the previous section shows.** *However,* **a much faster and less expensive method of detecting fractures is increasingly being used in exploratory wells: wire-line logging analysis.**

Paragraph Length

One last way to revise your rough draft at the structural level is to check for paragraph breaks.

Paragraphs are odd creatures—some scholars of writing believe they don't exist and are just arbitrary break points that writers toss in whenever and wherever they please. This idea may be true for creative or expressive writing, but in technical writing, the paragraph is a key player in the battle for clarity and comprehension. Insert paragraph breaks where there is some shift in topic or subtopic, or some shift in the way a topic is being discussed.

Here are some suggestions for paragraph length:

- If your technical document needs a great deal of expository writing and will be printed in hard copy, you can probably use relatively long paragraphs. A single spaced page full of text will probably contain one to four paragraph breaks. (There's nothing magical about that average, so don't treat it as if it were law.)
- If your technical document does not require long blocks of text, consider breaking it up into short paragraphs. Three sentences per paragraph is a widely accepted average.
- If your technical document will be posted online, use short paragraphs. People generally find it easier to read short paragraphs online than to read long paragraphs online.

In any case, look at long blocks of text and think about breaking them up into bite-sized chunks.

Sentence-Level Revision

You've probably heard plenty of times that writing should be lean, mean, clear, direct, succinct, active, and so on. This statement is one of those self-evident truths—why would anyone set out to write any other way? But what does this advice really mean? What do sentences that are not "lean, mean" and so on look like? What sorts of things are wrong with them? How do you fix them?

Sentences do have ways of becoming flabby, redundant, wordy, unclear, indirect, passive, and just plain old hard to understand. Even so, they remain grammatically "correct"—all their subjects and verbs agree, the commas are in the right places, the words are spelled correctly. Still, these sentences are far more difficult to read than a sentence with just a comma problem.

The following sections can't pretend to cover all of the ways sentences can go bad at this higher level, but they do cover seven of the most common problems and show you ways of fixing them. And knowing these seven will probably enable you to spot others we have not trapped and labeled yet.

Nominalizations

Check your writing for sentences that use "to be" as the main verb and use a nominalization as the sentence's subject. (A nominalization is a verb that has been converted into a noun; look for -*tion, -ment, -ance,* and other suffixes. For example, "nominalization" is itself a nominalization; the root verb is "to nominate." The "to be" verbs are *am, is, are, was, were.*)

These sentences are probably weak and indirect. Revise them by changing the nominalization into a verb and replacing the "to be" verb. Your sentences will sound more active, and they will be easier for the reader to understand.

Sometimes, you can't convert a nominalization into a main verb, or a nominalization needs to remain a sentence's subject. (For example, "infomation" is a nominalization, but try converting "information" into a main verb. The sentence will be awkward, at best.) More often, though, you can convert that nominalization into a main verb.

The following examples demonstrate this problem and how to fix it. In each revised version, notice how a noun has been converted into the sentence's main verb and replaced the original "to be" main verb.

Problem:

The contribution of Quality Circles is mostly to areas of training and motivating people to produce higher quality work.

Revision:

Quality Circles contribute to the training and the motivating of people to produce high quality work.

Problem:

Measurement of temperature is done in degrees of Fahrenheit or Celsius, and its indications are by colored marks on the outside of the thermometer.

Revision:

Temperature is measured in degrees of Fahrenheit or Celsius and is indicated by colored marks on the outside of the thermometer.

Problem:

The beginning of the clonic phase is when the sustained tonic spasm of the muscles gives way to sharp, short, interrupted jerks.

Revision:

The clonic phase begins when the sustained tonic spasm of the muscle gives way to sharp, short, interrupted jerks.

Problem:

During speech, the generation of sound is by vocal chords and the rushing of air from the lungs.

Revision:

During speech, sound is generated by the vocal cords and rushing air from the lungs.

Problem:

The response of the normal ear to sounds is in the audio-frequency between about 20-20,000 Hz.

Revision:

The normal ear responds to sounds within the audio-frequency range of about 20-20,000 Hz.

Noun Stacks

Search your writing for sentences that contain long, piled-up strings of nouns. Their effect on a reader is similar being hit in the head with a large, blunt object.

Revise these sentences and "unpack" or "unstack" their long noun strings into multiple verbs, clauses, and phrases.

The following examples demonstrate this problem and how to fix it. In each revised version, notice how a long string of nouns has been broken apart:

Problem:

There is a growing awareness of organizational employee creative capacity.

Revision:

Awareness of the creative capacity of employees in all organizations is growing.

Problem:

Position acquisition requirements are any combination of high school graduation and years of increasingly responsible secretarial experience.

Revision:

To qualify for the position, you'll need to be a high school graduate and have had increasingly responsible secretarial experience.

Problem:

The Quality Circle participation roles and tasks and time/cost requirements of Quality Circle organizational implementation will be described.

Revision:

The tasks of the participants in Quality Circles and the time and cost requirements involved in the implementation of Quality Circles will be discussed.

Problem:

Proper integrated circuit packaging type identification and applications are crucial to electrical system design and repair.

Revision:

Identifying the proper type of packaging for integrated circuits is crucial to the design and repair of electrical systems.

Problem:

Cerebral-anoxia-associated neonatal period birth injuries can lead to epileptic convulsions.

Revision:

Birth injuries associated with cerebral anoxia in the neonatal period can lead to epileptic convulsions.

Redundant Phrasing

Eliminate redundant phrases in your writing. They can come from these three sources (but there are probably plenty more):

- **wordy set phrases:** Look for four- to five-word phrases; you can usually chop them to a one- to two-word phrase without losing meaning. For example, "in view of the fact that" can be reduced to "since" or "because."
- **obvious qualifiers.** Look for a word that is implicit in the word it modifies. For example, phrases like "anticipate in advance," "completely finish," or "important essentials" are examples of obvious qualifiers.
- **scattershot phrasing.** Look for two or more compounded synonyms. For example, "thoughts and ideas" (what's the difference?) or "actions and behavior" (if there is a difference between these two, does the writer mean to use it?) are common.

Here are some classic examples of wordy set phrases and their revised versions:

Wordy Phrase	Revised Phrase
in view of the fact that	since, because
at this point in time	now, then
it is recommended that	we recommend
as per your request	as you requested
in light of the fact that	since, because
being of the opinion that	I believe
in the near future	soon

during the time that	when
it would be advisable to	should, ought
due to the fact that	since, because
in this day and age	now, currently
for the reason that	since, because
in my own personal opinion	I believe, in my opinion, I think
to the fullest extent possible	fully
in accordance with your request	as you requested
four in number	four
predicated upon the fact that	based on
inasmuch as	since, because
pursuant to your request	as you requested
in connection with	related to
take cognizance of the fact that	realize
it has come to my attention that	I have learned that
with reference to the fact that	concerning, about
with regard to	concerning, about
in close proximity to	near, close, about
to the extent that	as much as
in the neighborhood of	near, close, about
until such time as	until
has the ability to	can
that being the case	therefore

Expletives

In grammar, an "expletive" is a word that serves a function but has no meaning. The most common expletive phrases in English are "it is/are" and "there is/are." They are sometimes useful, but they are more often redundant and weaken a sentence's impact. If you can, delete them from technical documents.

Here are some examples of sentences with expletives and their revised versions without expletives.

Problem:

When there is a very strong build-up at the front of the plane, it is what is known as a shock wave.

Revision:

When a very strong build-up occurs at the front end of the plane, a shock wave forms.

Problem:

When there is decay of a radioactive substance, there is the emission of some form of a high-energy particle—an alpha particle, a beta particle, or a gamma ray.

Revision:

When a radioactive substance decays, some form of a high-energy particle—an alpha particle, a beta particle, or a gamma ray—is emitted.

Problem:

It is the results of studies of the central region of the M87 galaxy that have shown that there are stars near the center that move around as though there were some huge mass at the center that was attracting them.

Revision:

Recent studies of the central region of the M87 galaxy have shown stars near the center moving around as though some huge mass at the center were attracting them.

Weak Use of Passive-Voice Verbs

One of the all-time worst offenders for creating unclear, wordy, indirect writing is the passive-voice construction.

Look for a "to be" verb coupled with a past participle (a past-tense verb, often ending in -ed). Change it to an active verb, and rearrange the sentence to make grammatical sense.

It's easy enough to convert a sentence from active voice to passive voice, and back again.

Passive Voice: The report was written by the student.

Active Voice: The student wrote the report.

However, the passive voice can be a shifty operator—it can cover up its source, that is, who's doing the acting, as this example shows.

Passive Voice: The papers will be graded according to the criteria stated in the syllabus.
Graded by whom, though?

Active Voice: The teacher will grade the papers according to the criteria stated in the syllabus.
Oh! That guy...

It's this ability to conceal the actor or agent of the sentence that makes the passive voice a favorite of people in authority—policemen, city officials, and, yes, teachers. At any rate, you can see how the passive voice can cause wordiness, indirectness, and comprehension problems.

Passive Voice: Your figures have been reanalyzed in order to determine the coefficient of error. The results will be announced when the situation is judged appropriate.
Who analyzes, and who will announce?

Active Voice: We have reanalyzed your figures in order to determine the range of error. We will announce the results when the time is right.

Passive Voice: Almost all home mortgage loans nowadays are made for twenty-five years. With the price of housing at such inflated levels, those loans cannot be paid off in any shorter period of time.
Who makes the loans, and who can't pay them off?

Active Voice: Almost all home mortgage loans nowadays are for twenty-five years. With the price of housing at such inflated levels, homeowners cannot pay off those loans in any shorter period of time.

Passive Voice: However, market share is being lost by ride-share operators, as is shown in the graph in Figure 2.
Who or what is losing market share, who or what shows it?

Active Voice: However, ride-share operators are losing market share, as the graph in Figure 2 shows.

Passive Voice: For many years, federal regulations concerning the use of wire-tapping have been ignored. Only recently have tighter restrictions been imposed on the circumstances that warrant it.
Who has ignored the regulations, and who is imposing them?

Active Voice: For many years, government officials have ignored federal regulations concerning the use of wire-tapping. Only recently has the federal government imposed tighter restrictions on the circumstances that warrant it.

Passive Voice: After the arm of the hand-held stapler is pushed down, the blade from the magazine is raised by the top-leaf spring, and the magazine and base.
Who pushes it down, and who or what raises it?

Active Voice: After you push down on the arm of the hand-held stapler, the top-leaf spring raises the blade from the magazine, and the magazine and base move apart.

Passive Voice: The solution was heated to 28.4 degrees Celsius and was stirred for 9 minutes and 1 second.
Who heated the solution, and who or what stirred it?

Active Voice: My lab partner and I heated the solution to 28.4 degrees Celsius and took turns stirring it for 9 minutes and 1 second.

Don't get the idea that the passive voice is always wrong. It is a good writing technique if

- the subject is obvious or too-often-repeated
- the actor is unknown
- the actor isn't important
- we want to stress the action more than who did it
- we need to rearrange words in a sentence for emphasis.

Notice that the passive voice is really all right in the last two examples above.

Subject-Verb Mismatches

In dense, highly technical writing, it's easy to lose track of the real subject and pick a verb that just does not make sense. The result is a noun physically not able to do what the verb says it is doing, or some abstract thing performing something nitty-gritty real-world action.

Check to make sure every sentence's noun matches the main verb.

Here are some examples and their revisions.

Problem: The causes of the disappearance of early electric automobiles were devastating to the future of energy conservation in the U.S.

Revision: The disappearance of early electric automobiles destroyed the future of energy conservation in the U.S.

Problem: Presently, electric vehicles are experimenting with two types of energy sources.

Revision: Presently, research on electric vehicles involves two types of energy sources.

Problem: Consequently, the body is more coordinated and is less likely to commit mental mistakes.

Revision: Consequently, workers will be more coordinated and commit fewer mental errors.

Readability, Sentence Lengths, and Sentence Structures

When you are writing about highly technical subject matter, it is easy to construct long sentences that become hard to read, or to bore your reader with highly repetitive sentence lengths and grammatical structures.

Readability

The reader of a technical document needs to be able to extract information from it as easily as possible, so most technical documents are written at the 8th-grade level. The average sentence length should be about fifteen words.

When you revise, look for long sentences that contain lots of information. Break them into shorter, bite-sized chunks that contain single ideas, and run the resulting sentences through a readability checker. For example, MS Word has a built-in readability tool that will tell you the number of words per sentence and the Flesch-Kincaid model's estimate of the text's grade level. (Open your document in MS Word, click *File > Options > Proofing*, check the "*Show readability statistics*" box, and run the spellchecker.)

Sentence Length

The average sentence in a technical document should contain about fifteen words, but you can use significantly longer or shorter sentences if necessary. Any sentence over thirty-five or forty words almost definitely needs to be broken up. An occasional short sentence (say, five to ten words) can be very effective, but lots of them can cause writing to be choppy and hard to follow.

Similarly, if the document contains a string of sentences that are close to the same length (for example, six sentences of exactly fifteen words each), the reader will fall into a rhythm and find it hard to pay attention. Break apart or combine sentences to create variety in their length.

Sentence Structures

In English, there are four basic sentence structures:

- **simple.** This type of sentence contains a single independent clause.
- **compound.** This type of sentence contains two independent clauses.
- **complex.** This type of sentence contains an independent clause and a dependent clause.
- **compound complex.** This type of sentence contains a compound sentence and at least one dependent clause.

Technical writing usually uses simple and compound sentences, and sometimes complex sentences. It very rarely uses compound complex sentences. Look for these sentence structures and revise your technical document accordingly.

Also, as with sentence lengths, if all your sentences use the same grammatical structure, your reader will fall into a rhythm and find it hard to pay attention. Break apart or combine sentences to create variety in their grammatical structure.

Here are some examples of overly long, complex sentences and their revised versions:

Problem: In order to understand how a solid, liquid or gas can be made to give off radiation in the form of a laser beam, one must understand some of the basic theory behind laser light.
Length: 35 words
Grade level: 15.2

Revision: A solid, liquid or gas can be made to give off radiation in the form of a laser beam. Understanding this process requires some knowledge about the basic theory behind laser light.
Average length: 16 words
Grade level: 9.0

Problem: Laser beams, which have many properties that distinguish them from ordinary light, result from the emission of energy from atoms in the form of electromagnetic waves whose range in most laser beams is 10^{-3} to 10^{-7} meters.
Length: 37 words
Grade level: 19.5

Revision: Laser beams are just beams of light, but they have special properties that distinguish them from ordinary light. Laser beams come from atoms that emit energy as electromagnetic waves. The average wavelength ranges from 10^{-3} to 10^{-7} meters.
Average length: 12.6 words
Grade level: 10.7

By: David McMurrey and Cassandra Race

Objectives

Upon completion of this chapter, readers will be able to:

- Explain and apply how to find information in libraries.
- Explain and apply how to indicate sources of borrowed information.
- Explain and apply how to cross-reference.

Information Search

This section focuses on finding information for your technical documentation projects online and in physical libraries. Your job is to get good, specific, up-to-date information for your formal report project. You may not be able to read it all—you're not writing a dissertation, nor is your knowledge about your topic expected to be anywhere close to that level. But at least you know what's out there.

Check out the library system at Kennesaw State University. Here KSU students will find research help 24/7.

How do I get started with research?

Find a Topic, Narrow It, Brainstorm It

Before you head for the library or its Internet equivalent, you need a topic, some idea of the specific aspect of the topic you want to focus on, and some ideas about what to say about that narrowed topic. Problems finding a topic and thinking of what to say about it are often called the dreaded *writer's block*.

Narrowing a topic is that process in which you go from an impossibly huge topic such as nanotechnology to something more manageable such as applications of nanotechnology in brain surgery.

Brainstorming a topic is that process in which you think of everything you can that you might write about in relation to your topic.

Know Your Booleans for Searching Online of in Databases

An important tool to have when you go searching for information—either in libraries or on the Internet—has to do with Booloean operators: AND, OR, NOT and a few esoteric others. The following table will help you become an expert in narrowing search parameters, especially in a huge database such as that provided by the university.

Table 1: Boolean Search Tools

Technique	What it Does	Example
Truncation — adding a symbol to the root of the word to retrieve related terms and variant endings for the root term. Some databases have left- and right-hand truncation.	Expands your search	structur* finds structure, structuring, structures, etc. *elasticity will find elasticity, aeroelasticity, viscoelasticity
Boolean AND — retrieves only those records containing all your search terms	Narrows your search	finite AND element AND methods

Boolean OR — retrieves records containing any of your search terms; especially useful for synonyms, alternate spellings, or related concepts	Broadens your search	energy OR fuel pollut* OR contaminat* sulfur OR sulphur
Boolean NOT, AND NOT — attempts to exclude a term that is not useful or relevant	Narrows your search	"Advanced Materials" AND composite NOT wood
Proximity — retrieves terms within a specified distance of one another; variations of proximity searches are phrase searches, where the terms must be retrieved exactly as entered; NEAR, ADJACENT, WITH, and WITHIN searches	Narrows your search	"Styrenic Block Copolymers" (quotation marks ensure that the multiple-word term is searched as a phrase, but are not required for all databases)
Parentheses ( ) — groups terms with Boolean for more complex searches	Combines searches	"mechanical engineering" AND (handbook OR dictionary)

Types of Resources for Information Research

Encyclopedias and Other Reference Works

If you are beginning at ground zero with your technical report topic, a good strategy would be to read some articles in general encyclopedias. As a researcher, you need to know something about the topic so you will know what kinds of questions to ask and how to organize your data. If you are knowledgeable, the entire research process will be more efficient and even enjoyable.

- World Book Online (yes, even this one!)
- Britannica
- Access Science for online access to the *McGraw-Hill Encyclopedia of Science and Technology*

Can you build a legitimate technical report based on encyclopedia articles that you summarize and paraphrase? NO! Most college level instructors will not accept encyclopedias as legitimate sources because their information is broad, not specific. You may not be able to gather enough information to create a report of any reasonable length. We could go on about this for a long time, but do not consider using an encyclopedia, not even wikipedia.com, as part of your cited research data...only as a place for you to begin building a background of knowledge.

You can find reference books like encyclopedias by typing in a couple of words of the title in an online library catalog (for example, mechanical engineer* handbook, "encyclopedia engineering", or "encyclopediaandengineering"), truncating any words that could have variant endings, and eliminating any prepositions or articles (*of, for, the, a, an*).

Here are some examples of what you might find:

1. *Prentice-Hall Encyclopedia of Information Technology*
2. *McGraw-Hill Dictionary of the Life Sciences*
3. *Robotics Sourcebook and Dictionary*
4. *Energy: A Guide to Organizations and Information Resources in the United States*
5. *McGraw-Hill Yearbook of Science and Technology*

Books

Books can provide excellent background, a historical treatment of your subject and depth. Check a book's table of contents and index to see if it has what you are looking for. For some current research topics, however, books tend to be too general. To obtain more specific information on technological advancements, go to journal articles, technical reports, or other sources discussed later in this chapter.

Try these resources. Search "drone aircraft" on each to see which has the most up to date resources:

- Online Books
- Library of Congress Catalog
- World Cat

Here are some sites that consolidate access to thousands of libraries worldwide:

- LibDex
- The WWW Library Directory
- LibWeb

Periodicals

Periodicals is a librarian's word for stuff that comes out periodically—like magazines, journals, newspapers. Magazines, which are by definition for general audiences, are not likely to have much that is useful to your report. At the college level, you will be expected to use scholarly, or peer reviewed, journals for research. You can find these in the university database, or you can borrow from other systems through an system of inter-library loans. When in doubt, pay a visit to your campus library and make friends with the librarians there.

Directory of Open Access Journals. DOAJ offers free access to over 3,500 full-text, quality-controlled scientific and scholarly journals, over 1,200 of which are searchable at the article level.

Most of the following are services you pay for; some offer a free 30-day trial. Your local library may subscribe to some of these, giving you free access:

- Applied Science and Technology
- Academic Search Complete
- INSPEC
- ScienceDirect

Technical Reports

- National Technical Information Service (NTIS)
- IEEE Xplore
- NASA Technical Reports Server

Associations and Interest Groups

Organizations like associations, special-interest groups, and advocacy groups are good potential sources for information on your topic—or a terrible ideological swamp. Keep in mind that associations and interest groups generally have agendas or biases about their topics. *Encyclopedia of Associations* may be a good resource. Ask your librarian for help with this kind of resource.

Library and Subject Guides

Research assistance, subject guides, useful resources and web sites compiled by the friendly librarians at Austin Community College, for example, occupational therapy, business and technical communications, and other department and field names. These are presented here.

Austin Community College Research Guides

Your own library at Kennesaw State University also has awesome resources for you to use.

KSU LibGuides

Other Information Resources

There are certainly other kinds of information sources such as patents, standards, product literature, conference procedings. Again, ask your librarian for help with these kinds of resources.

Evaluate Your Research Findings

The following is a system of evaluating the reliability of Internet information developed by the Cornell University Library. This information is especially important if you are using Internet sources and need to defend their validity and reliability.

- **Point of View**: Does this article or book seem objective, or does the author have a bias or make assumptions? What was the author's method of obtaining data or conducting research? Does the website aim to sell you something or just provide information? What is the author's purpose for researching and writing this article or book?
- **Authority**: Who wrote the material? Is the author a recognized authority on the subject? What qualifications does this author have to write on this topic? Is it clear who the intended audience is? What is the reputation of the publisher or producer of the book or journal? Is it an alternative press, a private or political organization, a commercial press, or university press? What institution or Internet provider supports this information? (Look for a link to the homepage.) What is the author's affiliation to this institution?
- **Reliability**: What body created this information? Consider the domain letters at the end of a web address (URL) to judge the site's quality or usefulness. What kind of support is included for the information? Are there facts, interviews, and statistics that can be verified? Is the evidence convincing to you? Is there any evidence provided to support the author's conclusions, such as charts, maps, bibliographies, and documents? Compare the information provided to other factual sources.
- **Timeliness**: Has the site been recently updated? Look for this information at the bottom of a web page. How does the copyright of a book or publication date of an article impact the information contained in it? Do you need historical or recent information? Does the resource provide the currency you need?
- **Scope**: Consider the breadth and depth of an article, book, website, or other material. Does it cover what you expected? Who is the intended audience? Is the content aimed at a general or a scholarly audience? Based on your information need, is the material too basic, too technical, or too clinical?

In addition to the above, if you are looking at Internet sites, pay careful attention to any advertising on page. Online gambling or magic weight loss solutions might not be the kind of company your research needs to keep.

As a rule of thumb, steer clear of any resource that has "wiki" or "about" in the title or url. Your safest bets are sites sponsored by the U.S. government (.gov) or educational institutions (.edu).

Citing Sources of Borrowed Information

When you write a technical report, you can and should borrow information like crazy—to make it legal, all you have to do is "document" it. If your report makes you sound like a rocket scientist but there's not a single source citation in it and you haven't even taken college physics yet, people are going to start wondering. (In *Night Court*, you'd be guilty of plagiarism. Fine—an F on the paper in question.) However, if you take that same report and load it up properly with source citations (those little indicators that show that you are borrowing information and from whom), everybody is all the more impressed—plus they're not secretly thinking you're a shady character. A documented report (one that has source indicators in it) says to readers that you've done your homework, that you're up on this field, that you approach these things professionally—that you are no slouch. Most importantly, you've shown that you respect the rights of the original authors, the owners of the intellectual property you are using.

The following resources will provide all the guidance you need to correctly document, or give credit to, your sources.

- Research and Citation Resources. Overview from the Purdue OWL with links to specific systems.
- APA Documentation. From Austin Community College.
- MLA Documentation. From Austin Community College.
- Turabian Documentation. From Austin Community College.
- CSE Documentation: Name-Year Method. From Austin Community College.
- CSE Documentation: Citation-Sequence System. From Austin Community College.
- IEEE Citation Style Guide . From Georgia Tech. (The IEEE system is very similar to the system described in the following.)

Number System of Documentation

If you've taken other college writing courses recently, you have probably been exposed to other documentation systems—specifically the MLA, or works cited system. The problem with that system is that it is rather limited to the literature and humanities field. Unfortunately, it is not widely used outside that field—especially not in technical and scientific fields. One of the more common systems used in technical fields is the *number system*, a formatting procedure that is easy to learn and use. The citation-sequence version of the *CSE (Scientific) Documentation* (see the link above) is one of the specific incarnations of the number system. (Notice here that we use brackets, not parentheses, for the source indicators.)

In this number system, you list your information sources alphabetically, number them, and put the list at the back of your report. Then in the body of your report, whenever you borrow information from one of those sources, you put the source number and, optionally, the page number in brackets at that point in the text where the borrowed information occurs. The illustration below shows how this system works. However, in a hypothetical example:

- [4] would refer to source 4 in the list.
- [4:231] would refer to page 231 of source 4.
- [4:231-235] would refer to pages 231 through 235 of source 4.
- [4;7] would indicate that the information was borrowed from source 4 and source 7.

What to Document

This question always comes up: how do I decide when to document information—when, for example, I forgot where I learned it from, or when it really seems like common knowledge? There is no neat, clean answer. You may have heard it said that anything in an encyclopedia or in an introductory textbook is common knowledge and need not be documented. Don't believe it. If it really isn't common knowledge for you, at least not yet, document it! If you just flat can't remember how you came by the information, then it has safely become common knowledge for you. (All that's really going on here is that we're trying to protect the efforts of those poor devils who worked themselves into the ground originating the information we want to borrow—give 'em a break, give 'em their due!) If you know you read it during your research process, you need to document it.

One other question that is often asked: do I document information I find in product brochures or that I get in conversations with knowledgeable people? Yes, most certainly. You document *any* information you did not create, regardless whether it is in print, in electronic bits, magnetic spots, or in thin air. While you probably studied this in high school, it becomes a very serious issue in a university that expects research to not only be useful, but also to be honest.

How to Place the Source Indicators

It's a bit tricky deciding exactly where to place the source indicators—at the beginning of the passage containing the borrowed information, at the end? If it makes sense to "attribute" the source (cite the name of the author or the title of the information), you can put the attribution at the beginning and the bracketed source indicator at the end (as is shown in in the following).

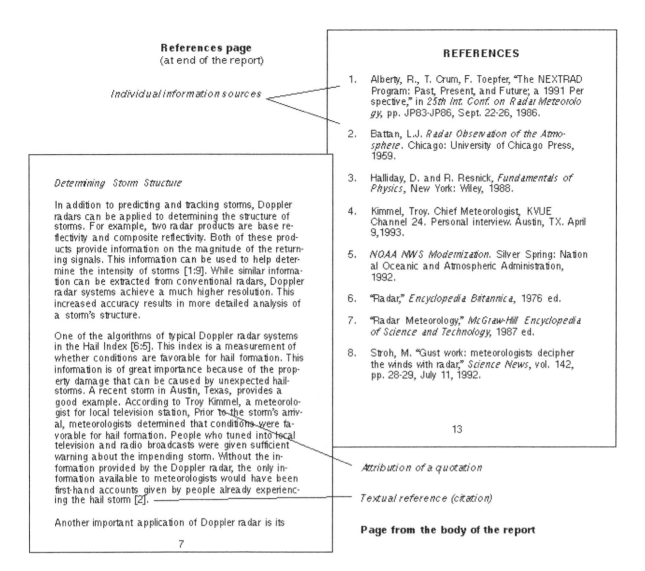

Figure 1: Example page with bracketed source indicators and corresponding source list

In the number documentation system, the code numbers in the text of the report are keyed to the references page. For example, [6:5] in the middle of the page from the body of the report indicates that the information came from source 6 (in References), page 5. Notice that the attribution of the quotation indicates the beginning of the borrowed information and the bracketed source indicator marks the end.

How to Set Up the Sources List

A bit more challenging is setting up the list of information sources—that numbered, alphabetized list you put at the end of the document. (The context here is still the number system.) The best way to learn is to use examples. The following examples show you how to handle books, government reports, articles from magazines and journals, encyclopedia articles, and personal interviews.

Internet and web information sources. For format information regarding citing Internet and web sources, see any of the resources listed above. As you will see, there are quite a few variations. However, a simple functional practice would use this order:

- Author name, last name first. If that's not available, use the organization's name, followed by a period.
- Next, the title of the page.
- After that the publication date of the web page, if available; otherwise, use the "N.d" indicator.

- Next, the full URL of the page.
- And finally an indication of the date you accessed the page, for example, Accessed June 6, 1988.

Books. For books, first put the name of the author (last name first), followed by a period, followed by the title of the book in italics, followed by a period, followed by the city of the publisher, followed by a colon, followed by the publisher's name (but delete all those tacky "Inc.," "Co.," and "Ltd." things), followed by the year of publication, ending with a period. In this style, you don't indicate pages.

Burn, Duncan. *Nuclear Power and the Energy Crisis*. New York: New York University Press, 1978.

Magazine and journal articles. Start with the author's name first (last name first), followed by a period, then the title of the article in quotation marks and ending with a period, followed by the name of the magazine or journal in italics, followed by a period, followed by the date of issue of the magazine the article occurs in, followed by the beginning and ending page. If the article spread out across the magazine, you can write "33+." or "33(5)." The (5) in the preceding is an estimate of how many pages the article would be if it were continuous.

If there is no author, start with the article or book title. If there are two authors, add "and" and the second author's name, first name first. If there are too many authors, use the first one (last name first), followed by "*et al.*," which means "and others."

Idso, S. B. "Climate Significance of Doubling CO2 Concentrations." *Science* (March 28, 1980), 128-134.

Note: You may have seen complex entries indicating volume and issue numbers. While those may be required in some contexts, normally you can simplify things and just include the issue date. But ask!

Encyclopedia articles. Encyclopedia articles are easy! Start with the title of the article in quotation marks ending with a period, followed by the name of the encyclopedia (in italics if you have it; otherwise, underline), followed by the period, then the year of the edition of the encyclopedia.

"Nuclear Reactor." *Van Nostrand's Scientific Encyclopedia*. 1980 ed.

Reports. With reports, you're likely to dealing with government reports or local informally produced reports. With most reports, you may not have an individual author name; in such cases, you use the group name as the author. For government reports, the publisher is often the Government Printing Office; and the city of publication, Washington, D.C. Also, for government documents, you should include the document number, as is shown in the following example.

Committee on Energy and Natural Resources, *U.S. Senate Hearings on the Effects of Carbon Dioxide Buildup in the Atmosphere*. DOA 2.8/NAA 6655.3. Washington: U.S. Government Printing Office, 1980.

Personal interviews, correspondence, and other nonprint sources. With these sources, you treat the interviewee or the e-mail or letter writer as the author, follow that name with the person's title, followed by a period, then the company name, followed by a period, then the city and state, followed by a period, then what the information was ("Personal interview" or "Personal correspondence") followed by a period, ending with the date.

Smith, Eunice J., Public Relations Director. Fayette Power Facility. Fayetteville, TX. Personal interview. June 6, 1988.

Product brochures. For these kinds of information sources, treat the company name as the author, followed by a period, use something identifying like the product name (including the specific model number), followed by anything that seems like the title of the brochure, followed by a period, ending with a date if you can find one (otherwise, put "N.d.").

Society to Stop Nuclear Power Plants. *Stop the Nukes*. Political brochure. N.d.

Documenting borrowed graphics. It's certainly legal to copy graphics from other sources and use them in your own work—as long as you document them. You indicate the source of a borrowed graphic in the figure title (caption), which is located just below the graphic. In the figure title, you can show the source of the graphic in two ways—the long traditional way or the shorter way that uses the format of the number system:

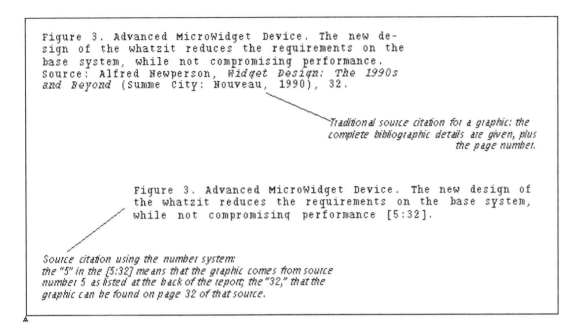

Figure 2: Two ways to indicate the source of borrowed graphics.

Cross-Referencing

Technical reports and instructions often require cross-references—those pointers to other places in the same document or to other information sources where related information can be found.

A cross-reference can help readers in a number of different ways:

- It can point them toward more basic information if, for example, they have entered into a document more complex than their level of understanding.
- It can point them to more advanced information if, for example, they already know the stuff you're trying to tell them.
- Also, it can point them to related information.

Related information is the hardest area to explain because ultimately everything is related to everything else—there could be no end to the cross-references. But here's an example from DOS—that troll that lurks inside PC-type computers and supposedly helps you. There are several ways you can copy files: the COPY command, the DISKCOPY command, and XCOPY command. Each method offers different advantages. If you were writing about the COPY command, you'd want cross-references to these other two so that readers could do a bit of shopping around.

Of course, the preceding discussion assumed cross-references within the same document. If there is just too much background to cover in your document, you can cross-reference some external website, book, or article that does provide that background. That way, you are off the hook for having to explain it all!

Now, a decent cross-reference consists of several elements:

1. Name of the source being referenced—This can either be the title or a general subject reference. If it is a chapter title or a heading, put it in quotation marks; if it is the name of a book, magazine, report, or

reference work, put it in italics or underline. (Individual article titles also go in quotation marks.) Choose italics over underlining when possible.

2. Page number—Required if it is in the same document; optional if it is to another document.
3. Subject matter of the cross-reference—Often, you need to state what's in the cross-referenced material and indicate why the reader should go to the trouble of checking it out. This information may necessitate indicating the subject matter of the cross-referenced material or stating explicitly how it is related to the current discussion.

These guidelines are shown in the following illustration. Notice in that illustration how different the rules are when the cross-reference is "internal" (that is, to some other part of the same document) compared to when it is "external" (to information outside of the document).

For details on creating graphics and then incorporating them into a document, see the section on graphics in this guide on page 16.	In this *internal* cross-reference, the section is referenced generically. It's standard to cite the page number in internal cross-references.
For details on creating graphics and then incorporating them into a document, see "Graphics" in the *Online Technical Writing Guide*.	The title of the chapter is in double quotation marks. The title of the book that the chapter occurs is italicized.
For details on creating graphics and then incorporating them into a document, see the chapter on graphics in the *Online Technical Writing Guide*.	If you don't want to cite the exact titles of the chapter, just use lowercase.
For details on creating graphics and then incorporating them into a report, see "Brighten Up That Monthly Report!" in the *Office Information Newsletter*.	If you cite an article in a periodical, put the article in quotation marks and italicize the name of the periodical.

Examples of cross-references. Internal cross-references are cross-references to other areas within your same document; external ones are those to information resources external to your document.

Activities and Exercises

- Locate several journals in your major field and find the information for writers section. What formatting protocols are expected if you want to be published?
- In small groups, visit the Purdue OWL Research and Citation Section and explore it. What can you learn about the different formatting styles? When would you use APA? MLA? IEEE? Chicago?
- In small groups or a discussion forum, share some of your own research techniques...what has been effective for you in the past? What advice would you offer others in the class for becoming a good researcher?
- Locate your school's policy on plagiarism and academic honesty. How important do you think this is? Find some sources that reveal cases of academic dishonesty...how does lack of integrity in research affect the individuals and the university?

5.7: Basic Patterns and Elements of the Sentence

By: David McMurrey

Objectives

Upon completion of this chapter, readers will be able to:

- Explain and apply basic patterns of the sentence as they relate to technical writing.
- Explain and apply basic elements of the sentence as they relate to technical writing.

This section is a quick review of the fundamentals of the sentence. If you encounter unfamiliar terminology in this textbook or in your class, refer to this section for help. For more on grammar, see the Purdue Online Writing Lab.

Basic Sentence Patterns

Subject + Verb

The simplest of sentence patterns is composed of a subject and verb without a direct object or subject complement. It uses an intransitive verb, that is, a verb requiring no direct object.

Control rods remain inside the fuel assembly of the reactor.

The development of wind power practically ceased until the early 1970s.

All amplitude-modulation (AM) receivers work in the same way.

The cross-member exposed to abnormal stress eventually broke.

Only two types of charge exist in nature.

Subject + Linking Verb + Subject Complement

Another simple pattern uses the linking verb, any form of the to be verb without an action verb.

The chain reaction is the basis of nuclear power.

The debate over nuclear power has often been bitter.

Folding and faulting of the earth's surface are important geologic processes.

Windspeed seems to be highest during the middle of the day.

The silicon solar cell can be difficult and expensive to manufacture.

Subject + Verb + Direct Object

Another common sentence pattern uses the direct object.

Silicon conducts electricity in an unusual way.

The anti-reflective coating on the the silicon cell reduces reflection from 32 to 22 percent.

Prestressing of the concrete increases the load-carrying capacity of the members.

Subject + Verb + Indirect Object + Direct Object

The sentence pattern with the indirect object and direct object is similar to the preceding pattern.

The walls are usually painted black.

The plant shutdown left the entire area an economic disaster.

The committee declared the new design a breakthrough in energy efficiency.

The low cost of the new computer made competition much too difficult for some of the other companies.

Passive Voice Pattern

The passive voice is not ordinarily considered a "pattern," but it is an important and often controversial construction. It reverses the subject and object and, in some cases, deletes the subject. Compare these example active and passive voice sentences.

Passive Voice: Saccharin is now permitted as an additive in food.

Active Voice: The FDA now permits saccharin as an additive in food.

Passive Voice: This report is divided into three main sections.

Active Voice: I have divided this report into three main sections.

Passive Voice: Windmills are classified as either lift or drag types.

Active Voice: Engineers classify windmills as either lift or drag types.

Passive Voice: The valves used in engine start are controlled by a computer.

Active Voice: A computer usually controls the valves used in an engine start.

Passive Voice: The remains of Troy were destroyed by later builders on the site.

Active Voice: Later builders on the site of Troy destroyed the remains of citadel.

Passive Voice: Some restaurant locations can be leased.

Active Voice: You can lease some restaurant locations.

Simple Sentences

A simple sentence is one that contains subject and a verb and no other independent or dependent clause.

One of the tubes is attached to the manometer part of the instrument indicating the pressure of the air within the cuff.

To measure blood pressure, a device known as a sphygmomanometer and a stethoscope are needed.
compound subject

There are basically two types of stethoscopes.
inverted subject and verb

The sphygmomanometer is usually covered with cloth and has two rubber tubes attached to it.
compound verb

Compound Sentences

A compound sentence is made up of two or more independent clauses joined by a coordinating conjunction (*and, or, nor, but, yet, for*) and a comma; an adverbial conjunction and a semicolon; or a semicolon.

In sphygmomanometers, too narrow a cuff can result in erroneously high readings, and too wide a cuff can result in erroneously low readings.

Some cuffs hook together; others wrap or snap into place.

Compound Predicates

A predicate is everything in the verb part of the sentence *after* the subject (unless the sentence uses inverted word order). A compound predicate is two or more predicates joined by a coordinating conjunction. Traditionally, the conjunction in a sentence consisting of just two compound predicates is not punctuated.

Another library media specialist has been using Accelerated Reader for ten years and has seen great results.

This cell phone app lets users share pictures instantly with followers and categorize photos with hashtags.

Basic Parts of the Sentence

Subject

The subject of a sentence is that noun, pronoun, or phrase or clause about which the sentence makes a statement.

Einstein's general theory of relativity has been subjected to many tests of validity over the years.

Although a majority of caffeine drinkers think of it as a stimulant, heavy users of caffeine say the substance relaxes them.

Surrounding the secure landfill on all sides are impermeable barrier walls.
inverted sentence pattern

In a secure landfill, the soil on top and the cover block storm water intrusion into the landfill.
compound subject

Verb Phrase

The main verb, or verb phrase, of a sentence is a word or words that express an action, event, or a state of existence. It sets up a relationship between the subject and the rest of the sentence.

The first high-level language to be widely accepted, FORTRAN, was implemented on an IBM 704 computer.

Instruction in the source program <u>must be translated</u> into machine language.
passive construction

The operating system <u>controls</u> the translation of the source program and <u>carries</u> out supervisory functions.
compound verb

Predicate

The predicate is the rest of the sentence coming after the subject. It can include the main verb, subject complement, direct object, indirect object, and object complement.

The pressure in a pressurized water reactor <u>varies from system to system</u>.

The pressure <u>is maintained at about 2250 pounds per square inch to prevent steam from forming</u>.

The pressure <u>is then lowered to form steam at about 600 pounds per square inch</u>.

In contrast, a boiling water reactor <u>operates at constant pressure</u>.

Subject Complement

The subject complement is that noun, pronoun, adjective, phrase, or clause that comes after a linking verb (some form of the *be* verb):

The maximum allowable concentration is ten <u>parts</u> H_2S per million parts breathable air.

The deadening of the sense of smell caused by H_2S is the <u>result</u> of the effects of H_2S on the olfactory nerves of the brain. Continuous exposure to toxic concentrations of H_2S can be <u>fatal</u>.

Direct Object

A direct object—a noun, pronoun, phrase, or clause acting as a noun—takes the action of the main verb. A direct object can be identified by putting *what?*, *which?*, or *whom?* in its place.

The housing assembly of a mechanical pencil contains the mechanical <u>workings</u> of the pencil.

Lavoisier used curved glass <u>discs</u> fastened together at their rims, with wine filling the space between, to focus the sun's rays to attain temperatures of 3000° F.

The dust and smoke lofted into the air by nuclear explosions might cool the earth's <u>atmosphere</u> some number of degrees.

A 20 percent fluctuation in average global temperature could reduce biological <u>activity</u>, shift weather <u>patterns</u>, and ruin <u>agriculture</u>.
compound direct object

The cooler temperatures brought about by nuclear war might end all <u>life</u> on earth.

On Mariners 6 and 7, the two-axis scan platforms provided much more <u>capability</u> and <u>flexibility</u> for the scientific payload than those of Mariner 4.
compound direct object

Indirect Object

An indirect object—a noun, pronoun, phrase, or clause acting as a noun—receives the action expressed in the sentence. It can be identified by inserting *to* or *for*.

In the application letter, tell *[to]* the potential <u>employer</u> that a resume accompanies the letter.

The company is designing *[for]* senior <u>citizens</u> a new walkway to the park area.

Do not send *[to]* the personnel <u>office</u> a resume unless someone there specifically requests it.

Object Complement

An object complement—a noun or adjective coming after a direct object—adds detail to the direct object. To identify object complements, insert *[to be]* between the direct object and object complement.

The superviser found the <u>program</u> *[to be]* <u>faulty</u>.

The company considers the new <u>computer</u> *[to be]* a major <u>breakthrough</u>.

Most people think the space <u>shuttle</u> *[to be]* a major <u>step</u> in space exploration.

Parts of Speech and Other Sentence Elements

Nouns

A noun is the name of a person (Dr. Sanders); place (Lawrence, Kansas, factory, home); thing (scissors, saw, book); action (operation, irrigation); or idea (love, truth, beauty, intelligence). Remember that, while a word may look like a noun, it must function in the sentence as a noun:

The one <u>experiment</u> that has been given the most <u>attention</u> in the <u>debate</u> on <u>saccharin</u> is the 1977 Canadian <u>study</u> done on <u>rats</u>.

The <u>Calorie Control Council</u>, a <u>group</u> of Japanese and American <u>manufacturers</u> of <u>saccharin</u>, spent $890,000 in the first three <u>months</u> of the 1977 <u>ban</u> on <u>saccharin</u> on <u>lobbying</u>, <u>advertisements</u>, and <u>public relations</u>.

A flat-plate <u>collector</u> located on a sloping <u>roof</u> heats <u>water</u> which circulates through a <u>coil</u> and is pumped back to the <u>collector</u>.

The <u>blades</u> start turning when the <u>windspeed</u> reaches 10 mph, and an <u>anemometer</u> is attached to the <u>shaft</u> to measure <u>windspeed</u>.

The multifuel <u>capacity</u> of the Stirling <u>engine</u> gives it a <u>versatility</u> not possible in the internal combustion <u>engine</u>.

The regenerative cooling <u>cycle</u> in the <u>engines</u> of the space <u>shuttle</u> is made up of high pressure <u>hydrogen</u> that flows in <u>tubes</u> connecting the <u>nozzle</u> and the combustion <u>chamber</u>.

Pronouns

A pronoun stands in the place of a noun. There are several types: personal pronouns, demonstrative and indefinite pronouns, and relative and interrogative pronouns. Pronouns have antecedents, a reference to a word they take the place of.

Personal pronouns include nominative case, objective case, and possessive case pronouns.

Nominative Case

Nominative case pronouns are used in the positions of subjects or subjective complements; they include

1. I
2. you

3. he, she, it
4. we
5. you
6. they

Objective Case

Objective case pronouns are used as direct objects, indirect objects, and objects of prepositions; they include

1. me
2. you
3. him, her, it
4. us
5. you
6. them

Possessive Case

Possessive case pronouns show possession; they include

- my, mine
- your, yours
- his, her, hers, its
- our, ours
- your, yours
- their, theirs

Demonstrative and Indefinite Pronouns

Demonstrative pronouns substitute for things being pointed out; indefinite pronouns substitute for unknown or unspecified things:

Demonstrative

- this, these
- that, those

Indefinite

- each, either
- any, neither
- anybody, some
- every, somebody
- everybody, someone

Relative and Interrogative Pronouns

Relative and interrogative pronouns link dependent to independent clauses; they link adjective or noun clauses to simple sentences. Relative pronouns include

- who
- whom
- whose
- when
- where

- why
- which
- whether
- that

Here are some examples of relative pronouns in use

Until the early 1960s, desk calculators, <u>which</u> performed only the basic arithmetic operations, were essentially mechanical in operation.

The invention of the transistor in 1948 and the integrated circuit in 1964 were two events <u>that</u> formed the basis of the electronic calculator revolution.

The form in <u>which</u> memory is presented to the software is sometimes called local address space.

George Boole, <u>who</u> was a self-taught man, is famous for his pioneering efforts to express logical concepts in mathematical form.

In 1855, Boole married Mary Everest, a niece of Sir George Everest after <u>whom</u> Mount Everest was named.

Lemaître proposed that all the matter in the Universe was concentrated into what he termed the primeval atom, <u>whose</u> explosion scattered material into space to form galaxies, <u>which</u> have been flying outward ever since.

Interrogative pronouns, similar to relative pronouns, are used in question sentences:

<u>What</u> is the fundamental unit of storage in a computer?

<u>When</u> did the first exhibit of computer graphics occur?

<u>Who</u> were the mathmaticians that arranged that first exhibit?

<u>Where</u> was the first computer graphics exhibit held?

<u>Why</u> is computer-aided art not considered art by some?

Verbs

Traditionally, verbs are divided into four groups: active verbs, linking verbs, auxiliary verbs, and modals.

Active Verbs

Active verbs express some sort of action and can be subdivided into intransitive and transitive verbs. Intransitive verbs do not take direct objects while transitive verbs do, as these two sets of examples show:

Intransitive Verbs

The rearrangement or division of a heavy nucleus may occur naturally (spontaneous fission) or under bombardment with neutrons.

The probability of an accident leading to the melting of the fuel core was estimated to be one chance in 20,000 reactor-years of operations.

The fuels used in ramjet engines burn in only a narrow range of fuel-air ratios.

Transitive Verbs

The generation of electric energy by a nuclear power plant requires the use of heat to produce steam or to heat gases in order to drive turbogenerators.

In an auxiliary relay, when the applied current or voltage exceeds a threshold value, the coil activates the armature, which either closes the open contacts or opens the closed contacts.

The solar power satellite absorbs the energy in geosynchronous orbit.

In the photovoltaic solar power system, solar cells convert the light energy into electricity.

Linking Verbs

A linking verb is any form of the verb *to be* without an action verb; it sets up something like an equal sign between the items it links. Linking verbs of a sentence can be longer than one word:

- had been
- was being
- had to have been
- would have been
- might have been
- will have been

A few linking verbs do not use *to be* but function like it:

That word processing program seems adequate for our needs.

This calculus problem looks difficult.

Since the oil spill, the beach has smelled bad.

He quickly grew weary of computer games.

Auxiliary Verbs

Auxiliary verbs "help" the main part of the verb. Here are some auxiliary verbs:

By 1967, about 500 U.S. citizens had received heart transplants.

Better immunosuppression management in transplant operations has yielded better results.

Researchers have found propranolol to be effective in the treatment of heartbeat irregularities.

Modals

Modal verbs change the meaning of the verb in a variety of ways as illustrated in the examples below:

Cracks in the welding can only be detected by x-rays.

Liquid oxygen could have leaked into the turbine and cause the fire.

The light metal fast-breeder reactor must be operated under extreme safety precautions.

Verbs are used together in a complex variety of tenses. In the chart below, keep in mind that "continuous" tenses are those that use *-ing* and "perfect" tenses are those that use some form of the auxiliary verb have.

Table 1: Variety of Tenses

Tense	Example
Simple Present	works
Present Continuous	is working
Present Perfect	has worked
Simple Past	worked
Past Continuous	was wroking
Past Perfect	had worked
Simple Future	will work
Future Continuous	will be working
Future Perfect	will have worked
Present Perfect Continuous	has been working
Past Perfect Continuous	had been working
Future Present Continuous	will have been working

Adjectives

An adjective provides more detail about a noun; that is, it modifies a noun. Adjectives occur just before the nouns they modify, or after a linking verb:

The armature is a rectangular ring about which another coil of wire is wound.

The generator is used to convert mechanical energy into electrical energy.

The steel pipes contain a protective sacrificial annode and are surrounded by packing material.

Adverbs

An adverb provides more information about a verb, adjective, or another adverb; that is, it "qualifies" the verb, adjective, or adverb:

The desk is made of an especially corrosion-resistant industrial steel.

The drilling bit actually tears rock apart to get at the oil.

The power company uses huge generators which are generally turned by steam turbines.

The debate over nuclear power has often been bitter.

Conjunctions

Conjunctions link words, phrases, and whole clauses to each other and are divided into coordinating, adverbial, and subordinating conjunctions. In this list, only the list of coordinating conjunctions is complete.

Table 2: Conjunctions

Coordinating Conjunctions	Subordinating Conjunctions	Adverbial Conjunctions
and	although	therefore

or	since	however
nor	because	in other words
but	when	thus
yet	while	then
for	if	otherwise
whereas	as if	nevertheless
as		on the other hand

Coordinating Conjunctions

Coordinating conjunctions link words, phrases, and clauses. Here are some examples:

Nuclear-powered artificial hearts proved to be complicated, bulky, and expensive.

In the 1960s, artificial heart devices did not fit well and tended to obstruct the flow of venous blood into the right atrium.

The blood vessels leading to the device tended to kink, obstructing the filling of the chambers and resulting in inadequate output.

The small clots that formed throughout the circulatory system used up so much of the clotting factor that uncontrolled bleeding from external or internal injury became a risk.

Current from the storage batteries can power lights, but the current for appliances must be modified within an inverter.

Adverbial Conjunctions

Adverbial conjunctions link two separate sentences, but require a semicolon or colon:

The Kedeco produces 1200 watts in 17 mph using a 16-foot rotor; on the other hand, the Dunlite produces 2000 watts in 25 mph winds.

The first artificial hearts were made of smooth silicone rubber which apparently caused excessive clotting and, therefore, uncontrolled bleeding.
This example does not contain two sentences; no semicolon, therfore, is needed.

For short periods, the fibers were beneficial; however, the eventual buildup of fibrin on the inner surface of the device would impair its function.

The atria of the heart contributes a negligible amount of energy; in fact, the total power output of the heart is only about 2.5 watts.

Subordinating Conjunctions

Subordinating conjunctions combine separate sentences in a different way: they turn one of the sentences into an adverb clause. Here are some examples of subordinating conjunctions:

The heart undergoes two cardiac cycle periods: a diastole, <u>when</u> blood enters the ventircles, and systole, <u>when</u> the ventricles contract and blood is pumped out of the heart.

<u>Whenever</u> an electron acquired enough energy to leave its orbit, the atom is positively charged.

If the wire is broken, electrons will cease to flow and current is zero.

Phrases and Clauses

Phrases and clauses are groups of words that act as a unit and perform a single function within a sentence. A phrase may have a partial subject or verb but not both; a dependent clause has both a subject and a verb (but is not a complete sentence). Here are a few examples (not all phrases are highlighted because some are embedded in others):

Phrases

Electricity has to do with those physical phenomena involving electrical charges and their effects when in motion and when at rest.
Involving electrical charges and their effects is also a phrase.

Electricity manifests itself as a force of attraction, independent of gravitational and short-range nuclear attraction, when two oppositely charged bodies are brought close to one another.

In 1800, A. Volta constructed and experimented with the voltaic pile, the predecessor of modern batteries.

In 1833, Faraday's experimentation with electrolysis indicated a natural unit of electrical charge, thus pointing to a discrete rather than continuous charge.
to a discrete rather than continuous charge is also a phrase.

The symbol that denotes a connection to the grounding conductor is three parallel horizontal lines, each of the lower ones being shorter than the one above it.

Electricity manifests itself as a force of attraction, independent of gravitational and short-range nuclear attraction, when two oppositely charged bodies are brought close to one another.

The symbol that denotes a connection to the grounding conductor is three parallel horizontal lines, each of the lower ones being shorter than the one above it.

These studies led Planck to postulate that electromagnetic radiation is emitted in discrete amounts, called quanta.

Since the frequency is the speed of sound divided by the wavelength, a shorter wavelength means a higher wavelength.

Nuclear units planned or in construction have a total capacity of 186,998 KW, which, if current plans hold, will bring nuclear capacity to about 22% of all electrical capacity by 1995.
if current plans hold is a clause within a clause.

Prepositional Phrases

A prepositional phrase, composed of a preposition and its object, shows relationships involving time, direction, or space:

An artificial heart was installed in a human subject for the first time in 1969.

The current leads to the field coils and into an external circuit. Alternators are not compatible with wind systems because of their high rpm requirements.

The operation of a wind generator is based upon Faraday's law of induced voltage which states that the voltage between the ends of a loop of wire is proportional to the rate / of change / in the magnetic field lines / within the

loop.
four prepositional phrases in the last highlighted area.

Appositives

An appositive, a word or phrase that renames a noun or pronoun, adds information about a noun but in a way different than do adjectives:

In 1972, Richard Nixon, president of the U.S., approved the development of a reusable space vehicle, the Space Shuttle.

Broad principles about space flight were laid down by the Austrian astronautical pioneer, Dr. Eugen Sanger.

The external tank of the Space Shuttle's main engines is composed of two tanks—a large hydrogen tank and a smaller oxygen tank.

An upper air inversion, a layer of stable air, is usually present over large areas of the tradewinds as a hurricane develops.

Participial Phrases

A participial phrase is a group of words acting as an adjective and modifying a noun or pronoun. A participle is the -*ed* or -*ing* form of a verb:

The Eagle Generator uses a 6-pole, shunt-wound generator designed to reach maximum power at 20 mph.

Because of the design created by Kwan-Gett, endothelial cells could grow on the fibrin layer, making the interior surfaces of the artificial heart similar to those of the natural heart.

The wire is wrapped around field cores made of steel laminations.

Gerunds and Gerund Phrases

Similar in appearance to a participial phrase, the gerund plays the role of noun. A gerund is a single word with -*ing* used as a noun. A gerund phrase is a single word with -*ing* accompanied by its objects, complements, and modifiers; it is a group of words acting as noun.

In the iron-core type transformer, the winding is wrapped around an iron bar.

The splitting of an atom produces a great amount of energy.

The cloning of a cell produces an identical cell.

Jarvik changed his artificial heart design in 1974 by fitting his model with a highly flexible three-layer diaphragm made of smooth polyurethane.

The Jarvik-7 design then in 1979 achieved a record time of sustaining life in a calf for 221 days.

Reversing the rotation of the electrohydraulic heart pump reverses the direction of the hydraulic flow.

Adjective Clauses

An adjective clause is almost a complete sentence—but not quite. It functions the same way a single-word adjective does: both modify, that is, add more information to our understanding of a noun. Adjective clauses contain (1) a relative pronoun, (2) in some cases, a subject, (3) a complete verb, and (4) any other accompanying predicates or objects.

Typically, one portable drilling rig, <u>which requires two tug boats to bring it to the site</u>, and several other boats are used in the exploratory drilling phase.

The company holds many patents on its wind energy systems, such as the flyball governor which varies the pitch of the blades in high winds and the slow-speed generator <u>whose performance curve matches that of the propeller</u>.

The idea of the artificial heart arose in part from the need to treat people <u>who cannot receive a donor heart</u>.

Nose designed a "biolized" heart <u>in which the surfaces that came into contact with blood were made from natural tissues</u> treated with chemical fixatives to make them tougher and immunologically inert.
an adjective clause within another adjective clause

The regular CPR class <u>people are taking everywhere</u> now only lasts an evening.

Adverb Clauses

An adverb clause is also nearly a complete sentence; it functions like an adverb does by explaining the how, when, where, and why of the discussion. The adverb clause usually contains a subordinating conjunction, a subject, a complete verb, and any other related phrases or clauses:

<u>Because the shortage in donor hearts is so severe</u>, transplant surgery is limited to people with the best chances of surviving.

<u>As long as the wind speed is sufficient</u>, the electrical energy will be continuously generated.

<u>If an oil spill occurs away from shore</u>, it is unlikely to affect many birds, unless they are directly in a major migratory path at a migrating season.

Noun Clauses

A noun clause is a group of words used as a noun. Introduced by a relative pronoun, a noun clause can play any of the functions a noun plays: subject, direct object, object of preposition, subjective or object complement. Here are example noun clauses, with their functions labelled:

Estimates indicate that 20 million Americans owned <u>hand-held calculators</u> by 1974.
direct object

Computer systems are often measured <u>by how much main memory their architectures allow</u> and <u>by how fast that memory can be accessed</u>.
object of preposition—two of them!

Lemaitre proposed <u>that all matter in the Universe</u> was once concentrated into what he termed the primeval atom.
direct object; in this sentence, <u>what he termed the primeval atom</u> is also a noun clause.

The choice of furnace wall construction depends <u>on how sophisticated the gas-cleaning equipment is</u> and <u>on whether a large amount of waste is to be recovered</u>.
object of preposition—two of them

Most microcomputers use <u>what are called flexible diskettes</u> for program and data storage.
direct object

The major disadvantage of sequential files is <u>that they are slow</u>.
subject complement

Coordinated Elements

Many of the sentence elements described above can be "coordinated"; that is, they can be doubled, tripled, or even quadrupled and linked with coordinating conjunctions like *and* and *or*. For example, in the phrase "a black and white Datsun 240Z," two adjectives are are coordinated. Here are some examples of coordinated sentence elements:

In 1800, A. Volta <u>constructed</u> and <u>experimented</u> with the voltaic pile, the predecessor of the modern battery.
two verbs

Maxwell's theory not only <u>synthesized</u> theories about electricity and magnetism, but also <u>showed</u> optics to be a branch of electromagnetism.
two predicates

Heat exchangers can be so designed <u>that chemical reactions</u> or <u>energy-generation processes</u> can be carried out in them.
two noun phrases

Heat exchangers find wide applications <u>in the chemical process industries</u>, <u>in the food industry</u>, <u>in the generation of steam for production of power and electricity</u>, <u>in aircraft and space vehicles</u>, and <u>in the field of cryogenics for low-temperature separation of gases</u>.
nine total prepositional phrases

5.8: Common Grammar, Usage, and Punctuation Problems

By: David McMurrey

Objectives

Upon completion of this chapter, readers will be able to:

- Explain and apply essential punctuation rules.
- Explain and apply essential grammar rules.
- Explain and apply essential capitalization rules.
- Explain and apply essential numbering rules.
- Explain and apply essential symbol and abbreviation rules.

Introduction

In this chapter, we will cover only those grammar, punctuation, usage, and spelling problems that give people the biggest headaches.

Technical writing professionals try to simplify grammar rules as much as possible without hurting the language or putting themselves in straitjackets. Typically, they work in teams and frequently move in and out of projects—so that the same document may be worked on by different writers and editors during the space of just a few years. That's why any guidelines based on interpretation or personal style or judgment must be avoided.

Commas

Punctuation is a good example of this effort to use clearly defined rules in technical writing. In journalistic punctuation style, you punctuate according to what you feel are the needs for clarity. But punctuating that way is likely to be viewed differently by different people. Therefore, punctuation style in technical writing is based on the *structure* of the sentence.

Introductory Elements

Use a comma after all introductory elements. *any* element, regardless of length, coming before the main clause should be punctuated with a comma. (The main clause is that core part of a sentence that makes it a complete sentence; that is, it expressed a complete thought.) Here are some examples:

When an atom acquires enough energy to leave its orbit, the atom is positively charged.

As for the energy required to produce plastic automobile parts, the auto makers view the additional cost as justified by the savings in petroleum by a lighter car during its lifetime.

Because the high-pressure turbopumps rotate at speeds of 30,000 rpm, the weight distribution on the turbine blades must be balanced with great accuracy.

Because there is no belt of doldrums in the Atlantic south of the equator, hurricanes do not usually occur there.

Between 40 and 50 degrees west and just south of 10 degrees north in the western end of the doldrums belt, calms do occur with frequency, and hurricanes originate there with great frequency.

In 1831, Michael Faraday discovered that if a magnet were moved in the vicinity of a coil, a current could be induced in the coil.
Punctuate even short introductory phrases like this one and the next two sentences.

Using this concept, Faraday arrived at a relation between the changing flux and the induced electromagnetic field.

Today, the computer consortium of IBM, Motorola, and Apple is announcing its new PowerPC chip.

Unnecessary Commas

Double check commas between parts of a sentence. A single comma should never break the flow of the main subject, verb, and object or complement of a sentence. Instead, commas should occur in pairs. Here are some examples (the bracketed commas indicate where commas are typically but mistakenly placed):

The discovery that moving a magnet within a coil could produce current[,] was a major breakthrough in the history of electronics.
Yes, it's a long way from the subject "discovery" to the verb "was," but there should be no comma.

Decreasing the radar operating frequency[,] increases the effective velocity coverage for the same sampling rate.
The whole phrase "decreasing the radar operating frequency" is the subject of the verb "increases"--no comma.

It can be assumed that[,] precipitation particles move with the air in their environment and are, therefore, good tracers for air motion.
Don't know why people would put a comma here--does it feel like a pause?

The separator between black mix and the zinc electrode[,] consists of a paper barrier coated with cereal or methyl cellulose.
No comma here either.

That European refuse incineration costs are substantially lower than U.S. costs[,] is particularly evident when income from by-product recovery and salvage operations is included.
The whole clause, "that European refuse incineration costs are substantially lower then U.S. costs," is the subject for the verb "is"--no comma.

Compound Sentences

Use a comma between all independent clauses. Whenever you have a compound sentence (those are the ones joined by *and, but, yet, or, not, for, whereas*), put a comma before the conjunction (the words I just listed). The length of the compound sentence does not matter. Here are some examples:

The tank is made of aluminum, but the outer surface is protected by a spray-on foam.

By the mid-1970s, the free-spending ways of the Apollo program were gone, and NASA now had to grapple with large technical challenges on a limited budget.

It first appeared that Hurricane Betsy would reach the eastern U.S., but a looping path took her around the tip of Florida and into the Gulf instead.

Gamma rays produce few pairs, but they travel farther.

One grate turns at 50 mph, but the others turn at 15 mph.

Type your name, and then press the Enter key.

You should type your name and then press the Enter key.
In this case, "you" is the subject for the compound verb--it's the subject for both "should type" and "press." This is not a compound sentence, and therefore there is no comma before "and."

Compount Predicates

Do not use a comma between two compound verb phrases. Watch out about what you think are compound sentences. A complete sentence has to be on both sides of the conjunction (that means subject, verb, object, or complement--the works). Compare the following examples.

Offspring exposed to significant amounts of alcohol in utero are much more active than controls[,] and sometimes seem to fly around the room.
This is a compound verb phrase, not a compound sentence: "offspring" is subject for both verbs.

Plastic parts are not weldable[,] and must be repaired by other methods.

The observation and measurement of such small frequency shifts require excellent radar frequency-stability characteristics that are not usually found in conventional radar[,] but can be added without a drastic increase in equipment costs.

Pulse Doppler radar effectively samples the backscattered signal at the radar repetition rate[,] and therefore can provide unambiguous Doppler frequency observations only in the frequency range allowed by the sampling rate.

The manganese dioxide used in batteries is usually obtained from natural ore (mainly from Gabon, Greece, and Mexico)[,] but can be a synthetic product by chemical precipitation or by electrolytic methods.

The last three sentences above probably seem incredibly long to you and needy of commas at *and* and *but*. Rather than break our rule (and remember it's not breaking the rule that matters; it's creating more and more exceptions that will drive us all crazy), why not split these into two sentences each as in the following?

The observation and measurement of such small frequency shifts require excellent radar frequency-stability characteristics that are not usually found in conventional radar. However, this same observation and measurement can be added without a drastic increase in equipment cost.

Pulse Doppler radar effectively samples the backscattered signal at the radar repetition rate. This type of radar therefore can provide unambiguous Doppler frequency observations only in the frequency range allowed by the sampling rate.

The manganese dioxide used in batteries is usually obtained from natural ore (mainly from Gabon, Greece, and Mexico). It can also be a synthetic product prepared by chemical precipitation or electrolytic methods.

Nonrestrictive Elements

Use commas around all nonrestrictive elements. Nonrestrictive elements are phrases and clauses that are nonessential to the grammar of the sentence. These elements can be taken out of the sentence without hurting its basic message. Use commas around these nonrestrictive elements. Here are some examples:

Eighty percent of the work done by the heart is carried out by the left ventricle, which pumps blood into the arteries serving the organs and the tissues.
Nice of the writer to remind us what the left ventricle does, but the sentence could live without it; it would still make sense.

The test produced a speed in the high-pressure hydrogen turbopump of 7000 ROM, which is 19 percent of the design speed.
This detail is additional and not essential to the sense of the sentence.

The Coriolis force, caused by the rotation of the earth, always acts at right angles to the pressure gradient in the northern hemisphere.
This definition is helpful but again is not essential to the sentence.

The bulky equipment, although placed on a rolling cart, must always remain within six feet of the heart transplant patient.
Nonessential stuff--put commas around it!

The formation of hurricane, a type of atmospheric vortex, involves the combined effect of pressure and circular wind.

Researchers also found that heavy drinkers--women drinking at least 1.6 ounces of absolute alcohol during

pregnancy--have infants averaging 59 grams less than the infants of lighter drinkers.
Nonessential stuff--put commas around it, or in this case dashes, which are commas by another name.

Adding waterproofing material to a fabric increases the contact angle, making the fabric water-repellent.
Nonessential stuff--put commas around it!

Molecules may also have some degree of ordering as well as disordered motion, in which case the total energy is the sum of the mechanical and thermal energies.
Nonessential stuff--put commas around it!

Restrictive Elements

Do not use commas around restrictive elements. Restrictive elements are phrases and clauses that a sentence desperately needs to make sense, to say what it means to say. If you take restrictive elements out of a sentence, you wreck the sentence!

Problem:

You can use the system[,] when the login prompt appears.

The way this sentence is punctuated implies that you can use the system any old time! The comma indicates that the clause beginning with "when" can be lifted from the sentence. **Revision:**

You can use the system when the login prompt appears.

The clause beginning with "when" is restrictive--it can't be omitted from the sentence and therefore should not be punctuated. Now the sentence means that you can use the system only when the prompt appears.

Here are some additional examples of this rather tricky rule.

A turbopump is essentially a pump that is turned by the action of a turbine that shares a common shaft with the pump.
It's not any old pump; it's the one that does what the latter part of this sentence says it does. Imagine this sentence ending at "essentially a pump."

Eighty percent of the work done by the heart is carried out by the left ventricle.
Imagine this sentence without "done by the heart," which is the restrictive element in this sentence. No commas here!

A drop of water almost flattens out when it is placed on a glass plate.
Imagine this sentence without "when it is placed on a glass plate," which is the restrictive element here. No commas need apply!

In one study, 11 percent of the offspring whose mothers consumed 2 to 4 drinks per day showed partial features of fetal alcohol syndrome (FAS), while 19 percent of those whose mothers consumed 4 or more drinks per day showed FAS features.
Imagine this sentence without "whose mothers consumed 2 to 4 drinks per day" or without "whose mothers consumed 4 or more drinks per day." The sentence simply wouldn't make any sense. No commas!

Series Elements

Use a comma before the "and" in a series of three or more. In a series of three or more words or phrases, go ahead and put the comma before the and that occurs before the final element. You may have heard that this series-*and* comma rule is optional. However, there are situations where the lack of the series-*and* comma (also known as the Oxford comma) can cause confusion. And when you consider that using the Oxford comma *can't* hurt the sense of the sentence, it makes sense to use it in all cases. Here are some examples:

Instrument panels, bumper components, door liners, seat covers, and grille panels are the most common parts produced directly by automakers.

A 12-ounce can or beer, a 5-ounce glass of wine, and a mixed drink with 1.5 ounces of 80-proof liquor all contain approximately the same amount of alcohol.

The development years involved designing the components for the Space Shuttle's engines, testing the original designs, and retesting the redesigned components.

In humans, the period of rapid brain development begins at mid-pregnancy, peaks in the third trimester, and ends by the postnatal year.

Two-Element Series

Do not use a comma between a series of only two. Be careful not to apply the Oxford comma rule to a series of only two elements. Watch out also for those situations where it looks like you have a series of three elements, but it is actually a series of two noun phrases and a compound verb phrase. See the example:

We brought bread and cheese and read poetry.
Sorry for the Dick-and-Jane sentence, but notice that "bread," "cheese," and "poetry" are not really in a series. No commas for either "and" here.

Series Adjectives

Punctuate series adjectives carefully. It gets tricky knowing how to punctuate when two or more adjectives pile up in front of a noun. One fairly reliable technique is this: if you can switch the order of the adjectives or if you can insert and between them without making the phrase sound weird, then you can consider using commas. (Remember that in no case is there a comma between the final series adjective and the noun it modifies.)

He's having his third mid-life crisis. Now he wants a new red sports car.
You couldn't say "mid-life third crisis" nor could you say "sports red new car"--so no commas in or amongst these adjectives.

Each door is held shut with an adjustable, spring-loaded door latch.
You probably could switch "adjustable" and "spring-loaded"--use a comma here.

As each rack passes through the wash chamber, the dishes get a thorough soil-stripping wash and a final, automatic hot-water rinse.
You probably could switch "final" and "automatic"--use a comma here.

These last two examples may have felt a bit "iffy" to you--the technique is only "fairly" reliable.

Colons

Although the colon has other uses in writing, its most important function is to act as a signal to the reader--it says something like "Okay, reader! Here it comes!" In the first example, notice the words before the colon make a complete statement--at least grammatically.

To make a kite, you need the following items: string, paper, thin sticks, glue, and scissors.

The main engines of the Space Shuttle consist of six main components: the external tank, the low-pressure turbopump, the high-pressure turbopumps, the preburners, the combustion chamber, and the nozzle.

Hurricane size is expressed in three ways: the strength of the maximum winds, the diameter of the hurricane-force winds, the diameter of the gale-force winds, and the overall size the cyclone circulation.

To make a metal dashboard, three steps are required: (1) the metal must be stamped; (2) the texture must be stamped into the metal; and (3) the part must be painted.

Notice in the last example that the first sentence introduces a series of complete sentences. You can use the colon to connect two complete sentences--as long as the first sentence introduces or prepares for the second. Here are some examples of this possibility:

The grades of the students in the caffeine research project told a dramatic story: the higher the caffeine intake, the lower the grades, both for semester and overall grade point average.

In general, shelf-life increases as the cell size of the battery becomes smaller: with well-constructed cells, shelf-lives of three years with a No. 6 telephone cell and ten years with a penlight cell are possible.

The line-of-sight in a communication satellite can be a problem: communication satellites can see the earth's surface only between about 83 degrees north latitude and 83 degrees south latitude.

Many of the new applications of microcomputer are "interactive": there is frequent interaction between the computer and one or more users.

However, don't use a colon inside a complete sentence. It should connect only complete sentences to complete sentences or connect complete sentences to lists.

Problem: The typical Doppler velocity sensor consists of[:] a transistor, an antenna, and a receiver.

Revision: The typical Doppler velocity sensor consists of a transistor, an antenna, and a receiver.

Problem: Three significant types of generating plants are[:] hydroelectic, fossil-fuel-electric, and nuclear-electric.

Revision: Three significant types of generating plants are hydroelectric, fossil-fuel-electric, and nuclear-electric.

Problem: You will need[:] string, paper, thin sticks, glue, and scissors, to make a kite.

Revision: You will need the following items--string, paper, thin sticks, glue, and scissors--to make a kite.

Look at this last example closely: the grammatical core of the sentence is "You will need the following items...to make a kite." You don't want to break up the core grammar of a sentence this way with a colon.

Semicolons

The semicolon could be called a strong comma. Its two main uses are to connect two (or more) sentences that seem very closely related and to clarify the punctuation of a series of items that have their own internal commas.

You may have had some unhappy encounters with run-ons and comma splices in the past. These two "comma faults" usually result from the writer's sense that the sentences involved in the problem are very closely related--the full stop signaled by the period seems like too full of a stop. (It's almost like music; makes you wonder why we don't have the equivalent of whole, half, quarter, and eighth rests in punctuation.) Often, these run-on sentences and comma splices can be fixed by substituting a semicolon for the offending comma.

But not always. Some writers go way overboard in sensing close relations between sentences. Well, yes, every sentence in a document is related to every other--they ought to be! But they need to be reeeaaally closely related. Here are some examples:

"Plaque-fissuring" refers to the formation of an opening from the lumen to the intima; it leads to an intra-intimal thrombus containing not just red cells but mainly firbrin and platelets.

In 1940, philanthropy accounted for 24 per cent of the total operating budget of nonprofit hospitals in New York City; in 1948, it had dropped to 17 per cent.

Gray mold is one of the most important fungal diseases in Italian viticulture; its growth causes serious production losses and adversely affects wine quality.

The other use of the semicolon worth noting here is how it can clarify items in a series that have commas within them already:

Injury caused by pollutants can easily be mistaken for injury caused by other stresses; or, just the opposite, injury symptoms from adverse temperature or moisture relations may resemble, and can be incorrectly attributed to, air pollutants.

Possible research areas announced recently have included genetics, fermentation microbiology, and immobilized biocatalysts; but environment biotechnology, such as metal recovery and waste recycling, is also included.

A typical membrane potential of about one-tenth of a volt sounds relatively small; but, because it occurs across a membrane that is only about 10 nanometers thick, it represents an enormous voltage gradient of about 10 million volts per meter.

The heart undergoes two cardiac cycle periods: diastole, when blood enters the ventricles; and systole, when the ventricles contract and blood is pumped out.

An organization may be functional, with responsibility assigned on the basis of buying, selling, promotion, distribution, and other tasks; production-oriented, with production managers for each product category and brand managers for each individual brand in addition to functional categories; or market-oriented, with managers assigned on the basis of geographical markets and customer types in addition to functional categories.

Electric power substations are used for some or all of the following purposes: connection of generators, transmission or distribution lines, and loads to each other; transformation of power from one voltage level to another; interconnection of alternate sources of power; and detection of faults, monitoring and recording of information, power measurement, and remote communication.

A common misuse of the semicolon is to plunk it down between what appear to be two complete sentences:

Problem: The slide rule was important device for scientists and engineers for many years[;] although its use has all but vanished since the advent of the pocket calculator.

Revision: The slide rule was an important device for scientists and engineers for many years, although its use has all but vanished since the advent of the pocket calculator.
The "although" clause is not complete; it can't stand on its own.

Apostrophes

Pity the poor apostrophe--it's practically an endangered species. The problem with the apostrophe is that it has some conflicting tasks: it is used primarily to show possession, mark contractions, and, minimally, to show plurals. But people have gotten it all mixed up. For example, the likes of "John love's Mary" was becoming pretty common in telephone booths before the rise of the cell phone. A scant two or three hundred years ago, people didn't even use apostrophes (yes--a world without apostrophes!). But the thing does add precision to writing; it does prevent confusion. The rules are super simple; here they are:

To show possession for singular words not ending in s, add 's:

- Earth's shadow
- the Moon's orbit

- this company's profits
- the fish's ear
- India's population
- the family's car

To show possession for singular words ending in s, x, or z; add 's or just an ':

1. Venus's (or Venus') orbit
2. James's (or James') calculator
3. Mars's (or Mars') shadow
4. tennis's (or tennis') popularity
5. the box's (or box') flap
6. the fez's (or fez') tassle
7.

To show possession for plural words ending in s, add ' to the plural form of the word (but don't add another s):

- these companies' employees
- these species' niches
- southern states' capitals
- planets' orbits
- these countries' populations
- these computers' capabilities

To show possession for plural words not ending in s, add 's:

- women's rights
- children's education
- men's rights
- geese's honking

To show the plural of numbers or letters when they are discussed as such, add 's (again usage varies on this, but this is a safe choice):

- Do you know how many c's and s's are in the word ne-e-ry?
- On a computer, O's are represented by O's and 0's with 0's.
- His speech was filled with annoying uh's, okay's, and you know's.

To show possession for possessive pronouns, don't use the apostrophe (don't ask me why):

- This book is yours.
- This CRT is theirs, not ours.

And, now, everybody's personal favorite—the one that English teachers and copyeditors can spot from outer space—the rules for its and it's. Its is the possessive form of it; it's is the contraction for it is (exactly opposite, I realize):

- The SGA density gauge is missing one of its adjusting knobs.
  possessive here
- It's unfortunate that our language has so many exceptions to its rules—or is it?
  contraction for "it is" here

Now, there are others rules involving apostrophes such as for contractions or for quotes within quotes, but we'll leave those for the reference books to handle.

Hyphens

Someone once said, "Take hyphens seriously, and you will surely go mad." They weren't lying!

Hyphens are supposed to keep us from misreading things and show us how words in complex phrases relate to each other. The problem is that the rules for hyphens just cannot be applied absolutely consistently—you end up hyphenating everything including the kitchen sink. Professional editors end up keeping long lists of exactly which word pairs they will hyphenate in a specific document (so that they don't end up in therapy).

Hyphens do matter, however (save the hyphen!). Our language culture seems to be very "into" piling up ambitious noun phrases. These sentences verge on having a problem called "noun stacks." To read this kind of stuff, we need hyphens—they show us what goes with what. Hyphens show that a pair of words is acting as a unit and must be read that way. The common types of unit modifiers—which are two or more words acting as a unit—are discussed in the following (but it's by no means exhaustive):

Although styles vary on this, do not hyphenate the common prefixes such as pre, anti, multi, and so on (unless it spells some other word or just looks hopelessly weird). However, do hyphenate prefix words such as self-:

- self-lubricating hinges
- multistep reaction
- antibotulism agent
- nonmaterial areas
- reusable
- re-sent
- nonprescription drugs
- precooked foods
- mid-1970s
- micro-universe
- subnuclear
- anti-icing

Hyphenate an elliptical form of a longer phrase that is acting as a unit modifier:

- below-average rainfall
- built-in scale
- start-up costs
- in-service accuracy
- immune-deficient animals
- warm-up period
- on-board timer
- pay-off period
- written-out number

Hyphenate a unit modifier ("5-year" in the first example) made up of a number followed by a unit of measurement:

- 5-year grant
- 20-megabyte memory
- 8-oz. cup
- 10-month period
- 3.5-inch diskette
- 4-gallon tub

Hyphenate a non-verb element and a verb-like element acting as a unit:

- drought-producing system

- coffee-flavored ice cream
- government-sponsored programs
- pressure-induced melting
- spring-balanced doors
- health-related costs
- water-repellent fabric
- nutrient-rich waters
- corrosion-resistent metal
- water-soluble reactants
- salt-free diet
- caffeine-containing substances

Watch out for three or more words acting as a unit to modify a following noun:

- case-by-case basis
- the right-to-die statutes
- on-the-job experience
- a three-to-one ratio
- the air-to-ground voice transmission

Don't hyphenate units in which the first word ends in -ly:

- highly developed country
- fully equipped computer

The toughest area for hyphenation are those combinations that look like *adjective + noun + noun* or like *noun + noun + noun*. (True, only the last noun is *really* a noun, but let's not worry about that.) If the initial adjective or noun modifies the final (and real) noun, do *not* use a hyphen. If the initial adjective or noun modifies the noun directly following it, consider using a hyphen.

These examples do not need a hyphen:

- embryonic stem cells
- high process yields
- poor economic performance

These examples could use hyphens according to some styles:

- cell-replacement strategies
- big-name automakers
- cell-surface markers
- large-scale production

If you are in doubt about whether to use a hyphen, don't use it. The best resource on hyphens is *Garner's Modern American Usage*; "Phrasal adjectives."

Once you get a partial feel for hyphens, watch out! You might start acting like Lucy in that show where she has been on the assembly line too long and starts going after everything and everybody with her wrenches. Everything will seem like it needs a hyphen! When that happens, back off, and ask yourself—could someone misread this sentence without a hyphen, even if they were just being mean? If it positively cannot be misread, then give your hyphen key a break.

Comma Splices and Run-ons

The comma-splice and run-on sentence (and the fused sentence, as a variant is called) are all examples of the problem in which two or more sentences are improperly joined. In the typical *comma-splice* sentence, two sentences are joined by a comma without an intervening coordinating conjunction (*and, or, nor, but, yet*). Technically, the *run-on* sentence is a sentence that goes on and on and needs to be broken up; it's likely to be a comma splice as well. A *fused* sentence is two complete sentences just jammed together without any punctuation and without any conjunction.

We write comma-splice and run-on sentences because we sense that the sentences involved are closely related—a full-stop period just doesn't seem right. Actually, the semicolon *is* the right choice in these situations (although it's easy to go semicolon crazy when you first start using them). Here are some examples of this type of problem and their revisions:

Problem: Sometimes, books do not have the most complete information, it is a good idea then to look for articles in specialized periodicals.

Revision: Sometimes, books do not have the most complete information; it is a good idea then to look for articles in specialized periodicals.

Problem: Most of the hours I've earned toward my associate's degree do not transfer, however, I do have at least some hours the University will accept.

Revision: Most of the hours I've earned toward my associate's degree do not transfer. However, I do have at least some hours the University will accept.

Problem: The opposite is true of stronger types of stainless steel, they tend to be more susceptible to rust.

Revision: The opposite is true of stronger types of stainless steel: they tend to be more susceptible to rust.

Problem: Some people were highly educated professionals, others were from small villages in underdeveloped countries.

Revision: Some people were highly educated professionals, while others were from small villages in underdeveloped countries.

Problem: This report presents the data we found concerning the cost of the water treatment project, then it presents comparative data from other similar projects.

Revision: This report first presents the data we found concerning the cost of the water treatment project and then comparative data from other similar projects.

Problem: Most of this firm's contracts have been with major metropolitan hospitals, included among them is Memorial East in Luckenbach.

Revision: Most of this firm's contracts have been with major metropolitan hospitals, included among which is Memorial East in Luckenbach.

Fragments

Fragments are simply incomplete sentences—grammatically incomplete. They usually come about because the sentence may already seem too long. Also, in conversation, we typically speak in fragments. Here are some examples and their revisions:

Problem: Mary appeared at the committee meeting last week. And made a convincing presentation of her ideas about the new product.

Revision: Mary appeared at the committee meeting last week and made a convincing presentation of her ideas about the new product.

Problem: The committee considered her ideas for a new marketing strategy quite powerful. The best ideas that they had heard in years.

Revision: The committee considered her ideas for a new marketing strategy quite powerful, the best ideas that they had heard in years.

Problem: In a proposal, you must include a number of sections. For example, a discussion of your personnel and their qualifications, your expectations concerning the schedule of the project, and a cost breakdown.

Revision: In a proposal, you must include a number of sections: for example, a discussion of your personnel and their qualifications, your expectations concerning the schedule of the project, and a cost breakdown.

Problem: The research team has completely reorganized the workload. Making sure that members work in areas of their own expertise and that no member is assigned proportionately too much work.

Revision: The research team has completely reorganized the workload. They made sure that members work in areas of their own expertise and that no member is assigned proportionately too much work.

Problem: She spent a full month evaluating his computer-based instructional materials. Which she eventually sent to her supervisor with the strongest of recommendations.

Revision: She spent a full month evaluating his computer-based instructional materials. Eventually, she sent the evaluation to her supervisor with the strongest of recommendations.

Problem: The corporation wants to begin a new marketing push in educational software. Although the more conservative executives of the firm are skeptical.

Revision: Although the more conservative executives of the firm are skeptical, the corporation wants to begin a new marketing push in educational software.

Problem Modifier

Modifier problems occur when the word or phrase that a modifier is supposed to modify is unclear or absent, or when the modifier is located in the wrong place within the sentence. A modifier is any element—a word, phrase, or clause—that adds information to a noun or pronoun in a sentence. Modifier problems are usually divided into two groups: misplaced modifiers and dangling modifiers.

To correct misplaced modifier problems, you can usually relocate the misplaced modifier (the word or phrase). To correct dangling modifiers, you can rephrase the dangling modifier, or rephrase the rest of the sentence that it modifies.

Misplaced Modifiers

Problem	Revision
They found out that the walkways had collapsed on the late evening news. *Was that before or after sports?*	On the late evening news, we heard that the walkways had collapsed.
The committee nearly spent a hundred hours investigating the accident. *Did they spend even a minute?*	The committee spent nearly a hundred hours investigating the accident.
The superviser said after the initial planning the in-depth study would begin. *Just when did she say that, and when will the study begin?*	The superviser said that the in-depth study would begin after the initial planning.

Dangling Modifiers

Problem	Revision
Having damaged the previous one, a new fuse was installed in the car. *Who damaged that fuse?*	Because the previous fuse had been damaged, a new one had to be installed. *or* Having damaged the previous one, I had to install a new fuse in my car.
After receiving the new dumb waiter, household chores became so much easier in the old mansion. *Who received the dumb waiter?*	After we received the dumb waiter, it was immediately installed. *or* After receiving the dumb waiter, we immediately installed it.
Using a grant from the Urban Mass Transportation Administration, a contraflow lane was designed for I-45 North. *Who used that money?*	When the Urban Mass Transportation Administration granted funds to the city, planners began designing a contraflow lane for I-45 North. *or* Using a grant from the Urban Mass Transportation Administration, city planners designed a contraflow lane for I-45 North.
Pointing out the productivity and health problems plaguing US workers, aerobic fitness programs may become much more common in American industry, according to the spokeswoman. *Who pointed that out?*	Because of the productivity and health problems plaguing US workers, aerobic fitness programs may become much more common in American industry, according to the spokeswoman. *or* Pointing out the productivity and health problems plaguing US workers, the spokeswoman said that aerobic fitness programs may become much more common in American industry.

One particularly effective way to correct dangling modifiers is to create a summary appositive, that is, a noun or pronoun summarizing what was just said followed by an adjective clause:

Dangling Modifier Problems	Summary Appositive Revisions
Stars that were formed relatively recently should have higher concentrations of heavy elements than do the older stars, which is confirmed by observation.	Stars that were formed relatively recently should have higher concentrations of heavy elements than do the older stars, a prediction that is confirmed by observation.
Most astronomers now believe that the energy of quasars comes from giant black holes in the cores of the quasars, which fits the growing belief that black holes are present in the cores of many galaxies, our own included.	Most astronomers now believe that the energy of quasars comes from giant black holes in the holes of quasars, a theory that fits the growing belief that black holes are present in the cores of many galaxies, our own included.

Parallelism

Parallelism refers to the way that items in a series are worded. You want to use the same style of wording in a series of items—it makes it easier on the reader. Widely varied wording is distracting and potentially confusing to readers. Here are some examples, with revisions and some comments:

Problem: The report discusses **how telescopes work, what types are available**, mounts, accessories, and techniques for beginning star gazers.
The "how" and the "why" clauses are not parallel to the "mounts," "accessories," and "techniques" phrases.

Revision: The report discusses how telescopes work; what types of telescopes, mounts, and accessories are available; and how to begin your hobby as a star gazer.

Problem: Customers often call the showroom **to inquire about pricing**, what items are available, and **to place orders**.
The "what items are available" clause does not go with the two phrases beginning with "to."

Revision: Customers often call the showroom to inquire about prices, check on the availability of certain items, and place orders.

Problem: While the dialysis solution remains in the peritoneal cavity, the dialysis is achieved, a process that includes **the removal of nitrogenous wastes** and correcting electrolyte imbalances and fluid overloads.
The "removal" phrase and the "correcting" phrase are not parallel to each other.

Revision: While the dialysis solution remains in the peritoneal cavity, the dialysis is achieved, a process that includes the removal of nitrogenous wastes and the correction of electrolyte imbalances and fluid overloads.

Problem: This report is intended for people **with some electronics background** but have little or no knowledge of geophysical prospecting.
The "with" phrase is not parallel with the "have little" clause—this one is not even grammatical.

Revision: This report is intended for people with some electronics background but with little or no knowledge of geophysical prospecting.

Parallelism problems have to do when same types of phrasing are not used in the same areas of a document: such as for list items in a vertical list, or for all headings at a certain level within a specific part of a document. At times, working on parallelism of phrasing is pedantic and unnecessary. However, in many instances, parallel phrasing can give readers important cues about how to interpret information. A jumble of dissimilar styles of phrasing for similar elements can be confusing. Shown below are those different styles:

- Questions
  - How are groundwater samples collected?
  - How should soil samples be handled?
  - Must monitor wells be used to collect groundwater for laboratory analysis?
  - What should the samples be analyzed for?
- Noun Phrasing
  - Method of groundwater sample collection
  - Soil sample handling
  - Purpose of monitor wells in groundwater collection for laboratory analysis
  - Purpose of soil sample analysis
- Gerund Phrasing
  - Collecting groundwater samples
  - Handling soil samples
  - Using monitor wells in groundwater collection for laboratory analysis
  - Analyzing samples
- Sentences
  - Groundwater samples must be collected properly.
  - Soil samples must be handled using the specified method.
  - Monitor wells must be used to collect groundwater for laboratory analysis.
  - Samples must be analyzed for specific elements.
- Infinitives
  - To collect groundwater samples
  - To handle soil samples
  - To use monitor wells in groundwater collection for laboratory analysis
  - To analyze samples
- Imperatives
  - Collect groundwater samples.
  - Handle soil samples properly.
  - Use monitor wells in groundwater collection for laboratory analysis.
  - Analyze samples.

Subject-Verb Agreement

With subject-verb agreement problems, either a singular subject is matched with a plural verb, or vice versa. (Remember that some singular verbs end in -s.) Sometimes it's hard to spot the true subject, particularly in these cases:

When several words come between the subject and verb:

Problem: The **communications** between the programmer and the rest of the company tends to be rather informal.

Revision: The communications between the programmer and the rest of the company tend to be rather informal.

Problem: The **purpose** of the monorails have changed from one of carrying food to one of carrying people to work in crowded urban areas.

Revision: The purpose of the monorails has changed from one of carrying food to one of carrying people to work in crowded urban areas.

Problem: The **shortage** of available infants and the **availability** of children with special needs <u>has</u> changed the focus of adoption for many parents.

Revision: The shortage of available infants and the availability of children with special needs have changed the focus of adoption for many parents.

When there are two or more subjects joined by *and* or *or*:

Problem: In the computer's memory <u>is</u> stored the **program** and the **data** to be manipulated by that program.

Revision: In the computer's memory are stored the program and the data to be manipulated by that program.

Problem: Either **BASIC** or **Pascal** <u>are</u> the high-level computer language you should take first.

Revision: Either BASIC or Pascal is the high-level computer language you should take first.

Problem: Skyrocketing **charges** for data preparation, the **need** to keep pace with rapidly increasing amounts of data, and **requirements** for fast system response <u>has</u> led to a search for more efficient input devices.

Revision: Skyrocketing charges for data preparation, the need to keep pace with rapidly increasing amounts of data, and requirements for fast system response have led to a search for more efficient input devices.

Problem: The magnetic-ink character-recognition **device** and the optical character-recognition **device** <u>is</u> two important advances in the preparation of batch input.

Revision: The magnetic-ink character-recognition device and the optical character-recognition device are two important advances in the preparation of batch input.

When the normal subject-verb order is inverted:

Problem: In the computer's memory <u>is</u> stored the **program** and the **data** to be manipulated by that program.

Revision: In the computer's memory are stored the program and the data to be manipulated by that program.

Problem: Introduced in 1968 by the Computer Machine Corporation <u>was</u> the **concept** of key-to-disk processing and the **concept** of shared processing.

Revision: Introduced in 1968 by the Computer Machine Corporation were the concept of key-to-disk processing and the concept of shared processing.

Problem: Equivalent to more than 3000 punched cards <u>are</u> the single **diskette**, first introduced in 1972.

Revision: Equivalent to more than 3000 punched cards is the single diskette, first introduced in 1972.

Problem: Through the center of the core <u>runs</u> several sense **wires**.

Revision: Through the center of the core run several sense wires.

When the subject is a word like each, every, none, either, neither, no one, and nobody, especially when followed by a plural object of a preposition:

Problem: Each of the steps in the process <u>are</u> treated in a separate chapter of this report.

Revision: Each of the steps in the process is treated in a separate chapter of this report.

Problem: Neither of the two high-level languages <u>offer</u> a facility for designing your own variables.

Revision: Neither of the two high-level languages offers a facility for designing your own variables.

When the subject is a phrase or clause acting as a unit:

Problem: Printing 54,000 chars. per 60 seconds <u>were</u> considered a high speed for printers at one time.

Revision: Printing 54,000 chars. per 60 seconds was considered a high speed for printers at one time.

Problem: Reversing the direction of currents through the wires <u>change</u> the magnetic state of the core.

Revision: Reversing the direction of currents through the wires changes the magnetic state of the core.

Problem: What is truly amazing about bits cells in integrated circuits <u>are</u> that 30 cells lined up side by side are about as wide as a human hair.

Revision: What is truly amazing about bits cells in integrated circuits is that 30 cells lined up side by side are about as wide as a human hair.

Pronoun Reference

Pronoun reference is an area that has caused international conflict and created major rifts in the women's movement—so don't expect this little section to explain it all. A pronoun, as you may know, is a word like "he," "they," "him," "them," "which," "this," "everyone," "each," and so on. It's like a variable in programming—it points to some other word that holds its meaning.

Problems arise when you can't figure out what the pronoun is pointing to (its "reference") and when it doesn't "agree" in number or gender with what it is pointing to. You may have experienced the first type of problem: you're reading along in some incredibly technical thing, and it up and refers to something as "this." You look back up at the sea of words you have just been laboriously reading through—you say "this what?!" You have just experienced one form of the pronoun-reference problem.

Problem: Lasers have also been used to study the reaction by which nitric oxide and ozone make nitrogen dioxide (NO2) and molecular oxygen. It plays an important role in the chemistry of the ozone layer that surrounds the earth and protects us from the sun's harmful ultraviolet radiation.
"It" what?

Revision: Lasers have also been used to study the reaction by which nitric oxide and ozone make nitrogen dioxide

(NO2) and molecular oxygen. This process plays an important role in the chemistry of the ozone layer that surrounds the earth and protects us from the sun's harmful ultraviolet radiation.
Okay, now we see...

The second kind of pronoun-reference problem arises over lack of agreement between the pronoun and what it refers to.

Problem: Motorola has just announced <u>their</u> new PowerPC chip.

Revision: Motorola has just announced **its** new PowerPC chip.

The problem here is that "Motorola" is a singular thing, while "their" is a plural thing—they don't agree in number! Now, maybe anyone knows what's being said here, but this writing is imprecise, and it can lead to serious problems, given the right situation.

Problem: These days, every **student** needs to own <u>their</u> own computer.

Revision 1: These days, **students** need <u>their</u> own computers.

Revision 2: These days, every student needs to own his or her own computer.

Revision 3: These days, every student needs to own a computer.

The problem in this example is that "student" does not agree with "their": one is singular; the other, plural. Some call this usage acceptable (*Merriam-Webster*). However, it is imprecise—and we care greatly about precision in technical writing. We have to search for the plural noun we think is being referred to by "their." Not a good idea in technical writing. As you can see from the revisions, there sometimes is no good way to fix the problem. Whenever it works, try converting the singular noun to a plural—the plural pronoun will then be okay (but don't forget to change the verb to plural). Here are some additional examples:

Problem: NASA hoped that, by using production tooling rather than by making each tool individually, <u>they</u> could save time and money.

Revision: NASA hoped that, by using production tooling rather than by making each tool individually, **it** could save time and money.

Problem: If an energy efficient system can be developed, electrical **vehicles** could become as popular as <u>its</u> conventional counterpart.

Revision: If an energy-efficient **system** can be developed, electrical vehicles could become as popular as **their** conventional counterpart.

Problem: Currently, Houston has $328.2 million in their 1984-1985 budget to help fund a new form of mass transportation

Revision: Currently, **Houston** has $328.2 million in **its** 1984-1985 budget to help fund a new form of mass transportation.

Problem: Aerobic fitness programs help to improve **an employee**'s physical condition by strengthening <u>their</u> circulatory, muscular, and respiratory systems.

Revision: Aerobic fitness programs help to improve **employees'** physical condition by strengthening **their** circulatory, muscular, and respiratory systems.

Problem: American **industry** should implement aerobic fitness **programs** for the betterment of their employees even if there is some opposition to it at first.
A double dose of pronoun-reference grief! ***It*** *refers to what?*

Revision: American **industry** should implement aerobic fitness **programs** for the betterment of **its** employees even if there is some opposition to such **programs** at first.

Pronoun Case (Who, Whom)

Yes, you too can learn the proper usage of *who* and *whom*. *Who* is used in the same slots that words like *he, she, they*, and *we* are used; *whom* is used in the same slots that *him, her, them*, and *us* are used. So if you can run a little replacement test, you can figure out which to use.

Step 1

Imagine that you start out with sentences like these (admittedly not an eloquent crew but they'll do):

It was the NBS engineers [who, whom?] Sen. Eagleton's office contacted on July 17.

It was the NBS engineers [who, whom?] performed the tests on the walkways.

Send a copy of the report to [whoever, whomever?] wants one.

No one is sure [who, whom?] will be the next mayor.

It was the NBS engineers to [who, whom?] Sen. Eagleton's office made the request for technical assistance.

Step 2

Now, strike out all the words up to the *who* or *whom* including prepositions:

~~It was the NBS engineers~~ [who, whom?] Sen. Eagleton's office contacted on July 17.

~~It was the NBS engineers~~ [who, whom?] performed the tests on the walkways.

~~Send a copy of the report to~~ [whoever, whomever?] wants one.

~~No one is sure~~ [who, whom?] will be the next mayor.

~~It was the NBS engineers to~~ [who, whom?] Sen. Eagleton's office made the request for technical assistance.

Step 3

Next, juggle the remaining words so that they make a complete sentence:

Sen. Eagleton's office contacted the NBS engineers.

The NBS engineers performed the tests on the walkways.

[Who, whom] wants one?

[Who, whom] will be the next mayor?

Sen. Eagleton's office made the request for the technical assistance to the NBS engineers.

Step 4

If it sounds right to substitute *I, he, she, they, we*, use *who*. If it sounds right to substitute *me, him, her, us, them*, use *whom*:

Sen. Eagleton's office contacted them. => (whom)

They performed the tests on the walkways. => (who)

He wants one? => (who)

She will be the next mayor? => (who)

Sen. Eagleton's office made the request for the technical assistance to them. => (whom)

Step 5

Here are the results:

It was the NBS engineers whom Sen. Eagleton's office contacted on July 17.

It was the NBS engineers who performed the tests on the walkways.

Send a copy of the report to whoever wants one.

No one is sure who will be the next mayor.

It was the NBS engineers to whom Sen. Eagleton's office made the request for technical assistance.

This trick works without having to toss around terms like *nominative* case and *objective* case. (Incidentally, the third example, which contains "whoever wants one," is typically missed by people who pride themselves on their grammar. The rule about always using *whom* when it comes after a preposition does *not* work!)

Caution: You can get *whom* exactly grammatically right but sound fussy and pedantic. The famous day-time quiz show in which Johnny Carson got his start was called *Who Do you Trust?* not *Whom Do you Trust?*. You have to have an ear for the language. If it sounds fussy and pedantic to use *whom*, use *who*.

Capitalization

One of the big problems in technical writing involves capitalization. Technical people, developers, and other nonprofessional writers tend to use capital letters for everything that feels important—particularly the stuff that they've worked on. Problem is that this practice breaks all our standard capitalization rules and, more importantly, makes text harder to read. Most professionals in publishing, writing, and editing believe that excessive and unnecessary capitalization is distracting and confusing for readers. Capitalization should *not* be used for emphasis (use underscores or italics for that, or for really important things, use special notices).

Capital letters should be used for proper names—formal, official names of things and people. For example, Tandem Corporation is a proper name; Mosaic is the proper name of a software product. However, a loose reference to the "development area" at IBM does not need caps; it's not the official name of that area. Similarly, WordPerfect is a proper name, but not its grammar-checking feature. In technical writing, the impulse is often to use caps for the components of a thing—no! For example, if we were discussing the disk drive, the monitor, the CPU unit, the modem, the mouse, or the printer of a computing system, none of it should be capitalized. However, if we were talking about the the Dell NL40 Notebook computer, the Microsoft Mouse, or the IBM 6091 Display, then certainly caps are in order.

Of course, there are some exceptions. For example, in instructions, you want to reproduce the capitalization style shown on buttons, knobs, and other physical features of products as well as on the display screens of computer programs as they are shown on the hardware—but not if all caps are used. If I have a Service button on my computer, I'd write it as Service but not SERVICE, no matter how it is shown on the machine.

A common misuse of capitalization involves acronyms. You know that whenever you use an acronym in your text, you should spell it out first then show its acronym in parentheses. Writers often want to put the spelled-out version in initial caps; you would do so only if the spelled-out version were a proper name in its own right:

The North Atlantic Treaty Organization (NATO) was formed just after Word War II.

When you turn your computer on, it normally goes through a process called initial program load (IPL).

Standard Rules for Caps

Use capital letters for names of people, races, cities, regions, counties, states, nations, languages, and other such proper names:

The Early Bird satellite was launched by Intelst, a consortium of Western countries including the United States, France, the United Kingdom, and Germany.

Samuel Morse invented the coding system called the Morse code.

Among Muslims, Ramadan commemorates the first revelation of the Koran and is celebrated by fasting.

The population of Quebec is largely French speaking.

The Middle East, culturally speaking, refers to those lands in that part of the world that are predominantly Islamic in culture.

The Midwest includes Ohio, Indiana, Illinois, Michigan, Wisconsin, Minnesota, Iowa, Missouri, Kansas, and Nebraska.

In her sophomore semester Gilda took English, French, astronomy, biology, geology and a special course called "Key Concepts in Western Science."

Use capital letters for points of the compass only when they refer to well-established regions, but not when they simply refer to a direction of travel:

In the 1970s and 1980s, the major population and economic growth regions of the United States have been the South and Southwest.

The dam is located to the west of the city.

Oil imports from South America have been decreasing recently.

Drive ten miles north from Baldwin City, Kansas, and you'll be in Lawrence.

Use capital letters for titles of offices when the title precedes the name of an officeholder but not when the title occurs alone. This rule is often ignored within organizations that need to use capitalize titles of positions. Another exception to this rule involves the president of the U.S.; some styles require this title to use a capital letter, even when it occurs alone:

The first electronic computer was assembled in the years 1940 to 1942 by Professor John V. Atanasoff and Clifford Berry, a student, at Iowa State University.

A professor and a student assembled the world's first electronic computer in the years between the wars.

In the U.S., the president holds the power of veto over any legislation passed by the Congress.

Last week, mayors from several cities in the region met to discuss an integrated system of health care.

Use capital letters for academic subjects only when they are part of a specific course title or when they are derived from the name of a person, country, or language. (This capitalization rule often get bent a little in resumes and application letters. Typically, names of occupations and fields, and job titles get initial caps. By standard capitalization rules, that's not correct, but the usage is so strong in these two types of documents that it has become acceptable:

She took a course in world history called "The Shaping of Western Thought" at Baker University in Kansas.

They consider Chemistry 301 a difficult course even though they are all chemistry majors.

This semester Majorie plans to take French, finance, and physics.

Use capital letters for the days of the week, months, special days, and holidays—but not for the names of the seasons:

On Monday, July 24, 1978, they celebrated her birthday at a local restaurant.

Last fall they spent Thanksgiving in Denmark.

In the United States, the national independence day is July the Fourth; in Mexico, it's called *Cinco de Mayo*.

Use capital letters for religions, religious groups, historical events, periods of history, and historical documents:

The telegraph played an important role in the Civil War.

The term *Protestantism* is used to distinguish this faith from the other major Christian faiths: Roman Catholicism and Eastern Orthodoxy.

At the Casablanca Conference, the Allies agreed to continue the war until the unconditional surrender of the Axis powers.

The Allies landed on Normandy Beach on July 6, 1944, a day known as D-Day.

The Great Depression in the United States was supposedly precipitated by the stock-market crash of 1929.

Under compulsion by English barons and the church, King John signed the Magna Carta in 1215.

Use capital letters for organization names (commercial, governmental, and non-profit) as well as their products and services:

In the late 1950s, the U.S. Department of Defense initiated a number of projects, such as Project Courier, which finally resulted in the Initial Defense Communications Satellite Program (IDCSP).

The IDCSP satellites were launched by the U.S. Air Force in 1966.

Saudi Arabia has its own air force and its own integrated defense system.

After the FCC's 1971 adoption of a "limited skies" policy, three domestic carriers initiated operations during 1974: American Satellite Corporation, a subsidiary of Fairchild industries, Inc.; Americom of RCA; and Western Union.

On March 24, 1980, Pennsylvania Governor Richard Thornburgh asked the Union of Concerned Scientists to make an independent evaluation of the krypton problem at the Three Mile Island nuclear power plant.

Recently, Apple Corporation introduced its Macintosh to compete with IBM's Personal Computer.

Use capital letters for references to most numbered or lettered items (figures, tables, chapters, parts, volumes, rooms, buildings, etc.):

In Figure 3 a simple telegraph arrangement is shown. Unfortunately, this small amount of krypton is uniformly mixed with the roughly 2 million cubic feet of air in the sealed Three Mile Island Unit 2 reactor containment building.

In this book, Chapter 6 discusses how to convert instructions written by engineers into instructions that can be read and understood by ordinary nonspecialists.

In Part I of this book, the basic patterns of technical writing are compared to those of traditional English composition.

Use capital letters for objects that have individualized names:

The first operational communications satellite, Early Bird, was launched in 1965.

Until the Challenger space shuttle, expendable launch vehicles such as the Thor Delta, Alpha-Centaur, and Titan were used for launching space communications satellites.

The Golden Gate Bridge was opened in 1937, and it is one of the most extraordinary bridges in the world.

Dr. Smith has her offices in the Woods Building.

Use capital letters for the earth, sun, moon, and universe when they are discussed with other celestial bodies or systems:

The Sun is 1.4 km from Earth.

The theory that the Universe is constantly expanding is based on the observation of red-shifts.

Use capital letters for most acronyms, although a few such as ac and dc are not. When in doubt, check your dictionary. Use capital letters for the spelled-out version of acronyms only if the spelled-out versions are proper nouns in their own right:

In 1969, an experiment at the Stanford Linear Accelerator (SLAC) shattered protons with electrons.

In 1977 and 1978, NASA launched the first two High-Energy Astronomy Observation (HEAO) satellites to study black holes.

The "brain" of the computer is the central processing unit (CPU).

Numbers vs Words

In the section on hyphens, it was pointed out that worrying too much about hyphens will drive you crazy—so will numbers. The main hurdle to overcome is to learn that in technical contexts, we use numerals in text—even ones below 10—if they are critical values. In other words, we break the rules that are taught in regular writing courses and that are used in normal publishing and copyediting practice. That's because in the technical and scientific context, we are vitally interested in numbers, statistical data, even if it's a 2 or 5 or—yes—even a 0.

The difficulty is in defining the rules. You should use numerals, not words, when the number is a key value, an exact measurement value, or both. For example, in the sentence "Our computer backup system uses 4 mm tape" the numeral is in order. Also in "This recipe calls for 4 cups of unbleached flour." But consider this one: "There are four key elements that define a desktop publishing system." A word, not a numeral, is preferable here because—well, how to explain it? The number of elements is exact all right, but it's just no big deal. Four, five—who cares?

To summarize the rules that we normally apply:

- Don't start sentences with numerals—write the number out or, better yet, rephrase the sentence so that it doesn't begin the sentence.
- For decimal values less than 1, add a 0 before the decimal point: for example, .08 should be 0.08.
- Make a firm decision on how to handle 0 and 1 when they refer to key, exact values and stick with it. (Style varies wildly in technical writing on these two villains.) Some technical styles choose to use words for these; they resign themselves to the slight inconsistency but better readability.
- Use numerals for important, exact values, even when those values are below 10.
- Use words for numerical values that are unimportant, such as in the sentence "There are six data types in the C programming language."
- When you must use fractions, avoid the symbols that may be available in the character set used by your software. Construct the fraction like this: 5-1/4. Be sure and put the hyphen between the whole number and the fraction.
- It would be nice if all fractions could be reset as decimals, but such is not the case when you have things like 1/8 floating around. Stay consistent with either decimals or fractions in these situations.
- Don't make numerical values look more exact than they are. For example, don't add ".00" to a dollar amount if the the amount is rounded or estimated.
- For large amounts, you can write things like 36 million or 45 billion, but, for some reason, *not* 23 thousand.
- Apply these rules in specifically technical, scientific contexts only. Be sensitive to what the standard practices are in the context in which you are writing.

Some 19 million tons of sulphur dioxide are discharged from US sources alone each year, and another 14 million tons from Canada.
Using the number "19" and the word "million" indicates an approximate amount. "19,000,000" might make some readers think it was an exact amount.

It was not until after December 1952, when 4000 people died in London from air pollution in just a few days, that real gains in pollution-control legislation were made.

The US Army's standard airborne Doppler navigator weighs 28 lb (12.7 kg), requires 89 W of power, and operates at 13.325-GHz frequency.

All vitrain of the European classification, if more than 14 micrometers thick, has been regarded as anthraxylon.

In 1971, 11 countries accounted for about 91 percent of world production of coal.

The Department of the Interior has just published a report that reviews 65 different coal gasification processes.

Combustion turbines total about 8% of the total installed capability of US utility systems and supply less than 3% of the total energy generated.

Internal combustion engines in small power plants account for about 1% of the total power-system generating capability of the US.

The water-cement ratio will generally range from 4 gal of water per sack of cement to about 9 gal per sack.
These are exact values here; in technical writing, use the numeral even if it is below 10.

The problem is located in piston number 6.

When there are enumerated items or parts, technical writing uses the number, as in this example. But notice that no "#" or "No." is used.

The signal occurs in 6-second intervals.

The order is for 6-, 8-, and 12-foot two-by-fours.

Use Code 3 if a system shutdown occurs.

Mined coals commonly contain between 5 and 15 percent mineral matter.

The above illustration shows a 20-unit coaxial cable with 9 working coaxial pairs and 2 standby coaxials, which automatically switch in if the electronics of the regular circuits fail.

There are 59 different species of the coffee shrub, but only 4 are of commercial importance.

Most grinds of coffee contain particles ranging in size from 0.023 to 0.055 inches in diameter.

Using carrier frequencies between 0.535 MHz and 1.605 MHz in the US, AM broadcasting stations sprang up all over the country beginning in the 1910s.

As a base from which to work, 2-1/2 to 3 gal of water are needed for each sack of cement for complete hydration and maximum strength.
These are exact values; therefore, in the technical-writing context, we use numerals. Notice how fractional values are handled: put a hyphen between the whole number and the fraction to prevent misreading.

The order for twelve 30-foot beams was placed yesterday.

The order was for 30 fifteen-gallon tubs.

They used six 8-pound sacks of nails.

The microprocessors of the 70s and 80s operated under the control of clocks running at 1 to 5 MHz, that is, 1 to 5 million counts per second.

Your eye has a bandwidth of 370 trillion Hz, the visible spectrum.

Transmission rates on ETHERNET range from 1 to 10 megabits per second (0.125 to 1.25 million bytes per second).

In 1978, the satellite carriers' revenues were about $88 million, and by 1986, they are expected to reach $800 million.

Most communications satellites are in geostationary orbit: at an altitude of 22,300 miles over the surface of the earth and at a distance of 26,260 miles from the center of the earth (the earth's radius being 3960 miles).

Aggregates constitute about 70 percent of a concrete mix.

Uniform compaction of 95% or better of standard AASHO densities is recommended.

In this book, Chapter 7 discusses the different audiences of technical prose and translation techniques for communicating effectively with the less specialized ones.

The wheels of the four-wheel tractor give it increased speed over the Crawler, but because of the weight distribution over four wheels rather than over two wheels or tracks, this vehicle has less traction.

Hundreds of thousands of people will have purchased microcomputers by the end of 1980. Tens of millions of them will bought them by the end of the century.

There are two telephones in service today for every three people in the US.

In 1965, Dr. Gordon Moore announced his "law" that the complexity of a chip would double every year for ten years. *Use the word "ten" here because it is not an exact amount.*

The typical stand-alone microcomputer system consists of seven physical components. *Use the word "seven" here because, even though it seems like an exact amount, it is not a key value. It doesn't have the same significance as the "7" would have in "7 quarts of oil."*

If you are using page-zero addressing, use a RAM for memory page zero.

Primary fuel cells are those through which reactants are passed only one time.

Before recharging, a zinc-carbon battery must have a working voltage not less than one volt. *Even in technical-writing contexts, rules for one and zero vary. Just pick a style and stay with it. Using the word "one" is the standard in this example.*

Japan has roughly one-third of the US production of dry batteries. *In running text, always write out fraction like this, and hyphenate them. However, you'd still write "5-1/2 inches."*

The radial fractures are so extensive that they are the dominant structural element over half of Mars's surface. *And just to be sure, "half" by itself in running text is always a word.*

A nanosecond is one-billionth of a second.

Inside the UP are three 16-bit registers. *When you have two separate numerical values side by side, one has to be a word, and the other a numeral. Styles vary here, but make the numeral the higher number. Contrast with the next example.*

Data from the frequency counter take the form of 16 seven-bit ASCII words.

Sales of batteries have increased from $510 million on the average during 1957-1959 to $867 million in 1966 and are projected to exceed $1.8 billion in 1980.

The speed of light is roughly 300 million meters per second.

Fifty-three representatives of different software development companies showed up at the meeting. *Never start a sentence with a numeral in any writing context. With this example, some rewriting might be a wise idea to get the numerical out of the beginning of the sentence, as in the following rewrite.*

At the meeting, 53 representatives of different software development companies showed up.

Symbols and Abbreviations

In technical-writing contexts, you may often have to decide whether to use " or ' for "inches" or "feet" or whether to use "inches," "in," or "in."

First of all, remember that symbols and abbreviations are distracting to readers; they are different from the normal flow of words. However, there are plenty of cases where the written-out version is more distracting than the symbol or abbreviation. Also, the context (specifically, technical or nontechnical) has a lot to do with which to use.

Imagine a technical document which has only one or two references to numerical measurements in inches. There is no reason to use symbols or abbreviations here—just write the thing out. But imagine a technical document with numerous feet and inch references: using symbols or abbreviations in this case is better, more readable, more efficient for both reader and writer. But which? Imagine the amount of foot and inch references there would be in a carpentry project (for example, a dog house). In this case, the symbols, " and ' would be greatly preferable. However, this example would be an extreme case; otherwise, use the abbreviations.

When you do use symbols, especially for feet, inches, and some math symbols, use a symbols-type font. Avoid the "smart" quotes for feet and inches. Use the multiplication symbol for measurement contexts.

Which are the standard symbols and abbreviations to use? Go with the standards in the field in which you are writing, or with those found in a standard reference book such as a dictionary. Don't make them up yourself (for example, "mtrs" for meters)!

What about plurals? Very few abbreviations take an *s* to indicate plural: for example 5 in. means 5 inches. For the few that you think might take the *s*, check a dictionary.

What about obscure abbreviations and symbols? If you are concerned that readers might not recognize the abbreviation or symbol, write its full name in regular text and then put the abbreviation and symbol in parentheses just after the the first occurrence of that full name.

High resolution displays use larger video bandwidths, up to 30 MHz or more.

Most touch-sensitive displays use a matrix of either LED/photodiodes or transparent capacitor arrays to detect a physical touch.

The part of the memory that is easily alterable by the operator consists of RAM chips.

A satellite in geostationary orbit looks at the earth with a cone angle of 17.3θ corresponding to an arc of 18,080 km along the equator.

The arc from 53θ W to 139θ W will cover 48 states (excluding Alaska and Hawaii) and is said to provide conus coverage.

Fairchild Industries, Inc., was an early participant in commercial satellites.

The voice was compressed from the usual 64-kb/s pulse code modulation (PCM) to 32 kb/s per channel by near-instantaneous companding (a modified PCM technique).

Terrestrial microwave radio communications require repeaters spaced every 20 to 40 mi from each other.

Over a period of several days the spacecraft is tracked from the ground and positioned on station (i.e., in the preassigned orbital spot) in order to commence operations.

A velocity increment of approximately 155 ft/s per year is required to correct drift problems in satellites.

The ancient battery-like objects made by the Parthians in 250 BC were thin sheets of copper soldered into a cylinder 1.125 cm long and 2.6 cm in diameter.

The standard electrodes are the normal and the 0.1 normal (N) calomel electrodes in which the system is $Hg|KCl$ solution saturated with $HgCl$.

Such batteries contain 4400 cc of water in which $NaOH$ is dissolved.

Water pressure in the heat recovery loop can be as much as 25 psig.

Resources

Here are some other sources to consult:

Grammar Girl Quick and Dirty Tips for Better Writing

Brian Garner. *Garner's Modern American Usage*. Oxford.

Grammar Book. Provided by Jane Straus.

Guide to Grammar and Writing. Provided by Charles Darling at Capital Community College.

5.9: Common Spelling Problems

By: David McMurrey and Tiffani Reardon

Objectives

Upon completion of this chapter, readers will be able to:

- Identify and correctly spell commonly misspelled words.
- Define and distinguish between similar-sounding words.

Who Made Up This Language?

For some writers, their main spelling problem is similar-sounding words, for example, *principle* and *principal* or *affect* and *effect*. These problems cannot be flagged by software spell-checking functions.

Here is a list of these commonly confused homophones (different spelling; same or very similar pronunciation), with examples of their correct use.

All definitions in this section are from the Merriam Webster dictionary via the Merriam Webster Dictionary mobile application.

accept, except

The construction form *accepted* the offer to build the bridge.

Everything has been finished *except* for the paint job.

Merriam-Webster Definitions

Accept - (verb)to receive or take (something offered): to take (something) as payment: to be able or designed to take or hold (something)

Except - (preposition) not including (someone or something): other than (something or someone)

advice, advise

The construction firm ignored the engineer's *advice*.

The engineer *advised* the firm to use single-suspension walkways.

Merriam-Webster Definitions

Advice - (noun) an opinion or suggestion about what someone should do

Advise - (verb) to give an opinion or suggestion to someone about what should be done: to give advice to (someone): to recommend or suggest (something): to give information to (someone)

affect, effect

The *effect* of the increased oil prices has been devastating on our economy.

The increased oil prices have *affected* our economy drastically.

Merriam-Webster Definitions

Affect - (verb) have an effect on; make a difference to

Effect - (noun) a change that results when something is done or happens: an event, condition, or state of affairs that is produced by a cause: a particular feeling or mood created by something: an image or a sound that is created in television, radio, or movies to imitate something real

cite, site, sight

The consulting engineer *cited* a paragraph from the building code.

At the construction *site*, the workers carefully erected the scaffolding.

The collapse of the walkways was a terrible *sight*.

Merriam-Webster Definitions

Cite - (verb) to write or say the words of (a book, author, etc.): to mention (something) especially as an example or to support an idea or opinion: law: to order (someone) to appear before a court of law

Site - (noun) the place where something (such as a building) is, was, or will be located: a place where something important has happened: a place that is used for a particular activity

Sight - (noun) the sense through which a person or animal becomes aware of light, color, etc. by using the eyes: the ability to see: the act of seeing someone or something: a position in which someone or something can be seen

complement, compliment

The programmer has received many *compliments* on her new system.

The colors that have been selected for the room do not *complement* each other.

Merriam-Webster Definitions

Complement - (noun) something that completes something else or makes it better: the usual number or quantity of something that is needed or used: grammar: a word or group of words added to a sentence to make it complete

Compliment - (noun) a remark that says something good about someone or something: an action that expressed admiration or approval

counsel, council, consul

She was appointed *consul* to the embassy in Beirut.

There was lengthy debate on the tax proposal at city *council* last night.

He *counselled* her to get a degree in technical communication.

Merriam-Webster Definitions

Counsel - (verb) to give advice to (someone): to suggest or recommend (something)

Council - (noun) a group of people who are chosen to make rules, laws, or decisions about something: a group of people who provide advice or guidance on something

Consul - (noun) a government official whose job is to live in a foreign country and protect and help the citizens of his or her own country who are traveling, living, or doing business there: either one of two chief officials of the ancient Roman republic who were elected every year

its, it's

It's time to go home; *it's* getting late.

The car has lost one of *its* headlights.

Merriam-Webster Definitions

Its - (adjective) relating to or belonging to a certain thing, animal, etc.: made or done by a certain thing, animal, etc.

It's - (contraction) it is: it has

lose, loose

Your car *loses* power when it is out of tune.

I have some *loose* change in my pocket.

Don't let Mamie get *loose*!

Merriam-Webster Definitions

Lose - (verb) to be unable to find (something or someone): to fail to win (a game, contest, etc.): to fail to keep or hold (something wanted or valued)

Loose - (adjective) not tightly fastened, attached, or held: not pulled or stretched tight: of clothing: not fitting close to your body: not tight

personal, personnel

They plan to take out a *personal* loan to build the deck.

Send your application to the *personnel* office.

The CEO wants to have a *personal* chat with all this company's *personnel*.

Merriam-Webster Definitions

Personal - (adjective) belonging or relating to a particular person: made or designed to be used by one person -- used to describe someone whose job is involved working for or helping a particular person

Personnel - (noun) the people who work for a particular company or organization: a department within a company or organization that deals with the people who work for it

principal, principle

The *principal* component of the solar panel is the collector.

Explain to me the *principle* of convection.

stationary, stationery

Use company *stationery* for company business purposes only.

The derrick may not remain *stationary* during the gale-force winds.

than, then

My utility bill was higher this month *than* it was last month.

The hurricane reached the Texas coast; *then* it plunged right into the heart of Houston.

their, there, they're

Their calculus course is much harder than ours.

Over *there* on the table is your calculus book.

They're not taking calculus this semester.

to, too, two

Are they going *to* pave the street today?

It is still *too* rainy to pave the street.

Two hours ago, the sky was clear.

whose, who's

Whose technical writing book is this?

There is the woman *whose* technical report won top honors.

Do you know *who's* in charge around here?

He's a man *who's* not afraid of criticism.

your, you're

Your technical writing book is on the table.

You're going to have review to Part 1 before writing that report.

5.10: Strategies for Peer Reviewing and Team Writing

By: David McMurrey

Objectives

Upon completion of this chapter, readers will be able to:

- Explain and apply strategies for peer reviewing.
- Explain and apply strategies for team writing.

Be a Thoughtful Reviewer; Be a Good Team Member

Peer reviewing (also called peer-editing) means people getting together to read, comment on, and recommend improvements on each other's work. Peer-reviewing is a good way to become a better writer because it provides experience in looking critically at writing.

Team writing, as its name indicates, means people getting together to plan, write, and revise writing projects as a group, or team. Another name for this practice is collaborative writing—collaborative writing that is out in the open rather than under cover (where it is known as plagiarism).

Strategies for Peer Reviewing

When you peer-review another writer's work, you evaluate it, criticize it, suggest improvements, and then communicate all of that to the writer. As a first-time peer-reviewer, you might be a bit uneasy about criticizing someone else's work. For example, how do you tell somebody his essay is boring? Read the discussion and steps that follow; you'll find advice and guidelines on doing peer reviews and communicating peer-review comments.

Initial Meeting

At the beginning of a peer review, the writer should provide peer reviewers with notes on the writing assignment and on goals and concerns about the writing project (topic, audience, purpose, situation, type), and alert them to any problems or concerns. As the writer, you want to alert reviewers to these problems; make it clear what kinds of things you were trying to do. Similarly, peer reviewers should ask writers whose work they are peer-reviewing to supply information on their objectives and concerns. The peer-review questions should be specific like the following:

1. Does my expanation of virtual machine make sense to you? Would it make sense to our least technical customers?
2. In general, is my writing style too technical? (I may have mimicked too much of the engineers' specifications.)
3. Are the chapter titles and headings indicative enough of the following content? (I had trouble phrasing some of these.)
4. Are the screen shots clear enough? (I may have been trying to get get too much detail in some of them.)

Peer-Reviewing Strategies

When you peer-review other people's writing, remember above all that you should consider all aspects of that writing, not just—in fact, least of all—the grammar, spelling, and punctuation. If you are new to peer-reviewing, you may forget to review the draft for things like the following:

1. Make sure that your review is comprehensive. Consider all aspects of the draft you're reviewing, not just the grammar, punctuation, and spelling.
2. Read the draft several times, looking for a complete range of potential problem areas:
    1. Interest level, adaptation to audience
    2. Persuasiveness, purpose

3. Content, organization
4. Clarity of discussion
5. Coherence, use transition
6. Title, introduction, and conclusion.
7. Sentence style and clarity
8. Handling of graphics

3. Be careful about making comments or criticisms that are based on your own personal style. Base your criticisms and suggestions for improvements on generally accepted guidelines, concepts, and rules. If you do make a comment that is really your own preference, explain it.

4. Explain the problems you find fully. Don't just say a paper "seems disorganized." Explain what is disorganized about it. Use specific details from the draft to demonstrate your case.

5. Whenever you criticize something in the writer's draft, try to suggest some way to correct the problem. It's not enough to tell the writer that her paper seems disorganized, for example. Explain how that problem could be solved.

6. Base your comments and criticisms on accepted guidelines, concepts, principles, and rules. It's not enough to tell a writer that two paragraphs ought to be switched, for example. State the reason why: more general, introductory information should come first, for example.

7. Avoid rewriting the draft that you are reviewing. In your efforts to suggest improvements and corrections, don't go overboard and rewrite the draft yourself. Doing so steals from the original writer the opportunity to learn and improve as a writer.

8. Find positive, encouraging things to say about the draft you're reviewing. Compliments, even small ones, are usually wildly appreciated. Read through the draft at least once looking for things that were done well, and then let the writer know about them.

Peer-Review Summary

Once you've finished a peer review, it's a good idea to write a summary of your thoughts, observations, impressions, criticisms, or feelings about the rough draft. See the peer-reviewer note below, which summarizes observations on a rough draft. Notice in the note some of the following details:

- The comments are categorized according to type of problem or error—grammar and usage comments in one group; higher level comments on such things as content, organization, and interest-level in another group.
- Relative importance of the groups of comments is indicated. The peer-reviewer indicates which suggestions would be "nice" to incorporate and which ones are critical to the success of the writing project.
- Most of the comments include some brief statement of guidelines, rules, examples, or common sense. The reviewer doesn't simply say "This is wrong; fix it." He also explains the basis for the comment.
- Questions are addressed to the writer. The reviewer is doublechecking to see if the writer really meant to state or imply certain things.
- The reviewer includes positive comments to make about the rough draft and finds nonantagonistic, sympathetic ways to state criticisms.

Excerpt from a note summarizing the results of a peer review

Spend some time summarizing your peer-review comments in a brief note to the writer. Be as diplomatic and sympathetic as you can!

Strategies for Team Writing

As mentioned earlier in this chapter, team writing is one of the common ways people in the worlds of business, government, science, and technology handle large writing projects.

Assembling the Team

When you begin picking team members for a writing project in a technical writing course, choose people with different backgrounds and interests. Just as a diverse, well-rounded background for an individual writer is an advantage, a group of diverse individuals makes for a well-rounded writing team.

If you are the team leader, you might even ask prospective team members for their background, interests, majors, talents, and aptitudes. These following writing teams combine individuals with diverse backgrounds and interests:

Writing Team 1

Project: A report on current cloaking technologies

Team members; backgrounds, skills, interests

- *Shawn S. - Electrical engineering major, currently doing basic office-management chores at a law firm*
- *Tracey K. - Senior English major, hoping this course helps with employment prospects*
- *Sanjiv G. - Computer science major, currently doing computer graphics at a software development shop*
- *Jeon Chang Y. - Soon-to-be electrical engineering major, still developing English language skills*
- *Alice B. - Undeclared major with a nontechnical focus, possibly in the wrong course, no stated skills*

Planning the Project

Once you've assembled your writing team, most of the work is the same as it would be if you were writing by yourself, except that each phase is a team effort. Specifically, meet with your team to decide or plan the following:

Planning Stages

- Analyze the writing assignment.
- Pick a topic.
- Define the audience, purpose, and writing situation.
- Brainstorm and narrow the the topic.
- Create an outline.
- Plan the information search (for books, articles, etc., in the library).
- Plan a system for taking notes from information sources.
- Plan any graphics you'd like to see in your writing project.
- Agree on style and format questions (see the following discussion).
- Develop a work schedule for the project and divide the responsibilities (see the following).

Much of the work in a team-writing project must be done by individual team members on their own. However if your team decides to divide up the work for the writing project, try for at least these minimum guidelines:

- Have each team member responsible for the writing of one major section of the paper.
- Have each team member responsible for locating, reading, and taking notes on an equal part of the information sources.

Some of the work for the project that could be done as a team you may want to do first independently. For example, brainstorming, narrowing, and especially outlining should be done first by each team member on his own; then get together and compare notes. Keep in mind how group dynamics can unknowingly suppress certain ideas and how less assertive team members might be reluctant to contribute their valuable ideas in the group context.

After you've divided up the work for the project, write a formal chart and distribute it to all the members.

	Team writer 1 (Kerry) *Library/interview specialist*	
	Team writer 2 (Jim) *Graphics coordinator*	
Team leader (Julie) *Production coordinator Team writer 5*	**Team writer 3** (Sterlin) *Chief style/edit guru*	
	Team writer 4 (Anh) *Technical lead*	

Figure 1: Chart listing writing team members' responsibilities for the project

Scheduling the Project and Balancing Workload

Early in your team writing project, set up a schedule of key dates. This schedule will enable you and your team members to make steady, organized progress and complete the project on time. As shown in the example schedule below, include not only completion dates for key phases of the project but also meeting dates and the subject and purpose of those meetings. Notice these details about that schedule:

- Several meetings are scheduled in which members discuss the information they are finding or are not finding. (One team member may have information another member is looking everywhere for.)
- Several meetings are scheduled to review the project details, specifically, the topic, audience, purpose, situation, and outline. As you learn more about the topic and become more settled in the project, your team may want to change some of these details or make them more specific.
- Several rough drafts are scheduled. Team members peer-review each other's drafts of individual sections twice, the second time to see if the recommended changes have worked. Once the complete draft is put together, it, too, is reviewed twice.

Schedule for a Team Writing Project

Task	Deadline
Individual prototypes due	October 1
Team meeting: finalize the prototype	October 1
Rough-draft style guide due	October 5
Team meeting: finalize style guide	October 5
Twice-weekly team meetings: progress & problems	October 5-26
Graphics sketches due to Jim	October 14
Rough drafts of individual sections due	October 26
Review of rough drafts due	October 28
Team meeting: discuss rough drafts, reviews	October 28
Update of style guide due from Sterlin	October 31
Revisions of rough drafts due to reviewers	November 3
Final graphics due from Jim	November 5

Completed drafts to Sterlin: final edit/proof	November 7
Team meeting: review completed drafts with final graphics and editing	November 12
Completed drafts due to Julie for final production	November 15
Team meeting: inspection of completed project	November 15
Project upload due to McMurrey	November 16
Party at Julie's	November 19

When you work as a team, there is always the chance that one of the team members, for whatever reason, may have more or less than a fair share of the workload. Therefore, it's important to find a way to keep track of what each team member is doing. A good way to do that is to have each team member keep a journal or log of what kind of work she does and how much time she spends doing it.

At the end of the project, if there are any problems in the balance of the work, the journal should make that fact very clear. At the end of the project, team members can add up their hours spent on the project; if anyone has spent a little more than her share of time working, the other members can make up for it by buying her dinner or some reward like that. Similarly, as you get down toward the end of the project, if it's clear from the journals that one team member's work responsibilities turned out, through no fault of his own, to be smaller than those of the others, he can make up for it by doing more of the finish-up work such as typing, proofing, or copying.

Setting Up a Style Guide or Style Sheet

Because the individual sections will be written by different writers who are apt to have different writing styles, set up a style guide in which your team members list their agreements on how things are to be handled in the paper as a whole. These agreements can range from the high level, such as whether to have a background section, all the way down to picky details such as when to use italics or bold and whether it is "click" or "click on." See the excerpt from a project style sheet in the following.

Before you and your team members write the first rough drafts, you can't expect to cover every possible difference in style and format. Therefore, plan to update this style sheet when you review the rough drafts of the individual sections and, especially, when you review the complete draft.

Highlighting

- Use bold for interface elements that function like commands (for example, the **Exit** button).
- Use bold for menu options that get you to commands (for example, **File>Open**).
- Use the > symbol to abbreviate menu traversal.
- Use Courier New for example text that users type in (for example, myfile.doc).
- Use italics for variables--placeholder text for which users substitute their own information (for example, *filename.doc*).

Hyphenation

- *Individual words.* Turn automatic hyphenation off. Do not hyphenate words except in tight places like tables or graphics.
- Compounds. Mr. Hyphen (Sterlin) will keep the hyphenated-compounds list. Use only those in his list, and submit new ones to him for approval and inclusion on the list. (Hyphenate compounds only for approval and inclusion on the list. [Hyphenate compounds only when they modify (for example, "back-up copy"), not when they act as nouns or verbs (for example, "to back up your files.")]

Terminology

1. Use only the words in **graph_project.dic**. Sterlin approves all new words for that database.
2. Use the same word for the same object, same process, or same action. No elegant variation, please!

Try to schedule as many reviews of your team's written work as possible. You can meet to discuss each other's rough drafts of individual sections as well as rough drafts of the complete paper.

A critical stage in team-writing a paper comes when you put together into one complete draft those individual sections written by different team members. It's then that you'll probably see how different in tone, treatment, and style each section is. You must as a group find a way to revise and edit the complete rough draft that will make it read consistently so that it won't be so obviously written by three or four different people.

When you've finished with reviewing and revising, it's time for the finish-up work to get the draft ready to hand in. That work is the same as it would be if you were writing the paper on your own, only in this case the workloads can be divided up.

By: David McMurrey

Objectives

Upon completion of this chapter, readers will be able to:

1. Define information structure.
2. Explain the contents and organization of different types of information structures.

Use a Logical, Natureal Structure: Content and Organization

The main parts of a technical-writing course focus on applications—ways technical writing skills are applied in the real world. However, these applications use varying combinations of information infrastructures. An *information structure* is (1) a type of information content (such as descriptive writing), (2) a way of organizing information (such as a comparison or classification), or (3) both.

The information infrastructures reviewed in this appendix are the ones commonly used in technical writing. Of course, there are other infrastructures—maybe some that scholars of technical writing have not yet pinned a label on, but these are the most common and the most readily visible. And of course some of these infrastructures blend together. The main thing is that by knowing these, you have the intellectual tools for quickly organizing and structuring just about any writing project.

Description

What Does it Look Like?

The biggest hurdle you may face in writing a description is remembering what the term means as it is used in this context. We all use the word *description* loosely to refer to practically any discussion or explanation. But in this context, it means *the detailed discussion of the physical aspects of a thing*. That means discussing things like color, shape, size, weight, height, width, thickness, texture, density, contents, materials of construction, and so on.

For example, this sentence is not really description in our sense of the word:

A computer diskette is a device used for storing electronic data.

It explains the function or purpose but provides little or no physical detail. However, this sentence is very definitely description:

The common computer diskette is 3.5 inches by 3.5 inches and approximately 1/8 inch thick.

Contexts for Description

As mentioned earlier, descriptions are common elements in technical writing—just not quite in the same way that instructions are. Descriptions appear more often as a sentence or two here, a paragraph there, or a whole section elsewhere. Certain kinds of technical writing feature description:

1. Accident reports requiring plenty of description.
2. Product specifications—documents that describe design and feature of a new or changed product—have plenty of description.
3. Instructions often require description to enable readers to visualize what they are doing and what they are working with.

Contents and Organization of Descriptions

The following is a review of the sections you'll commonly find in descriptions. As you read, check out the example descriptions.

Introduction. Plan the introduction to your description carefully. Make sure it does all of the following things (but not necessarily in this order) that apply to your particular description:

1. Indicate **the specific object** about to be described.
2. Indicate what the audience needs in terms of **knowledge and background** to understand the description.
3. Provide a **general description** of the object.
4. Include an **overview of the contents** of the description.

Background

If the thing you are describing is not likely to be familiar to most of your readers, consider adding some background before you plunge into the actual description. If you are about to describe an SGO/3 density gauge to nonspecialists, you'd better first discuss what in the world the thing is, what it does, and on what part of the planet it is used.

Discussion of the Parts or Characteristics

The main part of your description is the discussion of each part or characteristic. You must divide the thing you are describing into parts, or characteristics, or both. *Parts* are easy: for example, a wooden pencil has lead, a wooden barrel, an eraser, and a metal clip. *Characteristics* are describable aspects of a thing but are not parts: for example, the pencil has a certain weight, length, width, and so on. If you were a budding real-estate tycoon and had to describe a vacant lot for company files, you'd probably describe it by its characteristics: its location, square footage, terrain, vegetation, access to utilities, and so on. (Check out the description of the primitive stone scraper in the examples; part of it is arranged by characteristics, and part by parts!)

Once you've divided the thing you are describing into parts, characteristics, or both, your next job is to *describe each one*. For mechanical things, it works well to start by defining the part, by explaining its function. After that, you describe the part from general to specific, using any of the sources of description that are appropriate.

Notice that in description, you can mix other kinds of writing. You'll find yourself explaining functions, defining terms, discussing a bit of process as you describe. That's not a problem as long as the primary focus and the majority of the content is truly description.

Discussion of the Related Operation or Process

At some point in a description, often at the end, it is useful to summarize the operation or process associated with the object you're describing. For example, if you've just described a mechanical pencil, you could briefly explain how it is used. If you've just described a snowflake, you could discuss the process by which it formed.

Sources of Description

When you write a description, you need to think about the kinds of descriptive detail you can provide. Sometimes, descriptions are rather weak in this area. Use the following list to plan your description or to review a description you have written. Think of the categories of descriptive detail you could provide, or use the following list to identify categories you have not used:

Descriptive Details

- color
- height
- width

- shape
- weight
- materials
- texture
- location
- methods of attachment
- depth
- amount
- pattern, design
- ingredients
- age
- subparts
- length
- finish
- temperature
- moisture content
- smell

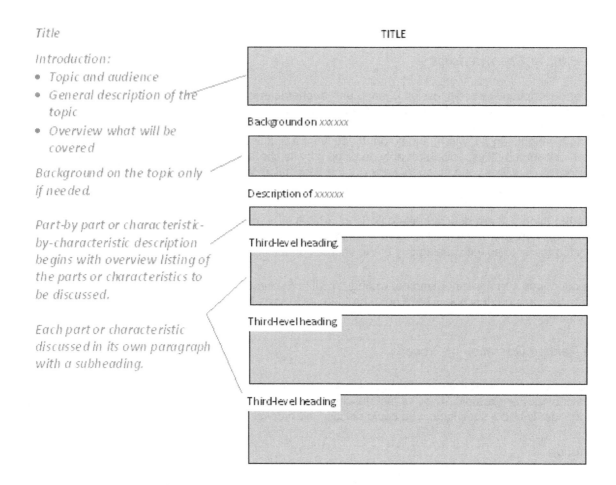

Figure 1: Schematic view of descriptions. Remember that this is just a typical or common model for the contents and organization—many others are possible.

Miscellaneous Concerns

Remember that technical writing breaks some of those rules you worked so hard to learn in past writing classes. In the technical writing context, we are often vitally concerned about numbers and want them to stand out. This concern means that you should use numerals in running text when the number indicates an exact, measured, or measurable amount or when it represents a critical value. For example, in these sentences, it seems to matter that the numbers are exact:

The cup is 3 inches in diameter. Use 4 tacks to fasten the poster to the wall.

However, this does not mean using numerals for indifferent values. For example, in this sentence, there is nothing heart-stopping about how many sections the report has: The report contains four major sections.

Anatomy of a Descriptive Paragraph

Typically, it starts with some statement about the purpose or function of the part, with the descriptive detail following. Descriptive detail draws upon the "sources" of description—such things as color, shape, width, and height.

Abbreviations

In technical writing, we expect to see abbreviations. Use them in your description freely. Remember the rule on punctuating abbreviations—punctuate them only if they spell a word (for example, "in."). Remember too that abbreviations do *not* go up against the number they are used with (for example, make that "8 mm tape" or "8-mm tape" but *not* "8mm tape").

Symbols

The most common problem with symbols in instructions and descriptions has to do with inches and feet. If you're writing instructions for a carpenter's dream project where there are feet and inches all over the place, use the symbols " (inches) and ' (feet). However, if you cite inch and foot measurements only a few times, use the word or abbreviation instead.

Graphics and Format in Descriptions

In most descriptions, you'll need at least one illustration of the thing you are describing, with labels pointing to the parts.

Headings

In descriptions, you'll want to use headings and subheadings to mark off the discussion of the individual parts or characteristics. Remember that, ideally, you want to describe each part in a separate paragraph or section—and flag that discussion with a heading. If you have a background section, use a heading for it too.

Lists

Lists are not nearly so important in descriptions as they are in instructions. However, if you itemize parts or subparts or list specifications, these are good situations for lists.

Special Notices

In descriptions, there is nothing like the important role for special notices as there is in instructions. After all, if it really is a description, readers should not be trying to follow any procedure, and, therefore, should not be running any risks of damaging equipment, wasting supplies, screwing up the procedure, or injuring themselves or others. However, you may find the *note* special notice to be useful to emphasize important points or exceptions.

Comparison

What's it Like—What's it Not Like?

Another important information structure often used in technical writing is comparison.

What is Comparison?

In technical writing, comparisons can be very important. Short comparisons to similar or familiar things can help readers understand a topic better; comparisons can also help in the decision process of choosing one option out of a group. An *extended comparison*, which is the focus in this chapter, is one or more paragraphs whose main purpose and structure is comparison. One type of comparison is the *analogy*, which is a special type of extended comparison of an unfamiliar thing to a familiar thing.

Extended comparisons can be *informative* or *evaluative*. An informative comparison seeks to compare the topic to something similar or familiar to help people understand the topic or, in some cases, to help people understand both better. An *evaluative* comparison seeks to recommend one or more of the options by comparing them.

How to Identify Points of Comparison

When you write an extended comparison, you must start by identifying the specific ways in which you are going to compare the things you plan to write about. These *points of comparison* are like categories of comparative detail. For example, in an evaluative comparison of smart phones, you'd probably want to compare the best four or five machines according to the following:

- cost
- ease of use
- reliability
- special features, and so on

If you don't start by identifying the points of comparison, your comparison can become uneven—for example, you might say that model 1 is easy to use but not say anything about the the ease of use of models 2, 3, or 4.

How to Organize Comparisons

One of the most important concepts to learn in writing comparisons has to do with organizing the contents. There are two basic ways to organize a comparison:

- whole-to-whole approach
- point-by-point approach

To get a sense of how these two approaches work, take a look at the following illustration of these two approaches. In the whole-to-whole approach, details about each of the options being compared are lumped together. This is our natural tendency—however, it does a sloppy, uneven job of stating the comparisons. The better way is to use the point-by-point approach. In the schematic diagram in the illustration, you'd have one paragraph comparing the costs of Models A, B, and C; then another paragraph comparing the warranties of the three models; and so on.

Use the point-by-point approach unless something about your topic, purpose, or audience dictates otherwise. With the whole-to-whole approach, the comparison is often uneven—you might forget to tell about the warranties for Model B; you might neglect to state the actual results of comparison—that Model C is better in terms of special features. In the whole-to-whole approach, writers often leave the actual comparisons up to the reader, thinking that just supplying the raw data is enough.

In the point-by-point approach, each of the comparative sections should end with a conclusion that states which option is the best choice in that particular category of comparison. Of course, it won't always be easy to state a clear winner—you may have to qualify the conclusions in various ways, providing multiple conclusions for different conditions.

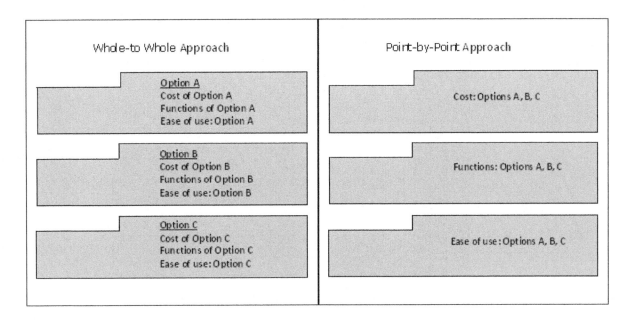

Figure 2: Schematic view of the whole-to-whole and the part-by-part approaches to organizing a comparison. Unless you have a very unusual topic, use the point-by-point approach.

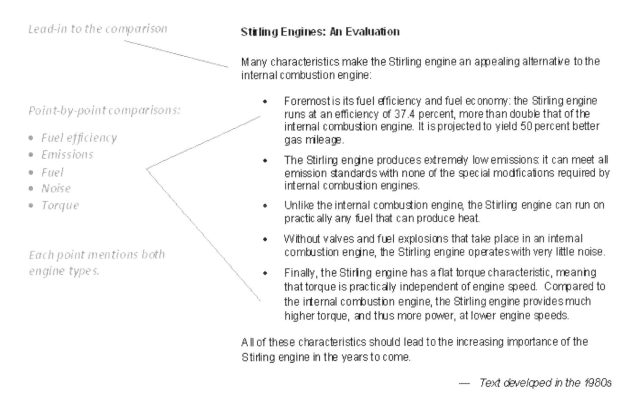

Figure 3: Short paragraph-length comparison

How to Write Comparisons

As with causal discussions, comparisons are not distinctive because of a certain kind of content. Instead, it's the special transitional words that make comparative writing work: for example, "similar," "unlike," "more than," "less than," and other such words that draw readers' attention to comparisons and highlight the results of the comparisons. Notice how many are used in the illustrations in this chapter.

When you write comparisons, take special care to use these transitional words. Emphasize the similarities and differences—don't force readers to figure them out for themselves.

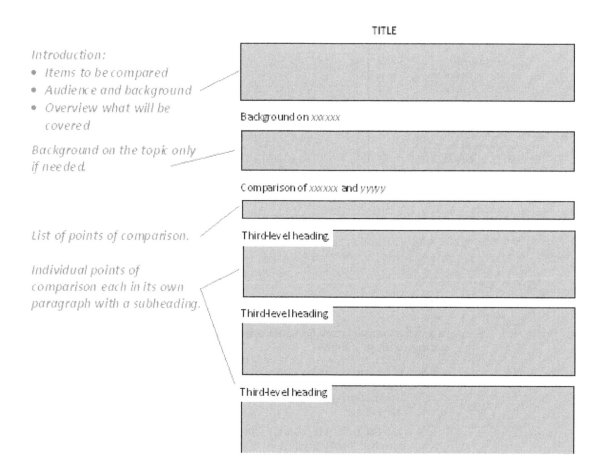

Figure 4: Schematic view of comparisons

Remember that this is just a typical or common model for the contents and organization—many others are possible.

How to Format Comparisons?

Comparisons don't call out for any special format; just use headings, lists, notices, and graphics as you would in any other technical document.

Classification

What are its Categories—into Which Does it Fit?

Another important information structure often used in technical writing is classification.

What is Classification?

In some technical reports, certain paragraphs or sections use a kind of writing and pattern of organization known as classification. Classification means either (1) explaining which class a thing belongs to or (2) dividing a group of things into classes. You may find that classification is an effective way to present background information to your readers.

True Classification

You are "classifying" (in the strict dictionary sense of the term) when you place an object, action, or person in one of several classes. For example, the XYZ Corporation may have just come out with its new ABC computer but cannot decide whether to classify it as a laptop or a notebook computer. A botanist may have discovered a new species of fungus and must now decide how to classify it. Written documents on these questions would resemble comparison because features of the new item (the computer or the fungus) must be compared to those of the established classes. The Jupiter example in the following shows an example of a true classification in which the writer shows why the object belongs to one specific category.

Division

Classification can also refer to breaking a thing down into its types, classes, categories, or kinds and then discussing each one. For example, computers for some time now have been divided into several classes: minicomputers, microcomputers, and macrocomputers. And, if you have ever taken biology, you know that terrestrial life is divided into into plant and animal "kingdoms"; the kingdoms, broken down into phyla (the plural of phylum); phyla, into classes; classes, into families; families, into genera; and genera, into species. Each of these divisions—except perhaps the last—represents a grouping of types.

Several key words indicate that classifications are being discussed: *classes, kinds, types, categories, sorts,* or *groups*. Classification can be quite useful in technical reports: it breaks the discussion of a subject into smaller chunks, and it can make the job of evaluation and selection much easier.

Jupiter can be classed as a Jovian planet because of its size and its average density. Indeed Jupiter is the largest planet in our solar system (as shown in Figure 16) and one of the brightest objects in the sky, having attained a magnitude of -2.5, more than a full magnitude brighter than Sirius, the brightest star in the sky. Jupiter's brightness results from its great size of course but also from its high reflectivity: it reflects about 44 percent of the light it receives. The size and composition of Jupiter's interior are open to much speculation. Some astronomers picture the interior as having a radius of over 30,000 miles and as possibly being composed of liquid hydrogen. The core is small and dense and may contain iron silicates. The other Jovian characteristic of the planet is its density. Even though its diameter is only 11 times that of the Earth, its total volume is 11 × 11 × 11, or over a thousand times that of Earth.

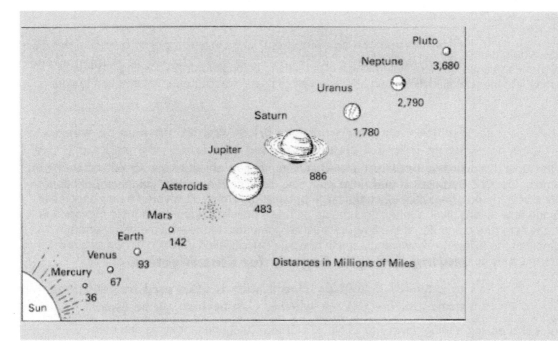

Jupiter more graphically, over 1000 Earths could be packed into the space occupied by Jupiter.

How to Identify Classes and the Principle of Classification

Once you know what you are going to divide into classes, your next step is to identify the classes and the principle of classification. For example, if you were classifying dialysis machines (used to treat people with kidney disease), you might list these classes:

- parallel flow design dialyzers
- coil design dialyzers
- hollow-fiber capillary dialyzers

The principle of classification is the design of the structure through which blood is filtered.

The *principle of classification* then is the method you use to sort the items into classes. If you sorted marbles into red, green, and blue ones, you'd be using color as the principle of classification. You must be careful to use only one principle of classification at a time. For example, you couldn't sort your marbles by color *and* size—you might have some big red ones and some small red ones!

Here are some additional examples of classifications and their principles:

Examples

Topic	Classes	Principle of Classification
Electrical circuits	Series Parallel Series-parallel	Pathway of electrical current
Anemias	Blood-loss anemia Iron-deficiency anemia Pernicious anemia	Main cause of the anemia
Hurrican track prediction methods	Total climatology and persistence methods Particular climatology and persistence method Circulation and climatology method	Combination of hurricane characteristics

	Dynamic model method	
Wind machines	Lift machines Drag machines	Interaction between the wind and propeller blade

How to Discuss the Classes?

When you write the discussion of the individual classes, you must choose sources of discussion that enable you to explain each class fully, add comparisons so that readers can see the differences between the classes, and plan for the length of your classification.

Choosing Sources of Discussion

Writing the discussion of individual classes is much the same as it is with extended definitions: you combine a variety of sources to explain the classes fully. To discuss the three types of dialysis machines for victims of kidney disease, you might use these sources:

Classification if Dialysis Machines

Definition: Kidney disease
Description: Main components of the different dialysis machines
Process: How the different machines operate
Comparison: Advantages and disadvantages of these machines

Of course, some classifications may use only one kind of writing. For example, in the discussion of different hurricane track prediction methods, the discussion would most likely be process—step by step how the methods work.

Adding Comparisons

No matter which sources you use in discussing the classes, comparison is an important ingredient. It helps readers distinguish the different classes from each other. Check out the following example of how comparisons work in classifications.

The higher-level heading would be something like "Types of Reactors."

Pressurized-water reactors (PWR). The first pressurized-water reactor was the submarine thermal reactor built in Idaho in 1953, which led directly to the first nuclear-powered submarine, the USS *Nautilis*. As the name implies, a pressurized-water reactor is both cooled and moderated by water under high pressure, thus permitting high temperatures. The hot water is pumped from a pressurized vessel containing the nuclear core to a steam generator in which heat is exchanged to produce the steam that drives a turbogenerator. . . .

First type of reactor is discussed—mostly in terms of how it works.

Boiling-water reactors (BWR). Boiling water reactors have much in common with pressurized-water reactors:

Second type of reactor is discussed, with direct comparisons to the preceding type. (Italics added.)

- The *main difference* is that the intermediate steam generator is omitted, and steam is supplied directly from boiling water in the reactor core.
- *Less pressurization* is needed because the water is allowed to boil, and *less pumping* is needed because of the large amount of heat absorbed by boiling water.
- An *increase in steam production* compared to that of the pressurized-water reactor is a result of an *increase in power level*, which *reduces the water volume* which *lessens its moderating ability*—a condition which in turn *lessens reactivity*.

—Text developed in the 1980s

Figure 5: Comparisons used in classification

Comparing the types to each other gives readers a clearer sense of the types as well as their distinguishing features.

Short and Extended Classifications

In short classifications, an overview of the types is packed into one sentence or into one paragraph. In an extended classification, you might have one or more paragraphs on each type. For an extended classification, you'll use a paragraph or more to discuss each of the classes, and a separate paragraph to introduce these classes—as illustrated in the extended classification in the following.

Lead-in to the types to be discussed

Three types of circuitry are used in automobile electricity:

The three types of circuits, with the text formatted as a bulleted list.

- *Series circuit.* In this type, the current flows in one path—for example, from the battery through the switch and through two light bulbs. In a series circuit, current must pass through all its electrical devices. If an devices fails to work, it will act as a switch and open the whole circuit.
- *Parallel circuit.* In the parallel type, there are two or more paths for current flow. If one device fails to work, the current still goes to the other devices, and they continue to work.
- *Series–parallel circuit.* Most automotive electrical circuits use a combination of series and parallel circuits. The series part works like a series circuit, as described above; the parallel part, like a parallel circuit.

Notice the italics on the name of the type

Figure 6: Single-paragraph classification. All the classes are discussed briefly in this one section.

Notice how much definition and causal discussion is used to prepare for the discussion of the types.

Italics used to indicate that a term is defined at that point.

Lead-in to the types of anemia to be discussed, formatted as an in-sentence list.

Each type discussed in its own paragraph with a bolded run-in heading.

Types of Anemias

One of the most important classes of disorders of the hematological system involves the various types of anemias (disoders of the red blood cells). The term *anemia* is used to indicate a deficit in the amount of iron expressed as hemoglobin in the blood. Anemia is further defined by the mechanism that causes the inability of the erythrocytes to deliver enough oxygen to the individual cells.

Anemia can be the result either of a lack of the total number of red blood cells or by low amounts of hemoglobin in the individual erythrocytes. *Hypoxia* is the universal symptom of this condition where the patient's blood cannot carry sufficient amounts of oxygen.

The most common classes of anemia include (1) blood-loss anemia, (2) iron-deficiency anemia, (3) pernicious anemia, (4) aplastic anemia, (5) hemolytic anemia, (6) sickle cell anemia, and (7) secondary anemia.

Blood-loss anemia. Obviously, with any great loss of blood, one will become anemic. If a patient loses some of the red blood cells needed to carry oxygen, the only oxygen that can get to the tissues is that carried by the erythrocytes that are left.

Iron-deficiency anemia. The normal nonanemic male loses approximately 1 mg of iron per day principally from the gastrointestinal tract . . . .

Figure 7: Extended classification with classes treated each in their own paragraphs

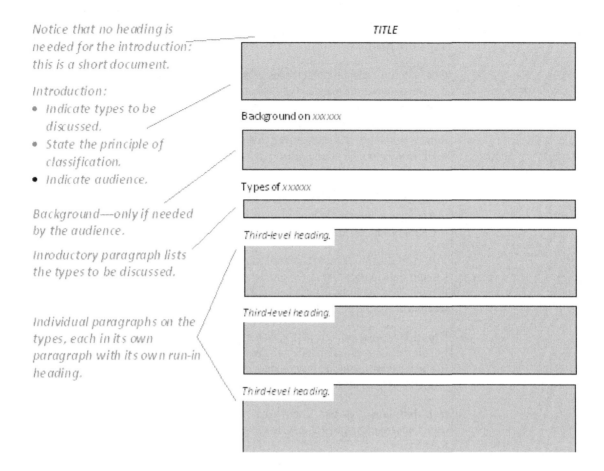

Figure 8: Schematic view of classification. Remember that this is just a typical or common model for the contents and organization—many others are possible.

How to Format for Classifications?

Classifications don't call out for any special format; just use headings, lists, notices, and graphics as you would in any other technical document. For details, see:

- Headings
- Lists
- Notices
- Graphics

Causal Discussion

What happened—why did it happen?

Another important information structure often used in technical writing is the discussion of causes and effects.

What Is a Cause–Effect Discussion?

Discussions like these answer questions such as the following:

- What are (or were) the causes of this? How and why does (or did) this happen?

- What brought about a situation, problem, or accident?
- What are (were or will be) the effects, results, or consequences of this? What will happen if a certain situation or problem continues?
- How does this work? What causes this to function as it does?
- Why won't this thing work? What's wrong with it?
- What changes will occur if a certain plan or action is taken?
- How can a certain problem or situation be avoided?
- What are the advantages, benefits, or disadvantages of an action or object?
- What are one or more potential solutions to a problem?

Some examples:

- What causes tornadoes? What sorts of damage do tornadoes cause?
- What will happen if the world continues to use petroleum resources at its current rate?
- What were the causes of the Great Depression?
- What are the effects of an economic recession?
- How does a photocopier work?
- What makes a microwave oven work? (Does this sound like your seven-year-old?)

As you can see from these examples, we can discuss the causes and effects of human or social processes, natural processes, mechanical or physical processes, historical or economic processes, meteorological or biological processes, and on and on.

If you think about it, there's not much difference between process discussion and causal discussion. Both occur over time; steps in a process often involve causes and effects. The distinction depends on your purpose and emphasis: process discussions are primarily concerned with *how* an event occurs; causal discussions, with *why* an event occurs. Process discussion focuses on the chronology of something; causal discussion focuses on the causes and effects.

- I can tell you step by step how to take a photo or what events occur inside the camera when you take a picture—that's process.
- But I can also explain to you what physical and chemical principles are at work when you take a photo, what principles actually enable you to take a photo—that's causal discussion.

For some topics, however, such as explaining tornadoes, it's almost impossible to make a distinction. Here are some contrasting examples:

Subject	Process Discussion	Causal Discussion
Lightning	How to safeguard home appliances from lightning	What natural phenomena cause lightning
Instruction writing	How to set up understandable instructions	What causes instructions to be unclear
Acquisition of language by children rapidly	How to help children learn language more rapidly	Why certain children learn language more rapidly
Growing tomatoes	How to plant and care for tomatoes	Reasons why tomatoes are less productive
Air conditioning	How cool air is produced by conventional systems	Why your air conditioning is costing you more this summer

Here are some common reasons why you may need to discuss causal and effects:

- You need a record of the damage done by something. Photographs work, but words may also be needed.
- You need an account of the scientific principles at work in a process so that you can understand what you are doing in an instructional procedure.

- You need to understand the causes of something so you can have a better understanding of how to control or eliminate it.
- You need to understand the effects of something so that you can work to prevent it or increase its likelihood.

How to Organize Causal Discussions?

How you organize the contents of a causal discussion depends on how many and what combination of causes and effects you discuss:

- Single cause–single effect—A single cause can lead to a single effect; for example, a radiator leak can cause the car to overheat.
- Multiple causes–single effect—Many different causes can be seen as leading to one effect: for example, high unemployment, high interest rates, and high real estate costs (causes) might lead to decreased real estate sales (effect).
- Single cause–multiple effects—A single cause can be seen as producing numerous effects. For example, proponents of the greenhouse effect believe that increased CO_2 in the atmosphere (cause) will lead to changes in weather patterns, higher temperatures, drought, increased storm activity, and higher sea levels (effects).
- Sequential causes and effects—One cause can bring about an effect, which in turn becomes the cause of another effect, and so on. For example, proponents of the greenhouse effect argue that increased burning of fossil fuels (cause) leads to increased CO_2 in the atmosphere (effect) which in turn is the cause of less thermal energy being reradiated out of the system (effect) which in turn becomes the cause of increased global temperatures.
- Alternate causes and effects—Causes and effects can be alternating. For example, if the car won't start (effect), it may be because of a dead battery (alternate cause 1), no gas in the gas tank (alternate cause 2), or a faulty part (alternate cause 3).

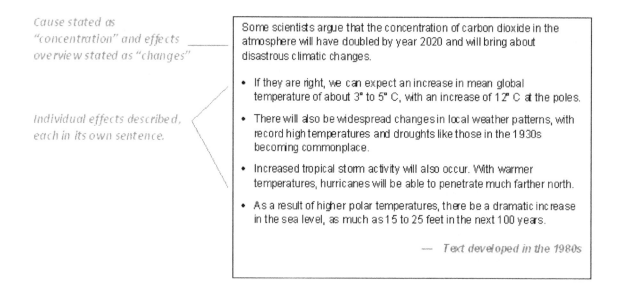

Figure 9: Organization of effects in a short causal discussion. First, the cause is stated; then the effects are discussed one after another.

Consider a simple example: imagine you want to discuss how a single situation has led to a number of problems, in other words, one cause leading to several effects. In a single paragraph, the first couple of sentences might focus on the cause; each of the following sentences would focus on the effects. In an extended discussion, there might be a paragraph on the cause, and a paragraph on each of the effects. The preceding schematic diagram of a causal discussion in shows you how the single-paragraph approach would look.

How to Discuss Causes and Effects?

Actual discussion of causes and effects is not as immediately identifiable as descriptive or process writing are. Typically, causal discussions talk about events and describe things. What makes causal discussions distinctive is the use of transitional words to indicate the causes and effects.

In this sentence:

Increased deficit spending by the government leads to increased inflation.

the verb "leads to" establishes the connection between a cause and an effect. In this excerpt, the connective "consequently" establishes a causal link between the increasing domestic anger over the Vietnam war and Johnson's decision not to seek reelection:

Meanwhile at home, anger, hostility, and outright revolt against the war grew. Johnson, sensing he could not get reelected in this atmosphere, consequently decided against running for another term.

In the "natural" greenhouse effect, less solar radiation is reflected back out of the earth's atmosphere than is absorbed by it, a process that causes higher mean temperatures within the earth's atmosphere. Specifically, 65 percent of solar radiation is retained by the earth and its atmosphere. Of that amount, 18 percent is absorbed by the atmosphere and 47 percent by the earth's surface. With radiative equilibrium—that is, a state in which incoming solar radiation matches outgoing thermal radiation from the earth, the mean global temperature would be -20° C. Instead, the mean global temperature is 14° C. The difference of 34° C is the result of the natural greenhouse effect in which the earth traps most of the long-wave radiation that enters its atmosphere.

Specific effect: earth traps some of the radiation it receives.

This trapping effect occurs largely because of minor constituents in the earth's atmosphere, mainly carbon dioxide and water vapor. These constituents block out a major portion of the 30- to 50-micron range of wave lengths—the infrared portion of the electromagnetic, within which excess thermal energy must be radiated back into space. Water vapor is a strong absorber of radiation over the entire thermal spectrum except in the 8- to 18-micron interval. CO_2 absorption retains excess thermal energy in the 12- to 18-micron range. The earth therefore is constrained to radiate its excess thermal energy in the small range of 8 to 12 microns. This increased absorption and retention of solar energy results in an overall warming if the earth–atmosphere system.

Exploration of the cause: how that trapping effect occurs.

Figure 10: Cause–effect relationship involving a single effect followed by an extensive exploration of its cause.

How to Format for Causal Discussions?

Here are a few suggestions on format as they relate specifically to causal discussions:

- Headings. If you write an extended causal discussion and have separate paragraphs for each of the causes or effects, then the headings should signal those causes. (See the examples in this chapter.)
- Lists. If you discuss sequential causes and effects, you're likely to need in-sentence and vertical numbered lists. If you have multiple causes or effects but no necessary order amongst them, then bulleted lists are appropriate.

- Graphics. Causal discussions often use conceptual diagrams to show the relationships between the causes and effects. In these you give a spatial representation of the causes and effects as they occur in time.
- Style. As with any other technical writing, you treat numbers, symbols, and abbreviations in process discussions the same. Exact measurement values should be numerals, regardless whether they are below 10.

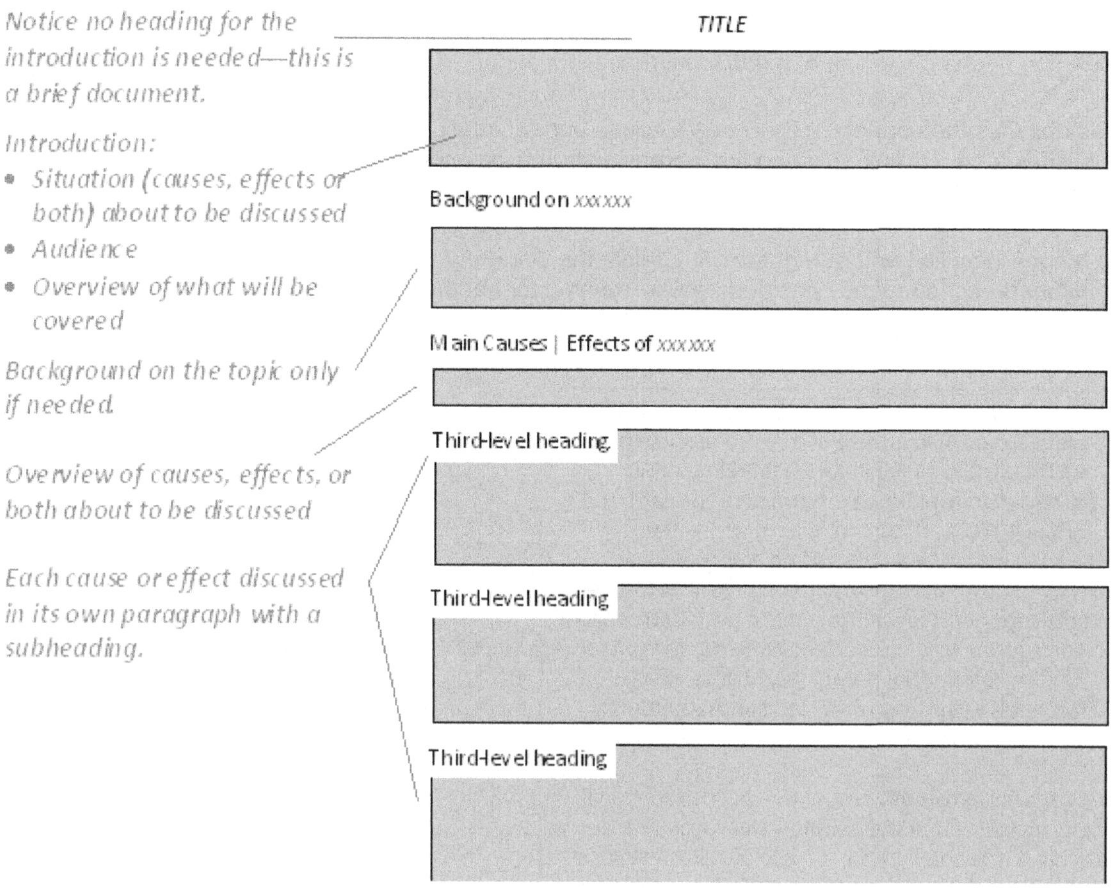

Notice no heading for the introduction is needed—this is a brief document.

Introduction:
- *Situation (causes, effects or both) about to be discussed*
- *Audience*
- *Overview of what will be covered*

Background on the topic only if needed

Overview of causes, effects, or both about to be discussed

Each cause or effect discussed in its own paragraph with a subheading.

TITLE

Background on *xxxxxx*

Main Causes | Effects of *xxxxxx*

Third-level heading

Third-level heading

Third-level heading

Figure 11: Schematic view of cause–effect discussions. Remember that this is just a typical or common model for the contents and organization—many others are possible.

Extended Definition

How Can You Define It?

An important writing tool you'll need, particularly if you are writing for nonspecialists, is definition—or more specifically, extended definition. An *extended definition* is a one or more paragraphs that attempt to explain a complex term. Some terms may be so important in your report, there may be so much confusion about them, or they may be so difficult to understand that an extended discussion is vital for the success of your report.

When you write reports, you may often discover that you need to explain certain basics before you can discuss the main subject matter. For example:

- in a report on new treatments for sickle cell anemia, you'd need a section defining the disease.
- In a report on the benefits of drip irrigation, you'd need to write an extended definition of drip irrigation, explaining how it works and what equipment is used.
- In a report showing small businesses how to weather economic recessions, an extended definition of the term economic recession would be needed first.

Writing Formal Sentence Definitions

One of the first things to do when you write an extended definition is to compose the formal sentence definition of the term you are writing about. Place it toward the beginning of the extended definition. It establishes the focus for the rest of the discussion. It is "formal" because it uses a certain form. Here are several examples:

Term defined (bold)   Class to which the term belongs (blue)

An **algorithm** is a finite description of a finite number of steps required to accomplish some well-defined task.

Carbohydrates are a food group including sugars, starches, and cellulose.

Computer memory is one of three basic components of a computer which stores information for future use—both the data that will be operated on as well as the programs that direct the operations to be performed.

Reservoir rock is that type of rock that has sufficient porosity and permeability to allow gas and oil to accumulate and be produced in commercial quantities.

Influenza is an acute highly contagious infection of the respiratory tract, which occurs sporadically or in epidemics and that lasts up to a month.

Characteristics: details about the term that distinguish it from other members of the class (red)

Formal sentence definitions: their components are the term being defined, the class it belongs to, and its distinguishing characteristics.

Take particular care when you write the reference to the class to which the term belongs; it sets up a larger frame of reference or context. It gives readers something familiar to associate the term with. The term may belong to a class of tools, diseases, geological processes, electronic components; it may be a term from the field of medicine, computer science, agriculture, reprographics, or finance. Avoid vague references to the class the term belongs to: for example, instead of calling a concussion an "injury" or botulism a "medical problem," call them something more specific like "a serious head injury" and "a severe form of food poisoning," respectively.

Similarly, provide plenty of specific detail in the characteristics component of the formal sentence definition. Readers need these details to begin forming their own understanding the term you are defining.

Be aware, however, that your formal sentence definition will likely contain additional potentially unfamiliar terms. Somewhere in your extended definition, you'll need to explain them as well, possibly by using short definitions (explained later in this section).

Formal sentence definition begins this extended definition.

Supplementary definition used within this extended definition.

Stress is a measure of the internal reaction between elementary particles of a material in resisting separation, compacting, or sliding that tend to be induced by external forces. Total internal resisting forces result from continuously distributed normal and tangential forces that vary in magnitude and direction and act on elementary areas throughout the material. These forces may be distributed uniformly or nonuniformly. Stresses can be categorized as tensile, compressive, or shearing, according to the straining action. Strain is a measure of deformation such as:

a. linear strain, the length per unit of linear dimensions
b. shear strain, the angular skew in a radians of an element undergoing change of shape by tangential forces
c. volumetric strain, the change of volume per unit of volume. The strains associated with stress are characteristic oif the material.

Figure 13: A formal sentence definition used in an extended definition.

Choosing the Sources of Definition

When you write an extended definition, you literally grab at any of the writing resources or tools that will help you explain the term to your readers. This means considering all of the various sources of information that can help define the term adequately (for example, description, process narration, causal discussion, and classification).

Notice how many different kinds of writing are indicated in the examples in this chapter.

The key to writing a good extended definition is to choose the sources of definition to help readers understand the term being defined. Use this checklist to select the kinds of discussion to include in your extended definitions:

Description	Does anything related to the term being defined need to be described?
Process narration	Is there some process (natural, social) associated with the term that should be discussed?
Additional definitions	Do unfamiliar terms occurring in the definition also need definition?
Historical background	Is there some history, some key individuals related to term being defined? Would that discussion contribute to he definition of the term?
Cause, causes	Does the reader need to know about causes related to the term being defined?
Effects, results, consequences	Does the reader need to know about effects related to the term being defined?
Problems, solutions	Does the term being defined represent a problem or a solution?
Statistics	Should you discuss numerical data related to the term defined—percentages, amounts, etc.?
Uses, applications	Would it help to discuss uses or applications related to the term?
Similarities, differences, analogies	Is the term similar to or different from something else? Would an analogy help define the term?
Classes, types, categories	Are there categories that the term can be divided into? Does it belong to a certain category?
Examples	Would examples contribute to the definition of the term?
Future developments, implications	Would an understanding of the roots, the etymology, of the word help define it?
Word origins	Should future developments related to the term be discussed? Does it have implications—good, bad, both?
Negatives	Would explaining what the term is *not*, what it does *not* refer to help?
Advantages, disadvantages	Are there advantages and disadvantages related to the term that can be discussed?

Figure 14: Checklist of sources for extended definitions

I. Introduction
II. Alzheimer's Disease: Overview of Current Knowledge
    A. Two Main Types of Alzheimer's Disease
        1. Alzheimer's disease (pre-65)
        2. Senile dementia of the Alzheimer's type (post-65)
    B. Demography of Alzheimer's Disease
        1. Age distribution
        2. Gender distribution
        3. Other demographics
    C. Process and Characteristics of Alzheimer's Disease
        1. Forgetfulness
        2. Speech disorders
        3. Difficulty calculating
        4. Visual disorientation
        5. Abnormal judgment and social behavior
    D. Brain Pathology of Alzheimer's Disease Victims
        1. Reduced brain size
        2. Neurofibrillary tangles
        3. Neuritic plaques
        4. Loss of specific populations of nerve cells
    E. Etiology of Alzheimer's Disease
        1. Aging
        2. Inheritance
        3. Infectious agents and toxins
III. Current Alzheimer's Disease Treatment

Classification: the disease is defined according to its main two types.

Description: demographic statistics are used in this definition.

Process: the stages of the disease are identified along with the effects of the disease at each stage.

Effects: clinical effects of the disease.

Causes: various possible causes of the disease.

Figure 15: Outline of a report that uses extended definition. This view shows how different sources of definition can be used to write an extended definition.

Formal sentence definition begins this extended definition.

Quick parenthetical definition of a potentially unfamiliar term.

Supplementary definitions used within this extended definition.

Demographics (statistics) used to further define the term.

Process of the disease

(Should "intercurrent" be defined for nonspecialist readers?)

First described in 1907 by Alos Alzheimer, a German physician, Alzheimer's disease is an adult-onset neurological disorder of unknown etiology (cause) manifested by loss of memory, impaired thought processes, and abnormal behavior. When the illness begins before the age of 65, it is termed *Alzheimer's disease*; when onset is after 65, it is referred to as senile dementia of the *Alzheimer's type*.

Approximately 5% of the U.S. population over 65 have severe dementia; an additional 10% have a mild-to-moderate impairment in memory and cognition. Of these demented individuals, approximately 40-50% have Alzheimer's disease, making this disorder the most common cause of dementia in middle and later life.

Affected individuals are, at first, forgetful. As the memory disorder gradually worsens, the individuals, although able to recall occurrences in the distant past, are unable to remember recent events. Subsequently, speech, the ability to calculate, visual orientation, judgment, and social behavior become progressively abnormal. Eventually, the individuals become profoundly demented and frequently die of intercurrent infection.

Figure 16: Another extended definition. This one uses additional definitions, description (demographics), process.

Adding Short Definitions

As mentioned earlier, you'll find that in writing an extended definition, you must define other terms as well. Typically, short definitions—a sentence, clause, or phrase in length—will suffice. Notice how many are added to the "after" version in the following.

Before Translation

Measles is an acute, highly infectious disease, with cough, fever, and maculopapular rash. It has worldwide endemicity. The infective particle is an RNA virus about 100-150 nm in diameter, measured by ultrafiltration, but the active core is only about 65 nm as measured by inactivation after electron irradiation. Negative staining in the electron microscope shows the virus to have the helical structure of a paramyxovirus with the helix being 18 nm in diameter.

Measles virus will infect monkeys easily and chick embryos with difficulty. In tissue cultures, the virus may produce giant multinucleated cells and nuclear acidophilic inclusion bodies. The virus has not been shown to have the receptor-destroying enyzme associated with other paramyxoviruses. Measles, canine distemper, and bovine rinderspest viruses are antigenetically related.

After Translation

Measles is an acute, highly infectious disease caused by a virus. The illness is characterized by a cough, fever, and maculopapular (raised red) rash. It has worldwide endemicity—that is, people throughout the world are vulnerable to the disease. The infective particle (organism causing the disease) is a virus about 100-150 nm (a nanometer being 10^{-9} meter) in diameter and contains RNA (ribonucleic acid) as it genetic material rather than DNA (deoxyribonucleic acid). The size of the measles virus as measured by ultrafiltration, in which filters with extremely small pore are used. The active core, or actual genetic material (RNA), is only 65 nm, as measured by electron irradiation which inactivates the core. Negative staining, a shadowing technique used with an electron microscope, shows the virus to have a specific helical structure common to a group of viruses known as paramyxoviruses. The helix, a spiral around a core (similar to a winding staircase) is 18 nm in diameter.

Measles virus will infect monkeys easily and chick embryos with difficulty. In tissue cultures (those involving living cells or tissues from other living organisms), the measles virus may produce giant cells containing many nuclei and acidophilic inclusion bodies (red-stained areas in the nucleus which are a laboratory sign for certain viral infections). The virus has not been shown to have the receptor-destroying enyzme, a protein capable of destroying or inactivating a cell-surface molecule, usually associated with other viruses in the paramyxovirus group. Measles, canine distemper (a flu-like disease affecting dogs), and bovine rinderpest (a virus affecting cows) are antigenetically related—that is, they possess similar antigens (molecules that stimulate production of an antibody on their surfaces).

Figure 17: Extended definitions often need additional definitions. These can be short, phrase-length definitions.

This process of supplying short definitions "on the fly" is critical in good technical writing for nonspecialists. Notice how many quick definitions occur just in the first two sentences of the preceding illusration. "Maculopapular" is defined in parentheses as "(raised red)." "Endemicity" is defined by restating the idea in other words: "that is, people throughout the world are capable of contracting measles." And "infective particle" is quickly defined by providing an alternative: "or organism causing the illness." Obviously, the passage is almost tripled in length—but that's the price for thorough explanation and clarity.

Format for Extended Definition

Extended definitions don't call out for any special format; just use headings, lists, notices, and graphics as you would in any other technical document:

- Headings
- Lists
- Notices
- Graphics

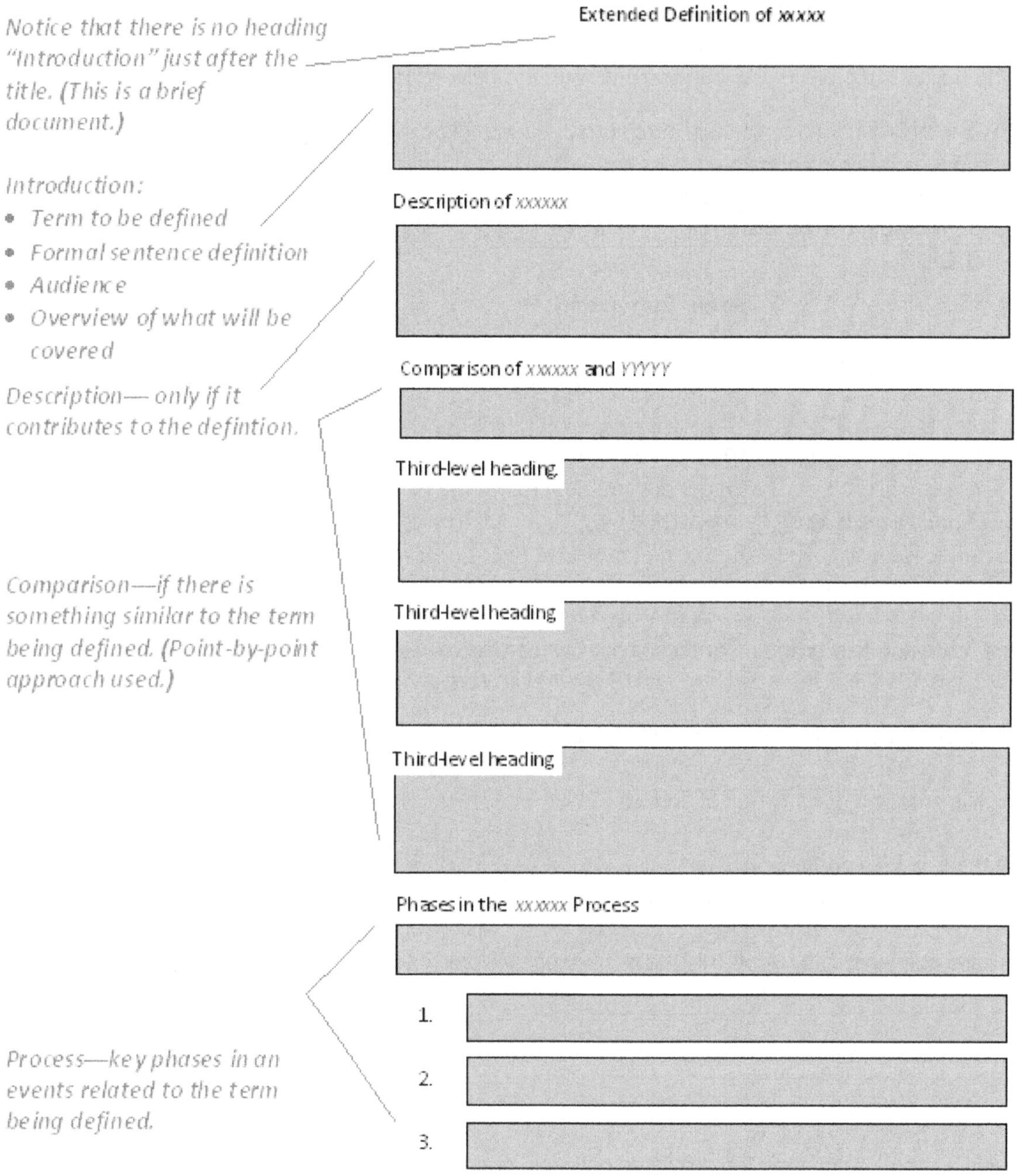

Notice that there is no heading "Introduction" just after the title. (This is a brief document.)

Introduction:
- *Term to be defined*
- *Formal sentence definition*
- *Audience*
- *Overview of what will be covered*

Description— only if it contributes to the defintion.

Comparison—if there is something similar to the term being defined. (Point-by-point approach used.)

Process—key phases in an events related to the term being defined.

Extended Definition of *xxxxx*

Description of *xxxxxx*

Comparison of *xxxxxx* and *YYYYY*

Third-level heading.

Third-level heading

Third-level heading

Phases in the *xxxxxx* Process

1.

2.

3.

Figure 18: Schematic view of an extended definition. Remember that this is just a typical or common model for the contents and organization—many others are possible.

How Does it Happen?

In technical writing, process discussion is one of the most important kinds of prose: people need to know how things happen, how things work, how to operate things, and how to perform certain actions. A *narration* tells how something occurs over a period of historical time. A *process* is an event or set of events that can be performed or that occurs regularly or repeatedly. The words "procedure" and "routine" are closely related. When you "narrate" a "process," you explain how something works or how something occurs. We'll use "process discussion" here.

What is a Process?

Process discussion is an information structure—it's one of those fundamental combinations of content and organizational patterns you use in many different situations in technical writing. For example, instructions are an application of technical writing; instructions make heavy use of process discussion.

The focus of this chapter is some basic guidelines for writing *noninstructional* process discussions. These process discussions answer such questions as:

- How does this mechanism work?
- What are the typical steps in this natural, mechanical, social, biological, psychological phenomenon?
- How does this event (mechanical, natural, human, social) happen?

When we ask questions like these, we expect a systematic step-by-step explanation of how the mechanism works or how the phenomenon happens. We're not looking to perform it ourselves, just to understand it. These are closely related to process discussions. In causal discussions, we're interested in why something happens, what causes it, what its results or consequences are. In process discussions, we are interested in how something happens, how it works, in a step-by-step fashion. Often the distinction between these two is blurry.

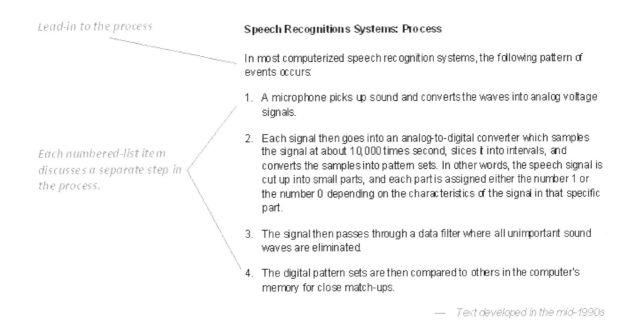

Lead-in to the process

Speech Recognitions Systems: Process

In most computerized speech recognition systems, the following pattern of events occurs:

1. A microphone picks up sound and converts the waves into analog voltage signals.

2. Each signal then goes into an analog-to-digital converter which samples the signal at about 10,000 times second, slices it into intervals, and converts the samples into pattern sets. In other words, the speech signal is cut up into small parts, and each part is assigned either the number 1 or the number 0 depending on the characteristics of the signal in that specific part.

Each numbered-list item discusses a separate step in the process.

3. The signal then passes through a data filter where all unimportant sound waves are eliminated.

4. The digital pattern sets are then compared to others in the computer's memory for close match-ups.

— *Text developed in the mid-1990s*

Figure 19: Process discussion. Step by step, this text explains how computers "recognize" speech.

Process discussions focus on things like formation of lightning, snow, hurricanes, cold fronts, tornadoes; gestation of a human embryo; pollination of a flower; automatic operations of a photocopier or a computer; occurrence of supernova, black holes, red giants, or white dwarfs. Process discussions explain the workings of such mechanisms as automobile batteries, light bulbs, telephones, televisions, microwave ovens, stereo receivers.

As mentioned previously, the focus in this chapter is *noninstructional* process. However, while explaining how doctors perform open heart surgery or how a nuclear power plant operates might sound like instructions, they aren't! Normally, documents on these topics would give people an overview of what goes on in these processes. This next illustration conveys a general idea of how seawater is converted into fresh water:

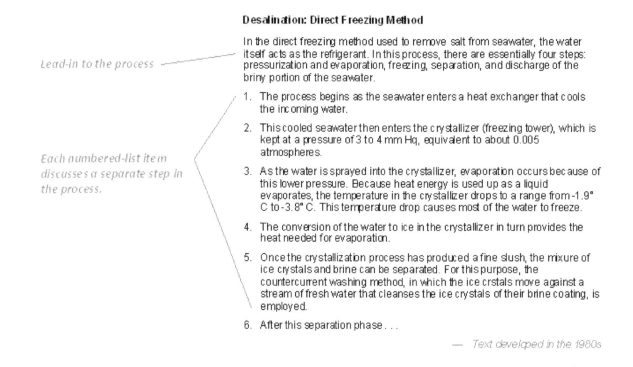

Figure 20: Process discussion. Step by step, this text discusses a method for the desalination of seawater.

How to Divide the Process into Steps?

When you write a process discussion—whether it's a single paragraph or a whole report—one of the most important tasks is to divide the process into its main steps, phases, stages, or periods. There are of course other ways to handle a process discussion, but division by steps is usually the best. For example, you might try organizing a process discussion by the key parts of a mechanism. Use whichever plan seems to work best for your readers, topic, and purpose.

A step is one action or event (or a group of related ones) that is performed or that occurs in the process. Consider a simple process such as making coffee with a drip coffee pot. Such an activity involves the following steps, each of which actually represents a group of actions:

- Boiling the water
    - Finding the kettle and taking it to the sink
    - Turning on the water and rinsing out the kettle
    - Filling up the kettle to the desired amount
    - Turning off the water and walking to the stove
    - Placing the kettle on a burner
    - Turning on the burner
    - Waiting for the water to boil
- Rinsing the coffee pot and the basket
- Measuring in the new coffee
- Pouring in the boiling water

Obviously, no one needs to be told all these specific actions; the example shows that a step usually stands for a group of related specific actions or events. If you look back at the preceding desalination example, you see a more realistic example of this process of division into steps. The discussion focuses on four steps in the desalination process: (1) pressurization and evaporation, (2) freezing, (3) separation, and (4) discharge of the briny portion of the seawater.

How are process discussions used in technical documents? First and foremost, processes are typically explained in instructions. For some situations, explaining how a thing works is almost as effective as providing the direct step-by-step instructions. And in any case, people understand the actions they are performing better when they understand the actions behind those actions. Process discussions are also vital in new product documents—either internal (meant for the product's designers and marketers) or external (meant for the product's customers and users). And finally process discussions are important in scientific research literature. You can imagine researchers studying acid rain or oil spills—understanding these processes might lead to controlling them better.

How to Discuss the Steps?

When you discuss a process, your goal is to enable readers to understand how that process works, the typical events that occur in that process. You use any writing tools at your disposal to accomplish that end. One of the most common ways of explaining a process is to divide it into steps, phases, periods, stages. These are essentially time segments—groupings of closely related events or actions. Take a look at any of the examples in this chapter; you'll see process sentences everywhere.

However, most process discussions aren't much without explanations of the causes and effects operating behind them. For example, it's not terribly exciting to read that when tornadoes form, it gets cloudy, wind and rain and twisters occur, wrecking things. We want more that just the bare-bones process: we want to know what causes them to form, what are the conditions favorable to their formation, how they behave once formed, and of course what sorts of damage they cause.

Other sorts of information can supplement the discussion of processes as well:

- Description: Explain how things look before, during, or after the process, or any phase within the process.
- Definitions: Explain the meaning of any technical terms used in the discussion.
- Comparisons: Compare the process, any of its phases or outcomes, to something similar or something familiar to help readers understand.
- Examples: Provide examples of the process you are explaining. For example, in a discussion of tornadoes, examples of tornadoes in history can help.

Mitosis is the process of cell duplication, during which one cell gives rise to two identical daughter cells. The process consists of four main phases: prophase, metaphase, anaphase, and interphase.

1. In prophase, the genetic material thickens and coils into chromosomes, the nucleus disappears, and a group of fibers begins to form a spindle.
2. In metaphase, the chromosomes duplicate themselves and line up along the mid-line of the cell. The halves are known as *chromatids*.
3. In anaphase, the chromatids are pulled at opposite ends of the cell by the spindle fibers. At this point, the cytoplasm of the mother cell divides to form two daughter cells, each with the number and kind of chromosomes the mother cell had.
4. In interphase, the daughter cells begin to function on their own, once their nucleus membranes and nucleoi reform.

How to Format Process Discussions?

Here are a few suggestions on format as they relate specifically to process discussions.

- Headings. If you write an extended process discussion and structure it by steps or phases, in other words, time segments, then the subheadings can be related to those steps or phases, as illustrated in the following schematic view of process discussions. If your process discussion has one section in which you explain the process and another in which you discuss some supplementary aspect of the process, your headings would need to indicate that structure as well.

- Lists. Because they focus on sequences of events, process discussions are likely candidates for in-sentence and vertical numbered lists as the examples in this chapter show.
- Graphics. Process discussions are prime territory for flow diagrams such as you see in some of the illustrations in this book. In these you give a spatial representation of things as they occur in time. Useful also are diagrams and drawings of the mechanisms that take part in the process.
- Style. You treat numbers, symbols, and abbreviations in process discussions the same as in any other technical document. Exact measurement values should be numerals, regardless whether they are below 10.

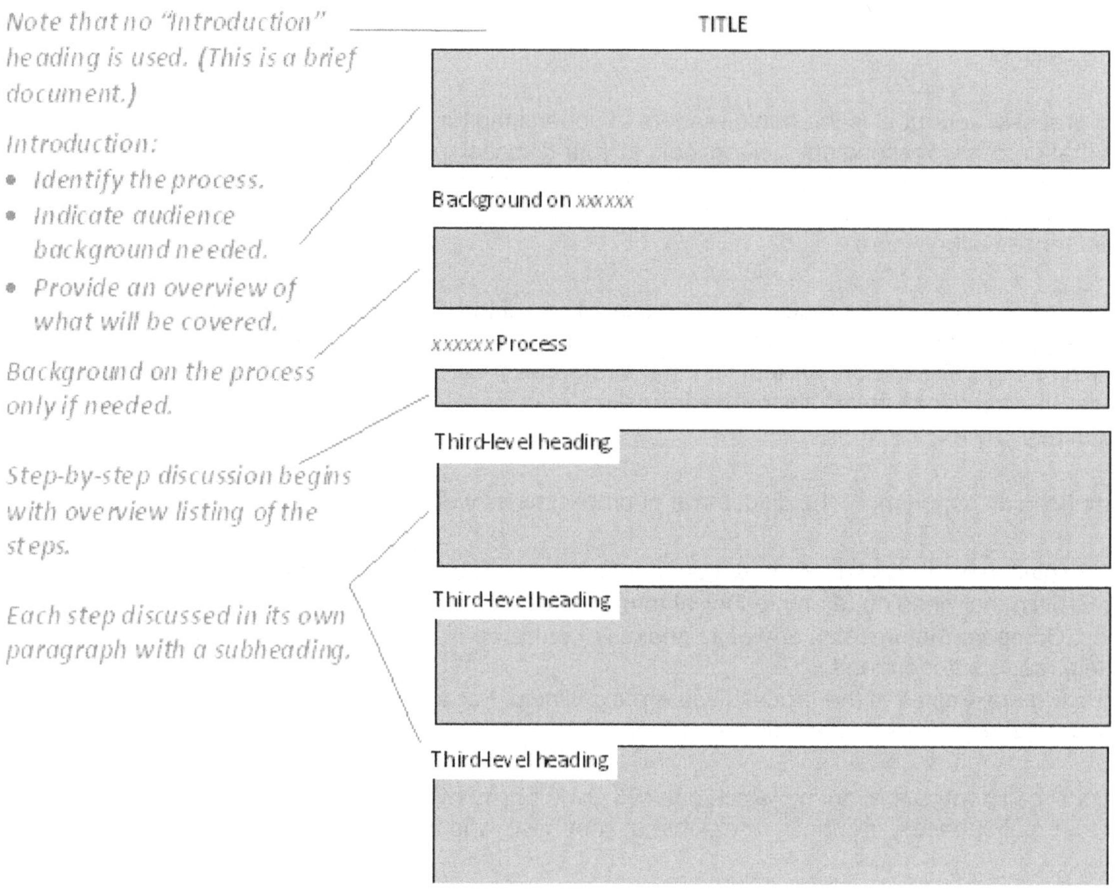

Note that no "Introduction" heading is used. (This is a brief document.)

Introduction:
- *Identify the process.*
- *Indicate audience background needed.*
- *Provide an overview of what will be covered.*

Background on the process only if needed.

Step-by-step discussion begins with overview listing of the steps.

Each step discussed in its own paragraph with a subheading.

TITLE

Background on *xxxxxx*

xxxxxx Process

Third-level heading

Third-level heading

Third-level heading

Figure 21: Schematic of a process discussion. A typical or common model for the contents and organization—others are possible.

Persuasion

Tell Them Why—Get Them on Your Side

When the teaching of technical writing first emerged in university engineering schools, it was defined as rigorously objective in writing style—even to the extent of using the passive voice instead of the first person singular "I." The standard model was the primary research report. However, since then, it has become clear that technical writers must often engage in persuasive communication efforts in their primary work.

What is Persuasion?

The infrastructure essential in proposals and progress reports is persuasion. To convince people to hire you to do a project and to reassure them that the project is going well, you need persuasive strategies. This chapter reviews the common persuasive strategies to get you ready to write those kinds of documents—as well as persuasive technical documents. Understanding general persuasive writing strategies, you will be well-equipped to develop these kinds of documents:

1. Resumes
2. Application letters
3. Proposals
4. Progress reports
5. Complaint letters

Persuasion is the communicative effort to convince people to think a certain or act a certain way—to vote for a city-wide recycling program, to oppose the building of more coal-fired electricity plants, and so on—or the opposite!

In the view of some, persuasion is not a legitimate tool for technical communication. For them, technical writing is supposed to be "scientific," "objective," "neutral." However, if you grant that proposals, progress reports, resumes, application letters, and even complaint letters are instances of technical communication because they often must convey technical information, then you see that persuasion is an important tool in technical communication.

What Are the Tools of Persuasion?

The classical approach to persuasion, laid down my Aristotle (384–322 BCE) in the *Art of Rhetoric*, involves these appeals to readers and listeners (remember your Rhetoric and Composition 101?):

- *Logical appeal*—When you use reasons and arguments, backed up by facts and logic, to make your case, you are using the logical appeal. We normally think of the logical appeal as the only legitimate method of argument, but the "real world" shows us differently.
- *Emotional appeal*—When you attempt to rouse people's anger or sympathies in a persuasive effort, you are using the emotional appeal. Showing a little girl fleeing from a burning village bombed by war planes or an oil-soaked seagull on a beach devastated by an oil spill—these images spark emotions like anger, horror, sympathy; but they don't make a logical case for or against anything. These images may, however, capture readers' attention and cause them to pay more attention to the rest of your persuasive effort.
- *Personal appeal*—When you present your qualifications, experience, expertise, and wisdom or those others, attempting to build readers' confidence, you are using the personal appeal. As with the emotional appeal, there is no logical justification for the personal appeal. It's like saying, "Trust me." Despite that, readers sometimes want to know who you are and what gives you the right to speak so authoritatively on the subject. Just as the emotional appeal can be used legitimately to get readers to pay attention and care about your message, the right amount of personal appeal can build readers' confidence in you—or at least a willingness to hear you out.

You may also have encountered the "stylistic" appeal: the use of language and visual effects to increase the persuasive impact. For example, a glossy, fancy design for a resume can have a positive impact just as much as the content.

In your rhetoric and composition studies, you may also have encountered something called the Toulmin approach to persuasion. The complete system involves claims, grounds, warrant, backing, and rebuttal, but a particularly useful element is the rebuttal, and another known as the concession.

- *Rebuttal.* In a rebuttal, you directly address counter-arguments that your persuasive opponents might bring up. You show how they are wrong or, at least, how they don't affect your overall argument. Picture yourself face to face with your persuasive opponents—what arguments are they going to come back at you with? How are you going to answer those arguments? In a written persuasive effort, you must simulate this back-and-forth, debate-style argumentative process. Imagine your opponents' counter-arguments (arguments they might put forth against your position) and then imagine your own rebuttals (your answers to those counter-arguments).

- *Counter-argument.* A persuasion can be structured entirely around tearing down the opponent's argument. Consider this example:

```
We're Not Running Out of Trees

Anti-recyclers rightly point out that more trees are growing in the U.S. than
ever before and that new forests are started as soon as trees are cut. However,
this perspective fails to take into account that, in the southern United
States, for example, where most of the trees used to make paper are grown, the
proportion of pine forest in plantations has risen from 2.5 percent in 1950 to
more than 40 percent in 1990, with a concomitant loss of natural pine forest.
At this rate, the acreage of pine plantations will overtake that of natural
pine forests in the South during the 1990s and will approach 70 percent of all
pine forests the next few decades afterwards. While pine plantations are
excellent for growing wood, they are far less suited than natural forests are
for providing animal habitat and preserving biodiversity. Paper recycling
extends the overall supply of fiber and can thus help reduce the pressure to
convert remaining natural forests to tree farms.
```

Figure 22: Example of a counter-argument. The paragraph begins by repeating an argument against recycling, then concedes a certain truth to it, but ends by showing that it is irrelevant. See the complete example.

- *Concession.* In a concession, you acknowledge that certain opposing arguments have some validity, but you explain how they do not damage your overall argument. Concessions build personal appeal: they make you seem more open minded.
- *Synthesis.* Modern rhetoricians urge us not to view the persuasive process as a win-lose, all-out war. When people are entrenched, they shut out the arguments of the other side. Such rigidity prevents us from resolving the issue and getting on with our lives. Instead, the process of counter-argument, rebuttal, and concession should be sincere and continuous until all parties reach synthesis—a middle ground where they drop their weapons and agree.

Main assertion: This paragraph begins with a straightforward thesis that recycling is not cost-efficient—that it costs too much.	One of the biggest problems with recycling is that it is not cost-efficient. In fact, recycling is a serious financial drain on all but a very few municipalities. As John Tierney pointed out in his 1996 *New York Times Magazine* article, collecting and handling a ton of recyclable materials is three times more expensive than putting them directly into a landfill. Why is that? Recycling programs require extra bureaucrats to manage them and enforcement officers to inspect people's recycling efforts and fine them if they are not complying. They require expensive public education campaigns to train people in the arduous process of sorting and storing their garbage correctly. (According to Tierney, "New Yorkers still don't know the rules.") Recycling programs are also more expensive because less garbage can be picked up at each stop. Tierney, in his aptly titled article, "Recycling Is Garbage," estimated that in 1996 New York City was spending more than $200 to recycle a ton of glass, plastic and metal than it would spend to bury the material in a landfill. He points out that market prices for recyclables has "rarely risen as high as zero." In fact, the city has to pay an additional $40 [per ton] to get rid of valueless recyclables.
Support: Relying primarily on the Tierney article, this writer goes through a series of reasons for the extra expense: extra city officials, public education programs, reduced efficiency of recycling pickup, and minimal market value for recyclables.	
Direct quotations: Notice that this writer quotes two pithy phrases from Tierney's articles, quotations that carry some of the attitude and personality of the original author.	
Documentation: even if this writer had not quoted, he's still obligated to cite his source for this information he has borrowed.	Source: John Tierney. "Recycling Is Garbage." *New York Times Magazine*, June 30, 1996: www.igc.org/nrdc/nrdcpro/recyc/appenda.html. Accessed January 18, 2000.

Figure 23: Single-paragraph example of persuasion. This paragraph would be one of several paragraphs attempting to discredit the recycling movement.

What Are the Common Flaws in Persuasion?

You should be aware too of the logical fallacies commonly found in persuasive efforts:

- *Hasty generalizations.* When you draw a conclusion based on too little evidence, that's a hasty generalization. For example, if you conclude that there is a big social trend to return to the 70's look because you see two or three bellbottoms and paisley shirts one day, you've drawn a hasty generalization based on a very limited, incomplete sample.
- *Irrelevant, ad hominem arguments.* When you base all or part of your persuasive effort on your opponent's character, behavior, or past, that's an *ad hominem* argument (meaning "to the man" in Latin). If a middle-aged political candidate were attacked for smoking marijuana in college, that might be an irrelevant personal attack.
- *Bandwagon effect.* If you base all or part of your persuasive effort on the idea that "everybody's doing it," you're using the bandwagon effect. Commercial advertisement commonly uses this tactic: everybody's buying the product—so should you!
- *False causality.* If you argue that because one event came after another, the first event caused the second, you may be making an argument based on false causality. For example, imagine that your father joined IBM in 1984 as a low-level regular employee and shortly thereafter the company began its historic slide to near-extinction. Imagine further that in 1995 he left the company, at which time the company began its remarkable comeback. Was it your dad who nearly brought the company to its knees? Did his departure save the company?

- *Oversimplistic, either–or arguments.* If you reduce the choices to the one you favor and to a totally unacceptable one, you are using an oversimplistic, either–or argument. Advocates of the nuclear power plant might argue that either we build the thing or we go without electricity
- *False analogies.* When you compare a situation to a simple object or process, that's an *analogy*. When you base an entire persuasive effort on an analogy, you may have problems. Some analogies are just wrong to begin with. And, at some point, all analogies break down. For example, arguments relating to global warming often use the analogy of how a car heats up when the windows are rolled up. The Vietnam war was justified using the analogy of how dominoes all topple over when they are lined up. Analogies can help readers understand, but not justify an argument.

How to Write a Persuasive Document

Here are guidelines on writing persuasively in a technical-writing content:

- *Carefully pick your topic and your approach to it.* Finding a project for persuasion is like trying to pick a fight. Think of the main issues of the day—global warming, ozone-layer depletion, alternative fuels, mass transportation, pesticides, zero population growth, solar energy, cloning (bioengineering), abortion, effects of computer- and video-game violence, capital punishment, nuclear armaments, chemical warfare. Each of these topics has multiple issues that are hotly debated. Technical-writing courses are not the place for the common pro-and-con and letter-to-the editor essays you may have written in past writing courses. However, these topics have a technical side that challenges your abilities as a technical writer. What are the logical arguments for recycling——more specifically, a city-based curb-side recycling program? They range from altruistic (for the city, for the planet) to selfish (to reduce waste management costs, to decrease taxes). Which arguments you use depends on your readers. Altruistic arguments may be of no use to certain conservative or business readers or to city administrators, but they may be vital in getting ordinary citizens to back such the program.
- *Define each of your arguments; plan how you will support them.* You must prove each logical argument, using supporting data, reasoning, and examples. You can't just baldly state that something costs less, works better, provides benefits, and is acceptable to the public—you've got to prove it! In your persuasive effort to get the city to consider recycling, you might use the logical appeal that such a program would reduce landfill requirements. How can you prove that? Do some research. What's the city's daily input to the landfill; what are the costs? Can you determine the percent made up by recyclables? If you can get believable numbers, calculate landfill savings in terms of volume and dollars.
- *Consider emotional appeals.* At best, emotional appeals capture readers' attention and get them to care about the issue. At worst, they rouse strong emotions such as fear and anger, preventing readers from thinking clearly about the issue. What emotional appeals could you use for the recycling promotion (not that you actually would, of course)? Images of overflowing landfills might work; images of dwindling natural habitats, replete with deer, chipmunks, hummingbirds——these might work. Would they pull at the heart strings of your readers, or would readers cynically mutter "give me a break"? How would you feel about using such tactics?
- *Consider personal appeals.* Like emotional appeals, personal appeals have no logical relevance to an argument. If you use the personal appeal, you attempt to build readers' confidence in you as someone who is knowledgeable and reliable. Citing years of experience and education is a common example of building a personal appeal. What personal appeals could this recycling persuasion use? To get people to accept your data, cite believable sources, such as government reports or leading experts. To give yourself credibility, describe your past experience and training in this area. Perhaps also describe yourself as a long-time resident of the city. These appeals shouldn't have any relevance, but they may cause people to hear you out.
- *Address any counter-arguments.* It's a good idea to address counter-arguments—objections people might raise in relation to your argument. Imagine people out there saying "but—but—but—!" Discuss their counter-arguments and show how they are wrong, how they can be addressed, or how they are irrelevant to your main point. Notice that the persuasive document advocating recycling is structured on counter-arguments: **Recycling: Not a Waste of Money or Time!** As for recycling programs, you must address the standard objections. *It's a hassle.* Your might counter-argue that recycling is no more of a hassle than taking out the garbage. *It's a hassle sorting everything and keeping in separate bins.* That one is easy——most recycling programs don't require sorting. *It's messy and attracts pests.* Hmmm, that's a hard one——time for some research.

- *Plan an introduction.* In an introduction to a persuasion, you cannot start out guns blazing and swords rattling. It's not necessary to state your main argumentative point right away. Instead, just indicate the subject matter—not your main point about it. Your readers are more likely to hear you out. Imagine that you've written the main sections of this persuasion. You have logical appeals, counter-arguments, and possibly some personal and emotional appeals as well. Instead of demanding that the city adopt a recycling program, begin with a quiet purpose statement that this document "looks at" or "investigates" the possibilities for recycling. Indicate that this document is for both city officials and ordinary citizens. Provide an overview, indicating that you'll be discussing current and projected landfill use and associated costs, amount of recyclables in municipal waste, their recyclable value, potential revenue from a recycling program, costs of a recycling program, and necessary administrative and citizen participation in such a program.
- *Consider the conclusion.* In a persuasion, the final section is often a "true" conclusion. If you have not yet overtly stated your main argumentative point, now's the time. When you do, summarize the main arguments that support it. While the introduction may be the place for quiet understatement, the conclusion is the place to pound home your main point. Come out and state vigorously that the city should implement a recycling program and then summarize the main reasons why.

How to Format Persuasive Documents?

Here are a few suggestions on format as they relate specifically to persuasive documents.

- *Headings.* If you structure your persuasion by individual arguments, then the subheadings can be related to those arguments. Notice that the headings in the example persuasion address the counter-arguments: **Recycling: Not a Waste of Money or Time!**
- *Graphics.* Factual information—data—supplies a great deal of the legitimate support for your presuasive effort. Make that data more dramatic and vivid by creating **tables, charts, and graphs**. **Graphics**—illustrations, drawings, photos—can also supply that essential logical support—but also the emotional support mentioned earlier.

By: Tamara Powell

Objectives

Upon completion of this chapter, readers will be able to explain and apply common paragraph organization patterns.

Organizing Paragraphs

Let's begin by learning more about organizing paragraphs.

This textbook has introduced you to various considerations regarding organizing information.

You need to know about a few more organizational strategies in order to have more tools in your toolbox for organizing information.

Classification and Partition

This type of organization is often confused with chronological. Remember, just because something is divided into parts does NOT mean it is divided up by time. My favorite meal, pasta alfredo with broccoli and garlic bread (hello, carbs!) has three main parts: the entrée and two sides. The entrée is whole wheat, radiatore pasta with from-scratch alfredo sauce including fresh basil, oregano, and garlic and topped with black olives. The first side is garlic bread with a dipping sauce of olive oil, balsamic vinegar, and oregano. The second side (notice these are partitions, not chronological steps) is broccoli with salt and butter. All together, pasta alfredo with broccoli and garlic bread comprise my favorite meal. Note the meal, a single unit, is divided into parts, and each one is described. I did not tell you how to make it. I did not divide it into time components (first, you boil the pasta. Then, you mix a tablespoon of butter with a tablespoon of all purpose flour. . .).

Cause and Effect

Beware of oversimplification. Just because two things occur in a similar time span does not mean they are linked by causation. Just because Terry was the last person to use the copy machine does not mean that Terry broke it.

Comparisons

Use part by part unless you have a good reason to use whole by whole.

Spatial Organization

Use spatial organization to describe something physically. You might use spatial organization to explain what a fountain pen looks like, for example. You would start the description at the top of the pen, the clicker. You would move, then, along the object spatially, describing the barrel of the pen down to the writing tip. Or, you might describe the pen starting at the tip and moving to the top. You move through SPACE to describe something (the space the object occupies), so that is spatial organization. You might use the spatial pattern to describe the physical scene of an accident. Or in a feasibility study, you might use this method to describe the property upon which a proposed facility would be built.

Chronological

A chronological description is one organized by time. Chronos is the Greek word for time.

How do I cook my favorite dish? Well, first, I boil water for the radiatore pasta. Then, I mix a tablespoon of butter with a tablespoon of flour. Next, I pour a cup of heavy whipping cream (unwhipped) into a pot. After it heats up, I lower the heat and add the butter and stir until the mixture thickens. I remove it from the heat. Next, I add garlic, parmesan cheese, and fresh basil and oregano to the mixture. As the sauce cools, I add broccoli to the steamer, add butter and salt, and steam the vegetables until tender and crisp. While the broccoli is steaming, I butter a slice of bread and grate fresh garlic over it. I place the bread in the toaster oven, and then I add the noodles to the boiling water. Finally, I pour olive oil and balsamic vinegar into a ramekin and add dried spices for dipping. Once all the cooked elements are ready, I assemble them on a plate: the noodles are topped with alfredo sauce; the bread is served with the ramekin of dipping sauce, and the broccoli is served to the side of the pasta and sauce.

Example

Sometimes, information is organized by an example. Such a paragraph usually starts with a statement that is then clarified by the example. For example (see what I did there?)...

A third mechanism of psychological defense, "Conversion," is found in hysteria. Here the conflict is converted into the symptom of a physical ilness. In a case of conversion made famous by Freud, a young woman went out for a long walk with her brother-in-law, with whom she had fallen in love. Later, on learning that her sister lay gravely ill, she hurried to her bedside. She arrived too late and her sister was dead. The young woman's grief was accompanied by sharp pain in her legs. The pain kept recurring without any apparent physical cause. Freud's explanation was that she felt guilty because she desired the husband for herself, and she unconsciously converted her repressed feelings into an imaginary physical ailment. The pain struck her in the legs because she unconsciously connected her feelings for the husband with the walk they had taken together. The ailment symbolically represented both the unconsious wish and a penance for the feelings of guilt which it engendered. (Wilson, 1964, p. 84).

Problem-Methods-Solution

This pattern does just what it says--it describes the problem, then outlines the methods used to solve it, and then provides the solution. For example,

The Problem

Earlier this year, we were proud to offer the industry's largest array of add-on multimedia products for both our own computers and those of other manufactureres. Our offerings in cards, CD-ROM drives, speakers, and other peripherals were unrivaled in both quantity and quality. And the response was terrific: in out first three months we sold more than 12,000 multimedia kits and 58,000 other peripheral units.

But growing pains soon became apparent: we logged more than 9,000 multi-media-related customer support calls in that same period. What was the cause of this unprecedented cusotmer-support problem? After considerable analysis of our customer-support data, we concluded that two factors were at work:Add-on multimedia kits, even those meant for our own computers, were not necessarily compatible with the hardware or the software our customers were using. We heard too many horror stories about how the kits were installed properly, but when the customer tried to reboot, the operating system was gone.

Some 70 percent of the customers were novices, as opposed to less than 40 percent for our other product lines, and our documentation was simply inadequate to the task.

Meeting the Challenge

We recognized that being a pioneer in the industry had its costs: we were the first to encounter the problems that are now pervasive in the industry and well publicized in the literature. And because we were first, we took our lumps from the trade journals for the resulting problems with customer satisfaction.

We instituted a four-point plan to meet the challenge:

We instituted a new quality-control program. Now every product is treated just the way a customer teats it. It is taken out of the box, plugged in, and turned on. We make sure that the printer setup is accurate and that the hardware and the bundled software are compatible. At our weekly audit meetings we revive that week's quality-control data; each team leader is now empowered to stop production to investigate a recurrent or unexplained problem.

We expanded our use of novices in our preproduction focus groups and in the quality-control program. We are concentrating on learning how the novice uses our products; in our expansion into the family market we expect to find that an increasing perentage of our customers are first-time computer owners.

We instituted a Process-Improvement Team, a group of 12 veteran employees committed to improving customer support and customer satisfaction. Among the first innovations of the Process-Improvement Team was the creation of more than 200 documents to assist users with common problems encountered when installing our kits and using common software. These documents are on our website and can be faxed to customers at no charge when they call a special toll-free number.

We instituted a Quality Team of 15 employees charged with the responsibility of seeking Manufacturing's ideas about quality and efficiency standards.

The Results

These measures have been in place for only two months, and it is too early to declare toal victory, but the preliminary data are encouraging. Customer-support calls on our multimedia kits are down more than 15 percent the last two months. As reported by Customer Support, the incident of catastrophic problems--such as destruction of the operating system--is down more than 30 percent. The increased use of novices in design and in focus groups has led to three interface improvements that were noted in a *PC Week* article earlier this month. The work of the Quality Team has resulted in a 7 percent decrease in rejection rates of our multimedia kits.

In short, I think we are on the right track. But quality improvement is a frame of mind and a commitment, not a goal that can ever be reached. I pledge to you that we shall continue to strive to make RST the best place to buy PCs and PC-related products.

General to Specific

General to specific is just as it says. It starts with a general overview, and then moves to specific details. This strategy is sometimes called an inverted pyramid. For example,

The proposed project involves transforming two currently existing electronic texts into a free, high-quality, interactive, multimedia textbook for the TCOM 2010 and WRIT 3140 courses at Kennesaw State University.

In order to achieve this overarching goal, we intend to

- create a textbook that satisfies both student and faculty requirements
- develop and incorporate materials that make the textbook desirable for both students and faculty members
- provide material that serves the distinct focus of each course
- make the textbook readily available for adoption and use
- encourage the textbook's adoption and use in onsite, hybrid, and online versions of the courses

and as a result, we believe we can increase student retention, progression, graduation, and employment rates.

Specific to General

This pattern is the opposite of general to specific, and it is sometimes called the pyramid. It starts with details and moves to a general statement. For example

Marsha's writing was filled with spelling errors. In addition, she was having problems using commas correctly, and she needed assistance with quotation marks. When I reviewed her sentence structures, I found that there were minor problems with subordination and coordination, and she needed to review and practice her parallel sentence skills. With regard to her choices related to organizational strategy, it seemed she had not thought through how she wished to organize her information. In general, for a three year old, I found Marsha to be a very good writer.

Order of Importance

Our two last organizational strategies are more important to less important, and less important to more important. They are exactly as they sound--organizing information from the most important reason for x to the least, or the least to the best. We are often asked "provide three reasons why x should happen." But as we do that, it's important that we consider the order in which we present our reasons. We want to present the reasons in the order of maximum impact. If your audience is likely to agree with you, then use least important to more important. That way, you end your paragraph on the most important note, and your reader should be highly motivated to follow through with your idea. If your audience is hesitant or even hostile to your idea, start with your most important reason for x. Use most important to least important to "hook" your reader early with your best evidence or argument so that they stay tuned for the supporting reasons. Following are some examples.

More Important to Less Important

Why should you learn Spanish? Recent research shows, learning a second language protects you against Alzheimer's and keeps your brain sharper, longer. Additional important reasons to learn Spanish are the same reasons for learning any language. It is very good for your brain. It helps you to speak your native language better and understand it better. It gives you insight into other cultures, which increases your global understanding and improves your human relationships. For Americans, learning Spanish can help you keep pace with popular culture. If you like to Zumba or listen to popular music, then Spanish will enrich your experience. Finally, learn Spanish so that you sound cool, amigo, when you order your dishes at your favorite Mexican restaurant or tapas bar.

Less Important to More Important

Why should you learn French? Well, to sound sexy, of course. Everyone knows a French accent makes you more interesting and assists you in sounding not-so-silly when you order food in a fancy (a.k.a. French) restaurant. A second reason to learn French is to assist you in your trip to Paris. Paris is the world's number one tourist destination, and if you go there, you need to speak French. French is also a language that is fun to learn and pretty easy for English speakers. If you have never learned a foreign language before, French is a great one to start with. The most important reason to learn French, however, is the same reason for learning any language. It is very good for your brain. It helps you to speak your native language better and understand it better. It gives you insight into other cultures, which increases your global understanding and improves your human relationships. And, recent research shows, learning a second language protects you against Alzheimer's and keeps your brain sharper, longer.

By: Steve and Cherie Miller

Taken with kind permission from the book *Why Brilliant People Believe Nonsense* by J. Steve Miller and Cherie K. Miller.

Logic and Logical Fallacies

> The dull mind, once arriving at an inference that flatters the desire, is rarely able to retain the impression that the notion from which the inference started was purely problematic.
>
> - George Eliot, in Silas Marner

Brilliant people believe nonsense [because] they fall for common fallacies.

Even the brightest among us fall for logical fallacies. As a result, we should be ever vigilant to keep our critical guard up, looking for fallacious reasoning in lectures, reading, viewing, and especially in our own writing. None of us are immune to falling for fallacies.

Until doctors come up with an inoculation against fallacies, I suppose the next best thing is to thoroughly acquaint ourselves with the most common fallacies. I chose the following fallacies by comparing a dozen or so university sites that list what they consider the most common fallacies that trip up students.[1]

> **Snoozer Alert!**
>
> Sorry, but this chapter and the next don't contain fascinating stories and intriguing intellectual puzzles. But please resist the temptation to skim to the following section. To think critically, we simply must familiarize ourselves with logical fallacies. Otherwise, we're fair game for all sorts of nonsense. Think of it like math. While the formulas themselves might be boring, we learn them in order to hopefully use them for something practical in the future. You'll assuredly find many of the below fallacies used in conversations and articles.
>
> Think of logical fallacies as the grammar you must master to learn a foreign language. Before you can use a language practically (like writing a note to that ravishing foreign exchange student in her native language), you simply must learn the vocabulary and grammar. Similarly, logical fallacies are a part of the vocabulary of logical thinking. I'll try to make understanding them as painless as possible.

So learn these well. Reflect upon them. Look for them in the media. Familiarizing yourself with errant reasoning goes a long way toward helping you to write, reason, speak, and listen with more critical precision.

Tip: If some of my definitions and examples don't sufficiently clarify, look up the fallacy in Wikipedia or other sources for alternate explanations.

Below this list of fallacies, I'll give you a bit of practice by asking you to connect a fallacy with an errant argument. Finally, I'll give a few tips on checking your own argumentation (particularly in writing and speeches) for fallacies.

Twenty-Seven Common Fallacies

Ad Hominem

Translated into English: "against the person", aka "damning the source," the "genetic fallacy," "poisoning the well," related to" "tu quoque" (you, too!). Defined as attacking the person (e.g. - can't be trusted, is a moron, etc.) rather than the argument.

> I don't believe anything he says because he's a biased political liberal.

Yet, shouldn't we assess his arguments based upon his evidence and argumentation, rather than solely because of his political label?

Caution: Sometimes a person has indeed been shown to be untrustworthy. Cautioning readers that he has been repeatedly caught in flagrant lies isn't an ad hominem fallacy. Noting a person's lack of integrity can be valid, if his argument requires us to trust him.

Tip: If the person's character is either irrelevant to the argument or unknown, focus on the facts and arguments.

Affirming the Consequent

AKA "converse error" or "fallacy of the converse." This is a formal fallacy (the *form* of the argument isn't valid) that assumes if the argument is valid going one direction, it's also valid when run the opposite direction.

Premise 1: If I get the flu, I'll be nauseated.
Premise 2: I'm nauseated.
Conclusion: Therefore, I have the flu.

This is invalid because while it may be true that if you get the flu, you'll get nauseated, the converse isn't always true. You can be nauseated and yet not have the flu. Perhaps you have a hangover, or are pregnant.

Tip: If you see an argument in the following form, it's affirming the consequent:

Premise 1: If P, then Q
Premise 2: Q
Conclusion: P

Appealing to Extremes

Taking an assertion to an extreme, even though the arguer may never take it to that extreme.

Avid health advocates blow out their knees by their 50s by running marathons. Therefore, don't prioritize regular exercise.

*But not **all** avid health advocates run long distances as their primary exercise. It's an extreme statement.*

AKA "*argumentum ab auctoritate,*" "appeal to authority." Claiming that a position is true because an authority says it's true.

Even when the referenced authority is a true authority in the field, arguments should ultimately be based upon facts and reasoning rather than quoting authorities. Also beware of people quoting false authorities, like football stars or models selling insurance or technology.

We know global warming is true because a number of great scientists assure us it's true.

Caution: Sometimes citing authorities can be a valid part of an argument. For example, if a hefty percentage of respected scientists who specialize in a related field are all warning us about the dangers of global warming, this in itself provides evidence that global warming is at the very least a viable theory that needs to be seriously considered. Alternately, if no respectable scientists took global warming seriously, then this would surely be a strike against it, even though ultimately we're looking for hard evidence rather than numbers of testimonies.

Tip: Ask yourself,

- Are these truly experts in the field I'm discussing? Would some view them as either biased or holding to fringe views on the subject?
- Have I explained clearly how I'm using these authorities as evidence, within the larger scope of my argument?
- Would it be relevant to explain the evidence that led the authorities to come to their position on the subject?
- Are you using their testimonies as helpful resources, quoting them as a part of a larger argument, or quoting them as a slam dunk argument to make your case? Make sure you're not saying something like: Dr. Authority believes x, so we should believe x as well.

Argument from Ignorance

AKA "appeal to ignorance," "argumentum ad ignorantium," related to "non-testable hypothesis." Assuming that a claim is true because it has not been or cannot be proven false (or vice versa, assuming that a claim is false because it has not been or cannot be proven true.)"

Nobody can prove that my client was at the scene of the crime, therefore he's innocent.

Of course, he may be in fact guilty. We may just lack sufficient evidence that he was there.

Caution: While some would say "absence of evidence is not evidence of absence," this isn't true in every case. For example, if I walk outside and see no evidence of rainfall (no puddles, the streets aren't wet), I'm justified in taking this as evidence that it hasn't rained recently. In this case, the absence of evidence for rain is indeed evidence for the absence of rain.

Band Wagon

AKA "ad *populum* fallacy," "appeal to widespread belief," "appeal to the majority," "appeal to the people." If a large number of people believe it, it must be true. It appeals to our desire to fit in.

Most people use Microsoft products, so they must be the best.

Everybody I know uses Meth, so it can't be that bad.

Caution: Some people naturally despise majority opinion and relish holding contrarian positions.2 Those who disagree with opinions held by a majority of intelligent people should at least make sure they understand the reasons informed people give to justify their beliefs.

Tip: Remember that popular opinion is often wrong, and what's cool today may seem foolish tomorrow. In fact, it's often those who stand against the crowd who change the world. As Apple, Inc. said it in their motto: "Think different."

Begging (Evading) the Question

AKA "circular argument,""petitio principii," translated "assuming the initial point." The conclusion is assumed in a premise. This typically isn't as obvious as it first sounds.

The Writing Center at the University of North Carolina gives a good example.

Active euthanasia is morally acceptable. It is a decent, ethical thing to help another human being escape suffering through death.

At first read, it may seem pretty straightforward. But let's examine it as a premise and conclusion:

Premise: It is a decent, ethical thing to help another human being escape suffering through death.

Conclusion: Active euthanasia is morally acceptable.

Look closely at these two sentences and you'll discover that they actually do nothing more than state the same thing twice; the conclusion merely dresses up the premise in different words. "Decent, ethical" in the premise is worded "morally acceptable" in the conclusion. "to help another human being escape suffering through death" in the premise becomes "active euthanasia" in the conclusion.

Thus, the argument doesn't tell us much, if anything, about *why* euthanasia is morally acceptable. It leaves us asking the implied question over again, "But *why* is it acceptable?", showing that the premise and conclusion merely begged (i.e., evaded) the question.

Tip: Typically, rewriting the argument in the form of premises and a conclusion reveals when a question is being begged. Do you agree with the premises? Are there gaps in the line of argument? Does the conclusion say nothing more than the premises already stated?

Bifurcation

AKA "false dichotomy," "black-or-white fallacy," the "either-or fallacy," related to a "false dilemma." The argument makes it appear that there are only two possible answers, but there are actually more.

Tip: Ask yourself, are there really two and only two options? If not, are any of the other options viable? Have all other options been sufficiently ruled out?

Dogmatism

Not even considering an opponent's argument, because of overconfidence in one's own position.

Statement: Mercedes makes the best car ever.

Retort: But according to *Consumer Reports*....

Dogmatic Defense: I don't care what those studies say; I *know*! Mercedes is the best.

Emotional Appeals

An appeal to emotion that is irrelevant (or largely irrelevant) to the argument.

The death penalty can't be right. Have you seen a person die in an electric chair?

Caution: Emotion can often be a legitimate part of an argument.

Look at these poor birds dying from an oil spill. This demonstrates one reason we should take great precautions to avoid such mishaps.

Equivocation

Related to "semantics," "playing with words." Using the same word with more than one meaning, thereby invalidating the argument.

Of all the animals, only man is rational. No woman is a man. Therefore, no woman is rational.

In the first instance, "man" means "mankind," whereas in the second instance, "man" means "the male gender." This change in meaning invalidates the argument.

Tip: Look carefully at the argument's important words. Are they used in a consistent way, or do they shift meanings?

Fallacy of Exclusion

Focusing on one group's behavior as if the behavior is exclusive to that group.

Watch those women drivers. They're always thinking of something other than their driving.

But are male drivers any better? Shouldn't this statement be based on psychological studies and statistics of accidents rather than personal observations of one sex?

False Dilemma

AKA "false dichotomy," "either/or," "black/white," "excluded middle." A form of bifurcation, this fallacy allows for only two extreme positions, although a legitimate middle ground might be arguable. Sometimes they paint one side as so extreme that nobody could ever agree with it.

You either support Israelis in Palestine or you're an anti-Semite.

Are you for George Bush or are you for the terrorists?

Tip: When only two extreme alternatives are given, look for middle ground.

Faulty Analogy

AKA "weak analogy." Comparing two similar things to make a point, but the analogy breaks down because of one or more significant dissimilarities.

The war in Afghanistan is nothing more than a modern day Vietnam war.

Tip: Is the analogy truly alike in all relevant respects?

Glittering Generality

AKA "Weasel Words." Using words in such a broad way that almost everyone resonates with them in the same way, thus lending credence to the argument. Thus, those who argue that their position is really about "freedom," "love," "human rights," etc., can gain a following, even though the words may mean different things to different people, or are being used in such a vague way as to be essentially meaningless.

Allowing this controversial artwork in our place of business is really about guaranteeing our freedoms, in this case our freedom of expression.

Perhaps, but what if the artwork trivializes or misrepresents your business, or disgusts and demoralizes your employees? Framing it as solely an issue of freedom seems to make it a glittering generality.

Hasty Generalization

Related to "non-representative sample," "fallacy of insufficient statistics," "fallacy of insufficient sample," "fallacy of the lonely fact," "leaping to a conclusion," "hasty induction," "*secundum quid* (converse accident). A conclusion was reached via inadequate evidence, such as when a sample cited was inadequate (e.g., atypical or too small) to warrant a generalized conclusion.

Most Hollywood stars have terrible marriages. Just read the tabloids.

Their conclusion may or may not be true, but reading tabloids is no way to decide the issue. News sources by their very nature select what's "newsy." Since a nasty divorce is more newsy than a stable marriage, the former gets the press, giving the impression that most Hollywood stars can't hold a marriage together.

I'll never fly again. I read about too many accidents and hijackings.

Again, you don't hear about the thousands of flights with no incidents. Thus, you're judging from the news you hear, which is both an atypical and small sampling. The National Safety Council calculated the odds of dying in a motor vehicle accident as one chance in 98 over a lifetime. The odds for dying in air travel (including private flights) was one chance in 7,178.[3]

Tip: Notice the sample size and where it's drawn from. Is it adequate to warrant the conclusion? Is the conclusion stated in terms that are too general and sweeping?

Inconsistency

AKA "non contradiction." The argument contradicts itself. (See the previous chapter for a more thorough explanation.)

Only statements that can be justified with scientific experiments can be believed.

Yet, this statement itself can't be justified by scientific experiments.

Our brains developed, not to think logically, but for survival in an agrarian society. Therefore, we can't trust our reasoning.

This statement uses logical reasoning, although it's claiming logical reasoning is not to be trusted.

Moral Equivalency

Arguing incorrectly that two moral issues are sufficiently similar to warrant the same treatment. It often compares lesser misdeeds to major atrocities.

Killing in war is legalized murder.

In some instances, this may be true. But in all instances?

Our local police act like Nazis—they have no respect for my human right to drive my car like I want.

Non Sequitur

Translated: "it does not follow." A general category that includes "hasty generalization," "slippery slope," "affirming the consequent," "missing the point," etc.) The conclusion does not follow from the premises.

Patrick always smiled at me and was so respectful. He couldn't have burned down the gym.

Is there some absolute law of nature that states that respectful, smiling people never burn down gyms? While Patrick's character in relation to you can be a relevant piece of evidence to be considered, it's a non sequitur to say that it proves he could have never burned down a gym.

Tips:

- Forget the conclusion for a moment. Looking solely at the premises, ask yourself what can be concluded from the premises.
- Now look at your conclusion. Ask yourself what kind and amount of evidence you'd need to support this conclusion. Do the premises provide that kind of evidence?
- Is your conclusion too extreme? Would it be closer to the truth if it weren't overstated?

Failing Occam's Razor

Prefer a simpler explanation (or hypothesis) to a more convoluted or complicated one.

Your best friend Ralph flunked Calculus. Possible reasons:

- If we were to run a psychological profile of both Ralph and his professor, we might find that they have diametrically opposed learning styles, thus making communication extremely difficult.
- Aliens kept Ralph up all night before both the midterm and final exam, questioning him and keeping him from adequate rest and preparation.
- Ralph admitted to never doing his homework and seldom attending lectures.

Occam's Razor would prefer the third, more simple and obvious explanation.

Warning: Occam's Razor doesn't decide all cases, since many explanations that end up being proven over time are indeed more complicated than their disproven counterparts. Typically, when choosing between competing scientific theories, the best fit with the observable data trumps simplicity. So it's wise to consider Occam's Razor a "rule of thumb" rather than a hard and fast rule.

Post Hoc Ergo Propter Hoc

Translated "after this, therefore because of this." Often shortened to "*post hoc,*" also called "faulty causality," "faulty cause," "false cause," or "correlation vs. causation"). Correlation and causation are confused in that one event follows another and the former is falsely assumed to be the cause of the latter.

Ever since his trip to India, Alfred's been sick. Obviously, he caught some-thing in India that our doctors can't diagnose

Tips:

1. When one event is claimed as the cause of another, look for other possible causes. In the above example, perhaps Alfred caught something the day he arrived back home, or already had an illness before going to India, but never developed symptoms until he returned.
2. Give evidence beyond "this happened after that," to support your claim. For example, you might discover that Alfred consulted with seven American diagnostic specialists, who all agreed that it was a malady they'd never before seen. This would lend credence to the "he caught it in India" theory.

Red Herring

Deflecting an argument by *chasing a rabbit* (an irrelevant topic.) The name "red herring" was originally used in fox hunting, when a herring (type of fish) was dragged across a trail to throw the dogs off the scent of the fox.

After Harry's wife caught him gambling away his paycheck and asked for an explanation, he responded, "At least with gambling I have a chance to get my money back. What about your weekly purchase of clothes that ends up in a bag for Goodwill? And why isn't your recent raise helping us to pay our debts?"

Harry's arguments deflect from the immediate issue: he gambled away his paycheck.

Sure, the mercury found in seafood is often unsafe, but fishermen have to make a living like everyone else.

Tip: If you're not sure, write the argument out as a line of argument. This typically shows clearly where the argument got off track.

Reductionism

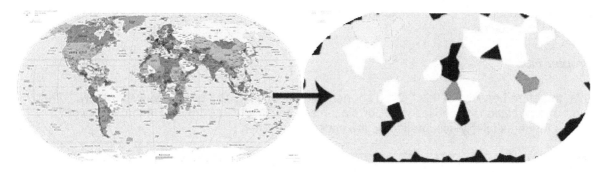

AKA "oversimplifying," "sloganeering." Reducing large, complex problems to one or a few simplistic causes or solutions.

The problem with our economy can be reduced to two words: trade imbalance.

What about other relevant issues, such as the drain of a huge national debt?

Tip: Ask yourself, "What other factors may contribute to this problem, or be a part of the solution?"

Slippery Slope

AKA "snowball argument," "domino theory," "absurd extrapolation," "thin edge of the wedge," "camel's nose." Arguing that one change or event will inevitably lead to another, eventually landing them at a place they never wanted to go.

If we allow more restrictions on purchasing guns, this will be followed by further restrictions and eventually the government will confiscate all our guns.

Caution: Slippery slopes do exist. The question is, just how slippery is the slope? Is it slippery enough to make the slide to the bottom inevitable?

Tip: Look closely at your argument for each link in the chain of consequences. Is there adequate evidence to conclude that each progression is either inevitable or fairly certain? Are there abundant historical precedents that back up the claim? Are there historical precedents that provide contrary evidence?

Stacking the Deck

AKA "cherry picking." Listing the arguments (or evidence) that support one's claim while ignoring the ones that don't.

Capitalism inevitably leads to a violent revolution by the proletariat. Here are fifty examples from history.

Tip: Ask yourself, "Are there counterexamples that the arguer is ignoring, or is she/he simply pulling out examples that support his/her theory?

Straw Man

Presents a weak form of an opposing argument, then knocks it down to claim victory.

Jack emailed his professor that he missed class due to a bad case of the flu and that he would bring a doctor's note. The next day, the professor announced in class that he would not excuse Jack's absence because his excuse was that he didn't feel like coming (not mentioning the flu or the note). Since the professor put Jack's argument in such a weak form, he was arguing against a straw man rather than Jack's actual defense.

Tip: Do you know the strongest arguments of your opponents? If so, are those the arguments you're arguing against?

Sweeping Generalization

AKA *dicto simpliciter*. Assumes that what is true of the whole will also be true of the part, or that what is true in most instances will be true in all instances.

All the preppies I know are materialists. Since Shawn dresses preppie, he must be a materialist.

Tip: Particularly when arguers use all inclusive words like "all," "always," "never," "nobody," or "everybody," ask yourself if the premises and/or conclusions should have been presented in less stark terms. Do you know people who dress preppie who don't appear to be materialistic? If so, then perhaps Shawn is a part of the subset of non-materialistic preppies.

Action Points

A Checklist for Spotting Your Own Fallacies

Ask these questions before turning in a paper, making a speech, or arguing with friends.

1. **How would your opponents respond to your argument?** What parts would they likely attack? Have you actually read the strongest arguments of your opponents and considered their side? Is there a way to strengthen your weak arguments?
2. **How would your argument look as a syllogism or line of argument?** Do you have adequate evidence for your premises? Does your conclusion flow logically from your premises?
3. **Is your conclusion presented with the degree of certitude that's warranted by the evidence?** (Be especially cautious if you use all-encompassing words like "always," "never," "everyone," etc.)
4. **Are there certain types of fallacies that you often fall for?** (Consider how professors responded to your earlier papers or speeches, and how your friends respond to your arguments.)

Flex Your Neurons!

Pursuing the Point of Know Return

Can You Connect an Argument with Its Fallacy?

Making it More Personal

Practical Takeaways

1. What are one or more ideas provoked by this chapter that you can apply to help you think more critically?
2. What are one or more ideas that you can apply to help you think more creatively?
3. What else do you want to make sure you don't forget?

Recommended Trails for the Incurably Curious and Adventurous

- For each fallacy that's still unclear to you, search it on Google to find more explanations and illustrations.
- Watch or read some advertisements. Write out their lines of argument or put them in syllogisms. Do any of them fall for one of the above fallacies?

End Notes

- I compared lists from:
    - the writing center at the University of North Carolina, Chapel Hill, which includes tips for spotting fallacies   http://writingcenter.unc.edu/handouts/fallacies/
    - the University of Idaho http://www.webpages.uidaho.edu/eng207-td/Logic%20and%20Analysis/most_common_logical_fallacies.htm
    - California State, Fullerton, includes nice, down home examples - http://commfaculty.fullerton.edu/rgass/fallacy3211.htm
    - from Purdue University   - https://owl.english.purdue.edu/owl/resource/659/03/
    - the University of Texas , El Paso -   http://utminers.utep.edu/omwilliamson/ENGL1311/fallacies.htm

- o Carson Newman, helpful for its division by categories - http://web.cn.edu/kwheeler/fallacies_list.html
- o the University of Louisiana , Lafayette, gives documented examples - http://www.ucs.louisiana.edu/~kak7409/Fallacies.html
- o Mesa Community College - http://www.mesacc.edu/~paoih30491/ArgumentsFallaciesQ.html
- o California State - http://www.csus.edu/indiv/g/gaskilld/criticalthinking/Six%20Common%20Fallacies.htm
- o Sacramento State University
- o the University of Wisconsin, Eau Claire http://www.uwec.edu/ranowlan/logical%20fallacies.html
- o St. Lawrence University
- o the University of Oklahoma
- o North Kentucky University.

It's interesting that some of these universities use contradictory definitions of various fallacies.

- Bertrand Russell demonstrated this tendency. He seemed to relish standing against the majority opinion. A person with his disposition should strongly consider that his assessment of evidence might be skewed by this character trait. See chapter 25 for an analysis of the passions that drove Russell.

- http://traveltips.usatoday.com/air-travel-safer-car-travel-1581.html.

By: Steve and Cherie Miller

Taken with kind permission from the book *Why Brilliant People Believe Nonsense* by J. Steve Miller and Cherie K. Miller.

Logic and Logical Fallacies

Anyone who denies the law of non-contradiction should be beaten and burned until he admits that to be beaten is not the same as not to be beaten, and to be burned is not the same as not to be burned.

- Avicenna

Brilliant people believe nonsense [because] they contradict, leave out valid options, and knock down straw men.

Those Who Question Logic

To the mind that's yet to be "enhanced" by some strains of modern thought, the above quote probably comes across as amusing, but useless. After all, who would deny something as basic as the law of non-contradiction or the basic laws of logic? If saying "My roommate annoys me" is no different than saying "My roommate doesn't annoy me," then how can we ever say anything meaningful? Moreover, the very act of denying non-contradiction assumes the law to be true.

Yet, some argue that our brains, like our opposable thumbs and other body parts, evolved not to perfect our logic, but to optimize our survival. According to these thinkers, when early man moved up in the world from hunter-gatherers to the African Delta, survival of the fittest favored those who learned to cooperate to grow crops, raise families, and breed domestic animals. Thus, our brains evolved to foster domesticity, rather than think through logically rigorous legal or scientific or philosophical arguments.[1]

(Digression: Surely it's equally plausible, even when reflecting upon recent history, that evolution should favor brains that are ruthless and conniving; employing a logic that's better suited to achieve selfish ends than to seek truth. When dispassionately objective intellectuals taught ideas that displeased Stalin, he removed them from the gene pool by the thousands. Thus, a large portion of 20th century man, under such regimes as Lenin, Stalin, Mao, Hitler, and Pol Pot, survived by suppressing their creativity and independent thought and perfecting a "don't piss off the morons in charge" type of thinking. In my mind, it would be difficult to prove that long ago, living in small communities on the Delta, brilliant misfits would have survived any better.)

Thus, following this naturalistic line of argument, our brains developed primarily for primitive survival, not to reflect accurately on the great scientific theories of cosmology or macroeconomics or to develop rigorous rules of logic. Those who walked about the early Delta with their minds distracted by such matters were almost certainly eliminated from the gene pool by animals higher up on the food chain.

Rather than being equipped for higher level thinking, according to this theory, we find our brains uniquely suited to think in ways that enhance our self-confidence, enable us to compete, socialize, and convince the opposite sex to mate with us.

As a result, today's brains should resonate more with *Glamour Magazine, Playboy* and *Sports Illustrated*, than *Physics Today* or *Philosophy Now*. In its favor, this theory successfully predicts the type and quality of magazines available for purchase at service station check-out counters. Such academics as Psychologist Susan Blackmore and Philosopher Alex Rosenberg similarly argue that our brains, in their present state of evolution, deceive us in many ways and can't be trusted. Why then should we trust in the ability of our empirical investigations or logical argumentation to help us find truth?[2] Without recounting the intricate details, I should also mention that eighteenth century philosopher David Hume argued, with breathtaking influence on modern thought, that taking empiricism to its logical conclusion leads to skepticism concerning any certain knowledge. His works, and many who built upon his foundation, have led some contemporary intellectuals to a thoroughgoing despair of finding truth through science or logic or any other means.[3] This is all to say that if you read widely, you'll run across many who teach that all truth is relative and a search for truth is futile. Rather than set forth a defense of our ability to find truth, or at the very least that we have the ability to weed through nonsense in order to get *closer* to the truth, I'll just note that I've never found a thoroughgoing skeptic who lives consistently with his skepticism.

As soon as he opens his mouth or wields his pen, he begins making statements that depend upon the very laws of logic he denies. When Blackmore argues that our minds deceive us and can't be trusted, why does she go on to write the next chapter? If *she* really believes what she wrote, she can't trust *her* reasoning. If *I* believe what she wrote, I can't trust in either the accuracy of her writings or my ability to interpret them. So why keep reading? After a professor teaches his students that we can't know truth, no sooner has he left the classroom and met his department chair than he engages her in an argument, based upon the facts and logic he denies in class, about his deplorable salary. And he certainly won't be satisfied if his boss responds that the argument is pointless because all truth is relative.

In the end, whether you claim to be a thoroughgoing skeptic or a believer in our ability to find truth, logic would seem useful, at least in arguing for a raise. So since this isn't a book on epistemology, let's proceed as if logic is indeed useful, and try to sharpen our ability to use it.

The Syllogism* as a Useful Starting Point

Syllogism - a type of argument that begins with two or more premises and draws a conclusion.

Increasingly, I find myself putting complex, convoluted, or long-winded arguments into the form of syllogisms in order to evaluate them. The value of this process was demonstrated to me at a recent philosophical conference. I was astonished to hear a philosopher attack a 450 page book by reducing the author's line of argument to a simple, three-line syllogism. If the philosopher succeeded, then no matter how many studies the author quoted, no matter how much data he accumulated, no matter how many more pages he wrote; if his line of argument was illogical, his conclusion wasn't warranted.

Here's the classic example of a simple, correctly formulated logical syllogism:

Premise 1: All men are mortal.

Premise 2: Socrates is a man.

Therefore: Socrates is mortal.

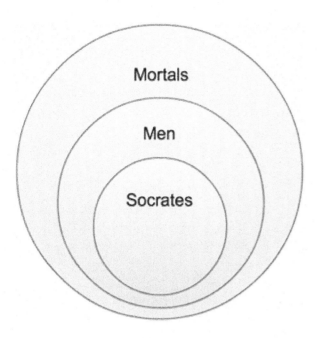

The beauty of a correctly formulated syllogism is that if we agree with the premises, then we must agree with the conclusion. Do you agree that all men are mortal? Do you agree that Socrates is a man? If so, then you *must* believe that Socrates is mortal. It's a logically air tight argument.

To evaluate someone's argument, try to put it in a syllogistic format and focus on two questions:

1. Do you agree with the premises? (Are they either intuitively obvious or well-supported by evidence?)
2. Does the conclusion logically follow from the premises?

Of course, arguments can get quite complicated, requiring complicated syllogisms to replicate them in logical form. If you're interested in exploring the more complex forms, study deductive logic. But I find that basic syllogisms suffice to evaluate the vast majority of meaningful arguments, even when evaluating chapters or entire books.

Let's Analyze an Argument!

Let's start with an argument proposed by a bright person and analyze it. Here are a couple of formulations of an argument put forth by Richard Dawkins, a popular science writer who once taught at Oxford University.

In his book, *The God Delusion*, Dawkins seeks to establish atheism, primarily by attacking theism. But he does present one positive argument for atheism, which he claims demonstrates that there is almost certainly no God. Dawkins believes the argument is devastating to theism— "an unrebuttable refutation."[4] It makes for a good argument to examine, since Dawkins states it in a few sentences rather than arguing it extensively.

Here's how he puts it:

"...any creative intelligence, of sufficient complexity to design anything, comes into existence only as the end product of an extended process of gradual evolution. Creative intelligences, being evolved, necessarily arrive late in the universe, and therefore cannot be responsible for designing it."[5]

Later in the book, he puts it this way:

"The whole argument turns on the familiar question 'Who made God?', which most thinking people discover for themselves. A designer God cannot be used to explain organized complexity because any God capable of designing anything would have to be complex enough to demand the same kind of explanation in his own right. God presents an infinite regress from which he cannot help us to escape."[6]

Think!

Before reading any further, try your own hand at responding to Dawkins. He says that he has "yet to hear a convincing answer" to his argument.[7] Do you think it's irrefutable? If the argument seems rather muddled to you, start by reading one sentence at a time and asking yourself, "Do I agree or disagree with this statement, and why?" Perhaps trying to put it in syllogistic format would help, or trying to express it as a line of argument. (Caution: Try not to let your personal worldview interfere with your reasoning. The question I'm asking is not "Is there a God?" but rather "Is Dawkins' argument irrefutable?")

Using a Line of Argument* and Syllogism to Clear Muddy Waters

If I understand Dawkins correctly, here's his line of argument:

There are only two possible ways that God's existence could be accounted for:

1. **He was created by another being.** But that explanation doesn't really help because then we have to ask, "Who made *that* designer, and the one who made him?" which leads to an infinite regress of questions which we can never fully answer.
2. **He slowly evolved through time.** But if He evolved, He would not have developed His incredible intelligence and power until *the end* of a long process of evolution. Yet, in order to create the universe, He needed this intelligence and power *at the beginning*. Thus, He couldn't have created the universe. Besides, what are the odds that such a complex being could evolve through purely naturalistic causes?

Dawkins thus concludes that since both of these scenarios are highly unlikely, it's highly unlikely that God exists.[8]

Put in a syllogism, it might read like this:

Premise 1: If God exists, he must have come into existence by either being created by another being or evolving slowly through time.

Premise 2: It's highly unlikely that God came into existence by either being created by another being or evolving slowly through time.

Conclusion: It's highly unlikely that God exists.

Think!

Does laying it out as a line of argument and as a syllogism help? Do you think I did it accurately? Now think through the line of argument and syllogism. Do you agree with each of the premises? (Is it sound?) Did Dawkins argue correctly from these premises? (Is it valid?*)[6]*

Sound Syllogism - *the premises are true and the form of the argument is valid.*

Valid Syllogism - *the form of the argument is correct, whether or not the premises or conclusion are true.*

As we continue with this chapter, we'll introduce some logical fallacies and apply them to both Dawkins' argument and the introductory discussion.

Fallacy #1: Bifurcation

Dawkins' argument seems to be a good example of a fallacy called bifurcation, whereby the argument assumes that only two (note the prefix "bi", meaning "two") possibilities exist, whereas there are actually more. This fallacy is particularly pernicious because it seems to contain an element of sleight of hand. If it is presented by a person we respect or agree with, we tend to assume that his premises represent all possibilities and we focus on the validity of the argument rather than the accuracy of the premises.

So here's how Dawkins' argument appears to be guilty of bifurcation.

He assumes that there are two and only two possible explanations for the proposed existence of God:

1. He was either created by another being, or
2. He evolved by natural means slowly over time.

To justify limiting the existence of God to these two options, Dawkins should have eliminated a third, seemingly viable option: that God could have simply existed from eternity past. After all, until well into the 20th century, the majority of scientists saw no problem in believing that *matter* existed from eternity past. Why then could *God* not have existed from eternity past? Is there evidence (either empirical or logical) that if God exists, He could not have existed from eternity past (or, alternately, could not exist outside of time and space)? If there is such evidence, then Dawkins should forward it. Otherwise, his premises are misleading and inaccurate in that they unnecessarily ignore this option.[9]

To put it another way, Dawkins claims that there are two and only two ways the existence of God could be explained. By explaining those two away, he claims to have explained away the existence of God. Yet, he's ignored (or deflected his readers from) a third possibility which he needs to explain away as well: that God existed from eternity past. By overlooking this third option, his argument fails, falling to the fallacy of bifurcation.[10]

Other Examples of Bifurcation

The Atlanta Falcons' loss to the New England Patriots was due to either inept play or poor coaching.

But aren't there more options than two? Perhaps they lost primarily because of a brilliant strategy by the opposing coaching staff, or the Patriots quarterback was on a roll, or the injury to the Falcon running back caused the Falcons to resort to "Plan B" rather than "Plan A", or any number of other possibilities that the armchair critic needs to rule out.

The president must be either insane or stupid to make that decision.

What other factors may explain the decision? Isn't it possible that the president was privy to facts we weren't aware of, or had made a wise political bargain that required that decision, or any number of other factors?

What a despicable child! He obviously either inherited bad genes or has inept parents.

What are some other possible contributing factors to the child's behavior? Perhaps he's sick or tired or teething.

Fallacy #2: The Straw Man

I'm dealing in this chapter with arguments that are very common. Familiarize yourself with them and you'll begin to see them everywhere—in articles, news broadcasts, Facebook discussions— everywhere!

The Straw Man fallacy presents a weak form of an opposing argument so that it's easy to destroy it and declare victory. The writer or speaker never actually attacks the opponent's arguments. Instead, he avoids the opponent's arguments by "knocking down a straw man."

Dawkins seems to have erected and knocked down a straw man in the argument we considered above. In brief, he argued that it's very unlikely that an evolved or created God exists. But the vast majority of theistic theologians and philosophers of the Western world would likely agree with this statement. In fact, I don't believe I've ever met a theist who believes in a created or evolved God. So arguing against this kind of a God says nothing about the existence of the eternal God that most of Dawkins' opponents believe in.

Thus, Dawkins has set up an irrelevant straw man (or in this instance, a Straw God), and tried to disprove His existence. If successful, he merely succeeds in knocking down a position that his opponents never held. The philosophers and theologians he's attacking overwhelmingly define God as one who existed from eternity past (or exists outside time and space). Dawkins should have attacked the position held by those he attacks.

Michael Ruse, Professor of Philosophy at Florida State University, himself an atheist, criticizes Dawkins' argument in part for this very reason. He concludes:

"...I want to extend to Christians the courtesy of arguing against what they actually believe, rather than begin and end with the polemical parody of what Dawkins calls 'the God delusion.'"

Another Example of Arguing against a Straw Man

A friend remarks to you: "The last three winters have been colder than average. So much for the theory of Global Warming!"

Your friend assumes that Global Warming advocates argue in this manner: "If temperatures are truly rising, *every year* and *every geographical location* should show increased warmth." But nobody argues this. It's arguing against a straw man. Global Warming advocates actually argue that *over long periods of time* the average temperature is increasing. Those who argue against global warming should argue against this rather than a straw man.

Fallacy #3: The Law of Non-Contradiction

Man has been accustomed, ever since he was a boy,to having a dozen incompatible philosophies dancing about together inside his head. He doesn't think of doctrines as primarily "true" or "false," but as "academic" or "practical," "outworn" or "contemporary," "conventional" or "ruthless.""[12]

- C.S. Lewis

In Chapter 9, I mentioned philosopher Alex Rosenberg's recent book. In it he argues, among other things, that:

1. **There's no free will.**[13] Thus, according to Rosenberg, we think only what we've been determined to think (by our genetics, etc.) How we think is determined by evolutionary processes that often have nothing to do with producing logical thinking. I can't direct my own thinking because there's no "I" outside my brain to direct my thinking. Our brains are just advanced computers, and computers can't think "about" things. Consciousness is thus an illusion.[14]
2. **Our thinking is flawed.** "Mother Nature built our minds for purposes other than understanding reality."[15]
3. **We can learn nothing from history or people's life stories.**[16]

With that background, here's where I see contradictions piling up.

1. **On changing people's opinions** - In his preface Rosenberg states that he wrote the book to help people discover the real answers to such questions as "Why am I here?" or "What is the meaning of life?" But if there's no free will, and all of our beliefs were therefore predetermined, how can he possibly hope to change anybody's opinion about anything? If evolution absolutely determines everyone's thought processes and beliefs, then how can he possibly trust his own mental processes or hope to change other people's thinking?

2. **On urging life change** - Why does he keep urging us to action, if everything's determined and his urgings are therefore worthless? Rosenberg preaches, "We need continually to fight the temptation to think that we can learn much of anything from someone else's story of how they beat an addiction, kept to a diet...." But what does it mean to "continually fight" a temptation if we're already destined to fight or not fight, to either beat the temptation or fall for it?

3. **On recommending a course of action** - By the end of the book he's recommending that we adopt the philosophical nihilism of Epicurus, not take ourselves so seriously, and take Prozac if you're unhappy that life has no meaning.[17] Can't he see that if we believed what he said earlier about that we can't learn anything from other people's life stories, we can also learn nothing from his own experiences and recommendations?

4. **On learning from history** - He says we can learn nothing from history: "History, even when corrected by science, is still bunk."[18] But then he recounts history to make his points.[19] For example, how can we know if Prozac works, unless we accept the testimonies of other patients and rely on their stated medical histories?

Thus, it seems evident to me that Rosenberg's book is riddled with internal contradictions. Now perhaps if I asked Rosenberg personally about the apparent contradictions, he could clear them up. But in the present state of his book, they seem flagrant, leading me to question many of his conclusions.

Sometimes contradictions are not so obvious. For example, a central tenet of Logical Positivists, whose views were very influential in the early 1900s (not only in philosophy, but also psychology and other sciences), expounded the verification principle, which can be stated as: "the only meaningful statements are those that we can verify through observation." Yet, their critics pointed out that this very statement (the verification principle) can't be verified through observation, making it self-contradictory, or self-defeating. In other words, they couldn't verify the verification principle with the verification principle, making it (to be consistent with Logical Positivism) a meaningless statement.

Well, that was rather embarrassing to Logical Positivists. This insight, in part, led to Logical Positivism's demise in the latter 1900s.[20]

Summary

The arguments we've examined in this chapter were put forth by bright people with topnotch education credentials—often PhDs holding prestigious positions. If *they* are subject to falling for logical fallacies, how much more the rest of us?

Why do brilliant people believe nonsense? Because they fail to sufficiently check their beliefs against logical fallacies. How can we guard ourselves from similar errors in thinking?

Action Points

How to Spot Logical Fallacies and Keep from Using Them in Our Own Communications

1. **Take time to think through arguments that are important to you.**

   Most don't. In fact, they barely even pay attention. Philosopher and scientist Francis Bacon once wrote: "Some books should be tasted, some devoured, but only a few should be chewed and digested thoroughly." For the latter books, articles or lectures, if the argumentation is complicated or unclear, I often summarize it with a line of argument, sometimes chapter by chapter. It takes a bit of time, but it keeps me from ending the book in a mental fog.

2. **Don't be intimidated by credentials and claims.**

   Surely this is, in part, why people take nonsense promoted by well-credentialed people at face value. Never listen to anyone without engaging your critical thinking.

3. **Beware of the tendency to uncritically accept the arguments of those you agree with, or arguments that have an agreeable conclusion.**

   Professor H. Allen Orr, in the *New York Review of Books*, reflected on Dawkins' argument and his way of arguing. According to Orr:

   "Indeed he suffers from several problems when attempting to reason philosophically. The most obvious is that he has a preordained set of conclusions at which he's determined to arrive. Consequently, Dawkins uses any argument, however feeble, that seems to get him there and the merit of various arguments appears judged largely by where they lead."[21]

4. **Ask yourself, "Are there facts or personal experiences that don't fit with either the premises or the conclusion?"**

   When I read Rosenberg's argument that we can't learn anything from history or life stories, I couldn't help but reflect on the wealth of valuable lessons I've learned from observing people's lives and reading great biographies. For example, by watching people make wise and poor financial and health decisions, I've learned much from their successes and failures. My personal experience represents one strike against his conclusion, causing me to look more critically at his argumentation.

5. **Put it in a syllogism (or line of argument) and ask yourself two questions:**

1. Are the premises supported by sufficient evidence?
2. Does the conclusion follow logically from the premises?

(To remember this point, reflect back on the **D.R.** of Dr. Cackler. Is the data complete and accurate? Is the reasoning from that data clear and accurate?)

6. **Have others look at the argument.**

Learn from Hewlett Packard's practice of running an idea by the person next to you. If the idea is important to you, discuss it with others. We all think a bit differently and it's very likely that others will see aspects of the issue that you don't see.

For example, Einstein once observed that scientists are typically poor philosophers. Whether he's right or not, psychologists do find people typically having strong and weak areas of reasoning. If a scientist is trying to reason philosophically, he might be wise to run his arguments by a philosopher. It's often wise to run important arguments by people who think differently from you.

7. **See how others in the field respond.**

Dawkins' argument is philosophical and the field of philosophy has a rich history of arguments concerning the existence of God. It would seem unlikely, though not impossible, that an expert in animal behavior (Dawkins) would dream up a slam dunk argument than never occurred to any great philosophical thinker from Plato to Immanuel Kant to Bertrand Russell. If Dawkins' argument were truly original and significant, I'd expect a loud chorus of respected philosophers to be hailing this argument's arrival.

Yet, the responses I've seen by philosophers and academics have been underwhelming at best. Philosopher William Craig went so far as to declare it "the worst atheistic argument in the history of Western thought."[22] Academic biologist H. Allen Orr noted that the argument was "shredded by reviewers."[23] For example, some attack the argument by noting that an explanation doesn't typically require an explanation of the explanation (responding to Dawkins' contention that theists must forward an explanation as to where God came from). In other words, if we were to visit the dark side of the moon and find an advanced, but long-abandoned (at least a century old, deduced from its state of natural aging) mining operation, where all the inscriptions were in a non-human language, wouldn't we be justified in positing that alien intelligences were behind it, *even if we had no idea how the aliens came to be or where they were from*? And it's not just theistic philosophers who find Dawkins' argument lacking.

Atheist Michael Ruse attacks Dawkins' argument in this way:

> "Like every first-year undergraduate in philosophy, Dawkins thinks he can put to rest the causal argument for God's existence. If God caused the world, then what caused God? Of course the great philosophers, Anselm and Aquinas particularly, are way ahead of him here. They know that the only way to stop the regression is by making God something that needs no cause. He must be a necessary being. This means that God is not part of the regular causal chain but in some sense orthogonal to it. He is what keeps the whole business going, past, present and future, and is the explanation of why there is something rather than nothing."[24]

Surely such rejoinders are legitimate challenges that Dawkins should respond to. Had he run his argument by some philosophers prior to publishing, perhaps he could have responded to their objections.[25]

Think Different (Creative Thinking)

One of philosopher Immanuel Kant's most valuable contributions to practical human thought was his insight that we don't experience things entirely as they are. While some people insist that seeing is *believing*, we all know that seeing can also be *deceiving*. For example, Kant notes that we don't see objects directly. Rather, we're a step removed in that we see reflections of objects on our retinas. We take another step back from real objects when our brains bring our own interpreting mechanisms to those objects, such as "quality" or "cause and effect."

Modern psychology confirms and extends Kant's insight. We don't "see" the reflections on our retinas in the same way. While *you* may see a green object on your retina, *I* may see it as brown, since I'm color-blind to certain greens. And we're well aware of common optical illusions and misperceptions. That's why eye-witness testimony is often contradictory, even when the witnesses are honest. Often, what we see shouldn't be believed.

You've probably seen illustrations such as this, where our minds fool us. How many "F"s do you see in this passage?

FINISHED FILES ARE THE RE

SULT OF YEARS OF SCIENTI

FIC STUDY COMBINED WITH

THE EXPERIENCE OF YEARS.

Most people see only three. That's all I saw the first two times I read it. Actually, there are six. (Look slowly at each letter and count again, perhaps starting at the end.) This is similar to the problem drivers have spotting motorcycles on streets where they are rare. We're watching for cars and trucks and may not see the motorcycles at all.

Are the horizontal lines below curved or straight? Use a ruler or straight edge to see.

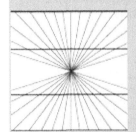

Fallacies such as bifurcation, like a good magician or an illusion, play on our brains' tendencies to see certain things incorrectly or to be distracted from crucial details. How can creativity help us to overcome distractions and wrong directions in order to innovate productively?

- **Broaden your range of input.**

    Who would you prefer to edit your writing?

    - A dyslexic, who struggles to read well?
    - Slow readers?
    - A top academic who teaches grammar and literature?
    - A person so proficient at reading that she can polish off an entire novel in an evening?

    Intuitively, most authors seem to seek out exclusively d) and e) types, and I agree that their input has a place. After all, shouldn't avid readers and top grammarians have valuable input?

    But I'm increasingly seeking editorial input from a wider range of people. While fast readers may excel at telling you if your story is interesting and flows well, the slow reader may be better for thinking through your line of argument, spotting places that need more documentation, or helping you with the rhythm produced by combinations of long and short sentences. Literature professors tend to love clever analogies and brilliant descriptions, whereas the average reader may see these as distractions from the story line. That's why I like input from both.

    Academics have a high tolerance for detailed argumentation and theory. While I'll get their input on this book, I can't quite trust their verdict if they tell me it's interesting. If I'm writing, not primarily for professors, but for their students and the broader public, I treasure input from those who aren't naturally interested in my subject matter. I'm blessed with dyslexic twins, and love their input. That's one reason I use lots of white space, bullet points, and illustrations. Dyslexics cringe when they see a page full of unbroken words. I've found that if I can hold the attention of struggling readers, I'm more likely to captivate a broad range of readers, and in the end delight academics as well.

- **At times, ignore the current theory that drives your research, and allow non-experts to offer ideas; or just throw a bunch of stuff against the wall to see what sticks.**

Sometimes our theories and methods keep us from trying potentially fruitful experiments. Since we seldom recognize that the ruling theory may have deflected us onto a side road, it sometimes helps to toss it and try something new.

Isn't this the way inventor Thomas Edison often proceeded? I still picture him in his later years, stopping beside the road to sample plants that might be used as a substitute for the rubber used to make tires, which was in short supply during World War II.

  - A thirteen year old, Jack Andraka, took an intense interest in trying to cure pancreatic cancer, after it killed a family friend. Being new to the field, he took a different direction from the standard research, resulting in his inventing a simple, cheap test to detect pancreatic cancer early, when it can be successfully treated.[26]

  - Don Valencia, a cellular biologist who developed tests to diagnose autoimmune diseases, had worked on isolating molecules in human cells without destroying them. It occurred to him that this technique might work for making a concentrated extract of coffee that could capture its flavor more successfully than other extracts. He experimented with it in his kitchen, trying out different flavors on his neighbors. Once perfected, he took it to Starbucks. They eventually hired him and used the technology to expand their product line to coffee ice cream, bottled beverages, etc.[27]

2. **Employ higher levels of reasoning.**

Bloom's Taxonomy (most refer to the "revised" taxonomy), distinguishes different types of thinking, suggesting ways for us to move past rote memory. Unfortunately, many students seem to seldom move past merely identifying and memorizing the important parts (what might be on the test) of texts and lectures.

Yet, to succeed in real life, we must go further than recognition or rote memorization (see Level 1 in the below graphic.). We need to develop the skills of comprehending (Level 2), applying (Level 3), analyzing (Level 4), synthesizing (Level 5) and evaluating (Level 6). Search "Bloom's Taxonomy" in Google and you'll find many lists of specific characteristics of each level of thinking. Referring to such lists when working through an issue can suggest new ways to approach it.

For example, in our discussion of Richard Dawkins' argument, I first stated it (Level One) and several times put it in my own words to try to clarify it (Level Two). We skipped application, but analyzed it (Level Four) by putting it in a line of argument and syllogism, so that we could identify and examine the premises. We did a bit of synthesis (Level Five) when we brought in outside ideas of how theists conceive of the eternal existence of God, and how other thinkers have responded to the argument. Finally, evaluation (Level Six) came to play when we noted that there seems to be an element of smoke and mirrors involved in the fallacy of bifurcation.

So if you're evaluating an argument or a proposal, consider running it through Bloom's Taxonomy to expand your ways of looking at the issue. Note how several levels involve creativity.

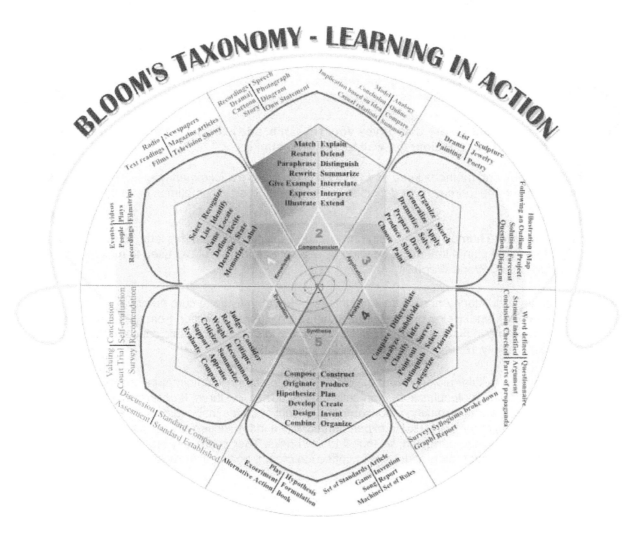

BLOOM'S TAXONOMY - LEARNING IN ACTION

Flex Your Neurons!

Pursuing the Point of Know Return

1. Write your own example of a "straw man" argument.
2. Write your own example of a "bifurcation" argument.
3. If you agree that Dawkins' argument makes no sense, why do you think such a smart person would forward such a nonsensical argument? If you believe that the argument could make sense if reformulated, how would you change it to overcome the difficulties scholars have brought forth?
4. How could you use Bloom's Revised Taxonomy as a practical tool for thinking more critically about issues you study and write about?
5. How could you use Bloom's Revised Taxonomy to think more creatively?
6. Since our brains often deceive us, how can we protect ourselves against such deceptions?

Making it More Personal

Practical Takeaways

7. What are one or more ideas provoked by this chapter that you can apply to help you think more critically?
8. What are one or more ideas that you can apply to help you think more creatively?

9. What else do you want to make sure you don't forget?

Recommended Trails for the Incurably Curious and Adventurous

1. To more fully understand a fallacy, it's often helpful to read other people's explanations and examples. To do this, Google "bifurcation" or "straw man."
2. Learn more about "Bloom's Taxonomy." This Wikipedia article is a good starting point to introduce it, discover the main controversies, and find other resources: http://en.wikipedia.org/wiki/Bloom%27s_taxonomy
3. Here's a TED talk of Jack Andraka talking about his development of a test for pancreatic cancer. Why do you think a young teen was able to develop such a test, when the experts had failed? http://www.ted.com/talks/jack_andraka_a_promising_test_for_pancreatic_cancer_from_a_teenager?language=en

End Notes

1. Analytical philosopher Alvin Plantinga argues that this line of reasoning is consistent with, and even demanded by, philosophical naturalism. http://www.nybooks.com/articles/archives/2012/sep/27/philosopher-defends-religion /.
2. Susan Blackmore and Alex Rosenberg argue that since our brains were constructed solely through naturalistic evolutionary processes—for survival than for finding truth—our brains build mental models that we can't control (there is no "I" or "self" directing the brain, in the view of both authors) and they can't be trusted to lead us to truth. Susan Blackmore, Dying to Live (Buffalo, New York : Prometheus Books, 1993), pp149-164; 221-225; Alex Rosenberg , The Atheist's Guide to Reality (New York: W. W. Norton & Company, 2011).
3. For example, Hume's radical empiricism led him to deny that we can establish cause/effect relationships—a belief which would obviously wreak havoc in science.
4. Richard Dawkins , The God Delusion (New York: Mariner Books, 2008), p. 187.
5. Ibid., p. 52.
6. Ibid., p. 136.
7. Ibid., p. 187.
8. Ibid., see also pp. 186-188.
9. Academic biologist H. Allen Orr suggests that Dawkins failed to consider that, rather than ending in an infinite regress ("Who made God?" "Who made the being that made God," etc.), God could be a brute fact, like subatomic particles or matter. "It could, after all, be a brute fact of the universe that it derives from some transcendent mind...." H. Allen Orr, "A Mission to Convert," The New York Review of Books, January 11, 2007. http://www.nybooks.com/articles/archives/2007/jan/11/a-mission-to-convert/
10. In The God Delusion, Dawkins doesn't even mention the option of God being eternal, much less argue against it. In one of his earlier books, The Blind Watchmaker, he least acknowledges that some would argue that God exists eternally, but brushes this option off (rather than forward an opposing argument) with a sentence: "You have to say something like 'God was always there', and if you allow yourself that kind of lazy way out, you might as well just say 'DNA was always there', or 'Life was always there', and be done with it." Richard Dawkins, The Blind Watchmaker (New York: W. W. Norton & Company, 1996), p. 200. But why does Dawkins consider "something was always there" an invalid option? After all, prior to the 20th century, the majority opinion of scientists was that the universe was always there, extending into eternity past. Was that "lazy" on their part? In fact, when we consider ultimate origins, we'd seem to be left with two options: either there was nothing prior to the Bang (the standard scientific view of the Big Bang, according to Dawkins), so that something appeared out of nothing, with nothing to cause it, (that's absolutely nothing—no empty space, no vacuum), or that the beginning of the universe was caused by something that existed in some non-material form outside of time and space, existing from eternity past. Is the latter option really stranger than something coming from nothing on its own accord? If not, then why does Dawkins think it so inconceivable (or lazy) that God could have existed eternally? He fails to address this question.
11. Gary Gutting, Does Evolution Explain Religious Beliefs? The New York Times (July 8, 2014) http://opinionator.blogs.nytimes.com/2014/07/08/does-evolution-explain-religious-beliefs/?_php=true&_type=blogs&_php=true&_type=blogs&_r=1&
12. C.S. Lewis , The Screwtape Letters (New York: HarperOne reprint edition, 2009), p. 1.
13. Alex Rosenberg, The Atheist's Guide to Reality (New York: W.W. Norton & Company, 2011), pp. 2,3.
14. Ibid., pp. 164-193.

15. Ibid., p. 16.
16. Ibid., pp. 2,3,310,311.
17. Ibid., pp. 313-315.
18. Ibid., pp. 311.
19. Ibid., for example, pp. viii, 304-306. For a helpful critique of this book, see James N. Anderson, Analogical Thoughts (blog), August 13, 2013, http://www.proginosko.com/2013/08/the-atheists -guide-to-reality/.
20. "Minus logical positivists, tremendously influential outside philosophy, especially in psychology and social sciences, intellectual life of the 20th century would be unrecognizable." Yet, "By the late 1960s, the neopositivist movement had clearly run its course. Interviewed in the late 1970s, A. J. Ayer supposed that "the most important 'defect' was that nearly all of it was false." http://en.wikipedia.org/wiki /Logical_positivism#Critics. For a brief history of Logical Positivism, see articles such as "Logical Empiricism" or "Theism" in The Stanford Encyclopedia of Philosophy , Edward N. Zalta (ed.). It's a wonderful (free!) resource for all things philosophical.
21. H. Allen Orr, op. cit. Dawkins would seem to be a master of the straw man . Perhaps he gives us a clue as to why in his introduction to The Divine Watchmaker, where he states his opinion that Darwin's first edition of Origin of the Species was more persuasive than the last edition, because in the first edition Darwin didn't deal with all the objections. Apparently, in Dawkins' mind, Darwin's stating other people's objections took away from his argument. So perhaps Dawkins knows many of the objections people would give to his arguments, but is afraid that if he presents the strongest arguments for all sides of his statements, that this will take away from his persuasiveness. Thus, he presents straw men , which are much more easily knocked down. Example: if you look carefully at his arguments against the existence of God in chapter three of The God Delusion, he doesn't present the arguments as his strongest opponents present them. In the form he presents them, they're easily destroyed. For example, on Dawkins' critique of the Cosmological Argument for God's existence, see philosopher Edward Feser's critique at http://edwardfeser.blogspot.com/2011/07/so-you-think-you-understand.html. Also, view Dr. William Craig 's presentation at Oxford on the same topic at https://www.youtube.com/watch?v=fP9CwDTRoOE.
22. Ed. by Paul Copan, William Lane Craig, Contending with Christianity 's Critics (Nashville: B&H Academic), p. 5.
23. H. Allen Orr, replying to Dennett's response in the New York Review of Books, http://www.nybooks.com/articles/archives/2007/mar/01/the-god-delusion/.
24. See Michael Ruse 's response in Does Evolution Explain Religious Beliefs?, op. cit.
25. Note other objections to this argument:
    1. Going along with our argument concerning the mining operation on the moon, philosophers argue that an immediate explanation doesn't require an ultimate explanation. Example: William Craig suggests that if we found artifacts of a lost civilization, that's sufficient evidence that the civilization actually existed, even if we have no ultimate explanation of where the civilization came from. Contending with Christianity's Critics , op. cit., p. 4.
    2. From a purely naturalistic perspective, we have no ultimate explanation of anything. For example, you may ask why this cat is sitting on my desk looking at me? I may respond, "It wants to lick the milk out of my bowl of cereal." But what if you counter, "That's no explanation, where did the cat come from?" I may say, "Its mom." And you may complain, "Yes, of course. But if you can't give me the ultimate explanation of where the cat came from, I refuse to believe that it even exists." Yet, from a naturalistic perspective, all scientific explanations end with the Big Bang, a place at which physics as we know it breaks down and at which scientists tell us all scientific questions stop. All reductionist scientific explanations end with the Big Bang, and if we ask one more "Why?" beyond the Big Bang, science lets us down, because the Big Bang is a singularity. Thus, if all arguments about the existence of this or that must answer the ultimate question of origins to be meaningful, aren't we stuck with no meaningful arguments at all? Thus, from a naturalistic perspective we can't ultimately answer the question, "Where did this cat come from?" But would Dawkins thus concede that we therefore can't argue for its existence? Surely not.
26. Jack Andraka , A Promising Test for Pancreatic Cancer...from a Teenager?, A TED talk , (Filmed Feb., 2013) http://www.ted.com/talks/jack_andraka_a_promising_test_for_pancreatic_cancer_from_a_teenager?language=enhttp://www.ted.com/talks/jack_andraka_a_promising_test_for_pancreatic_cancer_from_a_teenager.
27. For the story of the development of Starbucks ' instant coffee, see Schultz , Howard and Dori Jones Yang, Pour Your Heart Into It: How Starbucks Built a Company One Cup at a Time (New York : Hyperion, 1997), pp. 216-218.

By: Steve and Cherie Miller

Taken with kind permission from the book *Why Brilliant People Believe Nonsense* by J. Steve Miller and Cherie K. Miller.

Logic and Logical Fallacies

Read not to contradict and confute; nor to believe and take for granted; nor to find talk and discourse, but to weigh and consider.

- Francis Bacon, Of Studies

Brilliant people believe nonsense [because] they either fail to recognize fallacies, or misapply the ones they know.

Warning

Learning fallacies can be fatal to your argumentation and detrimental to your relationships. For these reasons, I teach logical fallacies with a great deal of hesitation. It's a bit like selling firearms to a person with no training in how to use them. I'd hate to be known as one who arms Internet trolls*.

Troll - A participant in social media who delights in haughtily slamming other people's positions before fully understanding either thei position or the context of the discussion.

So before I present a large list of fallacies, I'll acquaint you with a particularly pernicious type of fallacious reasoning that's running rampant on the Internet, but which is strangely absent from lists of fallacies. I call it "The Fallacy Fallacy."

The Fallacy Fallacy: Debunking Debunking

I often read comments on blog posts or articles or Facebook discussions which accuse the writer of committing a specific logical fallacy and thus declaring the argument thoroughly debunked, typically with an air of arrogant finality. While the debunker may feel quite smug, intelligent participants consider him quite sophomoric*. In reality, he's typically failed to even remotely understand the argument, much less apply the fallacy in a way that's relevant to the discussion.

Sophomoric - *A statement that is immature and poorly informed, but is spoken with overconfidence and conceit. The word is a composite of two Greek words meaning "wise" and "fool."*

Surely this fallacy deserves a proper name and should be listed with other fallacies. Thus I'll define "The Fallacy Fallacy" as "Improperly connecting a fallacy with an argument, so that the argument is errantly presumed to be debunked.[1]

Don't be a troll. Here are a few ways people misapply fallacies, thus committing "The Fallacy Fallacy":

1. **They misunderstand the fallacy.**

   "YOU'RE ALWAYS ARGUING WITH JAMIE, WHICH IS OBVIOUSLY *AD HOMINEM*." (Trolls delight in using all caps, confusing *louder* with *smarter*.) If the person was actually arguing against Jamie's arguments, rather than putting Jamie down as a person, then the arguments weren't *ad hominem* at all.

2. **They fail to appreciate nuance. (They understand the fallacy, but apply it errantly.)**

   Someone quotes Albert Einstein to bolster his argument. "THAT'S AN APPEAL TO AUTHORITY!" shouts the troll. But citing authorities isn't always fallacious. If a person cites Einstein concerning a question of relativity theory, then Einstein is a legitimate authority. Thus, quoting him can be a legitimate part of an argument, although it's typically not a slam dunk in itself. While arguments concerning establishing facts should be argued on the basis of the evidence, in many cases citing authorities can help to substantiate the evidence.[2]

3. **They assume a thorough debunking when there's typically more to the argument.**

   While trolls are celebrating their "brilliant" comments with a victory dance and a handful of Skittles, their opponents are often typing a clarification that makes the Trolls' comments irrelevant. We simply must take the time to thoroughly understand the arguments we're evaluating.

Making Arguments More Fruitful

For those who sincerely want to learn from one another by hashing out issues, consider this: Trolls "flame" opponents by either calling them morons or presenting their arguments dogmatically, as if they have crushed their opponents. If you're concerned about the truth, seek more to understand than to demonstrate your brilliance. To accomplish this, *suggest* rather than *slam*; express tentativeness rather than dogmatic finality; ask questions rather than accuse.

Does it in any way weaken a counter-argument to word it in a cautious, humble manner, such as: "At first glance your argument appears to be an unwarranted appeal to authority. Are you really saying that your position is correct solely because Einstein believes it as well?"

In this way, the opponent is more likely to respond in a reasonable manner and you save face in case you took the comment out of context or otherwise misunderstood it.

Benjamin Franklin on Fruitful Argumentation

Franklin was one of the most influential people in American history. He learned a lesson early in life which he considered of such significance that he discussed it at some length in his autobiography. He describes learning Socratic argumentation, which he delighted to use in humiliating his opponents. (As an annoying ass during this phase of a few years, he was a predecessor to the modern day Internet troll.)

But over time, he realized that this method failed to either persuade others or to help him learn from them. Rather, it disgusted people. So he changed his method of argumentation. In Franklin's own words, he discovered the value of:

As a result, Franklin became a skilled negotiator and persuader, allowing him to help start America's library system, organize firefighters, run a successful printing business, improve our postal service, negotiate with the French to aid us in the Revolutionary War, and assist in finalizing and adopting the Declaration of Independence, just to name a few of an astonishing array of accomplishments.[4]

Some Helpful Ways to Organize Fallacies

The plethora of known fallacies can be quite unwieldy, so let's first of all look at some helpful ways of classifying them. In this way, when you sense an argument is invalid but can't remember the name of the specific fallacy, at least you might be able to identify the category in order to better evaluate or research it.

(Example: "That sounds like a fallacy of definition.") Although no single categorization scheme has become standard, you'll find some of the categories (such as "formal" and "informal") used widely.[5]

Aristotle

Aristotle was perhaps the first to categorize logical fallacies in his *De Sophisticis Elenchis* (Sophistical Refutations). He lists 13 fallacies under two categories: **Verbal** (those depending on language) and **Material** (those not depending on language). In modern times, those building on Aristotle's two divisions often add a third: **Logical or Formal**—fallacies that violate the formal rules of the syllogism.

Philosopher J. L. Mackie

Mackie divided fallacies into:

Fallacies in a Strict Sense

Invalid forms of deductive reasoning; the conclusion doesn't logically follow from the premises.

Formal Fallacies - The conclusion is invalid because of the argument's form. Example: Exerting the consequent—If there are too many cooks, there's chaos in the kitchen. There's chaos in the kitchen, therefore there are too many cooks. (If p then q. q, therefore p)

Informal Fallacies - The conclusion is invalid for reasons other than its form. (Example: Using vague or ambiguous terms.)

Fallacies in Non-Deductive Reasoning and in Observation

Errors in inductively reasoning from evidence to a conclusion or hypothesis.

Induction and Confirmation - example: *post hoc ergo propter hoc* - the fact that event "b" followed event "a" doesn't absolutely prove that event "a" *caused* event "b".

Analogy - A weak analogy, one that has few or trivial points of resemblance, may have no evidential value at all.

Statistics - Example: If students from City High School outperform students from County High School on standardized tests, this doesn't necessarily imply City High School has better teachers. Perhaps administrators skew the scores, or one district has more high risk students.

Probability - Example: Although the probability of flipping a coin five times and getting heads every time is low, that doesn't mean that if you got heads four times in a row, it's very unlikely that you'll get heads in the next flip. The odds are still 50/50.

Observation - Example: Often what we observe is skewed by what we want or expect to observe.

Fallacies in Discourse

The argument fails because of some reason other than invalid deductive reasoning or arguing from evidence.

Inconsistency- You can't have it both ways. **"Petitio Principii"** - Including your conclusion in your premises (aka begging the question or arguing in a circle).

A Priori Fallacies - Bringing to the argument unfounded preconceptions that influence the conclusion.

"Ignoratio Elenchi" - Missing the point: An argument concerning something that was never meant, in the context of the argument, to be proven.

Fallacies of Interrogation - Demanding a narrow and specific answer to questions that demand broader answers. Example: "Answer yes or no: Have you stopped beating your wife?"

Fallacies in Explanation and Definition - Example: using the same word in two different ways in an argument, thus invalidating the argument.[6]

Historian David Hackett Fischer

In Fischer's instructive and delightful book, *Historians' Fallacies*,[7] he discusses 112 fallacies under 11 categories. Note that these apply far beyond professional historians. Whenever we blog about an event, summarize our family vacation on Facebook, or write that first high school paper on "What I Did for My Summer Vacation," we're telling history, and risk committing these fallacies. Here are Fischer's categories:

Question-framing - Historians begin their research by asking one or more questions. If these questions are vague or ill-conceived, they will yield the wrong answers. Example: asking a complex question and expecting a simple answer.

Factual Verification - Failure to rigorously employ the best methods for verifying historical data.

Factual Significance - Historians can't report every fact from a period of history; they must be selective. If they select based on the wrong criteria, their conclusions will likely be wrong as well.

Generalization - Improper statistical reasoning from historical data. Example: Drawing a general conclusion from an insufficient sampling of data.

Narration - Historians gather threads of historical data and weave them into stories. Yet, "nothing but the facts" is often at odds with great storytelling, which assigns feelings and even time sequences that may not be warranted by the historical data.

Causation - Example: The reductive fallacy reduces a complex historical cause to a simplistic one.

Motivation - Historians often assign motives without sufficient evidence; for example, assuming that a Roman Emperor thinks, reacts, and is motivated by the same things that motivate a middle-aged academic historian at Berkeley.

Composition - Historians tend to study and write about groups, or individuals as part of groups, whether the groups be social, religious, nation al, ideological, cliques, castes or economic. One fallacy of composition is assuming that the character of one member is shared by the rest of the group.

False Analogy - Example: People often reason from a partial analogy to declare there's an exact correspondence; but in reality, analogies are seldom exactly parallel.

Semantical Distortion - Problems with unclear or imprecise prose. For example, the failure to clarify definitions of terms.

Substantive Distraction - The argument shifts the reader's attention to issues that are irrelevant to the discussion.

While categorization schemes are helpful for getting an overview of types of fallacies, none seem to be without their downsides. For example, some fallacies seem to fit snugly into multiple categories.

A Great Big List of Fallacies

In my first Appendix, I list a great number of fallacies. I don't recommend trying to memorize them. Rather, familiarize yourself with each of them so that in the future, when you run across an argument that doesn't sound quite right, you can return to the list to search for a fallacy that might apply. If you're reading this for a class, your teacher or professor may single out certain fallacies that they deem the most important or the most frequently abused in literature and the media.

Conclusion

There are many ways to go wrong in our arguments. Some are a bit technical. But by familiarizing ourselves with fallacies, learning to apply them correctly, and discussing disagreements in a civil and humble manner, we can learn from each other and mutually come closer to the truth.

Matching Exercises

Flex Your Neurons!

Pursuing the Point of Know Return

1. What do you think motivates trolls to flame people in social media or to start arguments in social settings?
2. How do trolls hinder the process of finding truth?
3. How can we keep from behaving like trolls?
4. Write your own examples (lines of reasoning that contain the fallacy) of five fallacies (from the list in the appendix) that especially interest you.

Making it More Personal

Practical Takeaways

1. What are one or more ideas provoked by this chapter that you can apply to help you think more critically?
2. What are one or more ideas that you can apply to help you think more creatively?
3. What else do you want to make sure you don't forget?

Recommended Trail for the Incurably Curious and Adventurous

For any fallacies that seem unclear or are of special interest to you, Google them to find other explanations and illustrations.

1. Aristotle was the first I'm aware of to discuss examples. Apparently, back in 350 BCE, Greek predecessors to today's trolls strolled about annoying the great philosophers, imagining that they were spouting profundities. Thus, Aristotle wrote a work about "Sophistical Refutations," which he defined as "what appear to be refutations but are really fallacies instead." While mainly writing about logical fallacies, he also spoke of assigning fallacies incorrectly. See Aristotle, *Sophistical Refutations,* written c. 350 B.C.E., translated by W. A. Pickard-Cambridge, available digitally here: http://classics.mit.edu/Aristotle/sophist_refut.1.1.html.

2. Aristotle describes this issue: "By a sophistical refutation and syllogism I mean not only a syllogism or refutation which appears to be valid but is not, but also one which, *though it is valid, only appears to be appropriate to the thing in question.*" (Italics mine, Part Eight, *Sophistical Refutations.*)

3. Benjamin Franklin , *The Autobiography of Benjamin Franklin* (New York : Dover Publications, 1996), p. 13.

4. Tetlock, in his respected work, *Expert Political Judgment*, suggests that those who use more temperate language tend to be more accurate in their predictions. He brings together a wealth of research showing that the foxes (who know many little things) predict better than the hedgehogs (who know one niche area in depth), although the latter are typically considered the experts and practically everyone (e.g., news sources) wants to hear from them. Those who speak in terms of "perhaps," and "possibly" are far better predictors than the dogmatic, assured experts. Philip E. Tetlock, *Expert Political Judgment* (Princeton , New Jersey : Princeton University Press, 2005, 2006).

5. Many such schemes of categorization have been proposed through the centuries. For example, John Stewart Mill proposed five general categories: Fallacies of Simple Inspection (or *A Priori* Fallacies), of Observation, of Generalization, of Ratiocination, of Confusion. *A System Of Logic, Ratiocinative And Inductive* (New York: Harper & Brothers, Publishers, 1882, available digitally at Project Gutenberg). According to Mackie, "Of other classifications of fallacies in general the most famous are those of Francis Bacon   and J.S. Mill." See "Fallacies" in *The Encyclopedia of Philosophy* (Vol. 3), pp. 169-179.

6. *Encyclopaedia Brittanica*, 1910 edition, see the article entitled *Fallacy*.

7. From his article "Fallacies," op. cit.

8. David Hackett Fischer , *Historians' Fallacies* (New York: Harper & Row, 1970).

Chapter 6: Usability

By: Cassandra Race

Objectives

Upon completion of this chapter, readers will be able to:

1. Explain the characteristics of a usable document.
2. Conduct a usability test.

Usability: Evaluating Documents and Websites

I will never forget a Christmas Eve many years ago, when the kids were finally asleep and Mr. and Mrs. Santa Claus began the assembly of the much desired "brand name" doll house. Out came the tools, out came a hundred or so tiny plastic parts, and out came an instruction sheet written by someone clearly from another land far away. After several hours of attempting to decipher some of the worst instructions ever written, we recruited a neighbor's 12 year old, a seasoned veteran in the world of dream houses, and the assembly was completed in time for Christmas morning.

Whenever *usability* is mentioned, this incident comes to mind. **Usability**, a term that refers to how easily and effectively a person can use a document, website, or product to achieve a purpose, is an integral element of workplace and technical writing and must not be overlooked at any level. On the web, it's critical for survival...if users can't figure out how to purchase that awesome table lamp, they will quickly go elsewhere on the web to shop. The vendor loses money. If users can't find the information they need, they will move on...there is plenty else out there that will meet their needs. And someone loses money. In the office, if employees spend large amounts of time figuring out unclear documents or deciphering poorly written instructions, the company loses money.

The concept of testing usability is relatively new...in the 1960's the rise of the computer industry brought about a need for user manuals and engineers realized that it would be important to know how users interacted with the materials and the technology. When personal computers became available in the 1980's and the 1990's brought the World Wide Web into households and businesses, engineers and designers...and technical writers...recognized that research into how people used and interacted with computers and documents was essential for the development of not just programs and software, but for instructional materials. (Jameson p399).

As a technical writer in the 21st century, you must incorporate some level of usability testing or evaluation in the documents you create. Think back to Chapter 1, The Nature of Sexy Technical Writing, and to the standards that determine if your document will be effective. Without some level of testing, you won't know if you have done the job...or if your reader is annoyed or frustrated by writing that is not accurate and comprehensible, a design that is not accessible, information that is missing, or even links and design features that simply don't work.

Characteristics of Usable Documents

According to Jakob Nielsen (2012), a usable document or web site must have several key elements.

1. It's easy to learn so that the person can quickly accomplish the desired tasks
2. It's efficient, enabling the person to accomplish the task in a timely manner
3. It's easy to remember the process needed to use the document or web site to accomplish this task
4. It's free from errors, enabling the user to complete the task without mistakes
5. It's satisfying to use...the user will find it pleasant or enjoyable to use this design

In addition, a usable document or website combines utility...it has the functions needed...with usability...how pleasant or easy it is to use.

In addition, it has some other attributes, one of which is utility. Does the document or website do what the user needs it to do? If it meets the criteria above, then it is useful. And useful is essential to effective technical writing or design.

Think about the last time you paid a bill online, or shopped from an Internet site. How easy was it to do what you needed to do? Did you experience any frustration?

Usability Evaluation

The best way to guarantee that your site or document is usable and useful is to evaluate it or test it. How does this work? The methods you choose will largely depend on the size and significance of the project and can range from the simple to the complex.

At the first level, careful proofreading or evaluation of the document using a checklist may reveal areas that need development or clarification. Ask someone to review your draft or prototype and offer suggestions that will improve the design of the document. Most types of usability evaluations involve 3 groups of individuals: Users, the primary audience for the document; subject matter experts (SMEs) who are knowledgeable about the topics of the document or web site; and usability experts, who are trained to determine what questions to ask about the draft or prototype and how to best acquire the answers that will be most useful (Markell, 2015) Usability evaluations also come in different forms, and may include interviewing users ,using a questionnaire or survey, conducting focus groups, and observing users.

Usability Testing for User-Centered Design

Dr. Carol Barnum (2002) identifies the following characteristics of usability testing:

1. The goal is to improve the usability of a product
2. The participants represent real users
3. The participants do real tasks
4. The researchers observe actions and record what the participants say
5. The researchers analyze the findings, diagnose problems, and recommend changes

The important thing to notice here is the inclusion of paid participants, or users, who are representative of the target audience, and a researched protocol that the testing follows. There are a number of testing models, including *lab testing*, *testing without a lab*, and *field testing*.

In the *usability lab* (which is the most expensive and time consuming process) a number of users come into a controlled environment and are given a task to complete in a specific time frame. Observers may watch from behind 2 way mirrors and record what they see or hear or use a television monitor to observe and listen to the participants. Typically a lab requires dedicated space and lots of equipment, including video or audio recording devices.

Figure 1: Usability Lab

Testing without a lab requires a space like an office or conference room where the participants and observer will not be disturbed. The observer may sit next to the participant and record manually or with a recorder what the participants does, or have the participant "think aloud" during a process. Modern technology, like computers or phones with cameras and microphones, make this form of testing easily available and economically feasible, but, according to Jakob Nielson (2012), a notepad and pen are the only equipment you will need.

Figure 2: Usability test without a lab

Field testing means that the observer goes to the user and "tests" in the actual environment that the document or device will be used, and as an added bonus, can observe users in their natural environment with supports and distractions.

What if I Just Skip this Process All Together?

Yes, usability testing can be expensive and time consuming, but in most cases will be worth the time and expense. The costs of not testing a product or program are reflected in the amount of additional training needed to support the users, the competitive advantage of the product or program, the image and reputation of the organization, and the efficient use of employee and client time (Barnum p.23).

Start by Making a Plan

If you are going to conduct a usability test, you have to start with a plan. That's how you will document what you're going to do, how you're going to do it, how many participants you need to recruit, and what you will have them do. In this case, you will be the usability specialist.

For your plan, you need to identify the scope and purpose of the testing, decide when and where you will do the testing, identify the equipment you will need, determine how many sessions you will conduct and how long each will be, and how many participants you think you will need. You must determine what tasks you will be testing, and develop the metrics for evaluation. For example, subjective metrics include the questions you'll ask the participants about ease and pleasure, and quantitative metrics indicate what data about errors, completion rate, or time to complete a task you will collect. You may need to identify your staff and what role other members of the team will play (usability.gov Planning a Usability test).

Recruit the Participants

Once you have a plan, you will recruit your participants. You will try to find people who are as close to your target audience as possible, and you may have multiple users groups. Its okay to use your own colleagues for testing during piloting stages, but not during actual testing. If you are seeking insights, Jakob Neilson states that 5 users will give you as much information as you will need. For quantitative data collection, seeking statistics, you will need at least 20 users. If you are going to conduct iterative testing over the course of developing a document or site, you should have a different group of participants for each test. Lastly, since participants are usually compensated, you will need to decide how you will pay them. Keep in mind that you cannot pay federal employees.

Run the Test!

A typical usability test might look like this:

The facilitator welcomes the participant, explains the test session, and asks any demographic questions. The facilitator will then explains what the participant will do, then explains the task scenario. The participant begins working on the scenario and may think aloud during the process while the observer or facilitator takes notes of what is said and the participant's actions. The session ends when tasks are complete or the mandated time is up, and the facilitator either interviews the participant with end of session subjective questions or thanks the participant, offers the compensation, and escorts the participant from the testing area.

Jen Bergstrom (2013) observes that choosing the best moderation technique for the session depends on the goals of the session. A concurrent think aloud (CTA) is useful for understanding participants thoughts as they work through the task. The retrospective think aloud (RTA) has the participants retrace their steps when the session is complete. Concurrent probing (CP) requires that the facilitator ask follow up questions whenever the participant makes a comment of does something out of the ordinary. Retrospective probing (RP) waits until the end of the session and then asks questions about the participants' thoughts and actions as a follow up. Each method has its pros and cons, and none of them contribute to collecting quantitative metrics data.

Interpret and Record the Data

After you finish conducting your tests, it will be necessary to turn all that data into information that you can use to improve the document or site.   Essentially, you will sort the quantitative data, like performance measures, and the subjective data, like attitude. You will analyze it carefully, looking for problems. Lastly, you will present your research in a report. Here's an example of a usability report for a study conducted on The Purdue OWL.

Don't Forget Accessibility!

Typically, usability testing does not consider the user with a disability.   As a technical communicator, you have a responsibility, both legally and ethically, to produce documents and sites that meet are compliant to Section 508 of the Americans with Disabilities Act. A site that is accessible presents information through multiple channels that allows users with disabilities to access the same information as users without disabilities. Check out the Americans with Disabilities web site, for more information.

Activities and Discussion

- For discussion: Why must you, as a sexy technical writer, need to consider usability evaluation and/or testing through all stages of generating documents or websites?
- For discussion: How does the concept of "usability" support the principle characteristics of effective technical communication?
- Activity or discussion: Take a look at your school's website. Imagine you are going to conduct a usability test on it. What tasks would you generate? What participants would you involve? For example: Find out how a community group not affiliated with the university can book a space to host an event.
- Activity or discussion: Locate a set of instructions for something you own and evaluate the instructions on the basis of the five characteristics of usability. Are you able to suggest improvements to the design?

- Activity or discussion: In small groups, choose some of your favorite websites, examine them, and create a user profile. Your profile will include gender and sex, age, education level, economic status, profession, or whatever else you determin. Then...turn it around. Create a different user profile and identify what changes you would make to improve the site for this new user.
- Activity or discussion: The FEMA (Federal Emergency Management Agency) website has resources for people who need assistance. Consider the usability of the site for an individual with limited computer experience...what would you do to improve the chances of this individual in a flood or hurricane?
- Activity: In the instructions chapter, you created an instruction manual. Recruiting friends or classmates, design a usability test for your manual, conduct it, and then write up the report following the format of a scientific or lab report.

References

Barnum, C. M. (2002). *Usability testing and research.* New York: Pearson Education, Inc.

Bergstrom, J. R. (2013). Moderating usability tests. Retrieved from http://www.usability.gov/how-to-and-tools/methods/running-usability-test.html.

Jameson, D. A. (2013). New options for usability teating projects in business communication courses. *Business Communication Quarterly*, 76(4), 397-411. Doi:10.1177/1080569913493460.

Nielsen, J. (2012). Usability 101: Introduction to usability. Retrieved from: https://www.nngroup.com/articles/usability-101-introduction-to-usability/

U.S. Department of Health and Human Services. (2013). Planning a usability test. Retrieved from http://www.usability.gov/how -to-and-tools-/methods/planning/usability.html.

U.S. Department of Health and Human Services. (2013).Usability evaluation basics. Retrieved from http://www.usability.gov/what-and-why-usability-evaluation.html.

Chapter 7: Collaborative Writing

By: Monique Logan

Objectives

Upon completion of this chapter, readers will be able to:

- Define successful and effective collaborative writing.
- Explain and employ strategies for effective collaboration.
- Explain and employ strategies for dealing with differences and conflict.

Perhaps you are just beginning your collegiate career, or you may be finishing it up. Either way, whether you're someone new to college or someone who has been around the block for a period of time, you've probably had some experience working in a group or on a team of some sort. You've probably been a part of an athletic or academic team. Perhaps not. Perhaps you have some group experience from being a cheerleader, a boy scout or girl scout or a member of the 4H Club. Either way, I'm sure you're familiar with the inner workings of a team or group environment.

But have you been fortunate enough to work collaboratively in a writing capacity? Whether your answer is "yes" or "no," this chapter is designed to help you look more closely at what it means to write collaboratively.

In this chapter, we will focus on writing in groups or teams. Specifically, we will discuss *collaborative writing*, which differs slightly from team and group writing.

1. Collaborative writing defined
2. Successful collaborative writing
3. Ineffective collaborative writing
4. Pulling together your team
5. Strategies for effective collaboration
6. Tools for collaboration
7. Dealing with differences
8. Dealing with conflict
9. Finalizing the project
10. Reflecting for future projects
11. Activities and discussion

What is Collaborative Writing?

Collaborative writing, group writing, team writing, distributed writing – all terms used interchangeably to describe what it generally means to perform collective writing in a professional atmosphere. For our purposes, however, we won't use all of those terms. Why? Because there is a vast difference between collaboration and working in groups or teams; thus, the terms collaborative writing differs greatly from team, group or distributed writing. We will refer to the act of writing together as collaborative writing.

Collaboration involves a mindset that sees the whole as more important than its parts. In other words, when people decide to collaborate, they are deciding to set aside their individual goals for the good of the group or company they represent. Collaboration seeks to combine multiple skill sets, knowledge bases, ideas and engagement from a number of people for the sole purpose of accomplishing a goal that benefits all – regardless of position or title. A collaborative mindset is focused on company success more than it is individual success.

Conversely, team and group writing tends to focus on gathering together for a period of time to accomplish a set goal for a certain project during a specific time or event. It does not necessarily entail a long-term, ingrained mindset that seeks constant success for the good of the company or group. So, collaboration differs from teams and groups because it requires every member of the group or team to take responsibility for the final outcome. It's what happens, for example, when the parents of a child see the success of that child as the responsibility of both parents, not just one. Collaboration is the reason that companies such as Cisco and Coca Cola thrive. According to Ron Ricci and Carl Wiese, authors of *The Collaboration Imperative* (2011), a company's success lies within the people they employ. "It's not hiding in a budget spreadsheet or a warehouse full of inventory. It lies within your people – in their ideas, their experiences, their focus, their energy. The more you empower them to share their knowledge and skills, the more successful your organization will be. From ideas come innovation and new forms of productivity."

In their 2015 book *Collaboration Begins with You: Be a Silo Buster*, best-selling author and management expert Ken Blanchard along with co-authors Jane Ripley and Eunice Parisi-Carew discuss what collaboration means. "Collaboration is a whole order of magnitude beyond teams. It's in the DNA of the company culture," they write. The authors continue, "It's an environment that promotes communication, learning, maximum contribution, and innovation – which, of course, all lead to healthy profits." Thus, successful collaborative writing stems from a company culture that invites collaboration not just writing by way of teams and groups.

Collaborative writing, then, can be defined as...

> *Writing that entails the collaborative efforts of a group of people who gather together to write documentation, produce images, provide subtext, and more in an effort to bring a project to completion. Members can work in spaces that are face-to-face or virtual. The main goal of collaborative writing is to produce the best work for the good of the company by including the ideas and skill sets of multiple authors.*

Why Write Collaboratively

In today's ever-changing, fast paced world of information, technology and social media, it is increasingly necessary to engage people who are able to contribute a varied set of skills, specialties and who come from various cultures in an effort to produce information that best reflects the company it represents. Today, people in government, science and technology are called upon on a regular basis to communicate large bodies of information in the best and most cost-efficient way possible with an outcome that allows a broad range of people from various backgrounds and walks of life to not only access the information, but to understand the information set forth. Thus, collaborative groups of writers have become more important than ever, making information even more accessible to multiple groups of people.

But collaborative writing is not something that happens in a vacuum, nor is it magically produced after a brief period of writing. Collaborative writing, like all other types of writing is something that requires exercising the process of writing. And it is something that requires time and labor. And, the results can be rewarding. Companies all over the world have found that writing collaboratively can produce favorable outcomes for their better interests. This, however, does not come without costs. While there are many benefits to collaborative writing, there are also disadvantages if the project morphs into team or group writing.

Successful Collaborative Writing

Collaborative writing has many benefits. Because many companies believe the advantages of collaborative writing outweigh the disadvantages, many companies choose to have employees work together on projects with writers as a part of those teams.

But the positive results often attained on company projects rely heavily on the formulation of the team, skill sets, and positive group dynamics, something we'll talk about a little later. For now, let's look at the advantages of collaborative writing below.

1. **Collaborative writing creates a more enjoyable work environment**. Because members of the team share the responsibilities of the project or writing, they must communicate verbally, electronically, and in some instances they must communicate virtually. These interactions often work to improve and foster a collegial atmosphere, producing a workplace that adds to the overall good of the company.
2. **Collaborative writing creates a product that considers diverse audiences**. When a team is created with the thought of diversity, the work they produce tends to be more sensitive to varied cultures and

audiences. If, for example, the team incorporates the skill sets of women, men, members of the LGBT community, cis and non-cis males and females as well as members of various races and cultures, the final product will have taken into consideration the complexities of multiple communities, something that is not so easily attained by a single community of writers .

3. **Collaborative writing provides an opportunity for employees – both new and not-so-new – to explore skills as both leaders and subordinate team members**. A sage once said, "To be a good leader, you must learn to follow." Now and then a true leader is born, but a really successful leader is one who has learned to follow. Employees who have been groomed and allowed to rise through the ranks often make the most successful leaders because they are able to understand the tasks at hand and empathize with the challenges created as a result of the task. Likewise, when organizations choose to rotate the roles of team members, it allows employees to participate in roles such as team lead, recorder, researcher, editor, reporter, and more.

4. **Collaborative writing fosters engagement through active learning**. When employees write collaboratively, they put themselves in a position to either learn from or hone their dormant skills as they work with colleagues who may be more adept at a certain skill than they are.

5. **Collaborative writing helps to grow the organization**. When all of the members of the team see their contribution as not just important but imperative to the success of the project, they contribute as an owner rather than a worker, ultimately affecting the bottom line – profit. And when a company has become successful as a result of fully engaged employees who see their contributions as the reasons behind the company's success, the longevity of the company is inevitable.

6. **Collaborative writing produces a superior product or outcome**. When performed correctly (see notes above about what true collaborative writing is and is not), the end result of the project will be more superior to anything produced outside of collaboration because the most advanced skills will have been utilized and because the members of the team will have drawn on their commitment to the end result for the good of not just themselves but for the good of the entire company.

7. **Collaborative writing draws on the use of technology**. With the emergence of so many new collaboration tools and other technological advances designed to make writing more efficient, employees are better able to engage with their colleagues and produce projects in less time and with fewer obstacles than they could without those tools. There are various types of collaboration tools, including e-mail, voicemail, instant messaging (IM), VoiP video call (or voice over IP), online calendars, wikis and shared document workspaces.

A Look at Successful Collaboration

Establish Clear Objectives and Tasks

Successful collaboration is created by the use of several strategies, including the ability to establish clear objectives and tasks. Just as with individual writing, team writing must employ clear objectives. It is imperative for the success of the project that the objective is clear from the outset. Clear objectives serve as a goal or end result the team aims to achieve. Those goals or objectives serve as a sort of "lighthouse" that can be seen from a distance to help guide the members to "safe harbors" or guide the members to a successful end result.

Each member of the team should know from the start what is expected of her. She should know her specific part and the connection of that part to the tasks and roles of other team members. Each member should see her role as important and one, which, if not completed with an inside-out mindset (a term created by Blanchard, Ripley and Parisi-Carew to indicate the need for collaboration to start on the inside of a person's heart, move to her intellect and finally to the hands – where the work occurs), will negatively impact the project.

It is important, then, that the team develop a space to meet and discuss the project – to ask questions, share ideas, provide input on the overall project, etc.

Conduct Effective Meetings

Another strategy of successful collaboration is the ability to conduct effective meetings that allow members to comfortably share their views and expertise. Being able to do so is often contingent on the ability of the team to employ careful listening skills versus just allowing a member to speak where team members just hear what is being shared. The difference in the two – listening versus hearing – is defined by intent and purpose. In *The Science and Art of Listening* (2012), Seth Horowitz delineates the two this way: "The difference between the sense of hearing and the skill of listening is attention." In order to listen versus hear what is being said, then, you must choose (or intend) to understand what is being said, you must give your attention to what is being said. "Listening is a skill that we're in danger of losing in a world of digital distraction and information overload." (Horowitz, 2012). "The richness of life doesn't lie in the loudness and the beat," he continues, "but in the timbres and the variations that you can discern if you simply pay attention." (Horowitz, 2012).

Set a Project Schedule

Successful collaboration is also dependent upon setting a project schedule. In today's technological world, there is an abundance of tools that enable teams to successfully achieve their end result by have a clear view of what is needed and when. Tools such as *WorkZone*, *Basecamp*, and *Microsoft Project*, among others, allow teams to know the schedule of their project and see the progress throughout.

Keep Them Honest

Maintaining a sense of ethical responsibility toward the project and team members is not only important, but it is imperative for the success of the project. In *Business Ethics: Concepts and Cases* (2011), Manuel G. Velasquez outlines ethical standards that are helpful to consider in collaborative situations.

- *Rights*: Everyone has a right to engage in intellectual discussions at work without fear of reprisal. Likewise, when a document or product is produced, the general public has a right to expect that honesty was central in its production.
- *Justice*: Everyone should receive the same justice regardless of race, gender, or sexual orientation. Team members should be treated the same. If not, the team can become divided into separate "camps," and the project can, in turn, become derailed.
- *Utility*: Consideration should be given for how group decisions will impact all involved. When the group operates as one unit, members will consider the impact that decisions will have on each of its members. The idea of operating as silos is thrown out of the window because it is understood that what affects one affects all.
- *Care*: Because the group operates from the "inside-out" mindset (heart-head-hand), care is given to those who are closest to members and with whom members work.

Encourage Discussion and Diversity

Finally, successful collaboration is contingent upon the very definition of collaboration as discussed earlier in the chapter – fostering an environment that promotes communication, learning, maximum contribution, and innovation. (Blanchard, Ripley, Parisi-Carew, 2012). In other words, team members must feel comfortable sharing and at times debating about their ideas. Members should be allowed to fully operate in the diversity they bring to the team. No team member should be made to feel that her contribution is less important than that of other team members because she may be differently abled. Likewise, a team member who is a part of the LGBTQ community, even if his sexual orientation is not considered a part of the majority in the workplace, should be allowed to communicate ideas on the project from his perspective. Allowing a contribution of ideas from diverse perspectives is best for the project because it takes into consideration the diverse audience who will most likely be the readers of the project. In the end, openness in discussion creates a product that considers the audience, a primary rule in writing for technical audiences.

In his article "6 Fundamentals of Effective Collaboration" (2010) that appeared in *Talent Culture World of Work*, Chris Jones, an IT Strategy and Change Management consultant, muses on his "secret sauce" ingredients for effective collaboration. Jones identifies six ideas he insists is necessary for effective collaboration.

- Engagement
- Keeping it real (being authentic)
- A bias for learning and discovery
- Respect for community members
- Driving a positive vibe
- Focus on results

Notice the similarities between the four standards identified by Velasquez (2011) and the six ideas listed by Jones (2010). Indeed, without these, collaboration in writing or in any other team setting will not be successful.

How is Collaboration Viewed in the Working World?: A View from the U.S. Office of Personnel Management (OPM)

In guiding federal employees on creating work environments that best reflect the vision and policies of the federal government, the Office of Personnel Management produced documentation that encourage collaborative team environments. The OPM cites the following as requirements for successful collaboration

- Have a common purpose and goal
- Trust each other
- Clarify roles
- Communicate openly and effectively
- Appreciate diversity
- Balance the team's focus

Ineffective Collaborative Writing

When collaborative writing morphs back to a team or silo mindset, it creates situations that work against the good of the group. Keep the following in mind as you establish your team and as you work through the project.

- **Avoid the "Me" syndrome** where too many people seek the role of leadership. When a clear hierarchy and roles have not been established in the group, the inevitable outcome is that you develop disjointed teams, thereby developing a disjointed project. This takes away from the collaborative environment.
- **Avoid the development of a multi-voice project** where an agreed upon voice does not come through in the project. Having an agreed upon style sheet can help to alleviate this problem. Another strategy to avoid creating a multi-voice project is to establish a team member or members as editors who review the final draft, checking specifically for the voice and tone of the message.
- **Avoid the tendency to have one or a few people shoulder the load of the team**. This is sometimes created when ethical standards are not maintained and when members feel de-valued. When this happens, other members of the team who feel alienated tend to lose motivation to work, often abandoning the project.
- **Avoid the tendency to engage in groupthink** where members care more about getting along and becoming friends than they do about the goal of the project.
- **Avoid the tendency to side with certain persons based on traits held in common** when a conflict arises. Always maintain the goal and purpose of the project so that conflict resolution is paramount for the good of the team and the project.

Scenarios for Consideration

Scenario #1

You work as a technical communicator for Apple, Inc. You have been charged with pulling together a team of writers, graphic artists, and subject matter experts (SME) to produce instructions for the latest Mac Book. The instructions must be produced in 30 days, a shorter time period than the three months typically given for such a project.

After assembling the team, assigning tasks and setting a schedule, you find that two of the team members, a subject matter expert and technical writer, have had past conflicts and have since found it difficult to work together. You pull the two team members aside, listen to each of their positions and insist that they leave the past behind them for the good of the project.

Two weeks pass, and you find that the two have not met to discuss their tasks. The problem with this is that other tasks given to other members of the team heavily rely on the SME and writer meeting to get the ball rolling.

As the project lead, you call the two together again to help them work through their differences. During the meeting you inform the SME that she must acknowledge her past fault for the good of the project. You say nothing to the writer about her contribution to the past conflict.

Consequently, the work on the project begins, but the spirit of the group is at an all time low at every group meeting. The project is finished, albeit two weeks late.

While presenting the finished product to the executive team, the response is negative, and you, the team lead find that the blame has been placed on you for not producing a superior product.

Questions for consideration:

- What, if anything, went wrong?
- What, if anything, could have been done differently to produce different results?
- Considering the suggestions above for successful collaboration, which guidelines were or were not followed?
- As a mentor to the team lead, what specific suggestions would you give her for her next project?

Scenario #2

Sherry, an environmental engineer working for the Environmental Protection Agency (EPA), was chosen as the team lead on a project designed to provide a clearer understanding for the community of the EPA's role in the new water project being instituted for the *Clean River Initiative* in the Greenspane Chattahoochhee Community. In order to fulfill her responsibility to her employer and the community, she recognized the need to produce documents – pamphlets, posters, blogs, radio advertisements, etc. in preparation for the upcoming festival a year away to unveil the project to the community.

Sherry enlisted the help of several members from various departments of the EPA, including Valarie, a production design assistant; Ricky, a systems engineer; Gabriella, community outreach coordinator; Myron, a health educator; and Erin, technical writer.

Once assembled, Sherry explained the project and the need for the group to understand the "," approach – the need to focus on the heart of the project followed by their intellect followed by the use of their hands. In other words, Sherry explained that the end result was contingent upon the entire team to see the project as something they all owned and were doing for the good of the organization and the community. "In the end," Sherry explained, "the community will benefit and have access to clean drinking water, which in turn will impact the cleanliness of all rivers."

The team came together to create a strategy for how best to communicate the message that clean rivers produce better health, which creates a stronger community. Working over a period of 12-14 months, the project came together as Sherry and her team created events that involved the community and that explained the connection of health to clean water vs. dirty water. The events included documents created by Valarie based on research produced by Diana and written by Sam. Ricky, in turn, saw to it that the documents created could be used across technological mediums such as social media, television, radio, and the internet.

The outcome was an event that the entire team and the organization could claim as their own, for they all played integral parts in making the project a success.

Questions for consideration:

- What, if anything, went wrong?
- What, if anything, could have been done differently to produce different results?
- Considering the suggestions above for successful collaboration, which guidelines were or were not followed?
- As a mentor to the team lead, what specific suggestions would you give her for her next project?

References

Blanchard, K., Ripley, J, Parisi-Carew, E. (2015). *Collaboration begins with you: be a silo buster*. Oakland: Polvera Publishing.

Horowitz, S. (2012). The science and art of listening. Retrieved from http://www.nytimes.com/2012/11/11/opinion/sunday/why-listening-is-so-much-more-than-hearing.html?_r=0

Jones, C. (2010). 6 Fundamentals of effective collaboration. Retrieved from http://www.talentculture.com/6-fundamentals-of-effective-collaboration/

Ricci, R. and Wiese, C. (2011). The collaboration imperative: executive strategies for unlocking your organization's true potential. Retrieved from http://thecollaborationimperative.com/wordpress/wp-content/uploads/2012/01/584_CiscoBook_Final-01-copy.pdf

United States Office of Personnel Management (1997). Retrieved from https://www.opm.gov/policy-data-oversight/performance-management/teams/building-a-collaborative-team-environment/

Velasquez, M.G. (2011). Business ethics: Concepts and cases. Upper Saddle River, NJ: Pearson.

Chapter 8: Technical Editing

By: Jonathan Arnett

Objectives

Upon completion of this chapter, readers will be able to:

1. Explain the general procedure for technical editing.
2. Explain the different levels of edit.
3. Explain the purposes of style guides and style sheets.
4. Use copyediting symbols appropriately.
5. Use proofreading symbols appropriately.

This chapter focuses on editing technical documents. In particular, this chapter will address some of the most common types of technical editing you can do, as well as processes, resources, and techniques you can use.

1. Overview of technical editing
2. General procedure for editing
3. Contracts
4. Levels of edit
5. Editors' resources
6. Strategies for writing comments
7. Strategies for marking up technical materials
8. Hard-copy editing marks
9. Special ideas for editing visual materials
10. Special ideas for editing websites

Overview of Technical Editing

You may find that technical editing is very different from what you expect. When people hear the word "edit," they think of rewriting an author's words; working with authors on issues such as character plot, and storyline; suggesting the most appropriate word in order to make a manuscript "sing." That's not technical editing.

Instead, technical editing is a highly rhetorical, detail-oriented process of ensuring that specialized information appears so that it is appropriate for end users, and technical editors make informed, thoughtful suggestions for improvement toward that purpose.

Technical editing is a collaborative process with authors, who are often subject-matter experts (SMEs, pronounced "smees"), to check correctness of such things as chemical formulas, specialized terminology, equations, and matchups between textual and visual elements, as well as more traditional aspects of writing.

Technical editing is a recursive process, not a one-and-done routine. Technical editors often review the same materials multiple times and have their edits reviewed before the materials are printed or posted online. Only rarely will technical editors make changes and then publish the materials immediately.

Technical editing covers a surprisingly wide variety of subjects, contexts, and materials. Job ads for technical editors seek people who can comment on—and create new—paper documents, electronic documents, images, visual designs, websites, audio and video files, and multimedia presentations, just to name a few examples.

This chapter will focus on editing text on hard copy, soft copy, and websites, but it will also provide you with concepts and techniques that you can use in graphics-heavy and multimedia editing tasks.

General Procedure for Editing

The way you go about editing technical materials will depend on multiple factors. You will need to consider the artifact you are editing—is it mostly text? does it contain visuals? is it mostly visuals? is it paper-based or in electronic format? does it contain multimedia content? is it static or interactive?—and the type of edits that you are responsible for making. Even so, you can use the same general strategy when approaching most technical editing projects:

1. Analyze the materials' purpose, audience, format, and uses.
2. Evaluate the materials to see if they fit. In particular, consider the materials'
    1. contents — completeness; appropriateness
    2. organization — order of contents; signals about order
    3. visual design — text; lists; tables; aesthetic appearance
    4. navigability — findable, working hyperlinks; section breaks
    5. style — writing style; authorial persona; sentence structures; cultural biases; grammar; mechanics
    6. illustrations — type; construction; placement
    7. accessibility — ADA compliance
3. Set up objectives and plan your project's sequence.
4. Review the plan with the author.
5. Edit the materials.
6. Evaluate the outcome.

Editor-Client Contracts

Sometimes, you and the technical materials' creator will work inside the same organization. In this case, your job title and job description likely already define your relationship with the creator, and both you and the creator will have set responsibilities and deadlines.

Other times, you may be editing materials for a client, a person who is not your coworker. In this case, you need to write a contract that defines your professional relationship with your client.

At the least, a contract should specify

- the type of materials you will edit
- the number of items
- the length (or size) of the materials
- the format of the materials
- the level of edit
- the deliverable (what you will return to your client)
- a schedule for completion
- your compensation

A clearly written contract benefits both yourself and your client. You will not be overworked or underpaid, and both you and your client will know what to expect and when to expect it.

As a general rule of thumb, if you are an inexperienced editor, double your estimate of how long it will take you to edit a project, and charge a per-hour or per-page rate. Once you are more experienced and know how quickly you can actually edit, you can charge a per-project flat fee.

Levels of Edit

When you begin an editing project, avoid the temptation of diving in and making any-and-all changes that you think will be valuable. Instead, find out what "level of edit" you need to perform, and stick to it.

A "level of edit" defines how "deep" you should go with your edits. Levels range from superficial to extremely deep. Many different levels of edit can exist; experts disagree about how many levels of edit are necessary and what the different levels should involve, and some types of materials may not require specific levels of edit. Even so, you can use three basic levels for most technical editing projects:

1. **Consistency and correctness.** Edit for surface-level issues such as spelling, punctuation, grammar, word use, page numbering, cross-references, and color consistency. Changes from these edits will not deeply impact the document as a whole.
2. **Visual readability.** Edit for substantive issues such as typeface choices and consistency; graphic elements' locations, sizes, labels, and captions; and document layout. Changes from these edits may have ripple effects across a document and create new errors with consistency and correctness.
3. **Content and structure.** Edit for deep issues such as internal organization, sentence structures, logical flaws, image appropriateness, and overall meaning. Changes from these edits often require fundamental changes in the document and may create entirely new problems with other levels of edit.

When you edit any technical materials, do multiple passes through the material, moving from the deepest to the most superficial level of edit. That way, you will avoid wasting your time on marking up or correcting surface-level problems that will be deleted anyway.

If you see a problem that is outside your responsibility as an editor—for example, if you see a logical problem but you're only responsible for fixing comma splices—note the issue and contact someone with the authority to correct the problem.

Editors' Resources

When you edit technical materials, consult a style guide or style sheet, and create a style sheet of your own.

Style Guides

A style guide is an existing, authoritative source that lays out rules for the materials you are editing. For example, you have almost definitely used a dictionary at some point in your life, and if you have taken a first-year composition course, you have used a writer's handbook. Both of these examples are style guides.

Many technical editors use their employers' own in-house style guides, but many technical editors also use commercially-available style guides. Some that are commonly used in technical communication include *Scientific Style and Format: The CSE Manual for Authors, Editors, and Publishers*, the *APA Publication Manual*, and the *Chicago Manual of Style*.

Specialized style guides for highly technical subject matter also exist. If you are editing materials that require specialized knowledge, consult an appropriate style guide. For example, if you're editing documentation for factory-control equipment that will be exported to Russia, refer to *The English-Russian Dictionary of Mechanical Engineering and Industrial Automation*.

Always be prepared to justify your edits with a style guide reference. If you make up your own rules or follow your gut instinct instead of following a style guide, your author may reject your edits, or worse, you may introduce new errors.

Style Sheets

Style sheets are small-scale, local style guides that provide consistent, quick-reference answers to common problems. Technical editors often develop style sheets to cover separate-but-related projects or different phases of a major project, and to make sure that all the editors on a project are following the same rules.

You should compile your own style sheet every time you edit anything. Do not simply list every error you encounter. Instead, list recurring errors or problems with answers that you need to look up frequently, and alphabetize the contents to make them easy to navigate.

Strategies for Writing Comments

When you edit technical materials, do not simply insert corrections unless the edits are simple or you have explicit permission to make final decisions. Instead, write comments to the author and suggest changes.

Before you write the comments, analyze the person you're writing to. Who is the author that created the materials you are editing? How will this person react to your comments? People are often very sensitive to criticism of their writing.

When you write the comments, actively think about the words and sentence structures that you use. Some authors are more open to criticism than others, but even receptive authors will ignore weak comments and balk at rudely stated commands.

Write your editorial comments using the strategies that Mackiewicz and Riley (2003) suggest:

- **Opinion**
  - *"I would use Verdana for the document's typeface."*
  - State your opinion if you mean the author should make a change.
- **Suggestion with an active modal verb**
  - *"You should probably use Verdana as the document's typeface. It'll make the text more readable onscreen."*
  - Combine a strong suggestion with "should," will," or "ought" if you mean the author should make a change. You can include a "downgrader" such as "probably" to soften the tone. You can, but don't have to, explain the payoff.
- **Command**
  - *"Use Verdana as the document's typeface, please. It'll make the text more readable onscreen."*
  - Issue a command if you mean the author should make a change. You can include a "downgrader" to soften the tone. You can, but don't have to, explain the payoff.
- **Possibility statement with an active verb**
  - *"You could use Verdana as the document's typeface. That's just an idea. It would make the text more readable onscreen."*
  - Make a suggestion with "can" or "could" if you are suggesting a non-mandatory option. You might also state the payoff.
- **Question**
  - *"Could you change the document's typeface to Verdana?"*
  - Ask a question only if you don't know the answer. Otherwise, avoid this strategy.
- **Suggestion with a passive voice modal verb**
  - *"The document's typeface should be changed to Verdana."*
  - Avoid this strategy.
- **Possibility statement with a passive voice modal verb**
  - *"The document's typeface could be changed to Verdana."*
  - Avoid this strategy.
- **Hint**
  - *"Using a sans serif font for a document that will appear onscreen increases the document's readability."*
  - Avoid this strategy.

Strategies for Marking Up Technical Materials

When you edit technical materials, your specific actions will depend on the type of editing and the materials' format.

Technical editors help develop technical communication artifacts as well as review them just before they are published. Before you begin editing, make sure you know which approach you should take.

Editing during the developmental phase is called **copyediting**. This type of editing may involve "shaping" the document through deep edits and multiple comments to the materials' author. Documents that are being copyedited in hard copy are often (but not always) double-spaced.

Editing during the pre-production phase is called **proofreading**. Ideally, proofreading should only require a superficial level of edit because it requires an editor to look for differences between the approved "dead copy" that has been edited multiple times and the first printed proof version—the "galley"—that will be reproduced and published. Documents that are being proofread in hard copy (on paper) are almost always single-spaced.

Procedural Markup vs. Structural Markup

Technical editors use different types of markup on text that depend on the editing goals and the edited materials' format. These approaches are complementary, not opposite.

Procedural markup involves going through a document and marking specific changes. A common example is correcting misspelled words or deleting blank spaces. You may also use procedural markup to provide instructions for changing a document's layout and design.

Structural markup involves "tagging" sections of a document to indicate they belong to specific categories. It is akin to using the Styles function of MS Word.

You can also combine the two approaches by using procedural markup to indicate textual changes and structural markup to indicate formatting changes.

(Times 12/14 FL RR) in one package, several areas of technical communication and rhetoric of science that are addressed separately in the present scholarship. The theoretical cornerstones of this project will be Habermas's concept of the ideal speech communication situation and pragma-dialectic argumentation.

Ideal Speech Communication Situation *(Trebuchet 14 bf)*

(Times 12/14 FL RR) Habermas's ideal speech communication situation is strongly analogous to how scientific discourse is supposed to work; *i.e.*, an unconstrained dialectic interchange among members of an intellectual community, oriented toward finding truth. In Habermas's terms, the ideal speech communication situation depends on communicative action that is free from strategic action and takes place in the public sphere, which is part of the lifeworld. In the paragraphs below, I define each of these terms and briefly explain how I will use them in my dissertation analysis.

Communicative Action *(Trebuchet 13 bf ital)*

(Times 12/14 FL RR) Communicative action can be thought of as the instantiation of critical discourse within the public sphere. Dayton (2002) describes it as "communication aimed at coming to an understanding with others, the primordial form of human communication from which all other forms are derived" (p. 365). In order to qualify as communicative action, though, Habermas provides four criteria—Comprehensibility, Truthfulness, Sincerity, and Legitimacy—that must be fulfilled.

I have reproduced, in rough form, a chart for applying these four principles:

(Trebuchet 10 centered ital bf) *(Trebuchet 10/12 FL RR bf)*

Norms of Practical Communication	Comprehensibility	Truth	Sincerity	Legitimacy
Corresponding questions	"What's this mean?"	"Is this true?"	"Can we trust?"	"Is this justified?"
Evidence of systematically distorted communication	Public exclusion by jargon	Information withheld; responsibility obscured; need misrepresented	Rhetorical reassurances; expression of false concern; hiding motives	Unresponsiveness; assertion of rationalizations; professional dominance
Suggestions for preventing distortions	Minimizing jargon; creating public review committees	Utilizing independent/critical third-party expertise	Organizing counteradvocates; checking with contacts, networks	Making decisions participatory; checking with affected persons

Figure 1: Procedural markup

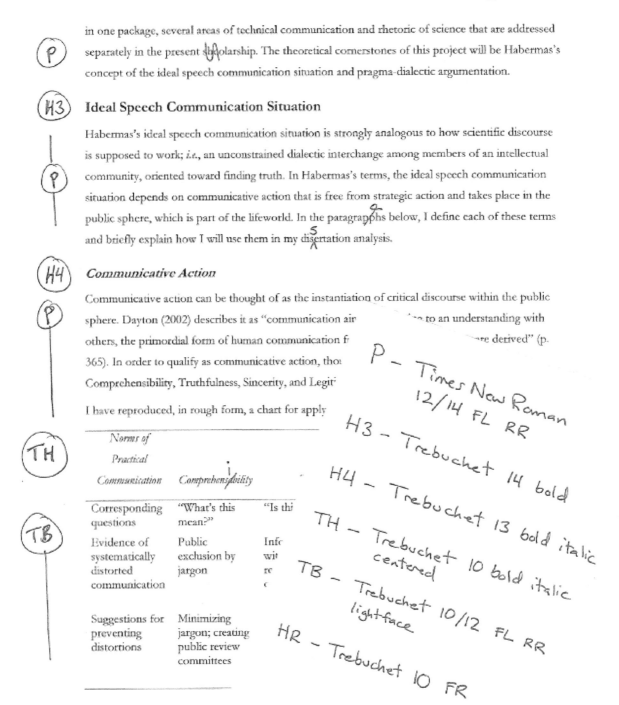

Figure 2: Structural markup

Hard Copy Materials

It is becoming less and less common for editors to work in hard copy (on paper), but it still happens. You may find that editing on paper is easier on your eyes, or that until you learn how to use a program's editing tools, editing on paper may be faster.

If you do choose to print out and mark up technical materials, you should follow a few standard procedures.

- Mark changes to text inside each page's main body. (Except if you're proofreading. In that case, mark changes in the margins.)
- Mark changes to layout in the margins.
- Write comments to the author in the margins, and label them as comments. "AU:" is a common label.
- Circle any marginal notes that are instructions.
- Use standard marks that other people will understand, not your own made-up marks.
- Choose the simplest markup.
- Clarify potentially ambiguous marks. (For example, if you insert a lower-case letter L, write it in cursive, and/or circle the letters "el" next to it.)

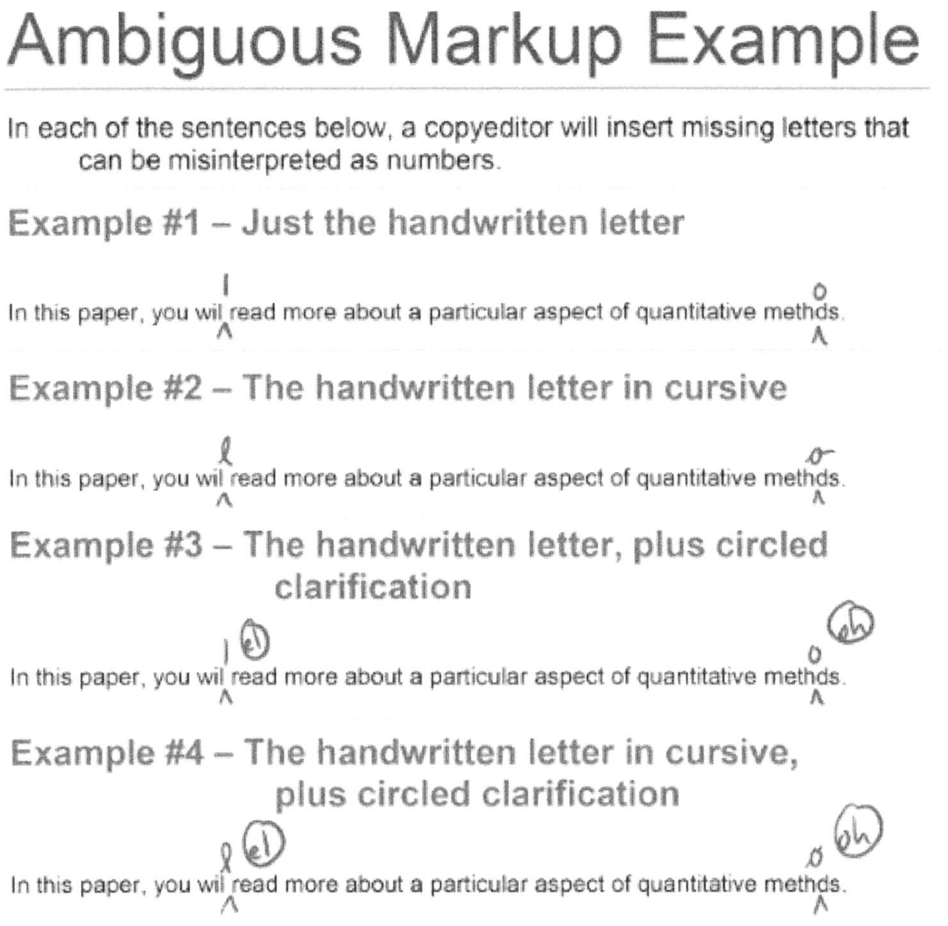

Ambiguous Markup Example

In each of the sentences below, a copyeditor will insert missing letters that can be misinterpreted as numbers.

Example #1 – Just the handwritten letter

In this paper, you wil read more about a particular aspect of quantitative methds.

Example #2 – The handwritten letter in cursive

In this paper, you wil read more about a particular aspect of quantitative methds.

Example #3 – The handwritten letter, plus circled clarification

In this paper, you wil read more about a particular aspect of quantitative methds.

Example #4 – The handwritten letter in cursive, plus circled clarification

In this paper, you wil read more about a particular aspect of quantitative methds.

Figure 3: Ambiguous markup

- Be consistent, and mark every instance of an error.
- Use a bright-colored (not blue or black) pen or pencil, with a medium tip.
- Erase all stray marks. They can be misinterpreted as instructions to make changes.
- Be neat. Scribbles, squiggles, and smears will only confuse the author and/or your fellow editors, and you may cover up important items.
- If you use structural markup, provide a legend that specifies each tag's formatting requirements.

Soft Copy Materials

More and more often, technical editors work in soft copy (on a computer). Doing so lets you avoid double-handling documents, erase mistakes, revise comments and markup, track versions easily, and automate repetitive tasks.

If you edit in soft copy, you should follow slightly different standard procedures:

- Use programs' built-in tools to write comments to authors.
    - On MS Word, highlight text and click **Insert > Comment**.
    - On Acrobat or Acrobat Reader, use the **Comment** menu. Click in the document and use the "Add sticky note" function, or highlight text and click "Add note to text."
- If you edit text on a word processor (for example, MS Word), activate the program's change-tracker and actually make changes. Don't just mark problems.
- If you edit text on a layout program (for example, InDesign) or a PDF handler (for example Acrobat or Acrobat Reader), mark up the document using the program's built-in commenting tools. Then, revise the text in a word processor and re-create the document.
- Apply structural markup instead of just marking for it. Use document templates, high-level formatting tools (such as MS Word Styles), and/or tagging languages (such as HTML or XML).
- Use find-and-replace tools to fix repeated errors.
- Use accept/reject functions to incorporate or reject changes and delete editors' comments.
- Toggle between viewing the edited document with markup and the document without markup. Without the change-tracker's highlighting, you may see new problems "hiding" in plain sight.

Hard Copy Editing Marks

Editors in many disciplines use two fairly standard sets of marks that you can use to tag hard copy documents. One set is specifically for **copyediting**; it assumes that the edited document will be double-spaced, with lots of room between the lines for an editor's scribbling. The other set is specifically for **proofreading**; it assumes that the edited document will be single-spaced.

There is some crossover between copyediting marks and proofreading marks, but they are not interchangeable. Keep them separate.

Copyediting Symbols

Symbol	Meaning	Example
ℓ	delete	I love edҩiting!
ℓ	delete, close up	I also love proof⌒reading!
✗ /	replace letter	Melinda went into a trᵉnce.
——	delete word	It's in the the back yard.
✗ ∧	insert	My telephone kept ringing all night.
|	insert space	Why won't he goaway?
#	insert space	The graffitiletters were unreadable.
∽	transpose	You should trasnpose the letters.
⌒	close up space	Eliminate the ext ra space.
≡	capitalize	john works at the ibm factory in ohio.
=	small caps	The alarm rang at 6 a.m.
/	lower case	It's not a Federal case.

Figure 4: Copyediting symbols - words and letters

Copyediting Symbols

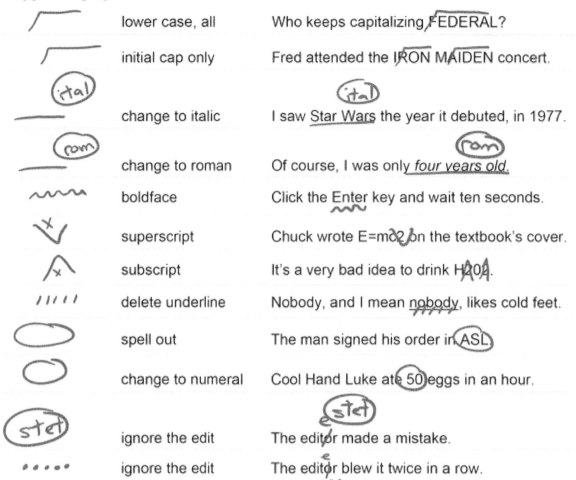

⌐	lower case, all	Who keeps capitalizing FEDERAL?
⌐	initial cap only	Fred attended the IRON MAIDEN concert.
(ital)	change to italic	I saw Star Wars the year it debuted, in 1977.
(rom)	change to roman	Of course, I was only *four years old.*
∿∿∿	boldface	Click the Enter key and wait ten seconds.
✓	superscript	Chuck wrote $E=mc^2$ on the textbook's cover.
∧	subscript	It's a very bad idea to drink H_2O_2.
/////	delete underline	Nobody, and I mean nobody, likes cold feet.
⬭	spell out	The man signed his order in ASL.
⬭	change to numeral	Cool Hand Luke ate 50 eggs in an hour.
(stet)	ignore the edit	The editor made a mistake.
• • • • •	ignore the edit	The editor blew it twice in a row.

Figure 5: Copyediting symbols - text formatting

Copyediting Symbols

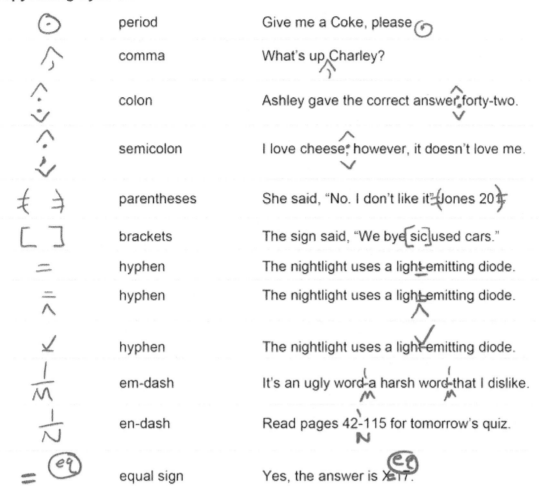

⊙	period	Give me a Coke, please⊙
⌄	comma	What's up Charley?
:	colon	Ashley gave the correct answer forty-two.
;	semicolon	I love cheese however, it doesn't love me.
( )	parentheses	She said, "No. I don't like it" Jones 201
[ ]	brackets	The sign said, "We bye sic used cars."
=	hyphen	The nightlight uses a light-emitting diode.
=	hyphen	The nightlight uses a light emitting diode.
⤫	hyphen	The nightlight uses a light emitting diode.
―M―	em-dash	It's an ugly word a harsh word that I dislike.
―N―	en-dash	Read pages 42-115 for tomorrow's quiz.
= eq	equal sign	Yes, the answer is X=17.

Copyediting symbols - punctuation marks

Copyediting Symbols

Symbol	Meaning	Example
¶	paragraph break	She liked it. Zhaleh raced out the door.
⌐	line break	Poetry often uses line breaks inside sentences.
∽	run together	You've gotta be crazy if you think I'm going to eat fricasseed squirrel.
≋	set as a paragraph, not as a list	Elise bought many kinds of books, including • paperbacks • hardbacks • ebooks
⌐ or (fL)	justify left	Why is this line indented?
⌐ or (fR)	justify right	Align this text to the right margin.
][	center	This line should be centered.
(RR)	ragged right	Full-justified text can look peculiar, especially when "lakes" and "rivers" of white form in its middle, or the words' spacing gets stretched, as is happening in this short paragraph. See?.
‖	align	No way, man. I don't follow your silly rules. Free spirits like me…we just gotta be free.

Copyediting symbols - spacing and positioning

Copyediting Symbols

Symbol	Meaning	Example
align	align	This should be fun. I'm going to align every line behind the first letter "e." Why? Because I can. Note the top and bottom vertical lines.
□	indent one em	□ You need to indent this line just a tad more.
2 or □□	indent two ems	□□ Indent this line twice as much.
2	indent all text by two ems	2 There is no need to update your information with any merchants who automatically bill to your account.
transpose	transpose words	What is going the heck on here?
(	close up vertical space	Charley started typing his paper at noon yesterday and has already hit a thousand pages. I'm worried about him.
#>	insert vertical space between lines	**Famous Movie Villains** Darth Vader is one of the most iconic baddies in the history of cinema.

Copyediting symbols - alignment and spacing

Proofreading Symbols

Special Rules for Proofreading

Put marks in both the margin and in the text.

If there is more than one error on a line, list them in order, and put slashes between their marks.

margin mark	in-text mark			
ϙ	ϙ	delete	ϙ	Deleteₑing extra letters is easy.
ϙ	ϙ	delete, close up	ϙ	Freeₑway is one word, not two.
the letter	/	replace letter	e	Melinda was a Ghostbustₑr for Halloween.
ϙ	ϙ	delete word	ϙ	Cut out extra extra words.
the letter(s)	∧	insert letter(s)	PP	The leaky faucet drₑed all night.
the word	∧	insert word	word	Oh, my...the most important is missing.
#	|	insert space	#	There should be space between the words.
tr	∽	transpose	tr	Switch the lettₑrs' order.
⌒	⌒	close up space	⌒	Delete the emp ty space inside the word.
Cap	=	capitalize	Cap	I think my keyboard's right shift key is broken.

Figure 9: Proofreading symbols - words and letters

Proofreading Symbols

Symbol	Mark	Meaning	Symbol	Example
(sc)	=	small caps	(sc)	The paper is due at 11:59 p.m.
(lc)	/	lower case	(lc)	Charlene visited the State capitol building.
(lc)	⌐	lower case, all	(lc)	You've gotta be KIDDING me.
(ulc)	⌐	initial cap only	(ulc)	I love KENNESAW State University.
(ital)	◯	change to italic	(ital)	Cletus subscribes to Cat Fancy magazine.
(rom)	◯	change to roman	(rom)	He breeds Maine Coon cats.
(bf)	◯	boldface	(bf)	Press the F5 key to reload the webpage.
(lf)	◯	lightface	(lf)	They don't need five wet wipes.
(wf)	◯	wrong font	(wf)	My cat simply adores me.
⋁	⋁	superscript		Journey's Time 3 box set is pretty good.
⋀	⋀	subscript		Dihydrogen monoxide is also known as H_2O.
(sp)	◯	spell out	(sp)	Michelle owes me seven $.
(stet)	······	ignore the edit	(stet)	The editor made a mistake while proofreading.

Figure 10: Proofreading symbols - text formatting

Proofreading Symbols

margin mark	in-text mark			
⊙	∧	period	🙂	Nobody likes Ramsay Bolton∧
⌄	∧	comma	∧	I asked∧"Why are you picking on Janet?"
(set)?	∧	question mark	(set)?	Are you serious?
:|	∧	colon	:|	There's one exit from this room∧the window.
;|	∧	semicolon	;|	Westley is mostly dead∧he can't speak.
ꞈ or ꞈ	∧	parentheses	ꞈ/ꞈ	Kennesaw State University∧KSU∧is awesome!
ꞈ or ꞈ	∧	brackets	ꞈ/ꞈ	The woman∧Charlene∧bought a box of bullets.
⌄	∧	apostrophe	⌄	You∧re right about that, I realize now.
⌄	∧	quotation marks	⌄/⌄	∧Go outside and play!∧said the boys' mother.
|=|	∧	hyphen	|=|	That Chevy has a four∧barrel carburetor.
M̄	∧	em-dash	M̄/M̄	My choice for the job∧Dave∧is well-qualified.
N̄	∧	en-dash	N̄	There were 40∧50 people at the party.

Figure 11: Proofreading symbols - punctuation marks

Spacing and Positioning

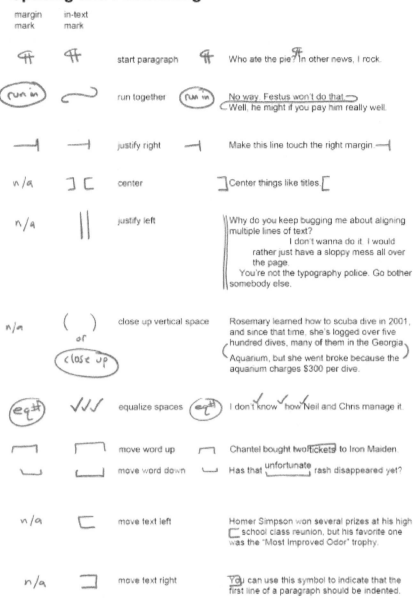

Figure 12: Proofreading symbols - spacing and positioning

For a downloadable, printable, and accessible PDF of the proofreading marks above, click here: Proofreading Marks.

Special Ideas for Editing Visual Materials

Most of the concepts and techniques described in this chapter focus on editing text, but they can also apply to other technical materials. This section will address ideas specific to editing visual elements.

Consider these six concepts when you edit visuals:

Appropriateness

- Decide if text, an image, or a combination of the two is most effective.
- Match the type of image (e.g., table, bar chart, scatterplot, pie chart, Gantt chart, flowchart, map, line drawing, cutaway, cross-section) to the idea/thing being discussed.
- Match the illustration's emotional tone to the subject matter's emotional tone.
- Follow established design conventions.

Clarity

- Use contrasting colors. Bright colors and dark shades attract the most attention.
- Make sure the visual elements' layout follows consistent rules on the screen or page.
- Omit any "non-data pixels" that do not carry information.
- Place an illustration next to the text that references the illustration.
- Explain every illustration's content and relevance in the text, preferably before the illustration appears.
- Label and caption every illustration.
  - Use the correct type of label.
  - Use a sequential numbering pattern.
  - Number tables and figures separately.
- Include "white space" (blank space) around illustrations.

Emphasis

Use arrows, callouts, and boxes to highlight elements that a user will find important, but don't go overboard.

Ethics

- Avoid images that exclude categories of people or play to stereotypes.
- Avoid inhumane images that downplay effects on people.
- Follow copyright law and create, cite, and/or pay for images.
- Use undistorted images of the actual object.
- Use realistic numbering scales that display quantitative differences in context.

Size

- Strike a balance between making images large enough to see details but not so large as to waste space.
- Minimize images' file sizes, but avoid making the images grainy.

Cost

Compare the cost of publishing images to your printing budget. Color pixels are free, but color ink is expensive, and projects that require a professional printer can be very expensive.

Special Ideas for Editing Websites

Technical editors are probably not going to code complete websites themselves. Even so, you may be asked to edit and possibly create web-based content, so you need to be familiar with the basics of web technology.

HTML and CSS

Hypertext markup language (HTML) is the backbone of internet content, and Cascading Style Sheets (CSS) are a vital part of how web programmers style that content. In short, HTML tells your browser what to put onscreen, and CSS tells the browser what it should look like.

This chapter cannot go into the details of how HTML and CSS work, but if you intend to edit websites, you need to be able to "read" basic HTML and CSS and understand how they work.

Many online tutorials for HTML and CSS exist; the W3 Schools website is one of the better ones.

General Web Design Principles

Websites' layout, design, purpose, and function vary tremendously, but most websites follow a set of basic concepts that you can use to evaluate and edit them. Consider these ideas when you edit websites:

- Are words used consistently across the whole website? Are these words meaningful to the users? If not, what words would the readers prefer or understand?
- Are related activities close to each other onscreen and in a logical location? If not, where would the user like to see those activities?
- Do the pages have plenty of headings? If not, where would headings be useful and appropriate?
- Are the sentences and paragraphs short? If not, how and where could you break up long blocks of text into bite-sized chunks?
- Are there any paragraphs that can become lists?
- Are the typefaces and font sizes appropriate for use onscreen? If they're hard to read, how could they be improved?
- Are the hyperlinks easily visible?
- Do the hyperlinks' visible text and mouse-over text describe the items that will open? (In particular, rename links that say "click here.")
- Do the hyperlinks work?
- Do the navigation menus appear in the same place and look the same on every page?
- Do the navigation menus work?
- Does the website include a sitemap?
- Does the website have an internal search engine? Does it work?
- Is the website usable on a mobile device?
- Does the onscreen layout follow an F-pattern? (Most people read websites in this pattern: they look across the top, scan down the left side a few inches, read across, and scan down again.)
- How long would it take for a user to realize s/he ran into a problem?
- Can the user start over if a problem occurs?

Accessibility

One editing issue that you need to consider very carefully is website accessibility. Some issues with accessibility deal with physical or mental disabilities, while others deal with limits on users' expertise and access to technology.

A federal law called Section 508 requires all government agencies that receive federal funding to make their electronic and information technology accessible to people with disabilities. Government agencies also want to make their websites usable for people with limited resources.

Similarly, corporations want to make their websites accessible to the widest possible variety of customers, so corporate websites should incorporate accessibility standards to accommodate these broad audiences.

As a technical editor, you may be responsible for evaluating a website's accessibility. Consider these ideas when you edit websites:

- Is the website usable by people with physical or mental disabilities? Examples include people who are
  - partially or completely blind
  - colorblind
  - unable to focus their eyes well
  - unable to see contrast
  - partially or completely deaf
  - easily distracted by noise

- unable to use a mouse accurately, or at all
- unable to use two hands
- unable to tolerate blinking lights
- dyslexic
- unable to form short-term memories
- unable to concentrate for long periods of time

Many of these users depend on assistive technologies such as screen readers and alternative keyboards. If the website does not work with these technologies, you should edit the website to make it accessible.

- Is the website usable by people who have limited experience with computers? Examples include
  - senior citizens
  - people from rural areas
  - people in developing countries
- Is the website used by people with limited or modified technological resources? Examples include people who have
  - dial-up internet connections
  - older computers
  - small or non-widescreen monitors
  - lack of access to computers other than mobile devices
  - lack of access to mobile devices
  - no software to open downloaded files
  - older web browsers
  - text-only browsers
  - disabled speakers
  - disabled cookies
  - disabled Javascript
  - ad-blocker programs
  - pop-up blockers

A detailed discussion of accessibility issues and goals is available online through the Web Accessibility Initiative section of the World Wide Web Consortium (W3C) website.

The W3C also hosts a page with an extensive and frequently updated list of accessibility checkers. You may wish to use them when editing a website for accessibility.

Website Markup Strategies

You have multiple options for how to mark up websites. None are innately better than the others, so choose the method(s) that best fits the project and your client's needs.

- Edit a website's unpublished text in a word processor as you would any other text document.
- Copy-and-paste a published website's text to a word processor, and edit it as you would any other text document.
- Capture and print screenshots, or print formatted web pages with your browser's "Print" function, then mark them up as you would any other hard copy documents.
- Capture screenshots, open them with a graphics program such as Photoshop or MS Paint, and mark them up with the program's drawing and/or text-creating tools.
- Export website pages to PDF and edit them with Acrobat or Acrobat Reader markup tools.
- Type a separate comments file.
- Directly edit the HTML and CSS code.
  - Use either a web-development program or a plain-text editor. *Never* use MS Word.
  - Tag your edits with highlighting, colored text, and/or comment codes (**<!-- commentgoeshere -->** for HTML, and **/** commentgoeshere **/** for CSS).
- Export the website's code or text to a collaborative online space such as a wiki or Google Docs, and edit it online, using the program's tools.

Chapter 9: HTML Basics

By: Tiffani Reardon

Objectives

Upon completion of this chapter, readers will be able to:

- Define HTML and identify what it stands for.
- Build a simple web page using HTML coding.
  - Identify and use common HTML tags.
  - Explain and apply basic tag rules.
  - Explain attributes and use them to stylize text and images.
  - Embed videos and other embeddable items into HTML web pages.
- Identify websites where readers can learn more and practice their HTML skills.

Introduction

There is a high probability that the readers of this chapter have at least heard the acronym HTML, although many may only know its most basic meaning: HTML is a code that makes web pages. You are not wrong, but there is a bit more to it. For example, did you know that HTML is actually a language with rules, just as English is? Or, perhaps, did you know that HTML actually stands for something, and is not just an all-caps name? Let's start from the beginning.

HTML stands for HyperText Markup Language. HTML is a coded computer language that, when read by a web browser, displays the web pages you see every day when exploring the Internet.

Don't believe me? See for yourself: In Mozilla Firefox, right-click on a web page and click "Inspect Element." The code of the page you are looking at should appear at the bottom of the page. This code is what Firefox reads to show you the page you are seeing in your browser. Pretty cool, huh?

> *Right-Click on a PC*
>
> *CTRL+Click on a Mac*

HTML is the baseline coding of every web page you see out there, and when combined with CSS, Javascript, and other languages, it can create cleanly-constructed and functional websites.

> ***CSS*** *- Cascading Style Sheet. This language is an advanced styling language that can be written into the HTML document or linked to from a separate CSS document.*

> ***Javascript*** *- High complexity programming language that makes the more complicated things you see on some websites, like games.*

Tag Rules

HTML is a language, and it, as all languages do, has rules that make it make sense to the web browser. Just as the English language doesn't make sense when you break grammar rules, neither does HTML when you break tag rules. The difference is, most English speakers will still understand what you are trying to say when you break a grammar rule; the web browser will not understand when you break a tag rule. So let's look at some of these rules.

When you look at a line of HTML, you'll see information enclosed in brackets **< >** throughout the code. This denotes a tag. A tag is what tells web browsers what each item on the page is; it tells the web browser how to classify that information. For example, a paragraph would be classified by a **<p>** tag.

Rule #1

Most tags have an opening tag and a closing tag that surround the information it is classifying or effecting. An opening tag is just the brackets with the tag enclosed, like so: **<p>**. A closing tag is the same thing, except there is a forward slash at the front of the tag, like so: **</p>**. When tagging a paragraph with the **<p>** tag, it would look like the example.

<p>This is a paragraph about how to properly tag a paragraph. To tag a paragraph, you have to start with an opening paragraph tag, type the paragraph, and then end with a closing paragraph tag. This is how most sections of simple paragraph text are tagged.**</p>**

Rule #2

Rule #1 does not *always* apply. Not all tags have to have a closing tag, and you just have to remember those. We will learn about some basic tags in the next section, where we talk about a few that do not require a closing tag.

Rule #3

Opening and closing tags must be *nested* to work. That is, the last tag you open should be the first tag you close, as shown in the example.

<body>

<p>This is a paragraph in the body of the webpage. As you see, I opened the body tag first, and then the paragraph tag; if I am nesting the tags, then I have to close the paragraph tag first, and then close the body tag.**</p>**

</body>

Basic Tags

There are tons of tags, and it's almost impossible to memorize them all. Luckily, we have the Internet, which means we don't have to memorize them. In this section, you'll learn about some of the basic tags that are needed in almost every web page.

Beginning Tags and the <head>

Every HTML web page starts with a **<!doctype html>** tag, with no closing tag. This is what tells the web browser what version of HTML the page is written in. The **<!doctype>** tag used to have several options in the last version of HTML, but in HTML5, there is only one: **<!doctype html>**.

After the **<!doctype html>** tag, there is an **<html>** tag, which is also required for every HTML document. Unlike the **<!doctype html>** tag, the **<html>** tag does require a closing tag of **</html>**. For nesting purposes, the closing **</html>** tag will always be the very last thing in your document.

Once the **<html>** tag has been opened, the page then has its head information in the **<head>** tag, which also has a closing tag of **</head>**. The **<head>** tag includes information that does not show up on the page, but is vital to the look and feel of the page. There is always a **<title>** tag with a closing **</title>** tag that encloses the information on the tab of the web browser. Users who are including CSS information in their document might also include CSS coding in the <head> tag.

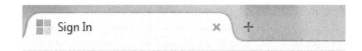

Figure 9: A browser tab with title information

The <body> Tag and Other Common Tags

After the **<head>** tag has been closed, the next tag to open is the **<body>** tag. This denotes the information that you actually see on the page when looking at a web browser. Everything you see within the browser window appears after the **<body>** tag and before the closing **</body>** tag.

For common tags used within the **<body>** tag and their purpose, see Table 1. Unless otherwise noted, all tags in the table below require a closing tag.

Table 1: Common HTML Tags

Tag	Function
<em>	Defines emphasized text. Text enclosed in an **<em>** tag will appear italicized.
<strong>	Defines important text. Text enclosed in a **<strong>** tag will appear boldface.
<img>	Defines an image. This tag requires an attribute that defines what image it shows. This attribute is called **src**. The **<img>** tag does not require a closing tag, however it does end differently. Instead of the usual closing tag, an **<img>** tag is closed by ending the opening tag with a space and then **/>**. For example: <img src="logo.jpg" />
<a>	Defines a link. This tag requires an attribute that defines where the link goes to. This attribute is called **href**.
<ul>	Defines an unordered list. This will start a bulleted list.
<ol>	Defines an ordered list. This will start a numbered list.
<li>	Defines a line in a list. This tag applies to both unordered and ordered lists. When you start a list, you must use **<li>** tags to open and close each line separately. See Figure 4 for an example of how a list looks in HTML.
<table>	Defines a table. This will start a table.
<tr>	Defines a table row. This will start a row in a table. You must have a **<tr>** tag for each row of a table.
<td>	Defines a table column. This will start a column in a row of a table. You must have a new **<td>** tag for each column of each row (each square) of the table. See Figure 5 for an example of how a table looks in HTML.
 	Defines a line break. This tag does not require a closing tag.

<h1> - <h6>	Defines headings. There are six HTML heading levels: **<h1>**, **<h2>**, **<h3>**, **<h4>**, **<h5>**, and **<h6>**. They each define headings of their specified order (**<h1>** being the first order heading and **<h6>** the sixth order).
<p>	Defines a paragraph. This is how most sections of text are tagged.

Table 2: Ordered and Unordered Lists Preview

HTML	Preview
<ul> <li>Item 1</li> <li>Item 2</li> <li>Item 3</li> </ul>	• Item 1 • Item 2 • Item 3
<ol> <li>Item 1</li> <li>Item 2</li> <li>Item 3</li> </ol>	1. Item 1 2. Item 2 3. Item 3

Table 3: Table Preview

HTML	Preview
<table> <tr> <td>Box 1</td> <td>Box 2</td> <td>Box 3</td> </tr> <tr> <td>Box 4</td> <td>Box 5</td> <td>Box 6</td> </tr> </table>	Box 1 Box 2 Box 3 Box 4 Box 5 Box 6

Basic Attributes

HTML attributes provide more information for tags or apply stylistic features to them that are not the default. For example, an **<a>** tag requires more information to know where it should link to, and a **<p>** tag can have a different font color than the default if you want it to. Let's take a look at some common attributes and what they do in Table 2 below.

Table 3: Common HTML Attributes

Attribute	What it Does	What it Looks Like in HTML
href	The **href** attribute	<a

	belongs to the **\<a\>** tag and defines where the link will go to.	href=""http://distanceed.hss.kennesaw.edu/technicalcommunication">This is a link to the textbook website.\</a\>
src	The **src** attribute belongs to the **\<img\>** tag and defines where the tag will pull the image from. This can be an image site or a file path from within the server.	\<img src="logo.jpg" /\>
width	The **width** attribute can be applied to images, iframe elements, tables, or other elements with a numerical width. It defines how wide the item will be.	\<img src="logo.jpg" width="300px" /\>
height	The **height** attribute can be applied to images, iframe elements, tables, or other elements with a numerical height. It defines how tall the item will be.	\<img src="logo.jpg" width="300px" height="300px" /\>
style	The **style** attribute allows you to add inline CSS elements to your tag. A few common ones are **color, font-size, font-family,** and **text-align**. You define a style element the same way as other attributes, however you then have to define the value of the style element. View the examples to the right to see how these style elements are defined.	\<p style="color:blue;"\> This is blue text.\</p\> \<h1 style="font-size:24px;"\>This is a 24pt font heading.\</h1\> \<a href="http://distanceed.hss.kennesaw.edu/technicalcommunication" style="font-family:Arial; font-size:12px;"\>This link to the textbook website is Arial 12 pt font.\</a\> \<h2 style="text-align:center;"\>This heading is centered on the page.\</h2\>

Embeddable Items

YouTube is the most popular video repository in America, if not the world. What if you want those videos on your web page? Perhaps you posted a video of a project you've been working on, and you want to show that video on your online portfolio. The answer is simple: embed codes. Most sites with hard-to-code items have an embeddable feature to them, and it essentially puts the information in a frame of one website into a frame on your own website.

You can usually find the embed codes in the share functions of items. The nice (and easy!) thing about embed codes is that they don't require you to add anything to them. You simply paste the code into your HTML page, and in that spot you will see the video or other item when you preview it. However, you can edit them. Let's analyze a YouTube embed code in Figure 6 below.

```
<iframe width="420" height="315" src="https://www.youtube.com/embed/zx_M-sWrDfc" frameborder="0" allowfullscreen></iframe>
```

iframe - Most embed codes use the iframe tag now, but not all of them. It depends on the website and what kind of code was used in creating the item.

height="315" - You can edit the width and height of embed codes, or add them in if it is not already in the code. This is good if the default size is not quite big or small enough for what you want to use it for. Just change the number in the quotations to change it.

src="https://www.youtube.com/embed/zx_M-sWrDfc" - The source of embed codes are usually some variation of the link to the item. If you put this link in your web address, it might not work (it also might just give you a full-screen version of the video). But if you take out the "embed/" part of it and replace it with "watch?v=", it would take you to a video fo my dog, Nutmeg, running around in her backyard on YouTube. Go ahead, try it.

Watch the video below to see tags, attributes, and embed codes in action!

Organizing Your Web Page

Web pages are a series of pages connected by hyperlinks, and they have unique needs. Let's think about it this way: you have a small child whom you keep in a playpen. In the playpen is a tiny toy box with a ball, a block, and a fire truck. You play a game where you tell her to show you the ball, and she points to the ball. You tell her to show you the block, and she points to the block. You tell her to point to the fire truck, and she points to the fire truck. This game works very well.

But then you take her into another room and put her in another playpen, and there's a pillow, a rattle, and a dolly. You tell her to point to the fire truck, and she looks around and shrugs her shoulders. Her mind is not advanced enough to understand that you wish her to point through the wall into the other playpen. And she does not have the physical ability to get out of the playpen, walk to the other room, and retrieve your fire truck for you. This game will not work.

You then try again. You put her back in the original playpen, but you take the small box of toys and scatter them around the house. You put the ball under the couch. You put the block in the bathtub. And you put the fire truck in the trunk of your car. You return to the playpen and ask the child to show you the fire truck. Again, she shrugs her shoulders. This game will not work.

Why does the first game work, but the other two do not?

What if you change the game by taking the child, playpen, toy box, and all into the next room and again ask the child for the block? Unless something distracts the child, the game will work! The child knows the block is in the box, and all functions as normal.

Your web page is the child, and its name is index. Your main folder is the playpen, and your subfolders are the toy boxes.

To be more clear, when you make the homepage of a website, you'll want to name it "index.html" and put it in a folder. In that folder, you can then put any pictures, documents, videos, or other HTML files that you might link to. You can also organize further by putting those things into subfolders. But no matter what, everything that is not already online must be put inside that main folder to be then posted online.

Where to Practice and Learn More HTML Skills

- Codecademy
- W3Schools
- Lynda

Examples, Cases, and Models Index

An Example is Worth Half a Thousand Words

The following are links to the examples and models of the kinds reports, letters, and other documents discussed in this book. (Some of the items are excerpts.) True, many of these examples are as much as twenty years old. However, the point here is technical writing, format, organization, style—not up-to-date technology. Even so, why not write a technology update on blood glucose monitoring systems, voice recognition software, laptop computers, wind power systems? (And then send it to us at reardont@outlook.com)

Resumes

Veterinary assistant

LAN system administrator

Maintenance technician for high-tech systems

Computer service and sales representative

Case management nurse

Technical writing intern

Curriculum Vitae

Instructional designer

Application Letters

Technical writing intern

Science editorship

Database programmer

Quality assurance manager

Programmer/analyst

The Ghost of Milagro - used with permission from Melanie Sumner, author of *How to Write a Novel*

Complaint Letters

Microwave problems

Printer problems

Cosmetics problems

Beginner's Guide to Eudora Lite for Windows

Operating the Minolta Freedom 3 Camera

How to Raise Potatoes in the Home Garden

Instructions for a Simple Window Curtain

Hand-washing policies and procedures for health care personnel

Accounting policies and procedures

Standard operating procedures: pouring dental impressions Thanks to Melissa Burke for making this SOP available.

User Guides

GIMP User Guide

Parallels User Guide

Recommendation and Feasibility Reports

Sport Utility Vehicles

Laptop Computers (annotated PDF)

Fire Ant Control

Blood Glucose Monitoring Systems

Uninterruptible Power Supply (UPS) Systems

First Telescope Purchase

Voice Recognition Software

Formal Technical Reports (annotated PDF)

DVD Technology and Applications

Cerebral Palsy and Its Treatments

Effects of Increased Atmospheric Carbon Dioxide

Report on Light Water Nuclear Reactors

Handbooks

Classification

Industrial Robots

Types of Solar Water Heaters

Causal Discussion

Effects of a Nuclear Attack

Lunar Organic Matter

Definition

Sickle Cell Anemia

Stratospheric Ozone Depletion and HVAC Refrigerants

Superconducting Quantum Interference Device

Process Discussion

Cardiac Cycle

Wind Turbine Power Generation

Shock

Persuasion

In Favor of Recycling

Opposed to Recycling

Graphics

Map of Hellbent - used with permission from Melanie Sumner, author of *How To Write a Novel*

Made in the USA
Monee, IL
06 August 2021